The
Well-Tooled
Kitchen

The Well-Tooled Kitchen

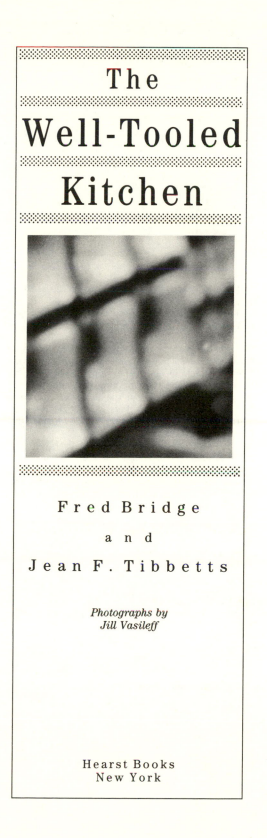

Fred Bridge

and

Jean F. Tibbetts

Photographs by
Jill Vasileff

Hearst Books
New York

Library of Congress Cataloging-in-Publication Data

Bridge, Fred.
    The well-tooled kitchen / Fred Bridge and Jean F. Tibbetts.
        p. cm.
    ISBN 0-688-12064-4
    1.Kitchen utensils.   2. Cookery.   I. Tibbetts, Jean F.
II. Title.
TX656.B75   1990
683´.82–dc20   90-37989
                                                            CIP

Printed in the United States of America

2 3 4 5 6 7 8 9 10

BOOK DESIGN BY RICHARD ORIOLO

For our very dear friend
Norman J. Alexander

Contents

From the Authors

When asked to describe myself and my contributions to the kitchenware industry in this country, I like to say that I'm its father and have very proudly nurtured its growth through nearly six decades of day-to-day activity. In fact, I have witnessed the development and evolution of fine kitchenware as it is known today: its transition from strict professional use to a more popular one; its constant upgrading with newer, sturdier materials and the ongoing introductions of more effective and efficient designs. That progress has been exciting to partake of as a merchant, gratifying to convey to new generations of promising chefs, and rewarding to contribute to design improvements.

I credit my father for teaching me the basics as I was growing up during the Roaring Twenties. He was a well-respected vendor of restaurant supplies in the Northeast, and, as I frequently accompanied him on his business rounds, I became as familiar as he was with his porcelain, silver, and glass.

In 1933 I enthusiastically entered that same kitchenware field by joining James N. Shaw, a supply firm that soon merged with Nathan Strauss Duparquet to become one of the largest of its kind in the country, selling to the most prestigious hotels, restaurants, and clubs, and outfitting the spectacular homes, chalets, and yachts of the famous Four Hundred.

With the onset of the Second World War I had the opportunity to serve as cook, baker, and chef, gaining the invaluable hands-on experience of those craftsmen with whom I would ultimately deal. The service was a constant source of new developments in cookware and cooking processes, all of which became useful when I returned to civilian life as an independent merchant of pots, pans, silver, and especially glass.

Just after the war proved to be the ideal time to focus on sales of domestic glassware because many of the great European firms were then in rubble and unlikely to be reliable sources for some time to come. My input and the high level of my manufacturers' know-how were the perfect combination to cause quality glassware to become available in America. Consequently, old clients like the Stork Club and the Waldorf-Astoria returned as new ones arrived—like the Beverly Wilshire in Los Angeles, the Blackstone in Chicago, and the Nationale in Havana.

The wholesale end of my business remains strong to this day, but back in 1955, when home cooking was becoming more sophisticated—growing from a necessity into a creative pastime—I began to offer the public the same heavy-duty saucepans and steamers, top-of-the-line knives and spatulas developed for chefs, yet ones that would help to expand the capabilities of those less experienced.

As retail requirements grew, so did the call for a broader selection of continental products. European importers had then centered on French copperware, but because the need to import French knives and the hand tools of the food finisher on a large scale was becoming evident, I became a direct importer of those goods in the late 1960s. It was also apparent that the state of cooking was evolving into a more exciting home hobby and these new implements would give my customers the opportunity to be more creative.

As such professional cookware was made more available to home chefs, many capable food writers, teachers, and chef-authors subsequently wrote or spoke about Bridge Kitchenware. Julia Child, Rudolph Stanish, and Maida Heatter are among them, but my all-time favorite piece remains the "discovery article" that the then *New York Times* food editor Craig Claiborne did on my store over thirty years ago.

Bridge Kitchenware continues to be a main focus for journalists preparing articles on food, editors securing kitchenware to enrich food photographs, and sincere nonprofessionals who might want to solve a food preparation problem. In fact, their questions and the kitchenware to solve them are constantly on my mind as my wife, Carolynn, is a prominent food stylist in the advertising business and it has become very much a family matter to talk about food, its preparation, and presentation at home. And I now enjoy the participation of my sons, Steven and Christoffer, in the business.

As the years passed, my travels abroad continued to expand the cookware selection at Bridge Kitchenware. Twenty years ago I began to import fine Italian stainless-steel pots, pans, and hand tools of various forms to complement the French ware and, more recently, to directly import German knives, which are now regarded as the finest in the world.

Close work with chefs and foreign manufacturers has also led to developing unique implements and specially sized and shaped vessels, while commissions to local craftsmen have produced novel variations of cookware for the commercial market.

The company's present site at 214 East 52nd Street in Manhattan is its third and largest retail location, and I am happy to say that our business has never been better. I am always impressed to see the number of young men and women now entering the business as either chefs or food provenders as it is they and the large number of emerging food hobbyists who speak for our future.

In their refreshing, creative approach to new foods, new techniques, and the ever-contemporary nutritional requirements, their progressive effort seems to set new standards for cookware.

I have many good and fast friends in the food and cookware world; we have intimately shared the last six decades, and as a result feel that we have collectively made major contributions to its success.

Quite often, I am mistaken for being curt, brash, and abrupt, but in truth I am direct and straightforward in dealing with problems or business matters. Bridge Kitchenware has a small staff and if I shout for assistance, it is done for expediency so that we can then help more customers. Those who know

me well appreciate that this is my style as it is very much a part of my background and I have always felt that getting quickly to the point best deals with any matter.

Friends in the publishing world have often asked me to do the ultimate book on kitchenware; frankly, I never thought that I could give it the time until I met my collaborator, Jean Tibbetts, who had frequented the shop as a journalist. We have worked well together and I regard the product of our effort as comprehensive. It is my fondest hope that we have delivered to the professional chef and home cook a constant, useful reference.

—FRED BRIDGE

A fantasy realized is the only way to describe that moment I first set foot in Bridge Kitchenware some years ago. It was a strange but real world of magnificent cookware including many commercial pieces of which I had only heard. Cavernous in scope, the array piled high on counters, dangled from rafters, and hung from every conceivable inch of wall space. Gleaming, state-of-the-art stainless steel stockpots and sauté pans stood alongside decades-old copper paella pans and casseroles. Literally hundreds of knives —from chef's to paring to butcher to oyster—shared their wall with mandolines, salamanders, shears, and spatulas. Above perched couscoussiers, zabaglione bowls and croquembouche molds; below were chopping boards, genoise tins, and pie plates. Marmites and flambé pans beckoned in one corner, truffle cutters and caramel pins did in another.

It was truly a Camelot of cookware, as if at the call of the knights who would practice the culinary arts. Indeed, one could easily imagine what delights a four-star chef might create with his twelve new terrines; how a food stylist would detail her soon-to-be-molded chocolate cigars; and in which magazine a pasta pin might eventually appear.

Such was—and remains—the constant environment where Fred Bridge presides in an imperious, peculiar fashion, perhaps akin to King

Arthur's Merlin the Wise among his retorts and reactors in the Crystal Cave.

"A fish poacher?" he might demand of one customer. "Make sure it's at least 24 inches long to hold a whole salmon." "A roasting pan? Its length and width should measure 2 inches less than those of your oven." "An aebelskiver pan? A cast-iron one retains heat longer than an aluminum one." The wand waved, and off would fly one of his modern-day sprites to retrieve the prescribed implement.

That ready knowledge of the perfect tool for the task—perceived as conceit by some but reliable by all —is, quite simply, the wisdom of experience—a nearly sixty-year familiarity with the trade, the materials, and their applications, all of

which Mr. Bridge openheartedly detailed to me over these past years for this book.

So, too, did those in the industry who believed that experts and aspirants alike should enjoy a definitive guide to kitchenware. Professional knife makers explained recondite designs and metallurgical advances; chemists simplified the maze of plastics and textiles; woodworkers clearly drew the lines between hard and soft varieties and their best uses.

Many respected practitioners who daily ply these tools very generously conveyed their techniques. One seafood merchant demonstrated the most efficient ways to fillet flat and round fish; another, how to contend with a recalcitrant clam. One butcher described the very distinct French and English ways to carve a baked ham, and another showed how to skillfully bone a leg of lamb.

The stellar chefs, restaurateurs, and food writers who continually enhance and advance the culinary arts generously contributed favorite recipes to demonstrate the use of specific tools. More than one hundred in all, their masterworks range from traditional to contemporary, rustic to elegant, and simple to complex. All dishes were tested and retested, and thoroughly relished on both occasions.

—JEAN F. TIBBETTS

Acknowledgments

Fred Bridge and Jean F. Tibbetts are indebted to the associates at Bridge Kitchenware for maintaining the high standard of quality at Bridge Kitchenware. They are Janine Bakker, Alan Bakker, Augustine Vidailhet, Michael Von Nostitz, and Richard Christensen.

We also thank the following people at William Morrow, Publishers: Ann Bramson and Laurie Orseck, our editors; Kathleen Morahan, our copy editor; Linda Kosarin for the jacket design. And thanks to Richard Oriolo for his art direction, Jill Vasileff for the photography, and Steve Eisenberg for the jacket photograph.

Jean F. Tibbetts wishes to thank the following for providing technical or commercial information:

Philip Runge, American Gas Association; Heather Hoins, Russian

Works of Art Department, Christie, Manson & Woods; Donald Beermann, Animal Science Department, Cornell University; Gertrude Trani, Library, Culinary Institute of America; Georges Henri while commercial attaché for the Government of the French Republic; Michael Bowdler, Hall China; Robert L. Topazio, J. A. Henckels Zwillingswerk; Karl Hipp, Karl Hipp & Associates; Saori Sugai, Korin Japanese Trading Corp.; Charles F. Lamalle, Charles F. Lamalle Housewares; Catharine Roehrig, Department of Egyptian Art, Metropolitan Museum of Art; Pierre Parisot, Matfer; Flora Miller, Miller's Magic Mill; Michael Fogarty, National Marine Fisheries Services; Bert D'Appolonia, Department of Cereal Science and Food Technology, North Dakota State University; Susan J. Black, Norton Company; Douglas Parrish, Parrish's Cake Decorating Supplies; N. William Pioppi, Russell Harrington Cutlery; Alain R. Guiol, Sitram; Lisa Barmann, United Fresh Fruit and Vegetable Association; Ralph P. Edwards, Wire Association International; Hans R. Rathsack, Wüsthof-Trident of America.

1. Knives

Each culture enjoys its own uniquely shaped, well-crafted general-purpose knife, as evidenced by a Chinese chef's boxy, rectangular blade, a Japanese chef's more elongated, snub-nosed complement, and a continental chef's spear-tipped blade.

These balanced blades can provide up to a 14-inch cutting edge to quickly chop, mince, dice, scrape, and shred vegetables and meats. Progressively lighter or smaller forms slice octopus, carve ham, bone fish, or flute mushrooms; the wealth of these are designed and manufactured by French and German cutlery firms.

The enormous selection of blade styles—a variety of which can be found in a professional chef's knife case—logically evolved from the hunter's and warrior's flint, obsidian, slate, and bone implements, and later their multipurpose metal daggers.

Among the earliest adaptations for kitchen use, depicted in New Kingdom butchering scenes, are daggerlike knives with double-edged blades and straight handles that lie on the same axis as the blade's midrib. The handle-to-blade juncture was generally clean and crisp, unlike the later Greek and Roman handles, which frequently overlapped onto their smaller straight and larger scimitar blades.

It is a far cry from early Christian days to the Middle Ages, but little is known about advances in Western knife design except that since table forks were not yet in general use, the distinctly tipped knife that the Romans carried with them to England was gradually transformed by the Saxons into one with a broader blade with a clipped tip to cut, pierce, and transfer food. That same Augustan butcher knife surfaced centuries later in Burgundian courts as an elegant carving tool—slightly narrower in profile with a dropped tip, upswept heel, and a well-ornamented handle that might be sculpted from ivory or rock crystal, enameled, or made of a precious metal.

Since the knives most frequently associated with this period were commissioned for carving before guests—an art that came to be called the honors of the table—the implements were highly decorative. Blades that once displayed their owners' etched names now cited proverbs or graces to be sung before the meal. As ecclesiastical influence remained strong, handles with different-colored inlays were used for different church festivals. Ebony-handled knives served their owners during Lent, ivory at Easter, and the two combined—usually in a checkerboard design—during Pentecost.

Those were extraordinary tableside tools that perfectly suited slicing; an accompanying blade with a broader, flat, round-tipped unsharpened edge eventually evolved for serving.

If contemporary woodcuts of kitchens and their furnishings are accurate, the later Renaissance chef was a lucky artist indeed with high-tipped and bird's-beak paring knives, round- and square-tipped cake knives, narrow and deep slicers, and clip-tipped and straight-backed butcher's knives. Save for modifications such as a straight heel, longer bolster, and more stylized handles in lieu of pistol or squared grips, we still utilize many of the same designs.

Those blades were traditionally struck in carbon steel, an alloy of iron and carbon that remained the knife maker's choice metal until forty-five years ago, when stainless steel became readily available. Carbon steel took and held a fine cutting edge, but it corroded easily and stained on contact with acidic foods because of its iron content. The chromium added to stainless steel prevented the iron from oxidizing and strengthened the metal, but it also produced a blade that is difficult to sharpen. Stainless steel is now recognized as great for specialty cutting tools while its successor—high-carbon stainless steel, which offers the benefits of both alloys but none of their liabilities—

Stamped vs. Forged Blades

Knife blades are either stamped or forged, and the difference in quality and handling is evident in balance, as it is in any fine hand tool.

A stamped blade—which is die-cut in a press bearing the basic blade configuration—is lighter and less expensive than a forged blade. Its steel is comparatively thin and flat to allow for stamping and reduced production costs, but the final product—after numerous processes including grinding and polishing—is a simple, clean-edged tool that is back-heavy in the hand. More forward pressure is needed to cut and more forward gripping to compensate for the weighting.

The better-balanced forged knife begins as a steel blank that is heated to a high temperature, set into a die, and struck with a multiton hammer to form the basic blade. The metal is then hardened through heating to temperatures up to 1700°F and cooled in a caustic chemical bath to contract the steel and make it dense. This produces a brittle blade, so a second heating and cooling treatment relaxes internal stress and makes the blade more flexible. Successive coarse to fine grindings create the taper and impart the desired amount of flexibility. The greater attention creates a heavier, tougher, more front-weighted blade with a distinct bolster, a thick band of steel that lies flush against and perpendicular to the handle.

is considered the finest knife-crafting steel now made. The small amounts of molybdenum and vanadium added to the iron, carbon, and chromium increase its ability to hold an edge; to resist rust, pitting, and abrasion; and to recover from bending without breaking.

As the end of the century nears, knife-manufacturing technology is bound to improve still further. Labor-saving and manufacturing innovations will surely be combined with space-age metallurgical advances. For those who care about knife quality, this may be just the beginning.

German-Style Chef's Knife

This high-carbon stainless-steel forged knife is distinctly German in style. Its spear-shaped blade rocks up the front half of the cutting edge to end at a sharp tip, and the bolster is thick to add heft and balance. It has a stylized, rectangular collar, characteristic of the German-class knives, and a full tang sandwiched between two form-fitted layers of plastic.

The blade is deep for uniform dicing and slicing; with all that heavy, rigid steel and a little momentum, it would be difficult to make rough, jagged cuts. Length ranges from 6 to 14 inches in 1-inch increments and is always a matter of personal preference, but the 10-inch blade seems to suit home use while a professional does better with a 12-inch one.

This knife is also available in carbon steel and various stainless-steel blends; some have full tangs and others rattails encased in hard rubber, plastic, or hardwood.

A number of Japanese manufacturers now forge high-carbon stainless-steel knives with full tangs and similarly angulated collars, but these usually have thinner, weaker bolsters.

Knife Nomenclature

A fine kitchen knife is composed of two parts, a blade and a handle, and their features include:

Point   This blade tip may resemble a spear; round spatula; sheep's foot (an outward arc from spine to flat cutting edge); cope (an abrupt, forward angle from spine to flat cutting edge) or clip (a slight concave arc from about mid-spine to the point. This secondary edge can be sharpened and called a swedge or left unsharpened and called a false edge).

Back or Spine   The thick, unsharpened edge of the blade

Cutting Edge   This sharpened edge of the blade can be plain, with a cross section revealing a gentle taper to a long or abrupt V-shape, or hollow-ground with a distinct concave area running down the length of each blade side. More complicated edges include: scalloped or wave-cut edges that resemble a series of small arcs, the short, sharp points of which end along the cutting edge; granton edges, whose elongated ovals are ground perpendicularly to the cutting edge and are staggered alternately on each blade side; serrated edges, which end as a series of tiny, V-shaped teeth; saw edges, whose teeth are bigger, more widely spaced, and can be variously shaped and outwardly flared; and corrugated edges, which look like accordion pleating.

Heel   The rear edge of the blade that extends below the bottom line of the handle

Bolster   The thick band of steel on forged blades that runs directly along the heel and up to the spine. (Some call this a shoulder.)

Tang   The unsharpened rear extension of the blade onto which the handle is attached with rivets or encased in plastic. A full tang runs the entire length of the handle with a shape to match; a three-quarter tang extends partially into the handle, while a rattail tang runs like a rod down the length of the handle. Generally speaking, the fuller the tang, the better the knife.

Handle   The hand grip that is frequently covered with metal, plastic, wood, or bone in one or two pieces. Occasionally it is simply an extension of the blade steel, like those on Far Eastern–made Chinese cleavers or French-made butcher's cleavers. It more often appears as a stylized rectangle, tube, bulb, or knob with a smooth, ribbed, or textured finish.

Butt   The rear end of the handle

French-Style Chef's Knife

Long, strong, and weighty, this classic, forged French knife may look like the German model, but it differs subtly. Its rock—the easy curve along the cutting edge from heel to tip—graduates to a more triangular shape, which many prefer. The collar design, rounded rather than angular, may have evolved from the time when the collar was capped with a ferrule, a metal ring that strengthened the knife and prevented its wooden handle from splitting.

This knife has a 10-inch carbon-steel blade, but it is also available in stainless and high-carbon stainless steels with blades that graduate in length from 6 to 14 inches in 1-inch increments.

Close, detailed cutting requires a small-bladed paring knife. Shown from left to right are bird's beak, miniature boning, fluting, clip point, sheep's foot, and spearpoint paring-knife styles.

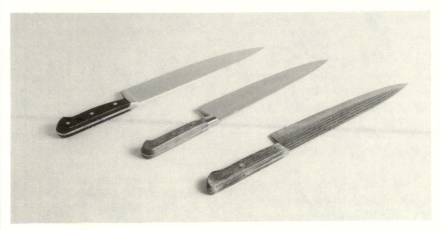

A long, sharp, broad-bladed chef's knife is the most essential tool in the professional kitchen. Shown left to right are forged German- and French-style knives and a stamped German-style blade.

Stamped Chef's Knife

The blade shape of this 10-inch stainless-steel stamped chef's knife is much the same as its forged French-style counterpart—long, wide, and triangular. It is also reputed to be a good value for the money; it performs the same tasks as a more expensive forged knife, and its stainless-steel composition assures as keen an edge as on any blade of similar steel.

But there are differences. Stamped blades must be cut from a thin sheet of steel, causing them to be 20 per-cent lighter than forged blades. Less weight means less leverage, which translates into more exertion for the chef. Sheet steel does, however, have an advantage over the steel used for forging: Because rolled steel is not as rigid as cast steel, any blade produced from it is more flexible and resilient.

Stamped blades can also be cut from carbon and high-carbon stainless steels—they are always bolster-free—and range in length from 6 to 12 inches. Many have full tangs, some have three-quarters, and either can be sandwiched or encased in hard rubber, plastic, or hardwood handles.

Fine German and French Cutlery Manufacturers

Just as Thiers outpaced Nogent, Paris, and Châtellerault as the cutlery manufacturing center of France, so did Solingen surpass Nuremberg and Remscheid in Germany. In Solingen the trade began in the fourteenth century as that of the swordsmith, becoming fully organized by 1412 with well-governed and supervised fraternities of smiths, grinders, temperers, and finishers. These guilds switched to crafting more knives than swords 450 years ago, with a number of the firms since established now recognized as the finest knife makers in the world. Among them are Wüsthof with its trident trademark and J. A. Henckels with its twins logo. These are separately displayed on the sides of their particular blades.

Sabatier is perhaps the most recognizable name on the blade of a French knife, and while there were once nearly twenty firms such as Maxime Girard and Therias L'Économe who were licensed to manufacture under the Sabatier name, there are now only twelve. Many of these firms still stamp their handles with their identifiable hallmarks, such as a crown, trumpet, lion, elephant, or a cluster of grapes. Others emblazon the company name on the blade itself.

Spearpoint Paring Knife

The traditional paring knife, a miniature version of the chef's knife, has two spear-shaped blade styles. The German-style one is visually balanced; the tip drops slightly while the cutting edge rocks up to meet it, forming a nearly perfect, rounded spear. The French-style blade is more triangular, the tip on much the same plane as the spine while the cutting edge approaches it in a direct line from the heel.

The stylized blades on other parers are often designed for a single purpose, but the versatile spearpoint blade allows the chef to cut, trim, and decorate with ease. Either style is recommended.

Look for a paring knife whose blade is rigid near the bolster, yet semiflexible at the tip; a slight limberness will make you more aware of the various textures in the food being cut and will help gauge the amount of pressure to apply. Also bear in mind that a paring blade must be short—3½ to 4 inches long; some manufacturers mislabel the similarly shaped but slightly larger 5-inch utility knife as a paring knife.

Sheep's-Foot Paring Knife

This knife's name is based on its vague resemblance to the silhouette of an animal's hoof. The tip lies on the same plane as the straight cutting edge, and the blade's spine arcs downward to meet it. This creates a wider angle of approach to the tip than on any other paring blade, which means that while the sheep's foot is equally adept at peeling and paring, it is not as efficient at the finer tip maneuvers required in garnishing.

The blade is usually semiflexible, 3 to 3½ inches long, and available either in carbon steel or high-carbon stainless steel.

Turnip Choucroute with Duck Sausage

Jean-Georges Vongerichten, Executive Chef: Restaurant Lafayette

4 servings

TURNIP CHOUCROUTE

2 *pounds turnips, peeled and julienned*

3 *tablespoons coarse salt*

3 *tablespoons distilled white vinegar*

1 *bottle dry white wine*

Combine the turnips, salt, vinegar, and half the wine (reserve the remainder) in a nonreactive bowl, cover with plastic wrap, and refrigerate 2 days; turn once or twice.

DUCK SAUSAGE

2 *7-ounce boned duck breasts, skinned and diced.*

4 *ounces boneless, chicken breast, skinned and diced*

3 *ounces duck foie gras, diced*

3 *tablespoons shelled pistachio nuts, peeled and coarsely chopped*

¾ *teaspoon salt*

Freshly ground black pepper to taste

Combine all the ingredients in a medium bowl, season to taste with pepper, and mix well.

Empty onto a 2-foot-long sheet of aluminum foil, shape into a long cylinder, and roll in the foil; twist the ends to close. Poach 12 minutes in simmering water, remove from the heat, and allow the sausage to cool in its cooking water, then refrigerate until ready to use.

ASSEMBLY

1 *tablespoon rendered duck fat*

1 *large onion, julienned*

1 *8-ounce slab double-smoked bacon, rind discarded, sliced ¼ inch thick, and blanched 5 minutes*

Reserved ½ bottle wine

8 *juniper berries*

Freshly ground black pepper to taste

12 *new potatoes, boiled in their jackets*

Preheat the oven to 400°F.

Rinse the turnip choucroute in warm water, drain, and squeeze to remove the liquid; place in a large ceramic casserole.

Melt the duck fat in a sauté pan set over low heat, add the onion, and cook 20 to 25 minutes, or until the onions become soft and transparent but not colored. Empty into the casserole with the turnips, together with the bacon, remaining wine, and juniper berries; season to taste with pepper. Cover and cook 1½ hours.

Slice the sausage and add it to the choucroute during the last 5 minutes of cooking.

Serve with the potatoes.

Bird's-Beak Paring Knife

With a spine that drops in a moderate curve to meet a slightly arced cutting edge, the blade of this paring knife looks like a very sleek bird's beak. Its unique curved shape makes it a particularly fine tool for trimming and shaping round vegetables such as pearl onions, Brussels sprouts, and radishes.

Bird's-beak blades run 2½ to 3 inches in length and are either forged (ideally) or stamped in high-carbon stainless steel or stainless steel.

A narrow, high-tipped blade enhances a knife's piercing and slicing capability. Shown at top is a spearpoint boning knife, and below, a high-tipped one.

Clip-Point Paring Knife

Many knife makers call this a granny paring knife and classify it as an American pattern. Its dropped tip lies near the cutting edge, and the spine is straight along the back half of the blade, abruptly angling 10 degrees downward to meet the tip. This design creates a long, slender point to make small, deep cuts in food; it is ideal for removing the eyes from a potato.

A clip-point paring blade is always stiff and 3 inches in length. It is available in the three major knife steels and can be forged or stamped.

Miniature Boning/ Paring Knife

The blade of this knife looks like a pint-sized version of the standard boning blade. Its tip lies at the end of a straight spine where it is met by a stylized S-shaped cutting edge. That high tip is meant to pierce flesh, and the gradual cutting-edge curve allows the blade to follow through with smooth, even strokes; this is particularly noticeable when trimming fat from steaks or boning small birds.

The blade is 2¾ inches long, available in high-carbon stainless steel, and can either be forged or stamped.

Fluting Knife

The wedge-shaped blade of this small knife looks like a cross between the German and French chef's blade styles. Its spine arcs slightly downward to the centered tip and its cutting edge rises almost directly from the heel to meet it. This produces a fairly small angle of approach to the tip, giving the blade a sturdy, yet delicate point that's unsurpassed for making or initiating shallow grooves, notches, and cuts. Its short length—2½ to 3 inches—ensures a close hand-to-tip placement for total control.

Fricassée de Poulet au Gingembre

Chicken Fricassee with Ginger

Alain Sailhac, Executive Chef while at The Plaza

2 servings

1 2½-pound chicken
4 to 5 tablespoons all-purpose flour
Salt to taste
Freshly ground black pepper to taste
3 tablespoons corn oil
2 ounces shallots, thinly sliced
2 ounces ginger, peeled and thinly sliced
1 garlic clove, crushed
½ cup dry white wine
Zest and juice from 1 lime
1 pound tomatoes, peeled, with ¾ pound seeded and diced and ¼ pound sliced
4 scallions, trimmed and thinly sliced

Use a chef's knife to cut the chicken into four pieces: Cut off the wing tips. With the chicken breast-side up, pull one leg away from the body and cut through at the top of the thigh. Firmly pull the leg away from the body to pop the ball joint from the hip socket. Cut through this, but do not sever completely. Rather, turn the bird on its side and cut to remove the oyster, then completely detach; repeat to remove the other leg. Cut along both sides of the backbone to remove, then cut down the length of the breastbone to separate it into two pieces, each with a halved breast and wing. Either discard the carcass or reserve for a future stock.

Preheat the oven to 400°F.

Season the flour to taste with salt and pepper, then use it to dredge the chicken pieces.

Heat the oil in a large ovenproof sauté pan set over medium-high heat, add the chicken, and sauté until golden; turn once. Remove, then add the shallots, continue to cook 2 minutes, add the ginger, cook an additional 2 minutes, then add the garlic and cook 30 seconds longer; stir frequently to scrape off the browned bits as they accumulate on the bottom of the pan. Drain off and discard the excess oil and fat.

Return the chicken to the pan, add the white wine, lime juice, and diced tomatoes, and stir to mix. Bring to a simmer, then cover and bake 30 minutes.

Correct the seasonings, then stir in the scallions. Top with the sliced tomatoes and lime zest just before serving with rice and snow peas.

Fluting knives are available in either high-carbon stainless steel or in carbon steel.

Curved Boning Knife

Boning a carcass and skinning one are similar operations; once that first cut is made, one hand pulls and liberates the meat or skin while the other uses the knife to separate further flesh. This calls for a blade with a high tip because the nearer it lies to its spine, the more it causes the front part of the blade to rock upward and slice as well as pierce the meat. This design rationale for the regular boning blade is also the reason why other boners offer still higher tips on upwardly canted spines, like those usually seen on skinning blades.

These higher-tipped blades are unparalleled when separating flesh from wide, flat flanks and shoulder blades, but they are unwieldly when maneuvering around the more contoured leg and shank bones.

Curved boning blades measure from 5 to 6 inches long and can be narrow or wide with varying degrees of flexibility. Most are available in high-carbon stainless steel or in stainless steel.

Boning Knife

The tip of this blade looks like a delicately bowed half spear; its point lies on the end of a straight spine where it's met by a cutting edge that rocks up at a 40-degree angle to the tip, creating a narrow, sturdy blade front whose point can initiate deep and accurate cuts and whose curved cutting edge can conclude with true slices.

Boning blades are either ⅝ or 1 inch wide and can be flexible or

Salade de Caille
Grilled Quail Salad

André Gaillard, Executive Chef:
La Réserve

4 servings

4 *quails*

¼ *cup distilled white vinegar*

12 *quail eggs*

1 *teaspoon butter*

1 *medium shallot, finely chopped*

1 *teaspoon drained green peppercorns*

2 *tablespoons sherry vinegar*

¼ *cup hazelnut oil*

¼ *cup quail stock (see page 211)*

Leaves from 1 fresh thyme branch

Salt to taste

Freshly ground black pepper to taste

1 *medium head Bibb lettuce*

1 *medium head radicchio*

1 *medium head frisée (curly endive)*

2 *medium mushroom caps*

1 *medium endive*

Use a small boning knife to remove the carcass from each quail: Run the blade behind and then under the wishbone to sever it from surrounding flesh, then pull it out. Insert the knife tip and inch the blade along and down one side of the breastbone to separate the flesh from the rib cage. When you get to the wing and then to leg joints, pull each back to snap and break it at the socket. Run the blade through each socket to separate cleanly, then repeat the procedure to free the flesh from the other side of the bird. Carefully run the knife along the backbone, then squeeze out the carcass through the front cavity and set aside meat and carcasses.

In a medium sauté pan set over high heat bring 2 inches of water and the distilled wine vinegar to a boil. Reduce the heat to a bare simmer, break the eggs directly into the water, and poach 1 minute. Remove with a slotted spoon to cold water to halt further cooking; trim if needed.

In a small saucepan set over medium heat, brown the butter. Add the shallot and green peppercorns, increase the heat to high, then deglaze with the sherry vinegar. Add the hazelnut oil and stock, season to taste with salt and pepper, then bring to a boil and cook 20 seconds to reduce. Set aside.

Season the quails with the thyme leaves, salt, and pepper and grill 2 minutes on each side.

Meanwhile, wash, dry, and julienne the lettuces; julienne the mushroom caps as well, then toss together to mix. Mound a little in the center of each plate, encircle with endive leaves and drained quail eggs, then top with a little sauce. Set a quail on each, drizzle the remaining sauce over the dish, and serve.

rigid. The wider blades, which are usually less pliant, are superb for boning large, simple cuts of meat. The narrow blades, limber enough to negotiate around intricate bone contours, are unsurpassed for boning poultry.

The blade of this knife ranges in length from 4 to 6 inches, and for most household boning chores the mid-sized, 5-inch flexible blade is recommended. It is available in any of the three major knife steels and can be forged or stamped.

How to Bone a Whole Leg of Lamb

Stanley Lobel, Co-Proprietor, Lobel's Prime Meats

One of the most luxurious ways to serve a leg of lamb is to season and roast it, then attach a manche à gigot, a decorative, viselike carving handle, to its trimmed shank bone. However, when you want to serve a uniformly seasoned or marinated leg of lamb, one that's stuffed, or one that must be consistently medium rare and therefore can't contend with the extra heat conducted through a bone, it's necessary to bone the leg before roasting it.

Before boning a whole leg of lamb, refrigerate it at least four hours to chill it completely; firmer flesh is easier to work with. If the fell—the tight, papery tissue that covers the leg—has not been removed, use the tip of a sharp knife to loosen it from the fat and flesh, then peel it off.

Place the rounded end of the leg toward you and, with the point of a boning knife, cut behind the length and around the contour of the pelvic bone; use short, forceful strokes to free it from the meat. When you encounter the ball-and-socket hip joint, cut inside the socket to sever the pelvic bone completely from the hip bone. Remove the pelvic bone and, if the tail is attached, remove it as well and either discard it or set it aside for a future stock.

Cut around the exposed ball joint, then carefully follow the femur's contours down to the knee. Use the same short cutting strokes, gently turning back the meat as you proceed.

Sever the tendon behind the knee. Cut around the knee joint and down and around the shank bone; pull up on this bone as you cut and scrape the meat from it. Carefully remove both bones.

Once the leg is boned, cut around and remove the popliteal lymph node located between the top and eye rounds; it is 1½ inches long and ¾ inch in diameter. If left in, this brings an unwanted texture, and some say it imparts a bitter flavor to the surrounding meat.

Filet d'Agneau Pané au Poivre Blanc

Sautéed Lamb Medallions with White Peppercorns

André Soltner, Chef-Proprietor: Lutèce

5 servings

1 5-pound saddle of spring lamb

Salt to taste

2 tablespoons cracked white peppercorns

10 tablespoons sweet butter

½ cup cognac

1 cup demiglace (see page 211)

Bone and completely trim the lamb. With the saddle rounded-side up, peel off the fell (if present) and remove the fat covering. Insert the blade of a boning knife and inch it down and across one side of the central backbone, cutting and scraping against this bone's contours to free one loin completely. Separate the other loin in the same manner. Turn the saddle onto its back, then cut along each side of the backbone to completely free each eye of loin. Cut off the stringy band of cartilage that runs along the length of each loin, then trim off any remaining fat and the underlying silvery membrane. Slice the meat into ½-inch-thick medallions and lightly season each with salt. Sprinkle on the peppercorns and press them in so that they adhere to the meat.

In a large sauté pan set over medium-high heat, brown the medallions in 4 tablespoons butter—about 1½ minutes per side. Transfer the meat to a warm platter.

Add the cognac to the sauté pan, flambé,* then add the demiglace; reduce the heat and simmer 4 to 5 minutes. Stir in the remaining 6 tablespoons butter, correct the seasonings, and strain over the medallions.

---

*To flambé successfully, use a spirit or fortified wine with a high (at least 70 proof) alcohol content and have it at room temperature for it to vaporize and ignite. Never pour alcohol from its bottle over the soon-to-be-flambéed foods; once ignited, the blaze could shoot up and into the bottle, which could then explode. Rather, pour the suggested amount into a small, wide-mouthed glass and add to the pan from this. Finally, if a dish to be flamed contains little or no sauce, angle the pan forward over the flame to create a thoroughly hot spot in its front third and add the liquor to this spot.

Cima alla Genovese
Stuffed Pressed Veal Breast

Giuliano Bugialli
Giuliano Bugialli's Classic
Techniques of Italian Cooking

18 servings

VEAL AND STUFFING

1 *7-pound breast of veal with rib bones*

6 *ounces veal spinal marrow, blanched 5 minutes in a bowl of boiling water, drained, and diced*

6 *ounces pancetta (or very fatty ground pork), coarsely chopped*

6 *slices white bread, crusts removed and soaked 10 minutes in 1 cup cold milk, then squeezed of excess liquid*

15 *raw shelled pistachio nuts, blanched 2 minutes in boiling salted water and peeled*

8 *extra-large eggs, 4 raw and 4 hard-cooked and shelled*

10 *fresh spinach leaves, washed, drained, stemmed, and cut into thin strips*

8 *ounces ground lean pork*

8 *ounces ground veal*

2 *ounces freshly grated Parmesan cheese*

2 *tablespoons fresh marjoram (or 1½ tablespoons dried)*

Salt to taste

Freshly ground black pepper to taste

Freshly grated nutmeg to taste

To bone the veal, remove the rib bones one by one: Hold the meat with the unattached ends of the bones up. Slit along both sides of the entire length of each bone, being sure not to cut any deeper than the thickness of the bone. Start at the free end of the bone and detach by cutting underneath to the end; repeat the procedure to remove the remaining ribs. Trim off the extra fat at the bottom end. There should now be about 4 pounds of meat.

To make a pocket for the stuffing, lay the meat flat and insert the knife at the top end on one side, precisely in the center of the thickness. As you cut across the meat, be careful to keep the knife in the middle of the meat all the way through. The opening should be in the middle, not close to either side. Insert the knife inside the opening to deepen it by cutting down to about 1 inch from the other end. Check to be sure there are no holes in the meat, but if there are, sew them up with a needle and twine before stuffing.

To prepare the stuffing, combine the marrow, pancetta, bread, pistachio nuts, raw eggs, spinach, ground pork and veal, Parmesan cheese, and marjoram and season to taste with salt, pepper, and nutmeg; gently mix with a wooden spoon.

Place half the stuffing in the veal pocket and top it with a centrally set row of hard-cooked eggs. Place the remaining stuffing over and along the sides of the eggs, being careful to keep them aligned. Sew up the pocket with a needle and twine.

Use your hands to roll the flat stuffed pocket into a shape that resembles a large loaf of bread, wrap it in cheesecloth, and tie it with twine.

POACHING BROTH

2 *tablespoons coarse salt (approximately)*

1 *large red onion, cut in half*

2 *medium carrots, coarsely chopped*

1 *large celery rib, coarsely chopped*

10 *whole black peppercorns*

1 *bay leaf*

Bring a large pot of water to a boil (or use a fish poacher) and add the salt. When the water returns to a boil, add the remaining broth ingredients and simmer 5 minutes. Add the meat and simmer, covered, 2½ hours.

When cooked, transfer the veal to a cookie sheet, cover with a 10-pound weight, cool 6 hours, then refrigerate at least 12 hours.

To serve, remove the cheesecloth, slice ¼-inch thick, and accompany with a basil or parsley sauce.

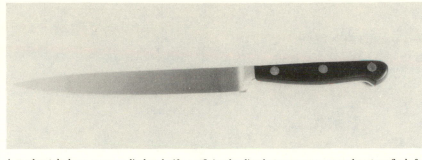

A moderately long, narrow, limber knife proficiently slips between carcass and watery flesh for filleting fish.

Fish Fillet Knife

Filleting sole and carving duck are comparable procedures: Tender flesh is pierced, then complex bone structures are followed with the point and edge of a blade, so the classic fillet and long slicing blades are similarly shaped. Both have dropped tips to pierce accurately into crevices and hollows, a lightly arced cutting edge to facilitate penetration or slicing, and limberness to follow carcass configurations. The only visible difference between the two is length: The standard fillet blade, generally used on smaller fish, is 1 to 3 inches shorter than that of the slicing knife.

Fish fillet blades, also styled with a high tip, most often measure 6 or 7 inches long. They are available either stamped or, better, forged, in any of the three major knife steels; high-carbon stainless steel is favored.

Cleaver

The blade of this knife is a thick, inflexible steel trapezium with a relatively flat cutting edge that splits cartilage and bone. A fine cleaver is also heavy and forwardly weighted to facilitate the drop-chop, downward-swing motion and armed with a powerful, axlike channel edge to protect the tool from heavy impacts.

Cleaver blades range in length from 6 to 9 inches and are usually available in three weights. The light chicken cleaver weighs under 1 pound, the medium kitchen cleaver weighs between 1 and 2 pounds, and the heavy market cleaver weighs over 2 pounds. Some have a noticeable saddle spine to push the blade's weight farther forward and others sport a curved edge that accomplishes some light cutting, but for general home purposes, a regular 6-inch medium-weight cleaver is sufficient.

How to Fillet and Skin Flat- and Roundfish

Robert N. Neuman, Proprietor: Rosedale Fish & Oyster Market

Many of the dishes that feature fish fillets do so out of sheer necessity; the even, airy texture of a salmon soufflé or pike quenelle couldn't possibly be achieved otherwise. But most recipes suggest using filleted fish for pure, practical dining ease. Not having to cope with a single bone in a stuffed trout or a pompano en papillotte might readily prompt the reaction that Thomas Jordan, a former London poet laureate, described: "Fish dinners . . . make a man spring like a flea."

To fillet and skin a flatfish, place the rinsed fish face up on a cutting board and, with the tip of a sharp knife, cut diagonally down from the central backbone and behind the gills to follow the contours of the head.

Keeping the blade almost flat, slide its tip through the skin and between the thick, meaty section and the rib bones. Use short strokes to scrape the blade toward the backbone and along the length of the fish; peel the flesh back once it's freed. Turn the fish around and, working from tail to head, separate the other half of the fillet. Flip the fish over and re-peat the procedure to remove the thinner top fillet; trim any peripheral bones from both fillets. Either discard the carcass or use it for a future stock.

To skin the fillet, place it skin-side down and, with the blade of a sharp knife, make a vertical cut ½ inch up from the tail and down to the skin. Using this as a tab to hold, slip the knife blade between the flesh and skin and run it down the length of the fillet to separate the two.

To scale, clean, and fillet a round-fish, use a pair of scissors to cut off the dorsal, anal, pelvic, and pectoral fins. Place the fish on a cutting board, firmly hold its tail, and use a fish scaler to scrape off the scales from tail to head with short, firm strokes. Rinse the fish.

Use a sharp knife to cut off the head behind the gill opening, then slit the belly to the vent and pull out the entrails.

Lay the cleaned fish on one side, hold it securely, and insert the knife blade between the flesh and backbone at the head end. Use short strokes and follow the contours of the bone to slice down its length; peel the flesh back once it's freed. Turn the fish over and repeat the procedure on the other side. Scrape off any ventral blood vessels and trim the fillets neatly.

Butcher's Cleaver

With its axlike cutting edge, backward-bowed blade front, and clipped spine beak, this large cleaver looks more like the fifteenth-century weapon of war brandished by halberdiers than a fine carcass separator. Its unique blade configuration throws most of the impressive 3¼-pound weight forward for an easier drop-chop motion, and a sturdy, 7½-inch channel edge withstands the constant heavy blows.

Butcher's cleavers are available in either carbon or stainless steels, usually with an uncovered handle.

Lamb Splitter

The lamb splitter is the largest member of the cleaver family. It has a 12-inch-long, 2½-inch-deep heavy blade whose cutting edge remains straight for most of its length until it sweeps up to a high, clipped tip. That strong angle adds extra length to an already impressive cutting surface and gives the splitter one of the longest cutting edges found in the batterie de cuisine. Its length and 2-pound weight make a tool that is part cleaver and part heavy knife.

The splitter cuts saddles and rib roasts from lamb carcasses. Lamb bones, which are not as hard as sheep bones, might splinter if cut by a typical cleaver. The splitter also uniformly slices steaks from large fish and halves lobsters.

A lamb splitter is most often available in carbon steel.

Round-Tipped Ham Slicer

This round-tipped blade shaves long, thin, even slices from roast ham and turkey, which, because they are drier and denser then other meats, should be cut as thinly as possible for maximum appeal. A thin slice shortens a meat's fibers to make its flesh seem more tender and the only way to slice sparingly is to use a narrow blade, in this case 1 inch wide. A

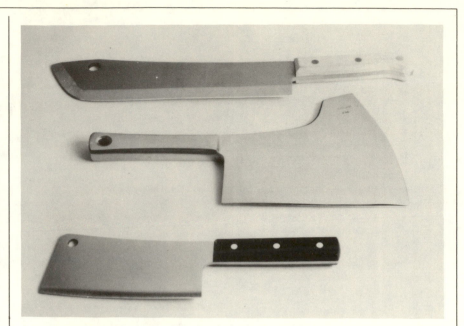

From top to bottom, the lamb splitter, butcher's cleaver, and kitchen cleaver are impressively heavy to help power through bones when sectioning meat, fish, or fowl.

All slicers are long; special shapes for special purposes include, from top to bottom, a salmon slicer, roast beef slicer, and ham slicer.

thick blade tapers more steeply from spine to cutting edge and, because the side of the slicer clings to the meat it's cutting, a slightly larger bevel pulls the blade off its straight course to cause progressively more diagonal, uneven slicing.

A slicer with a 10-inch-long blade is favored, in high-carbon stainless steel. It is alternatively finished with a spearpoint tip.

Spearpoint Roast-Beef Slicer

The spearpoint ham slicer and this one for roast beef are virtually the same, except that the roast-beef blade is heavier, stiffer, and 25 percent wider to slice and carve the juicier, softer beef into thicker slices. The blade's additional heft translates into extra power for clean pen-

How to Slice
Smoked Salmon

William Poll,
Proprietor: William Poll, Inc.

Many say there is an art to slicing smoked salmon, from extracting the fish's bones to executing smooth, clean, uniform slices. That's theory; in truth, it's not so much an art as it is knowing that the fish has 28 vertebrae and where they lie, recognizing the prime from the not-so-prime meat, then applying a set slicing procedure.

Smoked salmon that requires slicing is usually sold as a side—a portion half the whole length of the fish from shoulder to tail. An ideal side weighs five pounds and its woodsy, sweet/saline taste and satiny texture are best appreciated in paper-thin slices.

A side of smoked salmon can be sliced in one of two traditional ways. Some address the fish at a right angle and cut delicate, nearly ⅛-inch-thick, steaklike slices, but most prefer the long, wide, diagonal banquet-cut slices.

To slice a five-pound side of smoked salmon diagonally, place the fish, skin-side down, on a cutting board. Remove any skin and dorsal and pelvic bones that remain on this side of the fish, then trim off any fins and belly fat. Use a pair of tweezers or needle-nosed pliers to carefully remove the vertebrae that emanate from the center and run down the length of the fish.

Set the blade of a long, sharp slicing knife one-third of the way up from the tail and at a 15-degree angle against the flesh. Using the fingers of your free hand to steady the fish, apply a light, controlled, back-and-forth sawing motion to move along the top of the fish in cutting back toward the tail; this will produce a slice so thin you can read through it. Continue to slice the fish in this manner, working your way toward the shoulder with each successive slice. Try to avoid severing the skin that remains on the flip side of the fish.

Overlap the slices on four previously laid out sheets of plastic wrap; stack them, then tightly wrap in aluminum foil and refrigerate. The fish should be eaten within three days. (A five-pound side of smoked salmon will serve 24 as an appetizer.)

etration; the rigidity contributes to even slicing as the extra thickness provides the necessary backing for more substantial cuts.

Spearpoint roast-beef blades, also called long slicers, range in length from 8 to 12 inches. The round-tipped blades, less traditional for roast beef than for ham, are also available in the longer, 10- to 14-inch lengths. Both can have plain, wave-cut, and, in the case of the round-tipped blade, granton edges. A 10-inch-long, plain-edged spearpoint slicer in high-carbon stainless steel is recommended.

Salmon Slicer

This salmon slicer has the thinnest, narrowest, most flexible blade made today to slice scant sheets of smoked or cured salmon. A slight side bevel can't draw the blade diagonally off its course; a small surface area won't allow freed flesh to adhere, pull, and cause uneven cutting; and extreme pliancy lets the blade bend to conform to the thicker and thinner areas of the fish. A granton edge, a series of staggered ovals that run alternatively down the blade's two sides, makes this knife technically superb by shaving off even more steel from the sides of an already thin blade. During slicing, these alternating ovals constantly change the surface contact of meat against blade to further reduce the adhesion.

Granton-edge salmon slicers have blades that range in length from 11 to 13 inches, and for home use an 11-inch blade forged in high-carbon stainless steel is recommended. Plain-edged salmon slicers are also manufactured; their blade lengths can be 9 to 13 inches and they are available in both stainless and high-carbon stainless steels.

Gravlax

Christer Larsson,
Executive Chef: Aquavit

6 to 8 servings

Generous ½ cup salt

Generous ½ cup granulated sugar

2 *tablespoons cracked white pepper*

1 *4-pound side Norwegian salmon with skin on*

4 *bunches fresh dill, chopped (approximately 3 cups)*

Combine the salt, sugar, and pepper, mix well, and set aside.

Place the salmon skin-side down on a large nonreactive platter, rub the salt mixture into the flesh, then cover with the chopped dill. Cover with plastic, weight with about 5 pounds, and allow to sit at room temperature 4 to 6 hours. Refrigerate 48 hours; drain every 12 hours.

To serve: Transfer the salmon to a towel to drain and scrape off the seasonings. Slice diagonally into very thin slices and serve with crisp bread and mustard sauce (see below).

MUSTARD SAUCE

½ cup Dijon-style mustard

2 *teaspoons red wine vinegar*

2 *teaspoons granulated sugar*

¾ cup vegetable oil

¼ cup finely chopped dill

Combine the mustard, vinegar, and sugar in a small bowl and stir to mix. Whisk in the oil, then add the dill and stir to mix.

This carving knife has a gently upswept blade front to extend its cutting surface.

A steak knife's small, slender, lightly bowed razor-sharp cutting edge is the quintessential table-side piercing, cutting, slicing, and trimming tool.

Carpaccio

Arrigo Cipriani, Proprietor: Bellini by Cipriani

4 servings

12 *ounces beef sirloin, trimmed of all fat*

Salt

½ *cup mayonnaise*

4 *teaspoons Worcestershire sauce*

½ *teaspoon dry mustard*

3 *tablespoons milk*

Freshly ground white pepper to taste

Cut the meat across the grain into paper-thin slices, then overlap them on each of 4 serving plates so they cover the entire surface. Lightly salt the meat, then refrigerate it as you prepare the sauce.

Combine the remaining ingredients in a small bowl and mix with a wooden spoon.

Dip the spoon into the sauce and use it to drizzle a crosshatch pattern of sauce over each portion of carpaccio. Serve immediately.

Table Carving Knife

The 8-inch-long blade of this carving knife looks like a stylized bowie knife. Its cutting edge gently bows up to a high tip where it meets the second false edge that starts two-thirds up the spine, then graduates downward. These features expand the slicing and piercing capabilities of the blade's front; a longer cutting surface slices a greater amount of meat in one stroke, and a sharp narrow tip meticulously penetrates, to quickly free meat from bone.

Carving knives are designed expressly for table use and are often very decorative, with staghorn or buffalo handles and etched or inlaid blades whose styling stems from the Middle Ages. Most contemporary carving knives are equally effective yet free of the more extemporaneous designs. Their handles are either hardwood, impregnated wood, or durable plastic, and the blades are stainless or high-carbon stainless steel.

Steak Knife

The most popular steak-knife blade is narrow, barely flexible, and 4½-inches long with a straight cutting edge that gently sweeps up to a lightly clipped tip. Such delicate bowing extends the part of the blade most used during the down stroke and slicing, and a leaner tip allows for deft penetration when final trimming around a bone is necessary. Steak knives with serrated or wave-cut edges are inappropriate for slicing carefully cooked tenderloin and shell steaks. Since these cuts are devoid of tough muscle, the meats are uniformly tender and most easily cut against their grain with a razor-sharp straight edge. Serration is a substitute for sharpness; the teeth will bite and tear with the grain, but you wouldn't cut a steak that way because the sawing action produces ripped rather than clean slices.

Steak-knife blades range in length from 4 to 5 inches, are available in the three major knife-making steels, and should be maintained as diligently as any fine knife.

Deba-Bōchō

The three more common Japanese knives include, from left, a yanagi-ba-bōchō to cut sashimi, a nakiri-bōchō to cut, slice, and chop vegetables, and a deba-bōchō to fillet fish. (See discussion at right and on page 16.)

At first glance, this medium-length, wide, spear-shaped *bōchō* blade seems too awkward to fillet fish, but because the blade is ground on only one side, Japanese style (most western knife blades are ground on both sides to form a durable 25- to 30-degree-edge bevel angle), the extremely acute cutting edge created accomplishes surprisingly delicate boning tasks. Its broad tip can endure continued flesh penetration while the thin, 14-degree-edge bevel angle is so narrow that it readily slips across backbone and rib-cage contours for an efficient fillet.

The blade is traditionally single beveled and has been since 900 A.D. when craftsmen were perfecting samurai swords. Another blade construction technique that was developed then—laminating or folding blade steel—is also applied on today's Japanese knives. The blade's carbon-steel core is sandwiched between thin layers of stainless steel; when its single side is honed (unless specially ordered, this is done to the right side), the tougher stainless steel is ground off and the carbon steel exposed to form the cutting surface. The user enjoys all the benefits of a high-carbon steel cutting edge without the staining and rusting.

Laminated and full-stainless-steel blades are now commonly found in Japanese households, but professionals prefer all-carbon steel blades. A roughly 8-inch-long *deba* blade is the most popular size for home use.

How to Carve a Ham

Joseph Ottomanelli,
Proprietor: Ottomanelli Brothers

Three blind mice, see how they run!
They all ran after the farmer's wife,
She cut off their tails with a carv-
ing knife,
Did you ever see such a sight in
your life,
As three blind mice?

Old English nursery rhymes often seem silly initially, but on closer inspection, this one reveals how early in epicurean history the carving knife appears in the cook's hands. Before the advent of personal fork use, any hot meat, fish, or poultry served at a banquet had to be cut tableside into small pieces for the guests. This meant that carving and, as the art developed, a fine carving knife were indispensable to the feast. The cook who cut off the tails of those three mice could easily have been roasting a large ham in an open hearth for a banquet.

Baked hams are one of the glories of the banquet table; they are hand-some, richly flavored, and offer ample portions for a sizable crowd. With little effort, they are also easy to carve.

The French and English techniques are the two recognized ways to carve a ham. In the former, the meat is thinly sliced on a diagonal toward the bone, and according to the English style it is sliced vertically; both work well.

To carve a smoked ham according to the French method, use a sharp carving knife to cut three thin, lengthwise slices from the flat, less meaty side of the ham to form a secure base.

Turn the ham onto this base and insert a fork just above the shank bone. About 2 inches from the end of the shank make a straight, vertical cut into the meat down to the bone; make a second, diagonal cut 2 inches above this and to connect with the first. Remove and discard this fatty wedge.

Begin to slice at a 30-degree angle to the bone, making thin, even slices; remove the slices to a platter. After one-third of the ham has been sliced, the bone rises noticeably in the meat and it's necessary to start carving small, arclike slices from each side of the bone; when doing this, alternate the sides being sliced to keep the ham even.

To carve a fresh ham according to the English method, prepare a base on the ham as suggested above. Turn the ham onto this base and insert a fork into the meat just above the shank bone. Two inches up from the end of the shank, make a diagonal cut toward the meaty section of the ham and down to the bone; make a second, vertical cut one inch above this to connect with the first and to create a wedge of meat. Remove and discard this wedge.

Continue to make vertical cuts at ¼-inch intervals along half the length of the leg. At this point, the bone begins to rise and it's necessary to carve smaller slices from alternate sides of the bone. To detach the slices, run the blade of the knife underneath the slices and along the length of the bone.

Yanagi-Ba-Bōchō

One of the most frequently used knives at a sushi bar is this long, slender, swordlike *yanagi-ba*. Many call it the sashimi knife because it's the best tool to cut raw salmon, bass, and bream into elegant, paper-thin slices. The *yanagi-ba*'s cutting edge is sizable enough to cut cleanly through a large fish steak, yet not so unwieldly that it can't be equally effective with a small fillet. Like other Japanese knives, the blade on this one is ground on one side only for the necessary, dead-straight sashimi slicing. A second, slightly beveled edge facing the flesh being cut can alter a direct slice by causing it to angle off course.

The *yanagi-ba* has a barely dropped spearpoint tip and was once used strictly by chefs from Osaka, but it is now popular throughout Japan. Its brother blade, the *tako-biki*, which also cuts fish fillets, is equally long and narrow, but with a cropped tip. *Tako-biki-bōchō* means octopus cutter and, although readily available, still remains more or less a local favorite among Tokyo chefs.

Both knives have blades that range in length from 10 to 14 inches. A 12-inch blade in carbon steel is recommended; it is also manufactured in carbon-laminated and stainless steels.

Nakiri-Bōchō

The *nakiri-bōchō* blade looks like an elongated rectangle with a sheep's-foot tip. It usually has a straight, 8-inch cutting edge backed by a 2-inch steel width; the added support makes a tool manageable enough to slice vegetables decoratively, yet still sufficiently substantial to chop, shred, and mince. It is customarily ground on one side only so it can cut a crisp, continuous sheet from a daikon, style a turnip into a blooming chrysanthemum, and finely shred a carrot. Single-side

grinding brings an extra benefit: The angle created pushes freshly cut food out and away from its edge so that the chef can see clearly while slicing.

The *usuba-bōchō*, which resembles a narrow Western cleaver with a sheep's-foot tip, is the alternate and, some say, more popular vegetable knife. The *nakiri*, or *kanto*-style, *bōchō* was originally most prevalent in Tokyo and Yokohama, while the *kansai*-style *usuba* was first developed in the Kyoto-Osaka region. Both are available in stainless steel, carbon-laminated stainless steel, and the recommended carbon steel.

Chinese Cleaver

Even though it's as boxy as the Western cleaver, the Chinese version is less a cleaver than an oriental chef's knife. It is lighter, thinner, and, with its razor-sharp tapered edge, it slices and dices rather than hacks and hews. Its usual dimensions are 8 inches by 3 inches, although different sizes and shapes are designed for particular purposes. The elongated rectangle has a greater cutting edge that's especially good for mincing; the wider curved-edge cleaver, which can be rocked, is superb for chopping, and the popular boxlike cleaver, with its straight edge, excels at slicing and cutting.

Western cleavers are classified according to blade length, but the Chinese are delineated according to weight, with each allotted a specific number. Number 1 cleavers usually weigh 10 ounces and are used primarily for decorative cutting. The recommended Number 2 cleaver generally weighs 12 ounces and is used for mincing, dicing, shredding, and slicing. The Number 3 cleaver, at 20 ounces, is the heaviest and can quarter poultry and be used for hard chopping.

Chinese cleavers are available in carbon and stainless steels and recently, in a very fine, single, medium-weight high-carbon stainless steel from some of the German knife makers.

How to Cut Sashimi

Toshio Morimoto,
Chef-Proprietor: Kitcho

Few first courses strike the same artistic balance of flavor, color, and texture as the selection of raw sliced fish that the Japanese call sashimi. Freshness is crucial, so the seasons govern what is offered. A winter selection might include yellowtail and mackerel, and spring, sea bream and bonito; a summer platter might feature carp and perch, and autumn, bass and clams. The sushi chef must carefully clean, fillet, skin where necessary, and slice the fish into one of four presentation-style cuts, each of which measures three fingers wide.

The particular fish texture directs the slice. Bass and flounder are so delicate that, if thickly sliced, they would tear from their own weight when picked up. Resilient squid, on the other hand, is best appreciated in very thin, threadlike strips.

There are four basic sashimi cuts.

- *Hira-tzukuri* is the flat, rectangular slice most often used for such fragile-fleshed fish as porgy and flounder. After the fillet is skinned and trimmed to 2 inches wide, the meat is colorfully placed with its skinned side up. The knife is set straight down and drawn through to make successive half-inch-wide cross-grain cuts. (When the cleaned fish is set skin-side down and sliced diagonally, this cut is called *hegi-tzukiri*.)

- *Usu-tzukuri* is the paper-thin cut that best suits the semifirm-fleshed bass and bream. It is made by holding the knife at an acute, near-horizontal angle to the fish flesh and lightly drawing it through to make $\frac{1}{8}$- to $\frac{1}{16}$-inch-thick slices.

- *Kaku-tzukuri*, or cube cut, is used almost exclusively to slice the thick but soft-fleshed tuna and bonito fillets. Once the trimmed fillet is cut into $\frac{3}{4}$-inch-thick slices, they are then cut into $\frac{3}{4}$-inch cubes.

- *Ito-tzukuri*, or thread cut, is the only feasible way to slice cleaned, comparatively firm-fleshed squid. After its pouch is cut into 2-inch-long sections, these are then sliced into $\frac{1}{8}$- to $\frac{1}{4}$-inch-wide strips.

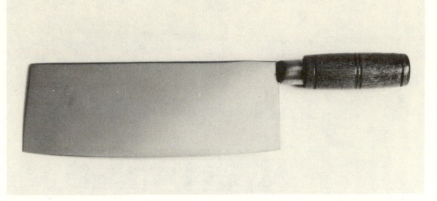

This Chinese cleaver, lighter and thinner than a western cleaver, is really more an oriental chef's knife.

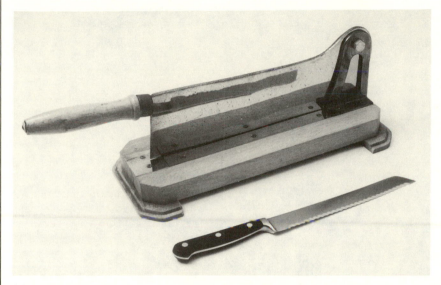

A long, rigid blade best contends with crusty bread. At front is a standard bread knife; behind it, a baker's bread-cutter.

Bread Knife

Long, moderately rigid, and upwardly canted with a wave-cut edge, this bread-knife blade is well equipped to slice across a large loaf in one stroke, to contend with the density of a dark rye or the airiness of a brioche. Bread knives with finely serrated blades work on the same principle as the wave-cut edge: They bite rather than slice into a hard crust, then quickly rip through the loaf's softer interior without compressing it.

Bread-knife blades range in length from 8 to 10 inches; all are bluntly tipped and are available in either stainless or high-carbon stainless steel. This is one of the few basic blades that, because of what it cuts, needn't have a full tang. A bread knife with a 10-inch-long blade—which can also be used to slice a torte horizontally for later layering or to remove the sugar bloom from a baked sponge cake—is recommended for household use.

Baker's Bread-Cutter

When cutting into a crisp-crusted loaf of French bread, this long, deep blade, attached to a platform, cleanly slices it. The blade's 10-inch cutting edge equally dispatches the successively wider loaves known as ficelles, baguettes, and bâtards; its 3½-inch steel depth adds weight and strength as the curved front, which is set with pivots to the base, keeps cutting edge and platform close for quick action. A corresponding slot in the wood base that receives the knife edge assures complete severing.

Frequently called a bistro bread knife because it's a hard-to-misplace near-staple in those small restaurants, these slicers are most often available with a 14-inch-long platform fitted with either a carbon or stainless-steel 10-inch blade.

Two-Pronged Tomato Knife

This rigid, wave-cut knife blade neatly saws through crisp fruit exteriors and pulpy interiors with little compacting or juicing, and its two prongs transfer newly cut slices to platter or plate while the 5-inch backup blade supplies leverage.

Many call this knife a European tomato knife, although it can also be used to slice salami, hull out small brioche for filling, or cut and serve hard cheese.

Grapefruit Knife

To free a grapefruit, orange, or lemon from its peel, you need a knife that has a narrow, medium-length, serrated or wave-cut blade whose flat plane curves near the blunt tip. This design conforms to the general size and shape of citrus fruit; the sawlike edge severs stringy pith and tough flesh, and a dull point can't pierce membranes and drain juices.

Grapefruit knives, which are also used to free melon from rind, hull tomatoes, and core onions, are generally made of stainless steel with blades that measure 3½ to 4 inches.

Decorating Knife

This blade serves two purposes. Its 1-inch tapered tip area, resembling the sheep's-foot parer, lightly peels and trims; the blade's remaining 3 inches are rigid and crenulated and shape tender root vegetables, crinkle-cut french fries, and score furrows in soft spreads and icings.

The grooves on some decorating blades can be shallower—even wavy—but these knives should be avoided because they only minimally ridge carrots and rutabagas, for instance. Some knife makers also offer decorating knives that have offset, or upwardly canted, handles, keeping the hand up and away from the cutting board while styling french fries and tofu.

Decorating knives are available only in stainless steel.

Chestnut Knife

Short, rigid, with a hooklike, curved cutting edge, this knife blade is used to score cross-marks through a chestnut's rounded, hard shell prior to boiling to prevent bursting. The arced cutting edge, which follows the contours of the nut, is employed to remove the shell and furry inner skin after draining.

Chestnut-knife blades are always 1 inch long and are available only in stainless steel.

Hard-Cheese Knife

Every fine hard-cheese knife is distinguished by a coped tip, flat cutting edge, and etched sides; the low tip ensures clean puncturing and slicing; the full, flat cutting surface provides an even steel spread for supersmooth cutting, while the etching prevents cheese from sticking, ragging, and pulling the blade off course. A usually offset handle allows forceful downward entry into

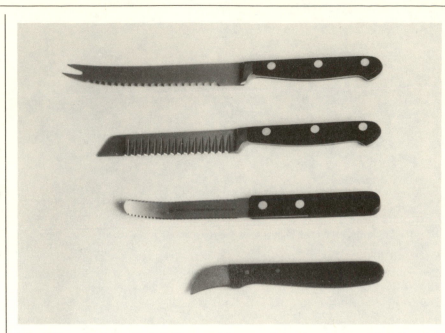

Inflexibility and unique edges help these special-purpose knives to cut, score, or tear. From top to bottom are a tomato knife, decorating knife, grapefruit knife, and chestnut knife.

A cheese's texture dictates which blade best cuts it. Shown top to bottom are a hard-cheese knife and two Parmesan blades.

a wheel without fear of jamming your knuckles against the cutting board.

For even slicing, the best blade should be slightly longer than the average diameter of the cheese you intend to cut. The blades range from 4½ to 12 inches long, and for household use the smallest size suits most needs. Cheese knives used commercially—those with blades longer than 12 inches and comparably deeper—are also available with two handles. Both styles are most often manufactured in stainless and high-carbon stainless steels.

Chestnut Salad with Walnuts and Pancetta

Paula Wolfert
Paula Wolfert's World of Food

4 servings

¾ to 1 pound fresh chestnuts

4 tablespoons sweet butter

½ teaspoon fennel seeds

1 6- to 7-inch celery rib with leaves

1 bay leaf

3 to 4 cups torn mixed greens: escarole, chicory, arugula, etc.

1 garlic clove

Salt to taste

4 thin slices firm white bread, crusts removed

4 ounces pancetta or thick slices of lean bacon (the latter first blanched, rinsed, and drained), cut crosswise into thin strips

Freshly ground black pepper to taste

3 tablespoons walnut oil

2 teaspoons aged red-wine vinegar

¼ cup chopped walnuts

Peel the chestnuts: Slit the flat side of each with a sharp knife—ideally a chestnut knife—then drop into boiling water for 2 to 3 minutes. Remove with a slotted spoon and keep warm under a kitchen towel. One by one, cut away the shell and skin together. If the inner skin is difficult to remove, return the chestnut to the hot water for an instant. If the skin still resists, spread on a baking sheet and place in a slow oven to dry. Once bone dry they can be rubbed with a coarse cloth.

Combine the chestnuts with 1 tablespoon butter, fennel, celery, bay leaf, and enough water to cover in a heavy, 8-inch skillet. Cover, and cook very slowly—15 to 45 minutes—until the chestnuts are tender; remove at once if the chestnuts begin to fall apart during this time.

Meanwhile, wash the greens thoroughly; drain and wrap them in a kitchen towel. Crush the garlic with salt and set aside. Cut the bread into croutons. Heat 2 tablespoons butter in a nonstick-surfaced skillet and, when hot, add the croutons and fry until golden on all sides. Add the garlic and toss for an instant; remove the croutons to drain on paper towels.

When the chestnuts are tender, transfer them with a slotted spoon to a flat plate to dry. Wipe out the skillet, then add the pancetta and fry until almost crisp. Add the remaining tablespoon butter and the chestnuts and season with salt and pepper; gently sauté 30 seconds or until glistening.

Just before serving, make a vinaigrette with the walnut oil, vinegar, salt, and pepper. Mix the greens with the vinaigrette and the walnuts, then add the chestnuts, being careful not to break them when mixing. Scatter the croutons on top and serve while the chestnuts are still warm.

Gorgonzola Knife

Gorgonzola and Stilton rank among the world's most luxurious cheeses, but the marbleization that helps to create the unique spicy/sharp flavors and velvety/rough textures in these well-aged blue cheeses frustrates the server who tries to cut them with an inappropriate blade. Crumbling won't occur, however, when a rigid, medium-length, broad, blunt-edged Gorgonzola knife is used. It's strong enough to dig down into a semisoft wheel and wide and dull to act as a wedge, splitting the cheese apart according to its veining for intact servings.

A Gorgonzola knife blade is nearly 6 inches long and expands from a ¾-inch base to a 4½-inch edge.

Oyster Knife

There are many types of stilettolike oyster knives—their blades are short and narrow with blunt tips and edges for shell penetration and to avoid shearing the meat, and each has a rigid central spine to give it prying strength. The most common blades are ⅝ inch wide and 3 inches long, notably the Providence and Galveston patterns; and some are beveled on only one side, like the Boston blade. There is one exception to this standard, however—the recommended curved and more sharply tipped New Haven blade. Its pointed tip stabs through a hinge faster and more easily than other knives and once inside, its slight 5-degree upward angle affords a greater axis for prying.

Oyster knives are available in carbon and high-carbon stainless steels with wooden or textured plastic handles.

Parmesan Knife

No blade can crack open a wheel, or drum, of Pecorino or prize a morsel from a large piece of Parmesan quite like this sharply tipped, leaf-shaped blade. Conventional blades work against the close grains of these dry cheeses and crumble rather than cut them. The Parmesan knife's sharp tip pierces into a hard wheel while its gradient cutting edges, which extend two inches up its flared sides, allow for enough penetration so that the broad blade can then be twisted to break the cheese cleanly apart along its natural grain.

The most utilitarian Parmesan knife blade measures nearly 5 inches long. A smaller, more decorative one is also available, and both are manufactured in stainless steel.

Arrow-shaped Oyster Knife

For those who hesitate to open an oyster with a needlelike blade, there is this fine, arrow-shaped alternative. It's shorter, tapered to two flared, blunt edges, and outfitted with a protective shield like a sword's hilt that prevents the blade from advancing beyond the width of any shell. The knife prizes oysters just as well as the traditional blade with one exception: It deals with the wide, flat Belon oysters far better. That narrow blade gains a foothold on a Belon, but it doesn't have as much leverage, so it usually cracks a Belon shell once the blade is inserted and twisted.

Arrow-shaped oyster knives are available in stainless steel.

Cherrystone-Clam Knife

Since a clam is opened from a point opposite its hinge and an oyster is broached from the hinge, the blades that open these bivalves differ dramatically. The needlelike oyster knife stabs and pries; the wide, spatula-shaped clam knife wedges and slices. Both are short, strong, and stiff, but the clam blade has a sharp cutting edge to slip through hard, pursed lips, and considerable width so the knife can be twisted to spread the two clamshells apart to break the vacuum.

Cherrystone-clam knives are generally 3 inches long, ¾ inch wide, and are available in stainless or high-carbon stainless steels.

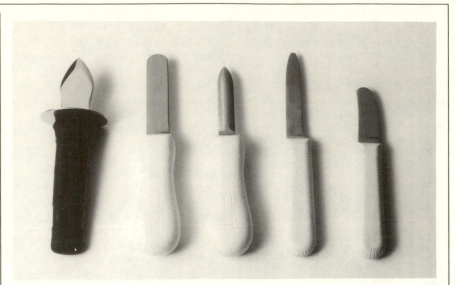

Shellfish knives, shown from left, are the arrow-shaped oyster knife, cherrystone-clam knife, oyster knife (described on page 19), littleneck-clam knife, and bay-scallop knife.

Littleneck-Clam Knife

The littleneck-clam knife is similar to the cherrystone blade in that it is thick, strong, and armed with one sharp cutting edge. However, the littleneck knife is slimmer and tapered to a point, since littlenecks are 25 percent smaller than cherrystones. Once a slender blade is slipped between a littleneck's less developed shells and twisted, it won't overwhelm, snap, and crack them as a bulky blade would. The tip makes it easier to maneuver into smaller shell hollows when severing adductor muscles.

Littleneck-clam knives are most often available in stainless steel.

Bay-Scallop Knife

This moderately wide, arced, rigid blade neatly prizes bay scallops from their shells. Its 2-inch length easily overcomes a small scallop; the blunt tip reduces flesh mutilation and the slight, upwardly curved profile that creates a broader area promises sure shell separation. Once the shell is open, the blade's slight cutting edge can then free the adductor muscle from its valves and trim off all viscera.

Bay-scallop knives are available only in high-carbon stainless steel.

How to Open an Oyster

Joseph Enea, Proprietor: Pisacane Mid-Town Corp.

Ernest Hemingway wrote, *"I began my second dozen of the flat oysters, picking them from their bed of crushed ice on the silver plate, watching their unbelievably delicate brown edges react and cringe as I squeezed lemon juice on them and separated the holding muscle from the shell and lifted them to chew them carefully."*

Connoisseurs have long held that the best way to appreciate the sweet taste and succulent texture of an oyster—be it a Belon, Blue Point, Malpeque, Olympia, Wellfleet, or other—is freshly opened and with a little lemon.

To open an oyster, hold it firmly in a thick cloth, hinge side out and flat shell up. Thrust the tip of an oyster knife about ½ inch deep into the hinge and twist it to break its vacuum and open the shell.

Slide the knife under the upper shell and, pushing upward, sever the muscle that attaches the meat to its shell; remove and discard the top shell. Run the knife under and around the oyster meat to release it from its shell.

Oyster Pan Roast

The Brody Corporation,
Proprietor: Oyster Bar &
Restaurant

1 serving

6 *to* 8 *large oysters, freshly*
shucked, with their juice
reserved

1 *tablespoon butter*

2 *tablespoons bottled clam juice*

1 *tablespoon bottled chili sauce*

1 *tablespoon Worcestershire*
sauce

Pinch celery salt

½ *cup heavy cream*

1 *slice toast*

Pinch paprika

Combine the oysters, their juice, butter, and 1 tablespoon clam juice in a small sauté pan set over high heat and cook just until the edges of the oysters begin to curl; remove from the heat and set aside.

Combine the chili and Worcestershire sauces, celery salt, and remaining tablespoon clam juice in a small saucepan set over high heat and bring to a boil; whisk constantly. Add the heavy cream and return to a boil; continue to whisk. Reduce the heat, add the oyster mixture, and stir gently; cook less than a minute to heat through.

Place the toast in a warm soup bowl, pour the pan roast on top, sprinkle with paprika, and serve immediately.

How to Open a Clam

Joseph Enea, Proprietor:
Pisacane Mid-Town Corp.

Although oysters and hard-shell clams are both bivalve mollusks with similar shell configurations, they should be opened differently to extract the meat. An oyster has two half-shells which taper to such a clean point that its lip is often imperceptible, so for safety, it is best opened at its hinge. A clam is not so streamlined; its two half-shells meet more bluntly and form a distinct lip that is easier to pry open.

To open a hard-shell clam, hold the clam firmly in one hand with the hinge against the palm. Lightly press the cutting edge of a clam knife between the half-shell directly opposite the hinge. Curl the fingers that hold the clam around the back of the blade to hold the blade in place, then simultaneously squeeze and push the knife to enter; immediately rotate the blade to pry the shell open.

Once the shell separates, run the knife up and around the inside of the top shell to sever the attaching muscles, then twist off and discard the top shell. Slide the blade tip under the clam to free the meat completely.

New England Clam Chowder

Edmund Lillys, Proprietor:
Gloucester House

6 servings

4 *tablespoons butter*

1 *large onion, diced*

4 *medium all-purpose potatoes,*
peeled and diced

1½ *cups water*

4 *quahogs or 2 dozen cherry-*
stone clams, shucked,
coarsely chopped, and their
liquor strained and reserved

1 *bay leaf*

½ *teaspoon dried thyme*

1 *cup milk*

1 *cup light cream*

Salt to taste

Freshly ground white pepper to
taste

Cayenne to taste (optional)

1 *tablespoon finely chopped*
parsley

Heat 2 tablespoons of butter in a large saucepan set over medium heat, add the onion, and sauté 10 minutes or until transparent and slightly golden; stir occasionally. Add the potatoes, water, clam broth, bay leaf, and thyme, increase the heat, and bring to a boil; skim off the rising impurities. Reduce the heat and simmer, partially covered, 20 minutes or until the potatoes are tender.

Combine the milk and cream in a small saucepan and scald over high heat.

Add the scalded milk, clams, and remaining butter to the chowder and cook 2 minutes to heat through; season to taste with salt, pepper, and, if desired, cayenne. Pour into warm soup bowls, top each with a little parsley, and serve.

Butcher's Knife

Long, broad, firm, and with a cutting edge that curves up 25 degrees to help create a bulging arrowhead tip, this butcher's knife blade is big and strong enough to initiate formidable incisions, to divide short loins, to reduce large top cuts into roasts and chops, and to section foresaddles.

Butcher's knives are available with 6- to 14-inch-long blades, and if you butcher your own meat you need one with a 10-inch blade; it will be long enough to tackle the largest cut in a single stroke. Most butcher's-knife blades are stamped in carbon or stainless steel.

Scimitar Knife

This blade evokes memories of Ali Baba in *The Arabian Nights' Entertainments*. Its extremely high tip and dramatically curved cutting edge extend the front cutting surface so that the blade can neatly draw through masses of bone-free loins and shoulder blades, then slice thick slabs of steak. And its moderate profile makes the blade light enough so it won't unduly compress and roughly cut these soft meat sections.

Scimitar knives have 8- to 12-inch-long blades, and if you are interested in one, choose a large, 10-inch scimitar. It is most often available in stainless steel.

Skinning Knife

When separating hide from flesh, you need a medium-wide blade whose cutting edge cants sharply upward to a high, broad tip. A 6-inch blade

From left to right, a skinning knife, scimitar knife, and butcher's knife help to either flay or section carcasses.

assures close hand-to-tip proximity for precision—flesh and subcutaneous fat may be punctured and ripped, but hide is more efficiently removed in one piece. Once the point penetrates the fine membranes between skin and flesh, the ¾-inch-wide blade is turned to further tear and separate. And an expanded blade front translates short twists of the wrist into more efficient, sweeping arcs when working through meat.

The beef skinner described above has a more highly canted blade than the one traditionally used for lamb. Beef-skinning blades are 5 to 7 inches long and available in high-carbon stainless steel. A lamb-skinning knife is usually 5 inches long and manufactured in high-carbon steel or high-carbon stainless steel.

Produce Knife

Vegetables often come to market with thick, woody stalks, fibrous stems, and gritty roots still intact, so greengrocers trim them with a rectangular-bladed produce knife. Its rigid, 1-inch depth offers good support to sever tough squash stems; a 6-inch length effectively reaches across a celery heart's unwanted ribs and roots and, since there is no need to pierce a stem, stalk, or root, the blade has no tip—simply one flat cutting edge.

Produce knives, which usually have finger shields to prevent accidental slips onto the cutting edge, are available with 4½- to 6-inch-long blades manufactured in high-carbon steel or stainless steel.

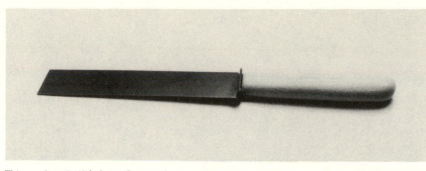

This produce knife's long, flat, sturdy cutting edge is used to quickly slice off the unnecessary stems and stalks from fresh fruits and vegetables.

Ideal for finishing cakes, slicing fresh candies, or apportioning tarts are, from top to bottom, a baker's knife, confectioner's knife, and cake knife.

Cake Knife

This knife is a fine instrument for slicing and serving wedges of flat-bottomed baked goods. A 6-inch blade readily portions 9- and 10-inch cake rounds; minimally set cutting-edge peg teeth cut through torte layers and tart crusts with little crumbling, and a flat, spadelike shape slips neatly under newly cut slices.

Many a serrated cake-knife blade does double duty as a pie slicer and server; it bends upward near the tang end to conform to a pie plate's angle and to offer a comfortable, offset handle.

Cake knives are available only with stainless steel blades.

Confectioner's Knife

Long, light, and with a wave-cut edge that cants 5 degrees upward toward a round, blunt tip, this confectioner's blade trims and slices blocks of nougat, cubes trays of fruit jellies, even dispenses with freshly made marshmallow masses. Its ample 10-inch cutting edge readily draws across the 8-inch square and 9×13-inch forms frequently used in non-industrial candy-making; a slight angle makes normal vertical slicing more comfortable, and $\frac{1}{4}$-inch-spaced teeth successfully tackle crisp meringues or dense chocolate blocks. It can also act as a spatula.

Confectioner's knives are usually available in stainless and high-carbon stainless steels.

Baker's Knife

This baker's knife, with its round, blunt tip, is well equipped to slice through tortes and genoises. Its 12-inch blade readily contends with 9- and 10-inch-round pastries; the tightly set, fine, straight teeth smoothly bite across flaky cream puffs and delicate angel-food cakes, while the nearly 1½-inch width hinders wobbling to promote straight slicing.

When buying a baker's knife, which is available only in stainless steel, keep in mind that pastry textures must be literally ripped apart by a serrated blade, and the smaller and more compact the teeth, the cleaner the cut will be.

Sandwich Spreader/Cutter

For those who need to spread and cut large quantities of sandwiches or canapés, a short, spatulalike tool with one dull and one serrated edge might be a wise investment. A 4-inch length ensures close contact with food so dipping and spreading are neatly and quickly done; a generous round tip, ample breadth, and dull, bowed edge scoop hefty amounts of chopped chicken liver, salmon mousse, or peanut butter, while the blade's moderate pliancy prevents soft, fresh breads from tearing as they're being spread. Use its serrated edge to cut and trim.

Sandwich spreader/cutters, which range in length from 3½ to 4½ inches, are manufactured in either high-carbon stainless or stainless steel.

Hachoir and Bowl

This perfect half-moon sheet of thin stainless steel with its nearly 9-inch cutting edge is designed to chop small quantities of fresh herbs. It's usually accompanied by an identically curved, slightly larger, hardwood or, most recently, polyethylene bowl, to accommodate bunches of parsley, tarragon, or dill to be minced.

A hachoir—from the French verb *hacher*, to chop—has a centered handle that is attached either perpendicularly or at a 75-degree angle. If you pick one up and mimic the recommended rapid up-and-down chopping motion, you'll notice that the canted handle offers the more comfortable grip. Hachoirs are available with 5½-inch diameters with stainless-steel blades.

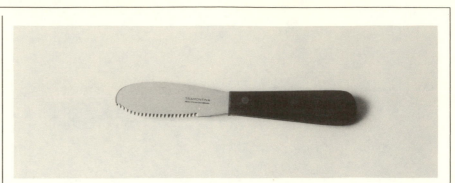

A sandwich spreader's small, flat, tongue-shaped blade can neatly scoop and spread small amounts of jams, jellies, and butters onto bread.

The curved blades of the mezzaluna on the left and the hachoir on the right can ease the rock/chop motion when mincing.

Mezzaluna

To chop vegetables and mince herbs effectively, most people hold down the tip of a chef's knife and quickly rock its blade back and forth with the handle. Others prefer to use a mezzaluna, a two-handled knife with a thick, crescent-shaped blade; it works according to the same principle, but two handles ensure even, less laborious downward pressure.

Mezzalunas, whose Italian name means half-moon, are available with single, double, and triple blades, most of which range in length from 5 to 12 inches. The greater the number of blades, the faster the chopping will be, so for general use, a double-bladed, 7-inch mezzaluna is recommended.

This frozen-food knife's saw and raker teeth swiftly cut through small boxes or blocks of fresh-from-the-freezer foods.

Frozen-Food Knife

Some frozen-food knife blades have a centered tip, others have two prongs, and still other blades end with a hooklike point that stabs, secures, and transfers small blocks of still-frozen foods. But the crucial feature on a frozen-food blade is its series of saw and raker teeth: saw teeth to nick, notch, and advance, and raker teeth to clean the bits of frozen food and their cardboard package from clogging the knife as it cuts. Some blades are fitted with two cutting edges—the main one for frozen foods and the secondary one, usually wave-cut, for slicing breads.

Frozen-food knives are truly an auxiliary tool; frozen-food saws, which are stronger and can also saw through bones, are more versatile. However, if you plan to buy one, select a 9-inch-bladed knife; you will want a blade that is bigger than the largest package you intend to cut. These knives are available only in stainless steel.

Grilled Veal Liver on a Bed of Onion Marmalade with Mustard Seeds and Vinegar Sauce

Wolfgang Puck
The Wolfgang Puck Cookbook

4 servings

4 6-ounce slices veal liver

Olive oil

Coarsely ground black pepper

2 to 3 red onions, cut into eighths

Salt

1½ cups chicken stock (see page 210)

1 tablespoon sherry wine vinegar

1 cup heavy cream

1 tablespoon yellow mustard seeds steeped in ¼ cup port, plus additional mustard seeds for garnish

1 large shallot, finely chopped

5 tablespoons sweet butter

¼ cup red-wine vinegar

1 cup dry red wine

¼ cup veal demiglace (see page 211)

Trim away any membrane or nerves from the liver, then brush both sides with olive oil and season with pepper; cover and refrigerate several hours.

Place the onions in a saucepan and season to taste with salt and pepper. Add the stock and sherry vinegar, bring to a boil, and cook over medium heat, partially covered, 15 minutes or until the liquid has evaporated.

In a small saucepan reduce the cream over low heat to 3 tablespoons. Add this to the onion mixture, bring to a boil, then set this marmalade aside in a warm spot. Bring the port and mustard seeds to a boil in another small pan, reduce over low heat to 1 tablespoon, then add this to the marmalade.

As the onions cook, prepare the vinegar sauce: Sauté the shallot in 1 tablespoon butter in a small saucepan set over medium heat for 2 to 3 minutes or until glossy. Deglaze with the red-wine vinegar and reduce to a 2-tablespoon glaze. Add the wine and reduce by half, then add the demiglace and continue to reduce until the sauce lightly coats the back of a spoon.

Gradually whisk in the remaining butter over low heat and season to taste with salt and pepper. If, when all the butter has been incorporated, the sauce needs more tang, reduce a little more red-wine vinegar by ⅔ in a separate saucepan, then gradually add to the sauce until you obtain the desired flavor. Strain the sauce into a clean saucepan and keep warm.

Preheat a grill, season the liver with salt, and grill over medium heat 2 to 3 minutes per side. The liver should remain pink inside, as longer cooking will make the flavor very strong.

To serve: Make beds of onion marmalade in the centers of 4 warm dinner plates. Place a liver slice on each and spoon a little vinegar sauce over them. Sprinkle with mustard seeds and decorate with colorful vegetables.

Butcher's Bone Saw

When you need to quarter a carcass, trim back a shank bone, or prepare a rack of lamb for roasting, nothing severs bone and cartilage more quickly, cleanly, and easily than a sturdy butcher's frame saw with a well-designed cutting edge of small, evenly spaced, alternately flared-rip teeth that are as long as they are wide. A span of ⅛-inch teeth neatly nicks and scores to inch gradually through bone while their opposite set creates a well-defined kerf, or groove, that thwarts blade wavering, snagging, and bending.

Butcher's bone-saw blades range from 12 to 30 inches long. Select a small, stainless-steel saw with a 12-inch replaceable blade that has plenty of tension.

Frozen-Food Saw

Armed with a rigid, moderately long blade with forwardly canted, flaring teeth, this saw is meant to cut through large pieces of frozen foods. A bone saw traditionally has a band of flared teeth that are either set vertically or angle back toward the handle. But since iced meat, fish, poultry, and vegetables have no uniform texture or obvious grain to follow, the serrated tool to cut them can't be designed to saw a narrow kerf, or channel; its teeth would catch on a partially severed tendon, bone, flesh, or stalk, would buckle, and perhaps snap the blade. The teeth should be crosscut, with a pronounced alternate flare to saw a larger channel that effectively divides the food. Stainless-steel frozen-food saw blades generally measure about 10 inches long.

Cake Saw

This long, horizontally set wave-cut blade braced by its C-clamp frame levelly cross-slices cake layers. Its near 21-inch span reaches across 18-inch tortes and genoises; unflared teeth create a narrow, crumb-free kerf, or groove, and a tautly held

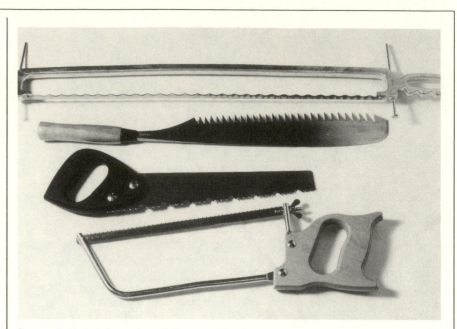

Saw teeth, shape, size, and set differ according to what must be cut. Shown from top are a wave-edged cake saw; large, rip-toothed ice saw; cross-cut frozen-food saw; and a small, rip-toothed bone saw.

carbon-steel blade won't easily buckle to cause off-kilter cuts. Adjustable pins in the C-clamp's shanks raise or lower the cutting plane to assure a straight cut.

When buying this 21-inch cake saw or a 14-inch cake saw, make sure its frame is sturdy for steady cutting and that its bow depth measures roughly 2 inches for adequate clearance.

How to Store Knives

The most damaging way to store a knife is unsheathed in a drawer together with other knives. Blades can rattle around, their edges can bump into one another, and dull blades result. This can be averted by using one of the storage devices currently on the market.

- Chefs favor the magnetic knife holder; up to 12 blades can be gripped by the two strong, 18-inch, horizontal magnets that run the length of a metal or wooden slat. The magnets hold the flat of each blade, and the knives are clearly identifiable and a snap to remove. Although it's also easy to clean, this storage method is not recommended for families with children or animals because the knives can be knocked off easily.

- A 14-inch wooden wall rack that holds up to 8 knives in a central slot created by two parallel strips

of wood is superb for display but not access. Most purchase this unit when the magnetic bar is unfeasible or unavailable. Attach the rack at chest height to a wall near the chopping area. Because blade edges are exposed, accidental cuts and nicks are possible when the rack is bolted lower.

- One of the most popular household methods of storing knives is the free-standing hardwood knife block that suspends up to 14 blades. Edges and points are separated and, when the unit is near the work area, the knives are very convenient. However, it is nearly impossible to keep dust free and the stored knives aren't readily identifiable.

- When wall or counter—but not drawer—space is limited, use graduated sizes of polystyrene sheaths; simply slip them over the blade and store carefully.

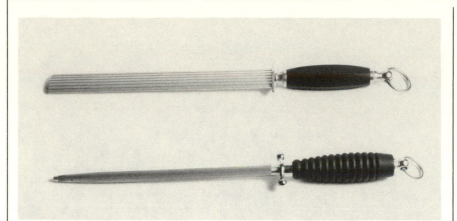

The multicut steel on top or straightening steel beneath it are as basic to the kitchen as knives are.

Ice Saw

Most bone and frozen-food saws have cross-cut teeth to cut on a push stroke; ice saws, however, should sport fangs that angle back toward the handle so the blade will cut on a pull stroke. Pulling rather than pushing a blade makes it less likely to catch, snag, and buckle, so the steel can be thinner and less flexible. Less steel and greater rigidity will, in turn, create straighter, narrower kerfs, or grooves, and prompt faster, less laborious sawing, both of which are particularly important when quickly preparing blocks of ice for scuplting.

Ice saws are available only with stainless-steel blades ranging in length from 12 to 30 inches.

Straightening Steel

This scored, chrome-plated carbon-steel shaft is the most popular style of straightening steel sold today. It provides ample surface area on which to realign a sizeable blade edge; it's moderately abrasive for measured trueing; magnetic to attract the small steel particles that wear off the knife as it is being realigned, and chrome-plated to ensure that the steel is harder than the blade being straightened. Steeling, or realigning, a blade can only occur when the steel is harder than the blade that scrapes against it.

With normal wear, the chrome plating eventually cracks and exposes the underlying carbon steel, which can rust. Always keep a steel dry, store it carefully, and only steel clean, dry knives.

Be sure a steel is long enough to service your largest blade. Steels are available with 6- to 14-inch shafts; a 12-inch shaft with a protective hand hilt is recommended.

Multicut Steels

Butchers and packinghouse workers once used two steels—medium-coarse to straighten the blade's cutting edge and fine-coarse to give it a keener finish. Butcher's steels—tapered cylinders with alternating ridges of medium and fine grits—were then introduced, followed by multicut steels with similarly ridged coarse- and fine-grained abrasive bands.

But rather than being rod-shaped like their predecessors, multicut steels are oval or flat, providing a broad contact area so that the drawn blade will connect with both grits.

Multicut steels are available with 12- and 14-inch shafts, and if you prefer this type, select one with a 12-inch-long abraded surface.

How to Remove Stains from Carbon-Steel Blades

The bane of owning a carbon-steel blade is that it rusts and stains even through normal use. Many knife makers call the inevitable oxidation "the honorable tarnish" but it and the discoloration caused by contact with, for example, citric acid or the sulfur in a hard-boiled egg can be removed. Dampen a cork, dip it into household scouring powder, then gently rub it against the sides of the blade and rinse. Scouring powder does the trick because it contains silicates—a light abrasive that polishes off surface stains—and because its strong reducing agent restores the steel's iron component by removing such chemically caused stains. Cork is recommended because it holds enough scouring powder to get the job done, it is moderately firm to convey ample pressure, and it distances the fingers from the cutting edge.

How to Use a Steel

Contrary to popular belief, a steel does not sharpen a knife blade, although that's a logical assumption. With routine chopping, slicing, and dicing, a blade's edge comes into continued contact with a hard chopping surface, causing the blade to make progressively duller cuts. After a few runs down the length of a steel, the knife appears to be sharper.

But a blade edge does not wear down like a pencil tip. Rather, the edge curls over microscopically during use, hampering its ability to cut cleanly and precisely. Proper steeling straightens out that curl and effectively realigns the edge.

Professional butchers recommend steeling a knife for every five minutes of blade use; it can be done in one of two ways.

Horizontally. Use the hand you favor to grip the knife in a chopping hold, as though holding a tennis racket, then point the blade tip slightly upward. Grasp the handle of the steel with the other hand and tuck your thumb safely behind its guard, pointing the steel away from your body.

Set the knife blade at a 20-degree angle against the shaft of the steel and, exerting light pressure, draw the blade down and diagonally across the steel, from the blade's heel to its tip, in one stroke. Do this five times on top of the steel, then go underneath the shaft and repeat the procedure to straighten the other side of the blade.

Vertically. Use the hand you favor to grasp the knife handle as you would a tennis racket. With the other hand, invert the steel so that its tip rests on a nonslip surface and grip its handle securely.

Set the knife blade at a 20-degree angle to the shaft of the steel, point the blade tip slightly upward, then smoothly and consistently draw the knife diagonally down along the length of the steel, from the blade's heel to its tip. Do this five times on one side of the steel, then repeat on the other side of the blade.

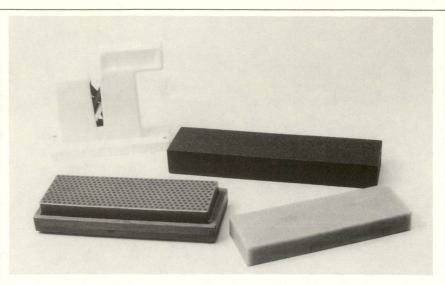

Most V-shaped abrasives like the one at upper left straighten a drawn blade; some units house sharpening rods. More conventional sharpeners include, from the left, a diamond-impregnated whetstone, Carborundum whetstone, and a natural Arkansas whetstone.

V-shaped Abrasive

Crock sticks and single-slotted edge straighteners work on the same steeling principle; both have small, anchored pairs of fused alumina, silicon carbide, chrome-plated carbon, or diamond-impregnated steel rods that are set at a 20-degree steeling angle. Crock sticks are two 4-inch-long steels fixed into a supporting base to form a V. The blade is drawn down and across each rod from blade heel to tip, straightening out its cutting edge. Diamond-impregnated steel rods also sharpen the blade. In a housed unit, the mini-steels are crossed and set on springs, rotating as the blade is drawn through them for controlled realigning.

Both reproduce the standard steeling method and either is recommended for those who hesitate to go with convention.

Carborundum Whetstone

When a blade develops small burrs or minute nicks, it should be sharpened as soon as possible, ideally with a Carborundum whetstone. Carborundum, which is nearly diamond-hard, is actually the trade name for several synthetic abrasives, most of which are composed of silicon carbide, a gray-colored sand-and-carbon preparation. Drum-tumbled with balls of iron or steel to a proper particle size, this abrasive is then

bonded, pressed into brick shapes, dried, and kiln-fired.

Carborundum stones are available with various grit sizes, from coarse to ultra-fine; a double-grit stone with a medium-coarse side and a medium-fine side is recommended. So is a superb kit whose hollow brick tray houses a triangular cartridge fitted with three $6'' \times 2'' \times 1''$ stones—medium-coarse, medium-fine, and fine. Stones measure from $4'' \times 1'' \times 1''$ to $8'' \times 2'' \times 1''$; and for general use, the medium size is most practical.

Diamond-impregnated Whetstone

The working surface of this whetstone is impregnated with diamonds, the hardest and most efficient substance for sharpening a blade. The stone's face is composed of a thin layer of perforated steel embedded with industrial diamond dust that is then molded onto its smooth plastic base. With water as a lubricant, filings from the blade drop into the lower, perforated areas so the higher, abraded surface remains clean and operative.

Diamond-impregnated whetstones are fine alternatives to traditional sharpening stones and can be purchased with one of three grits. A fine grit produces sharper-than-average edges, a medium surface hones average edges, and a coarse

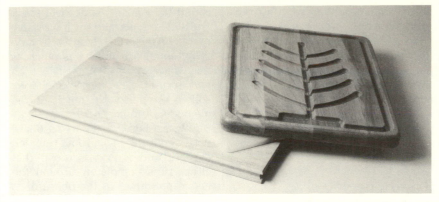

The hardwood chopping and grooved carving boards shown at left and right may be handsome, but the polyethylene board between them is more hygienic. (Carving boards are discussed on page 30.)

grit sharpens the more sizable edges on shears and axes. A medium-grit stone that measures 6″ × 2″ × 1″ is suggested for general use.

Natural Arkansas Whetstone

This whetstone is composed entirely of novaculite, a light-colored sedimentary rock that is essentially microcrystalline quartz. It is very dense, so its grit is far too fine to hone kitchen knives properly. Instead, it should be used, if so desired, to polish the knife edge after it has been sharpened with a coarser stone. On its own it is used as a sharpener for delicate hospital curettes, surgical instruments, and jewelry-making and engraving tools.

Arkansas stone is quarried from formations in Arkansas, Oklahoma, and Texas, then cut into bricks that most often measure from 4″ × 2″ × 1″ to 8″ × 2″ × 1″.

Polyethylene Chopping Board

Sturdy, warp-resistant, waterproof, and, most important, hygienic, polyethylene brings benefits to a chopping board that make it today's overwhelmingly favorite material. It's a thermoplastic, an ethylene-derived substance that is heated, molded, cooled, and cut to a simple shape. A rough-textured surface on most polyethylene boards prevents food from slipping as it's being cut, but the biggest advantage over wood is that it is easily restored to its pristine hygienic condition with a little bleach.

With today's diet, most of us eat less red meat and more poultry—especially chicken—which is known in its raw state to be rife with salmonellae. The only careful way to prepare poultry for cooking is on a polyethylene board that can be sterilized after use.

These boards are available in a wide range of sizes. Popular ones measure 8″ × 12″ or 12″ × 18″ with the most versatile being the largest, preferably with an inch depth and with grooving on one side. You can chop meat, poultry, fish, and vegetables—anything but hard cleaving and sawing—on the flat side, then reverse it and carve on the grooved one. The board also provides an excellent surface on which to roll pastry doughs; polyethylene is naturally cool, a necessity for making good pastry.

Hardwood Chopping Board

Despite its porousness and tendency to warp, split, and be less sanitary than plastic, many still prefer to cut on maple, cherry, or oak boards; they are warmer and more inviting looking than polyethylene, but their benefits end there.

For those who enjoy such a board, two basic types exist: the more durable linear, or edge-grain, style and the decorative end-grain one. The edge-grain, which looks like a series of parallel lines, is composed of kiln-dried boards cut into long strips, planed, glued, and sawed lengthwise. Ideally, these are then braced at each end with a wood cap that hampers buckling, but this

How to Use a Sharpening Stone

"The sharper the knife, the fewer the tears" is an appropriate adage because a well-honed knife would never initially bruise an onion, causing a chef to extend his chopping time and prolong his exposure to the onion's tear-producing essence. It allows him to complete this and any other cutting task swiftly.

Most agree that kitchen knives should be sharpened—reground with a two-sided abrasive stone—every six months, but any time a blade has an excessive drag when cutting or when extra downward pressure is needed, it should be sharpened immediately. Such signs indicate that the edge is dull or has minute rough spots called burrs.

To sharpen a knife, place a damp cloth on an even surface to create traction and center the stone on it, coarse side up. Place five or six drops of a light-grade machine or mineral oil down the length of the stone to prevent abraded grindings from clogging the pores of the stone.

Grasp the handle of the knife as you would a tennis racket and set the blade heel at a 20-degree angle to the stone. Place the fingers of your free hand across the side of the blade and exert enough pressure to keep the blade in constant contact with the stone.

Smoothly draw the blade diagonally across the stone from heel to tip in one quarter-arc movement. Do this ten times on one side, then transfer the knife to the other hand and draw it across the stone ten times to sharpen the other side of the blade.

After sharpening the blade against the stone's coarse grit, flip the stone over, oil it, and repeat the procedure along the finer-grit side.

Stroke the newly honed blade edge against a straightening steel two or three times on each side, wipe it with a clean, dry towel, and store it properly.

capping is more prevalent on European boards than American. Endgrain boards, which resemble checkerboards, are prepared like edge-grain ones except that they are sawed crosswise, so they have more glued joints and a greater inclination to crack from use and washings. They can only be suggested for ornamental purposes.

Both edge- and end-grain boards are available in 8- and 12-inch squares, while the edge-grain also comes as an 18″×36″ slab. Choose a board that is at least 1½ inches deep; shallow ones are sturdy enough to support only light chopping.

A hardwood board should be treated with a nontoxic mineral oil to seal against impurities; use a fine steel wool to rub the oil in, leave it on five minutes, then wipe off the excess. Do this once a week for the first month, once a month for the first year, and following each use. After using, clean the board with household scouring powder and a wire brush to remove food particles, then wipe with a cloth dampened with a water and chlorine-bleach solution to sanitize, then re-oil.

Hardwood Carving Board

Because carving a roast at the table is a true visual experience, few dispute the use of a wooden carving board over a polyethylene one; the latter may be more sanitary, but its appearance is almost sterile when compared to the warm, inviting glow of a wooden board.

Wooden carving boards have long been available in a variety of sizes and shapes; there are the medium-round ham plates, large oval steak and shad planks, and the impressive rectangular turkey boards. Thankfully, some are not as popular as they once were, such as slabs with nail inserts. The nearly inch-long spikes on these sap much of the meat's natural juices.

Select a hardwood carving board with smooth, snagproof rounded corners and a gravy groove that either runs completely around the inside perimeter of the board or is centered and resembles a stylized fir tree. Both should end with a full routed well for juice accumulation and easy spooning. Many boards are fitted with legs, but the more practical ones are legless. When turned upside down, they can serve as light-work chopping boards. A 12″×18″ board is suggested for household use. See page 30 for cleaning instructions.

Pot au Feu

Lydie Marshall
Cooking with Lydie Marshall

8 servings

BEEF STOCK

5 *pounds beef marrow bones, sawed into 2-inch pieces*

1 *veal knuckle*

4½ *quarts water*

1 *pound carrots, scrubbed and coarsely chopped*

2 *large onions, each stuck with 1 clove*

10 *parsley sprigs*

1 *medium parsnip, scrubbed and coarsely chopped*

1 *medium celery rib with leaves, coarsely chopped*

1 *medium leek, coarsely chopped, rinsed, and drained*

1 *bay leaf*

1 *teaspoon dried thyme*

5 *teaspoons salt*

5 *teaspoons black peppercorns*

Combine the beef and veal bones and water in a stockpot set over high heat and bring to a boil. Skim off the scum, then replace the amount of evaporated water with cold water—it should measure 1 inch above the bones. Bring to a second boil and reskim.

Add the remaining ingredients, reduce the heat to low, and simmer, partially covered, 7 hours.

Strain and clear the stock. (Yield: 2½ quarts)

POT AU FEU

2½ *quarts beef stock*

2 *pounds beef short ribs*

2 *pounds veal breast*

2 *pounds beef bottom round*

8 *russet potatoes*

8 *large carrots*

2 *teaspoons salt*

8 *leeks, dark greens reserved for a future soup, white part slit lengthwise to 1 inch from trimmed root end and washed*

Bring the stock to a boil in a casserole set over high heat, then add the short ribs and veal. Reduce the heat to medium and cook, partially covered, 1½ hours; skim off the impurities as they rise. Transfer the meats to a pan with ½ cup broth, cover, and keep warm over low heat.

Add the bottom round in one piece to the boiling broth and cook 30 minutes to remain rare. Again, skim off the impurities as they rise.

As the meats cook, peel and quarter the potatoes and cut the carrots into eighths. Boil the potatoes until tender in water to cover with 1 teaspoon of salt and steam the carrots for 15 minutes. Boil the leeks 10 minutes or until tender in water to cover with the remaining teaspoon of salt.

Thinly slice the beef and bone the short ribs and veal breast. Place the meats in the center of a large platter and surround with the carrots and potatoes; serve with leeks and additional broth separately. Accompany with Dijon-style mustard, horseradish, kosher salt, and vinaigrette dressing mixed with a finely diced hard-boiled egg.

2. Other Cutting and Piercing Tools

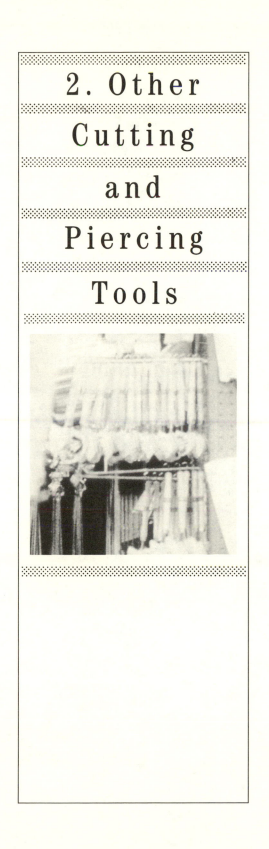

Implements that cut, pierce, gouge, scale, and shave are called kitchen *tools* after the carpenter's tools to which they're directly related. The single-point ice chipper that reduces large blocks of ice and notches small holes in ice sculptures breaks, bores, and looks like its awl predecessor. The long, troughed blade on a zucchini corer or boeuf à la mode needle penetrates and channels like a model gouge, and the deeply bowed harp cheese wire negotiates corners and edges like a coping saw.

The resemblances aren't always as evident as their applications and results. Lobster shears may suggest needle-nosed pliers, but they work like tin-snips to inch their way through a hard substance without disturbing surrounding matter. The wide, V-shaped melon cutter resembles a corner trowel, yet it grooves and hollows decoratively like a parting tool.

It's not surprising that these and other kitchen tools mirror those of the woodworker; since both chef and carpenter are craftsmen, it was only a matter of time—and a higher civilized state—before chefs applied the same tools to shape foods that had previously hewed, planed, and carved woods.

Yet it would take an anthropologist who had studied unearthed implements, knew which foods were available, and was aware of past cooking practices to correctly date the various crossovers. Closer to our own time, it's informative to peruse period cookbooks to discover which tools had already been incorporated into the cutting batterie de cuisine. Woodcuts in Bartolomeo Scappi's 1570 *Opera* show rasp-inspired nutmeg and sugar graters and a circular sawlike fluted pastry cutter. During Charles II's reign, *The Compleat Cook* from *The Queen's Closet Opened* recommended using a near-upholsterer's needle—a "larding pin"—to surface-draw lemon strips through a capon. And in 1817 Dr. William Kitchiner's *The Cook's Oracle* suggested getting the necessary stamplike octagonal and trefoil pastry cutters from local tinsmiths.

Over the centuries, designs for kitchen tools have been streamlined and become more specialized. The tines of a two-pronged chef's fork, for example, are now more closely set for today's smaller roasts, while two extra prongs were added to the wider, more diminutive and compact choucroute fork to enable it to snag, scoop, and transfer shredded cabbage.

The past fifty years in particular, because of newly developed and more readily available metals, have seen further advances. Harder-wearing stainless steel replaced carbon steel not just on knives but also on kitchen-shear blades to reduce their frequent disassembly for straightening and sharpening. Nickel-plated and stainless steels were employed instead of wood to frame mandolines and truffle slicers more durably.

Since each improvement added to the array of finely made, specialized kitchen tools, it's possible to track past and present popular food styles by reviewing the demand for the tools that prepared them. Twenty years ago, the fashion for vol-au-vent disks, Roquefort cutters, and hâtelets reflected our desire for haute cuisine. A decade ago, the drama of nouvelle cuisine sparked interest in the lemon strippers and melon-ball cutters. And today's intention to eat more healthfully—with less emphasis on red meat and more on carbohydrates—is indicated by the demand for poultry shears, fish scalers, and ravioli cutters.

Before buying any kitchen tool—and some are quite expensive—it's best to weigh its efficiency and user-ease against cost. To be a sound investment, a tool should save time, reduce labor, be simple to clean, and easy to maintain and store.

Fish Shears

Few shears look more ungainly than these—one blade is lean, serrated, and tapered while the other is broader, sharper, and rounded at the tip—yet they gut and fin fish easily. Poke the more tapered blade into flesh to make a ventral slit, angle it to follow the fish's contours, then run the blades down its belly and extract the entrails. The narrow tip spears well through flesh while its backwardly angled serration ensures firm grips. Use the shears to sever backbones from heads and tails, through the belly and to remove the dorsal, anal, pelvic, and pectoral fins prior to poaching and grilling. It's usually best to cut around both sides of the large dorsal fin and pull it out back to front to remove both fin and anchor bones, but when skin must remain intact for proper cooking and attractive presentation, shears should be used. This is particularly important when preparing a roundfish, whose bulging shape makes it impossible for a knife to get near the fin base for a close, clean cut.

Fish shears generally measure 9 inches overall and are available only in chrome-plated steel.

Poultry Shears

Industrial shears are designed so that the lower blade remains stationary while the upper one moves to execute cuts; the blades are large, non-uniform, and, in some instances, partially spring-powered. Shears differ dramatically from scissors, but for kitchen use, only size distinguishes the two. Scissors usually measure less than 6 inches while shears are longer.

Poultry shears operate in much the same way as the industrial variety. The lower blade has rear-angled serration to prevent backward slips while cutting slippery raw flesh and a notch to grasp slick legs and wings; the upper blade, with its clean, tapered cutting edge, executes most of the shearing as an internal spring kicks the blades apart, so that forceful cutting results with the closing effort. The blades bow 20 degrees upward to mirror the mostly rounded contours of chicken, capon, and duck carcasses.

Fine forged poultry shears range from 9 to a little over 10 inches long overall and are available in either nickel- or chrome-plated carbon steel or the more durable stainless steel. Be sure that their handles are textured for secure grip and that they have a pivot screw for pressure adjustment and disassembly and an end catch for safe storage.

Multipurpose Kitchen Shears

With their strong, sharply tipped blades—one serrated, the other tapered—handle tabs, ribbing, and flanged screwdriver heads, these shears are well equipped to tackle any number of household tasks. They have the strength to trim fibrous artichoke leaves and to divide pulled taffy; sharp tips notch dough, and keen edges cut decorative paper frills. Finning a fish? Serration grabs slippery rays so the blades advance rather than retreat. Tabs open poptop bottles; ribbing creates traction to open jars easily, and the exterior handle heads flip off fitted caps.

Like knives, shears and scissors are stamped or, preferably, forged (see page 3) in either chrome-plated carbon or stainless steel. Unlike knives, they are measured by their overall, tip-to-handle length.

General-purpose kitchen shears should be hardy, 8-inch stainless-steel ones joined by a pivot screw. The length provides two useful, easy-to-wield, 4-inch cutting surfaces and the screw allows cutting pressure to be adjusted and the parts to be disassembled for cleaning and sharpening. Many shears offer comfortable, plastic-coated handles that aid in gripping.

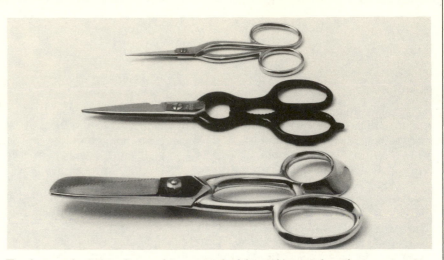

The shears and scissors often used to prepare food for cooking are, from the top, sea-urchin scissors, the recommended multipurpose kitchen shears, and fish shears (described on the previous page).

Roast Duck with Red Wine Butter and Gratin Dauphinois

Gérard Pangaud, Executive Chef while at Aurora

4 servings

ROAST DUCK

2 3- to 4-pound ducks, preferably Long Island ducklings, excess fat removed, wing tips clipped, ducks trussed and pricked with a fork

2 tablespoons corn oil

Salt to taste

Freshly ground black pepper to taste

1 cup red wine, preferably California Zinfandel

½ cup red-wine vinegar

6 medium shallots, finely chopped

2 ounces butter, cut into pieces

1 bunch fresh chives, finely sliced (approximately ½ cup)

Preheat the oven to 450°F.

Brush the ducks with oil, season to taste with salt and pepper, then set on a rack in a shallow roasting pan and roast 30 to 45 minutes, depending upon preference for doneness; baste frequently. Allow to rest 10 minutes, then cut in half lengthwise. Remove and discard the backbone.

As the ducks roast, prepare the sauce: Slowly cook the wine, vinegar, and shallots in a small saucepan set over low heat until all the liquid evaporates and the shallots are left dry. Gradually whisk in the butter, piece by piece, then add the chives at the last minute to preserve their color. Season to taste with salt and pepper.

GRATIN DAUPHINOIS

1 garlic clove, peeled and crushed

9 ounces butter, cut into pieces

1 quart milk

Salt to taste

Freshly ground black pepper to taste

2½ pounds red-skin-variety potatoes, peeled, rinsed, patted dry, and sliced in half lengthwise

1 pint heavy cream

Rub a large sauté pan with garlic, grease well with some of the butter, then add the milk and salt and pepper to taste.

Slice the potatoes very thinly with either a mandoline or a knife, add to the milk, and top with several pieces of butter. Bring to a simmer over low heat and continue to cook 30 minutes, stirring occasionally.

Preheat the oven to 375°F.

Once the potatoes are tender, strain them, then transfer them to a large gratin or baking dish. Cover with the cream and the remaining butter and season to taste with fresh pepper. Bake about 60 minutes, or until golden brown.

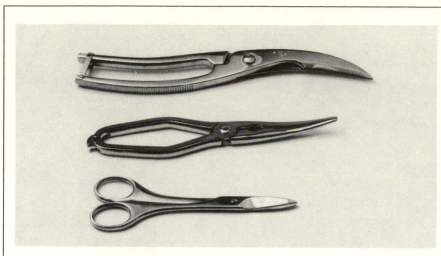

Shears and scissors frequently taken to the table for carving or apportioning include, from the top, poultry shears (see page 33), lobster pincers, and grape scissors.

Lobster Pincers

With its short, triangular blades and blunt tips, this pair of pincers looks more like a pair of needle-nosed pliers than a tool to snip through hard carapace to sever and remove lobster from its shell for broiling, grilling, or eating. The tapered 3½-inch blades are long enough to work under and around the shell and sandwich it for clipping; the ridged edges allow the blades to bite and break cleanly while the jaws' blunted tips, backs, and spines won't tear flesh in the process. The oval opening created just above the pivot by the jaws' slight bow neatly removes and cracks legs.

The best lobster pincers are spring-set. (Those that don't retract should be avoided, as they create double work for the chef.) They are generally 7½ inches long and are available in nickel-plated steel or the stronger stainless steel.

Sea-Urchin Scissors

These scissors are designed to expose sea urchins so they can be extracted from their shells. Their sharp tips easily penetrate mouth and flesh; narrow, tapered blades make them easier to drive in; and handles three times the blades' length give a high degree of leverage to make small, forceful snips and create a healthy distance from the urchin's porcupinelike spines. Once open and drained, a teaspoon is all that's needed to pry off the urchin's five coral tongues.

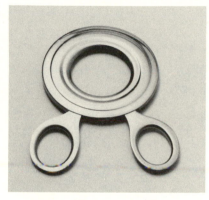

An eggshell cutter very tidily lops off the tapered tip of a soft-boiled egg.

These otherwise obscure scissors, since they're small—6 inches long—are strong due to chrome plating, and have an attractive appearance, can also be taken to table and used as grape scissors.

Grape Scissors

These scissors serve duty tableside, elegantly snipping small, manageable clusters from bunches of ripe grapes. The snub tips won't pierce fruit flesh or draw juice; their 1½-inch cutting edges still provide a long reach, while the cutting-edge combination—one concave and one straight—assures a firm hold during cutting. The triply long handles supply ample leverage for efficient snipping.

Nickel-, gold-, or silver-plated or stainless-steel grape scissors all measure about 6 inches long.

Eggshell Cutter

When this tool's ring front is set on the tapered tip of a soft-boiled egg and its two arms close, they simultaneously draw four tension-set, toothed blades inward to pierce, crack, and separate the top from the rest of the egg. The metal circle's 1¼-inch opening guarantees prudent, functional clipping; the four blades ensure the straightest possible break.

Eggshell cutters are manufactured in either chrome-plated or the preferred stainless steel and measure 4 inches in overall length. Although this tool is quite effective, its covered blades are impossible to clean thoroughly.

Swivel-Action Vegetable Peeler

The open, stainless-steel blade of this peeler won't trap germs; a slotted, U-shaped blade with two sharp edges suits right- or left-handed motions; a 105-degree swivel action allows waste-free paring on any potato, celeriac, or apple; and a tapered tip quickly plucks out vegetable eyes.

The slot sizes of the various peelers range in lengths from barely over an inch to 2 inches long, and the bigger the cutting edge, the faster the paring. Opt for a swivel blade over a stationary one and make sure the handle attachment is either open and washable or completely closed, to be hygienic.

Vegetable peelers are available with either carbon- or stainless-steel blades and plastic, wooden, or various steel handles.

Harp Vegetable Peeler

The harp peeler—although it more closely resembles a lyre—is as light, long in blade, and able to rotate and cut out eyes as its straight, older counterpart. However, a 2-inch handle breadth and new blade position create easier, less stressful wielding:

That extra width loosens the normally tight paring hold, and a perpendicular cutting edge induces a more natural up-and-down (versus lateral) peeling motion.

Harp peelers are occasionally available with straight handles, but chefs prefer the splayed types, usually those with aluminum frames over plastic; replaceable stainless steel over carbon steel; and the more precise single- over double-edged cutting blades.

Asparagus Peeler

What tool in the batterie de cuisine could eclipse this lean, sharp spatula with its tiny, jiblike attachment at preparing asparagus spears for cooking? A narrow blade is all that's needed to anchor the slicing regulator; a razor edge cuts through the most tenacious plant fiber; and an adjustable, cantilevered, removable band controls the depth of the shave. You can also use this peeler to destring celery or rhubarb or for light paring by detaching its slicing gauge.

Asparagus peelers are available only with 4½-inch long stainless-steel blades.

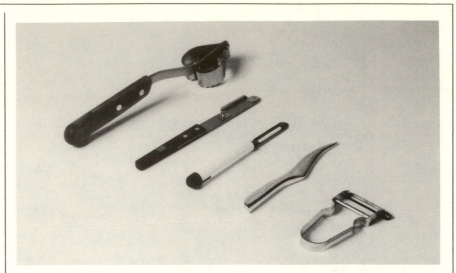

General- and single-purpose peelers and scalers include, from the left, a spade-shaped fish scaler, asparagus peeler, swivel-action vegetable peeler (see page 35), shrimp deveiner, and harp vegetable peeler (page 35).

Spade-shaped Fish Scaler

It's often said that the best place to scale a fish is in someone else's home. Once freed, the scales fly everywhere, only to be found months later in the most unlikely places.

This broad, inflexible, spade-shaped scaler with its four wave-cut surfaces achieves efficiency, if not neatness. Its 3-inch width quickly covers a wide swath; rigidity triumphs over the most firmly grounded scale; and its series of wave-cut edges, with well-spaced points, snag, pull, and rip out hard, gelatin-based flaps. Its dull end won't break fragile flesh, the offset handle provides generous hand clearance, and the stainless-steel composition won't rust.

Folded, serrated-blade scalers as well as those that look like hand-held rasps are also manufactured, but the sturdier, more effective spade-shaped scaler is recommended.

Sautéed Soft-Shell Crabs

Edmund Lillys, Proprietor:
Gloucester House

4 servings

2 *dozen silver dollar–sized soft-shell crabs (or 1 dozen regular size)*

¾ *cup all-purpose flour*

Salt to taste

Pinch cayenne

6 *tablespoons sweet butter*

2 *tablespoons corn oil*

1½ *teaspoons lemon juice*

1 *teaspoon minced parsley (optional)*

To dress each crab, hold it between its back legs and use kitchen shears to clip crosswise and sever just behind its eyes. Lightly compress the body, reach into this new cavity, and pull out the opaque gastric mill. Turn the crab on its back, lift up and pull off its tablike apron and the attached intestinal vein. Turn the crab over again, lift each pointed end flap, and scrape off the underlying spongy gills. Pat dry.

Season the flour to taste with salt and cayenne, dredge the crabs, and set them aside.

Heat the butter and oil in a large sauté pan set over medium-high heat, and without crowding, add as many crabs as possible in one layer; sauté 2 to 3 minutes per side until golden brown. (If using the larger crabs, sauté 3 to 5 minutes per side.) Similarly sauté the remaining crabs, adding more butter and oil if necessary. Sprinkle the crabs with lemon juice and the optional parsley and serve immediately with tartar sauce.

Troughed and ringed vegetable and fruit corers include, from the left, a zucchini corer (page 38), apple corer, and an apple corer/slicer (page 38).

Shrimp Deveiner

Not only does cleaning shrimp make for comfortable dining, but removing the gritty, dark intestinal tract also improves the dish's texture and appearance. Some use a paring knife to successively shell and devein a shrimp, but a bowed, dull-tipped, short-bladed shrimp deveiner that strips off both in one motion does the job in half the time. Its bare 15-degree arc mimics the upper curve of a shrimp; a stiff, blunt point penetrates and scrapes to separate vein from flesh, while its 3½-inch length slips beneath a beheaded shrimp shell, follows its contours, and emerges at its tail with vein and shell atop its spine.

The similarly long, curved blades found on the more intricate shrimp peeler operate on spring-clamp retractions rather than on hand-powered prying. Once the closed, narrow blade-tips are inserted through the flesh and along a shrimp's upper curve, squeezing the handles forces them open to separate vein and shell from flesh, frequently shredding the latter.

Both shrimp tools are equally well crafted. The former is most often seen in aluminum while the double-bladed peeler is made with stainless-steel blades and plastic handles. The single-blade deveiner seems the better tool to own because its lack of moving parts makes it less likely to break.

Apple Corer

When you want the classical accompaniment of golden-fried apple slices for a boudin noir or to end an autumn feast elegantly with poached pears in wine, those fruits must be cored before they can be cooked and enjoyed. This corer's rigidity withstands the necessary stabbing through flesh; its 4-inch blade reaches through the length of the largest Rome Beauty or Bartlett; the narrow trough holds the centers when cut, and a sharp, wave-cut ring encircles, then drives down and through a core's perimeter.

Center, plunge, twist, and withdraw is all it takes to remove these fruits' cores, but be advised that the corer's nearly 1-inch diameter extracts too much flesh from small apples and pears and too little from large ones.

Apple corers, pint-sized versions of pineapple corers, are available only with stainless-steel blades.

Creole Jambalaya

*Leah Chase, Proprietor:
Dooky Chase's Restaurant*

6 servings

8 *ounces smoked sausage, sliced*

8 *ounces chaurice (or chorizo),
    sliced*

1 *medium onion, coarsely
    chopped*

2 *cups rice*

8 *ounces large shrimp, peeled and
    deveined*

½ *medium green pepper,
    stemmed, seeded, deribbed,
    and coarsely chopped*

3 *garlic cloves, coarsely chopped*

1 *tablespoon finely chopped
    parsley*

1 *teaspoon salt*

1 *teaspoon paprika*

¼ *teaspoon dried thyme*

¼ *teaspoon cayenne*

3 *cups water*

Sauté the sausage, chaurice, and onion in a medium casserole set over medium heat for 12 minutes or until the onion becomes transparent; stir occasionally. Add the rice, stir to coat with the oil, then add the shrimp, green pepper, garlic, parsley, salt, paprika, thyme, and cayenne; stir well. Add the water, cover, reduce the heat, and cook 30 to 40 minutes or until the rice is tender. Toss to disperse the ingredients evenly before serving.

Zucchini Corer

In late summer when zucchini is at its prime, you might want to core, stuff, slice, and serve it with an herbed cheese or fill it with ground lamb and pine nuts and then bake it.

Coring is simple; some run a spoon down a halved length, but it is quicker to use a relatively sharp-tipped, rigid, troughed steel span. The strong point drives easily through the skin; a ⅝-inch-wide trough, inserted and turned, fully encircles a small to medium core; and a nearly 7-inch length reaches clear across a trimmed, standard-sized squash. You can also use this corer to seed cucumbers.

The better corers have slightly heavier steel blades and defined exterior-edge bevels.

Apple Corer/Slicer

This sturdy corer/slicer, whose centered cutting surfaces resemble the hub and spokes of a wheel, will come in handy for coring and sectioning large quantities of apples or pears. Its open, dropped center directs a neat downward stroke around the fruit's core as the spokes section the flesh into wedges; their rigidity eliminates buckling while two upwardly splayed side handles encourage uniform pressure and prevent the knuckles from hitting the cutting board.

The blades of an apple corer/slicer should be well soldered in their cast-aluminum frame. The corer/slicers with 12 or 14 sectioning blades cut wedges best used for baking or sautéeing, while those that cut 8 sections are better used when preparing preserves. Since apples and pears aren't uniformly sized, this tool, with its 3 ¾-inch cutting diameter, is effective only on small to medium fruits.

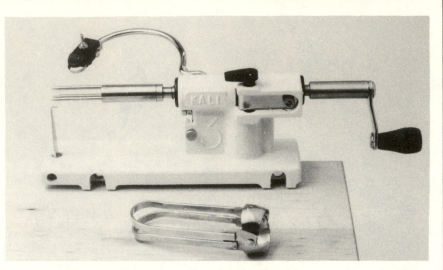

The very professional apple peeler/corer/slicer in the rear dispatches pears with equal authority; in foreground, a grapefruit corer's 1¼-inch-wide jaws pinch and snip to remove that fruit's pithy core and surrounding seeds.

Apple Peeler/ Corer/Slicer

When an apple or pear is fixed onto the three-pronged end of this tool's threaded spindle and the handle is turned, the fruit advances toward a tension-held, bowed blade, then onto and along a stationary, L-shaped slicing blade for the quickest, most efficient simultaneous peeling, coring, and slicing. Three nearly 2-inch-long prongs puncture a core's surrounding flesh for a sure hold, and a tension-set 1½-inch arced blade readily adjusts by means of the arm's spring to pare oncoming narrow and wide contours. The intercepting 2-inch L-shaped blade penetrates and cuts along the advancing core to cross-slice the surrounding flesh. Within thirty seconds, the resulting fruit spiral—either an apple or pear—is then sliced lengthwise with a knife and is ready to be added to tarts, turnovers, crisps, or crumbles.

An apple peeler/corer/slicer generally has a carbon-steel bowed blade, a stainless-steel L-shaped blade, and a chromed-steel C-clamp; its chassis is most often manufactured in cast-aluminum/plastic or the sturdier cast-aluminum/chromed-steel combinations. Its base measures 19″×2″×5″.

Grapefruit Corer

The sharp, prickly scent and bracing acidity of a Ruby Red, Duncan White, or Frost Marsh grapefruit is a favorite way to start the day. Sectioning isolates most of the bitterness caused by naringen and limonin, found in high concentrations in the pith, segment membranes, seeds, and core, while coring and seeding, most efficiently done in one step with a grapefruit corer, separate the remainder.

The corer works on the same hinge-and-pinch principle as a clamp. When its two pivoted handles are closed, their small, notched end scoops form a 1¼-inch-wide cutting circle that, with a twist and a thrust, plunges through the perimeter of a halved grapefruit's core to the inner peel. When the handles are opened, the scoops close to remove the core's base and seeds.

Grapefruit corers, which are usually nickel-plated and measure 5 inches in overall length, come with one cavil: The 1¼-inch diameter of the end scoops removes too much flesh from small fruit and visually too much from any sized fruit.

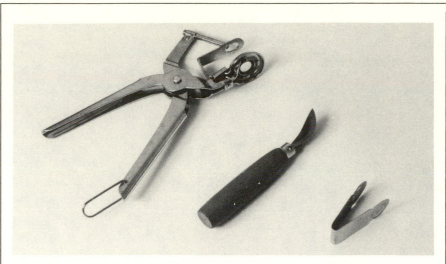

Clearly adpated from carpenters' and stationers' tools are, left to right, a cherry and olive pitter, fruit and vegetable pitter, and strawberry huller.

Fruit and Vegetable Pitter

This elliptical blade with its upward bow may be the twin of an artist's chip-carving knife, but it is actually used to pit and eye some fruits and vegetables. Its 2-inch length guarantees close hand proximity for precise, shallow cuts; inflexibility bests the densest Jerusalem artichoke or potato; and a curved, sharp-edged ellipse penetrates pineapples, then scoops out their eyes. To prepare fresh lychees with this tool, nick and remove the knobby, reddish-brown covering, slit through the flesh, and pry out the hard brown pit.

Fruit and vegetable pitters are available only with carbon-steel blades.

Cherry and Olive Pitter

During July and early August, with cherries overflowing greengrocers' shelves, many people get the urge to serve clafoutis, sample cherries with duck, or simply preserve them in vodka. Prior to cooking or canning, a cherry's tooth-breaking stone can be removed with a relatively sturdy, spring-loaded instrument that looks like a stationer's hand-held hole-punch. A cupped ring at the end of one blade holds the fruit—ideally, stem-side up—while the other blade's 1½-inch rod, when pressed, pokes through and punches out the cherry's pit with little loss of juice, then pulls back out of the cherry.

An unusual plastic-and-aluminum cherry pitter is manufactured whose slanted food tray funnels cherries two by two into separate slots for simultaneous pitting, but the sturdiest cherry pitter, which can also pit small olives, is nickel-plated, with plierlike handles that powerfully retract—you don't want to pull apart the handles after compressing them. The cup should be fairly deep and narrow to hold the cherry (or olive) securely.

Strawberry Huller

What device could more properly pluck the cottony core from a ripe strawberry than this short, wide, blunt-tipped tweezerlike huller? Its 2¼-inch length allows close, accurate leaf grips and pith pulls; its nearly 1-inch-wide, textured arms provide comfortable, slip-free surfaces, while rounded tips won't readily pierce or juice fragile flesh.

Tin-plated and stainless-steel hullers look exactly alike, but the slightly heavier, more durable stainless steel is preferable.

Clafoutis

*Patrick Verré, Executive Chef:
La Gauloise*

8 servings

½ *cup milk*

½ *vanilla bean*

3 *large eggs, separated*

1 *large egg yolk*

¾ *cup granulated sugar*

¾ *cup all-purpose flour*

½ *cup crème fraîche (page 123)*

1½ *to 2 cups pitted cherries (either jarred or fresh, the latter poached 3 minutes in a light sugar syrup)*

Pinch of salt

Preheat the oven to 350°F.

Combine the milk and vanilla bean in a small saucepan set over medium-high heat and bring to a boil; set aside to cool, then remove the bean, slit it, and scrape its seeds into the milk.

Combine the 4 egg yolks and sugar in a medium bowl and whisk to mix; add the milk with vanilla, ½ cup flour, and crème fraîche, whisking to mix after each addition.

Toss the cherries in the remaining flour and stir into the custard mixture.

Combine the egg whites and salt and whip until the meringue reaches its soft-peak stage. Add half this mixture to the custard and carefully fold it in; add the remaining and fold it in as well.

Pour into 8 lightly buttered and floured 6-ounce crème brûlée dishes, place in a shallow roasting pan, and pour in enough hot water to come halfway up the sides of the molds.

Bake 25 minutes and serve warm.

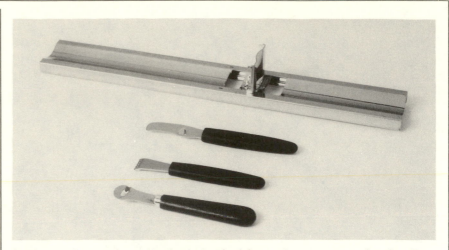

Stainless steel graces the working head of each of these strippers, zesters, and peelers. From the top are a corn stripper, orange peeler, citrus zester, and lemon stripper.

Corn Stripper

During mid-summer when golden and white sweet corn are readily available and a cob-free succotash, fritter, or timbale sounds appealing, this long, troughed steel stripper can do the scraping or shredding. A 17-inch span propels an uncooked cob toward the embedded cutter; a concave shape that mirrors the ear abets the proper press-push motion; and a convertible cutting area both scrapes and shreds. When the adjustable straight edge is raised, it wrests full kernels from a moving cob and when lowered, with guarded teeth exposed, the tool shreds, slits, and milks the kernels.

There is in addition a hand-held implement that has a curved, 1½-inch-long blade with shredding teeth, and a long, tonglike tool whose arms straddle a circular blade that encircles the ear and strips it bare. Both work with the same degree of effort and efficiency as the troughed device, but since this achieves both tasks, it seems the more prudent purchase. However, the recommendation comes with one caveat: Because no cleaned cob is uniformly cylindrical, pretrimming and frequent repositioning are mandatory for full kernel removal.

Lemon Stripper

The bulging V-shaped tooth that juts into the narrow horizontal slot near this tool's stiff blade front wrests thin, decorative strips from lemon and orange peels and grooves cucumbers and carrots for lively salad slices. A short, flat blade flattens the fruit or vegetable for even scoring, rigidity ensures the dropped, V-shaped cutting tooth's unwavering channel, and the freshly cut strips are fed out the V's slotlike plane for unhampered peeling.

Most lemon strippers, which are also known as canelle knives and can duplicate the tasks of the centered-toothed mushroom fluter, are geared for right-hand use. But for southpaws, blades with the cutting tooth set to the opposite side can occasionally be found.

All lemon strippers are manufactured in stainless steel.

Citrus Zester

The five tiny, sharp-edged holes that lie along this blade's downwardly curved front are unsurpassed at removing flavorful strips from lemon, lime, and orange rinds. The ¾-inch blade front covers the maximum possible area on a spherical surface, and the 20-degree downward angle ensures an incision only into the fruit's colored outer skin, called the flavedo, which houses the fruit's essential oils.

But don't restrict a zester's use to citrus; run it down a carrot or radish—even a daikon—for colorful or peppery ⅛-inch wisps for salads.

Straight-bladed and double zesters, with holes running down both blade sides, are also available, and while they are equally well constructed, the absence of that ideal front angle or forward cutting surface makes them a little awkward to maneuver. All are manufactured in stainless steel.

Orange Peeler

This blade's slight, concave scalloped-edged front and central, bowed cutting tooth quickly pare flesh and score strips from orange, lemon, or lime peels. The cutting edge's slightly crescent profile, which reduces compression while cutting spherical surfaces, restricts the amount of juicing; its scalloped edge severs membrane from pith as its ¼-inch-wide dropped-steel tooth, like a plane, rapidly channels and directs newly cut strips back, up, and out of the way as you work.

Orange peelers, which can also be used to groove carrots and cucumbers, measure just over 7 inches long and are manufactured only in stainless steel.

Four-sided Grater

Four-sided, or box, graters are usually 9 inches high with roughly 3-inch-wide grids. Coarse and fine rasplike perforations reduce hard Italian loaves to crumbs and file nutmeg kernels into near powder for custards. One of the two inclined planes will shred cheese, the other will slice rounds for a galette. All have at least four different grates and most are manufactured in stainless steel. Some are perfectly rectangular with identical base and top measurements, but the broader-based trapezoidal graters are more stable. Some handles are inset but it's better to select one whose handle is highly arced for hand clearance, wide to provide a comfortable working grip, and securely attached.

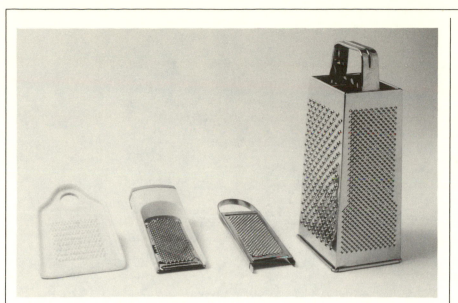

The general- and special-purpose kitchen graters include, from the left, a ginger grater, nutmeg grater, lemon grater, and four-sided grater.

Nutmeg Grater

Nutmeg is at its aromatic peak when freshly grated, but because only a small portion per kernel can be used in an eggnog, pâté, or pie, grating units are designed both to rasp and to store these seeds.

Since the kernel is so small, so is its grater, which looks like a halved cylinder with a back and cap. The curved grid, with its 3-inch-long band of tightly set teeth, provides ample grating area; a smooth top section allows for a comfortable working grip, and the back and lid hold up to five kernels.

Nutmeg graters—not to be confused with nutmeg mills—are almost always manufactured in stainless steel.

Ginger Grater

Most Westerners associate the use of fresh ginger with Chinese cuisine. Chopped, it accents stir-fried flank steak; it's sliced in roast Szechuan duck and shredded for steamed bass. Yet other Far Eastern cuisines, notably Japanese, also use ginger, not as a usual seasoning, but as a component in many dishes.

To be fully integrated into a dish, ginger should be very finely grated to offer plenty of juice and only a modicum of crispness. Flavor rather than texture must dominate, and this is best achieved by using an *oroshigane*, a small, spiked ceramic plate that vaguely resembles an old-fashioned washboard. Its 3-inch grating area is large enough to reduce a thin rhizome; ceramic is the traditional material, and a surface that looks like tiny thorns bruises, breaks, and juices plant fibers rather than a Western rasp, which tears, rips, and shreds them.

Japanese ginger graters are most often available in ceramic, although stainless steel and aluminum can occasionally be found.

Lemon Grater

At first glance, the narrow rasplike strip on this small, flat grater appears identical to that on a box grater, but its jagged perforations are noticeably smaller to ensure that none of the lemon's bitter white pith—the albedo—is included among the fragrant bits destined for a génoise or buttercream. It also has twice as many perforations per square inch for efficient strokes and to create smaller raspings whose texture is nearly undetectable in a madeleine or lemon curd. Choose the heavy, medium-thick–skinned varieties of lemons for grating.

Lemon graters usually measure 5″ × 2″ and are manufactured only in stainless steel.

Rotary Grater

If you had walked into a well-appointed French kitchen twenty years ago, you would have seen a device similar to this hand-held rotary grater, which grates nuts for tortes, chocolate for éclairs—even that last nugget of Parmesan that often gets thrown away. It also shreds carrots and slices cucumbers.

The tool is surprisingly small—7½ inches long—to accomplish so many tasks and remarkably safe for your fingers. The rotary grater has two joined handles; its lower one terminates in a small hinged hopper for the food which sits above a cylindrical cradle where one of three interchangeable drum graters is housed. The upper handle ends with a concave plate which clamps down on the food and pushes it toward the hand-turned drum's sharp, multi-edged surface to be grated, shredded, or sliced. The hopper holds approximately ⅓ cup, so unless the food being grated is already small, it must be trimmed first. A larger, 2-cup-capacity counter model is made, but for that much food, it's more practical to use a food processor.

The sturdiest rotary graters are manufactured in stainless steel. Check to see that its handle provides a smooth drum roll and always opt for the more useful, 3-drum rather than single-drum model.

Almond Grater

When the large rasp-drum that lies at the base of this grinder's hopper is fed shelled walnuts or skinned filberts or almonds and its crank is turned, it renders a fine flour for cakes, meringue shells, cookies, and sauces. Its 3-inch-wide cutting face snags, shaves, and chutes the ½ cup compressed feed into a bowl; the small and medium cutting teeth are set in opposite directions so that turning the drum one way produces fine gratings and the reverse, medium-fine gratings. A base clamp secures the apparatus to the countertop.

Nut flours are easily available in large cities and by mail order, but when their freshness is questionable, due to the substantial proportion of oil in nuts, self-grinding seems to be a safe hedge.

Sturdy countertop nut graters—also used for hard cheese and bread—are available in combinations that include cast iron and nickel-plated steel, aluminum and stainless steel, or nickel-plated and stainless steels.

Rotary Herb Chopper

A rotary herb chopper has a slotted hopper whose axle is fitted with four rows of perpendicularly set blades. The hopper, which has a ⅔-cup capacity, funnels the herbs to the chopping area where they are snagged, pushed, and broken, rather than truly chopped, by the crank-powered rotating blades.

Most prefer using a chef's knife to accomplish this, particularly when clean-up time is considered, but if you want this type of chopper, the most durable is crafted in stainless steel with a plastic-capped crank handle.

Roller-Mincer

When viewed from the side, this tool's sleek plastic housing could easily be mistaken for the clamshell fender from a tiny Bugatti. The roller-mincer's equally smooth, curved casing provides a comfortable working grip and acts as the axle brace for its five cutting edges. While most professionals still rely on their trusty chef's knives to mince, many less-practiced cooks like the efficiency promised by this tool.

The roller-mincer rolls back and forth over food to mince partially cooked spinach for ravioli, peeled and seeded tomatoes for a gratin, and parsley for soups, salads, and sauces.

Drum graters afford fine alternatives to flat graters. The most common are the rotary grater with its interchangeable drums at left and the almond grater at right. They are discussed on page 41.

The roller-mincer shown at left and the rotary herb chopper at right can be used in place of a chef's knife for mincing herbs.

The stainless-steel cutting wheels generally measure 2½ inches in diameter for long, easy sweeps, and the wheels are kept relatively clean by a fitted bottom plate that keeps foods from riding up into the casing. Handled roller-mincers, which work equally well, have 9 cutting wheels that are half the size of those in the 5-wheel type. They, too, have a wheel-shielding plate.

Be sure the parts are simple to clean—either totally immersible in hot water or easily disassembled to be so.

Melon Ball Cutter

To make sautéed sweet-potato balls, dilled beet spheres, or to accent a honeydew-Riesling soup with melon ovals, you'll need a sturdy, somewhat sharp melon ball cutter. A rigid stainless-steel form readily drives through the crispiest carrot or ripest cantaloupe, a relatively sharp cut-

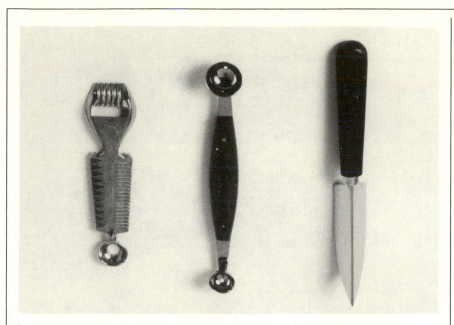

Decorative cutters in the batterie de cuisine include, from the left, a multifunction butter cutter, melon ball cutter, and V-shaped melon cutter.

Since this tool's side furrows are too shallow to define richly and the scoop's rim too dull to drive in effectively, the decorator is best reserved for curling and prizing off bottle caps. Multifunction butter decorators are manufactured only in cast aluminum in 6-inch lengths.

Butter Curler

For elegant dinners, some people like to serve individual butter pats, textured balls, or tight, scallop-shaped butter portions. The latter are easily achieved with a crenulated, hooked butter curler whose 1-inch breadth covers the width of a typical butter stick. Notching creates decorative ridging and a metal crook guides newly shaved butter into one specific shape.

Draw the blade down the length of a room-temperature stick of butter, drop the curl into a bowl of ice water to set, and refrigerate until ready to serve. Dip the blade occasionally into a bowl of warm water as you curl. It may take a few attempts before you understand how much pressure you should exert—too little causes curls that break and too much results in misshapen lumps.

Select a butter curler (which can also be used to make small chocolate shavings) that displays a full 180-degree curve—slightly bowed curlers won't produce the truly definitive shapes. Also look for deeply crenulated, rigid stainless-steel blades that flute emphatically.

Vegetable Garniture Set

A sherbet-filled melon, a soup-laden gourd, or ratatouille-packed eggplant suit a buffet wonderfully, but for a truly dazzling display, that same honeydew can resemble a celadon vase, the pumpkin a Strasbourg tureen, and the eggplant a piece of Chinese export porcelain. All that's needed is time, determination, and a minute, multibladed garniture set that gouges,

ting edge exacts clean shapes, and a tiny hole in the form breaks suction for easy releases.

Select a melon ball cutter whose oval or round shape is securely soldered to its shaft and one that seems heavy for its size—both translate into solid pressing and scooping power.

Round melon ball cutters range in diameter from ⅜ to 1¼ inches, while plain and fluted ovals measure either ⅝″×1″ or ¾″×1¼″.

V-shaped Melon Cutter

It used to take a small knife to do the zig-zagging for coronet-cut fruits, but nowadays a medium-length, rigid, V-shaped cutter more neatly and rapidly accomplishes the task. The nearly 4-inch blade reaches easily into the center of a large cantaloupe, its inflexibility prevents buckling, an inch-wide splay makes a distinct pattern, and an exterior bevel to the relatively sharp point allows smooth penetration.

The melon cutter also edges tomato baskets to hold braised pearl onions, trims grooved orange cases for fruit salads, and coronets onion cups for buttered carrot and turnip balls. When filling any hulled fresh-fruit or vegetable container, slice a little off its base to make it level.

The cutter's handle should be comfortable to accommodate strong grips, textured to prevent slips during plunges through firm peels, and well bonded to the blade. The same criteria apply to the slightly wider U-shaped cutter. A smaller, wider, multi-V cutter is also available, but because it has less well defined dents and a 2½-inch-wide front cutting surface, it can't address spheres as well as it does the flat, lengthy sides of zucchini and eggplant.

Multifunction Butter Cutter

When any one of this palm-sized tool's four surfaces is properly warmed in hot water, then pulled, pushed, or pressed into a semifirm butter block, it produces a shaped butter garnish—notched curls or crenulated slices or smooth balls. Its inch-wide plane end with a downwardly angled, crimped lip and open mouth successfully scrape, shape, and cradle developing curls; the small and large grooved edges on the central shaft, set in opposite directions, flute as they slice, while the other end's small holed scoop digs marble-sized butter or melon balls.

scrapes, and scoops those firmly fleshed fruits and vegetables.

The kit includes five blades, all under 2½ inches long, which are straight, skewed, and curved to score, cut, and carve at various angles. There are also four routers—one straight, two circular, and one diamond-shaped—to create hollows and notch grooves; four gouges in U and V shapes to produce small recesses and deep furrows; one chisel to initiate shapes; and a single saw to trim woody stalks and penetrate thick peels.

Well known to wood carvers, these sets afford interchangeable carbon-steel blades with a clamplike aluminum chuck to hold them at the end of a slip-free plastic handle. Few differences distinguish these tool sets from one another, so it's preferable to buy the most versatile 15-blade set, with which you can also work tallow. It is far better than the more commonly offered 3-gouge sculpting set.

Radish Decorator

The vegetable that gave sustenance to pyramid-building slaves, that together with eggs comprised Cowper's "spare feast," and that Ben Jonson claimed prepared the palate for wine is now generally regarded as a scarlet-and-white platter accent. The peppery radish is occasionally cooked with cream or dabbed with butter, but it's most often shaped into a chrysthanthemum, fan, coronet, or rose. It can take a paring knife and a little talent to accomplish such garnishes, but a tonglike radish decorator will produce that last rose in a snap.

The ringed end of one handle houses blades that form a spoke-and-hub pattern; the other's cupped end holds the trimmed radish, root end up. When the handles are squeezed, the blades drive their design into the vegetable; immersion in ice water then causes it to bloom.

Most radish decorators have an additional beveled, V-shaped notch

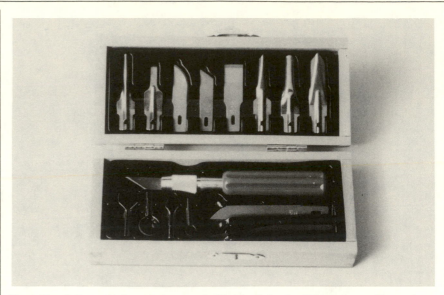

Vegetables, fruits, and tallow can be carved with this diminutive 15-bladed vegetable garniture set. (See page 43.)

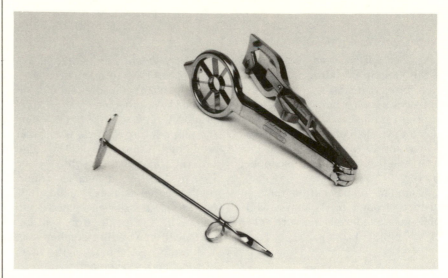

With a push and a twist through a root vegetable, the curl cutter at left produces potato, yam, and beet coils; with a press, the radish decorator at right scores radish roses.

at one handle end that snips through the rinds of halved citrus to create decorative cups.

These tools are available only with cast-aluminum handles and stainless-steel blades.

Curl Cutter

With a firm vegetable, a little pushing and twisting, and a corkscrew-fronted 6-inch steel span with side-set eyelets, you can create carrot coils, beet curls, and potato twists.

The conical tip drives through a raw or blanched vegetable, its flutes advance boring, and the near perpendicular eyelets—actually scorpers—carve through the surrounding flesh to cut crisp, clean, interlocking twists.

Once called quirlers after the German verb *quirlen* (to twirl), curl cutters are manufactured only in tin-plated steel. A good one should have a reasonably sharp tip, well-defined screw threads, carefully soldered scorpers, and a rigid lever.

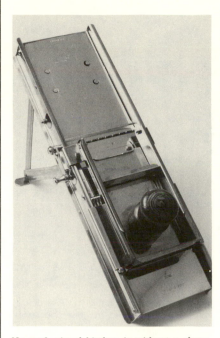

No professional kitchen is without a gleaming stainless steel mandoline that slices, juliennes, and waffle-cuts fruits and vegetables.

String-Bean Slicer

When green beans are at their peak and large quantities must be thinly sliced for freezing and canning, a

This hopper-fed, hand-cranked slicer rapidly juliennes fresh green beans.

sturdy, multibladed bean slicer clamped on the counter will seem like a gift from the gods.

Its six round blades, like a series of minute circular saws, are set along a single axle at ³⁄₁₆-inch intervals, providing a constant cutting surface against a grooved plastic wheel. The beans are dropped into the plastic hopper, the hand crank is turned, and the rolling blades, which initially nip the bean at a 45-degree

angle, cut it completely as the rotating blades pull the vegetable down against the cutting plate. A 1¼-inch span neatly shreds the largest bean, and a C-clamp base allows the free hand to feed the hopper constantly. The cavil about this machine is the difficulty in cleaning—in dismantling the casing and picking between sprockets and axles.

Easier to clean, but not even half as efficient, is a hand-held bean slicer, a nearly 5-inch-long piece of plastic with a single bean hopper, small cutting grate, and straight edge that cuts tops and tails. This tool is best used to slice small amounts of beans.

Mandoline

With its three cutting surfaces, smooth glide plates, and slice-thickness regulators, the mandoline is well equipped to do any number of cutting chores—slicing, julienning, and waffle-cutting among them. Its cen-

---

Tuna Tartare with Gaufrette Potatoes and Chive Oil

Jean-Georges Vongerichten, Executive Chef: Restaurant Lafayette

4 servings

TUNA TARTARE

1½ *cups ground raw tuna (approximately 8 ounces)*

¼ *cup olive oil*

3 *tablespoons finely sliced chives*

Few drops Tabasco

Salt to taste

Freshly ground black pepper to taste

Combine all the ingredients in a medium bowl and mix well. Set aside.

GAUFRETTE POTATOES

4 *large Idaho potatoes*

6 *cups vegetable oil (or clarified butter)*

Salt to taste

Peel the potatoes and trim crosswise into large ovals. Using the corrugated blade of a mandoline, cut gaufrettes: Hold the potato firmly against the glide plate and slide it down to remove a slice and cut a ridged design. Turn the potato 45 degrees and run it down the glide plate to criss-cross cut and produce a wafflelike slice. Adjust the mandoline if the slices are too thick or thin. You will need 36 slices. Rinse them in cold water, then dry on a towel.

Heat the oil in a deep fryer to 375°F and fry the potatoes in small batches until crisp and golden brown; turn once to be sure they brown evenly. Transfer to paper towels to drain, and sprinkle with salt.

ASSEMBLY

¼ *cup chive juice (extracted in a juice extractor from approximately 8 ounces fresh chives)*

¼ *cup vegetable oil*

12 *3-inch chive lengths*

2 *ounces salmon or flying fish roe*

Whisk the chive juice and vegetable oil together in a small bowl and set aside.

Mound 3 separately rounded teaspoonfuls of tuna tartare onto each of 4 serving plates and top each mound with a gaufrette potato. Similarly top with 2 more portions of tuna tartare and gaufrettes and insert 1 chive length through each pile. Sprinkle a few roe around each and encircle with a drizzling of chive oil.

Borscht

*Faith Stewart-Gordon,
Proprietor: The Russian
Tea Room*

6 to 8 servings

¼ *cup salad oil or bacon fat*

¾ *cup julienned onion*

¾ *cup julienned carrots*

6 *tablespoons tomato paste*

2½ *cups julienned beets*

1 *cup coarsely chopped cabbage*

2 *tablespoons red wine vinegar*

3 *tablespoons granulated sugar*

2 *quarts strong beef stock*

Salt to taste

Freshly ground black pepper to taste

¼ *cup finely chopped dill*

1 *cup sour cream*

Heat the oil in a large saucepan set over medium heat; add the onions and sauté 7 minutes or until transparent, stirring occasionally. Add the carrots, cook 1 minute longer, then add the tomato paste and cook another minute; stir occasionally. Add the beets, cabbage, vinegar, sugar, and stock, increase the heat, and bring to a boil. Reduce the heat and simmer, partially covered, 25 minutes. Season to taste with salt and pepper.

Empty into a tureen or individual soup bowls, garnish with dill, and serve with sour cream on the side.

A manual rotary vegetable shredder is the precursor to the food processor. If a selection is available, opt for a sturdy stainless-steel and plastic model, with up to five interchangeable cutting disks.

tral cutting head, flanked on each side by a glide plate, has one straight and one crenulated edge to make simple or rippled slices. An adjustable axle beneath the straight blade bears two series of perpendicularly set blades that can further cut simple slices into julienne or slightly wider french-fry strips. Their initial thickness is governed by the lever under each glide plate which raises or lowers its pitch from 1/16 inch to ½ inch.

Once called a mar-for after the now defunct Burgundian firm that popularized it here, the mandoline always has stainless-steel cutting edges but can have a wood, plastic, or stainless-steel frame. Avoid false economy and skip the inexpensive wooden ones, which warp, and the plastic ones, which buckle. The 16-inch-long stainless-steel mandoline may seem expensive, but it's a precise, peerless cutting instrument. Fine mandolines are frequently sold with an accompanying hand guard to anchor and slide foods along the glide plate and distance fingers from possible blade contact, so if your mandoline does not come with one, be sure to buy or order it separately.

Rotary Vegetable Shredder

This hand-cranked machine with its interchangeable cutting disks that shred, julienne, or slice vegetables, fruits, and cheeses is sometimes called the poor man's food processor. Its hopper exposes foods to the rotating cutting disk; its hinged cover simultaneously stabilizes food and presses it onto the sharp surface for cutting, while the manual crank acts as an axle to secure and turn the selected disk.

Vegetable shredders are usually available in tinned steel and plastic or the sturdier stainless steel and plastic. They generally measure 10″×7½″×2″ with a 1-cup hopper capacity.

French-Fry Cutter

Since the early twenties, manufacturers have produced a variety of tools to cut french fries, but none did so uniformly without an inordinate amount of attention. Potatoes needed frequent positioning, even pressure was essential, and, when using a knife, cutting had to be dead straight.

These earlier drawbacks have been overcome by this stainless steel french-fry cutter of choice. Gravity holds the potato in its small, slanted cradle at the correct angle to the cutting grid; a smooth, lever-powered plate allows methodical, even pressure; separately sold interchangeable grids easily produce delicate shoestrings, traditional

Uniform french fries are skillfully cut with the lever-powered device on the left; the pleated steel sheet on the right can render crinkle-cut vegetable slices or lengths.

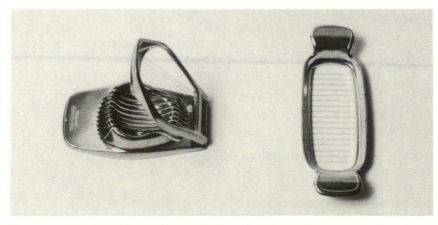

The framed, taut wires of the egg slicer on the left and the butter slicer on the right have almost no drag surface, so they cleanly slice through these semisoft foods.

strength and stability and its stainless-steel blade is generally longer and of a thicker gauge.

Egg Slicer

It's nearly impossible to slice a hard-cooked egg cleanly with a knife, as the blade creates a slight drag that pulls some of the yolk into the albumen. Attempting to contain a very supple substance is difficult, but an egg slicer will prevent slippage and inconsistent slices. Its 10 fine-gauge wires, held taut in the hinged top frame, first pinch and press, then cleanly and quickly slice through an egg positioned in the contoured base.

Egg wedgers, which vaguely resemble tongs and whose wires cut eggs into six sections, operate on the same hold, press, and cut principles. Both are manufactured in cast aluminum. Each wire should be soldered on the back of the frame as opposed to merely threaded around the pegs; the latter frequently come off.

Butter Slicer

The 17 stainless-steel wires stretched side by side across this tool's rectangular frame quickly and cleanly cut uniform, nearly 2-teaspoon pats from a chilled 4-ounce butter stick. Its single, multiple cut, allowing no time for softening, ensures tidy slicing; carefully spaced thin wires with no drag surface initiate smooth cuts while their frame's upwardly and outwardly set handle tabs, which lift fingers well above the work surface, encourage a full, even downward pressure.

Some butter slicers apportion only 14 pats, but all measure 8 inches long and are similarly manufactured with cast-aluminum frames and looped stainless-steel wires.

french fries, or the slightly larger pont-neuf cut.

A plastic-bodied cutter that employs the same brace and power-push principles is fine for occasional home use. Its horizontal bed directs the cradled vegetable toward the end cutting grid as a crank-driven back plate pushes it through. An accompanying guillotinelike blade can also be attached for cubing.

Crinkle Cutter

When you want to cut decorative cubes of tofu, notch uniform turnip sticks, or crenulate carrot crudités, you'll get good results with a medium-length, relatively sharp, accordionlike strip of steel. Moderately thick vegetable blocks or slices or anything with a final ½-inch width that can't be ridged by a mandoline can be served by a crinkle cutter. Its nearly 6-inch length can corrugate fries from a large Russet or Idaho, a 2-inch depth prevents wobbling during powerful downward presses, and a generous ¼-inch spacing between dents creates fine definition.

Select a crinkle cutter with a U-shaped frame rather than one with a standard handle; that frame adds

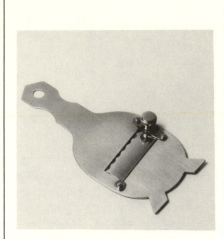

The perfect gastronomic tool is a paddle-shaped, stainless-steel truffle slicer; it can also be used to shave chocolate.

Truffle Slicer

This flat, stainless-steel, hand-held plane is so precise and of such high quality that it could only have been designed to slice something of enormous value: a truffle. Its smooth, polished surface allows for snare-free sweeps; a micrometer screw angles the centered blade up to a 15-degree pitch for relatively thick slices or to a bare 5 degrees for paper-thin ones, and the generous 2-inch cutting edge rifles through the most perfect, plum-sized truffle d'Alba or Perigordine, even though the latter is traditionally cut.

It's nearly impossible to present knife-cut truffle slices. A narrow, wave-cut blade like that on a ham slicer will cut superb slices, but those new shavings must then be transferred gingerly from cutting board to prepared dish. The thin, wave-cut blade on this portable plane can be employed directly over the risotto, fonduta, or omelet. You might also want to use this 7-inch-long implement to shave chocolate.

Cheese Plane

This slotted spade-shaped cheese plane originated in Norway, where it was designed to exact paper-thin slices from such strong-flavored cheeses as Gjedost and Gammelost—cheeses so assertive that they are virtually inedible if served any thicker.

The plane is a marvel of efficiency. Its cutting edge, which lies just below the horizontal blade and faces toward the handle, sits at a 25-degree pitch for controlled slicing; the angle lifts each shaving into the slot and then directs it onto the flat blade so it can't split or tear in the process.

Make sure your plane's blade is securely attached to the handle. It's recommended in durable stainless steel with a 2-inch-wide, slightly wave-cut cutting edge to gain a good purchase. The blade tip can be rounded, squared, or the favored pronged version, which exposes the most cheese for the easiest removal after cutting.

Lyre-shaped Cheese Wire

To portion large quantities of cheese properly for serving, the most practical implement is a medium-length, inflexible, lyre-shaped cheese wire. Its 8-inch span readily reaches across the widest lezay, the Y-shaped frame's 5-inch-deep bow cleanly cuts wedges from Corolle rounds or Pont l'Evêque bricks, and a tension-held, fine-gauge wire has little drag, so it cleanly severs the butteriest blue.

Since the lyre cutter slices, wedges, and cuts large blocks and rounds, its range is greater than that of a 4-inch slicing wire and, because it has a handle and a preset tautness, it's easier to wield than the 12- or 18-inch dowel-grip variety.

Fine lyre cheese wires are also available with 6-inch-wide spans. The 8-inch-wide cutter is fitted onto a 10-inch-long aligned stainless-steel frame and the 6-inch, on a 12-inch frame. Both come equipped with a tension-adjusting pin.

Risotto with White Truffles

Lidia Bastianich, Chef–Co-Proprietor: Felidia

2 to 4 servings

5 *tablespoons olive oil*

1 *cup finely chopped onions*

2 *tablespoons finely chopped shallots*

1½ *cups arborio rice, rinsed*

½ *cup dry white wine*

4½ *cups hot chicken stock (see page 210)*

¼ *cup heavy cream*

1 *walnut-sized white truffle, brushed clean*

2 *tablespoons butter*

½ *cup freshly grated Parmesan cheese*

Salt to taste

Freshly ground black pepper to taste

Heat the olive oil in a large saucepan set over medium heat, add the onions and shallots, and sauté 10 minutes or until golden; stir occasionally. Add the rice, toss to coat, and sauté 3 minutes to toast, stirring frequently. Add the wine, and when the rice has absorbed it, begin to add the chicken stock in 6-ounce ladlefuls. Once the rice has absorbed the first ladleful, add the next. Proceed until all the stock has been added, stirring constantly. Add the heavy cream. Shave the outer protruding pieces of the truffle into the rice; continue to cook until the cream has been incorporated into the rice; stir constantly.

Remove from the heat, add the butter and cheese, and stir quickly to mix. Season to taste with salt and pepper.

Empty onto 2 dinner or 4 first-course plates and serve; top by shaving some of the remaining truffle over each.

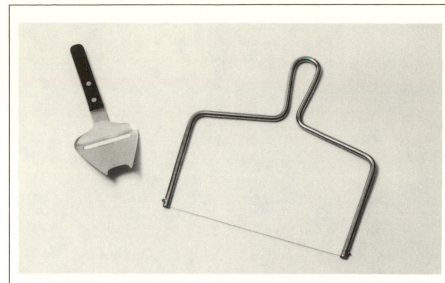

The cheese plane on the left handily slices semisoft and semihard cheeses; the cheese wire on the right quickly reduces drums of bricks to wedges or slabs.

On Serving Cheese in the Meal

Edward Edelman, Proprietor:
The Ideal Cheese Shop

Brillat-Savarin may have exaggerated when he professed, "Dessert without cheese is like a beauty with one eye," but his point of its importance within the meal was well made and one still taken. Few would dispute the fine final flavors of a flaky white Wensleydale and apple pie, ripe Gorgonzola and fresh pears, or winey Banon and Tokay grapes. Others who prefer an earlier sampling of cheese might instead serve Camembert and Saga with a postentrée salad or on its own as a predessert platter containing Brie, Saint-Paulin, Crottin, Pont l'Evêque, and Roquefort.

The foods and wines that precede and accompany cheese influence its selection. Lightly sweetened poached pears after a highly seasoned venison are perfectly matched by a tangy bleu de Bresse or fromage de Chaumes. A tart, tropical fruit salad following roast chicken is impeccably offset by a rich, buttery Saint-André. And vinaigrette-dressed greens succeeding grilled steak find great flavor contrast in a lightly sharp, creamy bûcheron or tomme de chèvre.

When served alone with crusty bread and perhaps some sweet butter, a three- to six-selection cheese tray takes its initial assembly cue from the entree: An emphatic main course should be balanced by at least one aggressively flavored cheese, and a delicate entrée by a similarly subtle offering. Such concern precludes serving cheese after curry or sushi, for example, as this would be ethnically inappropriate.

The link made, the remaining cheeses can then be selected for their variety in tastes, textures, and shapes. White, yellow, and blue-veined pastes look interesting and enticing; fruit, nut, and goat flavors provide harmonious contrasts, and soft and hard consistencies in log, loaf, wheel, and pyramid forms add tactile and further visual appeal.

Bearing these points in mind, a fine tray to suit any number of entrées could include a nutty disk of Saint-Nectaire, a rich triple-crème Belle Ètoile oval, and a mild, lightly goaty Montrachet cylinder. Another could offer a smooth, creamy-white Explorateur; a pale, supple Camembert round; a mild, straw-colored Gouda wedge; and a delicately sharp slice of blue Dolcelatte. A final tray with still greater variety could contain a hard, fruity Gruyère slab, a smooth, goaty taupinère cone, a soft-ripened, tangy Saint-Albray, and a mellow wedge of tomme de Savoie.

When buying cheese for a dinner party, plan on two ounces per person, then serve it at room temperature—well separated for slicing ease—on a platter.

A Roquefort cutter is as stately as it is effective at displaying and cutting that king of cheeses tableside.

Roquefort Cutter

The Roman scribe Pliny may have been the first to record the merits of this great blue cheese, but he was certainly not the last. The French epicure Grimod de la Reynière wrote that "Roquefort should be eaten on one's knees," while Casanova noted that "Roquefort and Chambertin restore love."

An elegant means to cut and serve it is this guillotinelike device. Its 8-inch-round split-marble slab holds the traditional 7-inch-wide cylinder of Roquefort; a taut cutting wire—too thin to draw buttery paste through crumbly veins during a downslice—hovers directly above this 4-inch-tall cheese; and the perpendicularly set handle—which gives shape to this tool's inverted-U frame—is spring-powered to ensure quick, clean cuts and rapid retractions. The wire is driven downward into a grooved base so complete severs can be made. After portioning, the 12-inch-high apparatus acts as a visual frame for the remaining cheese.

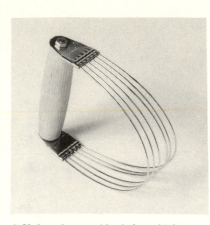

A U-shaped pastry blender's multiple wires quickly combine butter and flour with minimal warm hand contact.

Special-purpose circular blades found in the kitchen include, clockwise from left, a pastry cutting wheel, a pastry crimper/cutter, and a pizza wheel.

All Roquefort cutters come equipped with heavy iron frames, but their bases can be made of wood, hard plastic, or marble, of which the latter is the most authentic.

Pastry Blender

The ideal pie, tart, or turnover pastry has a texture that's tender, flaky, and crisp, qualities that are only achieved when the cold dough is quickly worked and minimally handled. Prolonged mixing or slight warmth encourages the gluten in flour to develop its long, elastic strands, the microscopic webbing that gives body to firm French bread but makes pastry dense and tough. To retard gluten growth, ingredients are preassembled, water chilled, and many people use a multiwire, U-shaped, semiflexible pastry blender. Six wires rapidly reduce flour and cubed butter into small flour-coated pieces, a deep, smooth curve creates a nearly 9-inch working length that can be used even in narrow bowls, moderate pliancy facilitates the proper press/bounce action, and a 4-inch distance between handle and dough separates warm hands from cold ingredients.

A 4-pronged pastry-blending fork is likewise designed to cut butter into flour. Its tines are widely spaced, triangularly shaped, and back-bladed, so they are technically superb for breaking butter into small bits.

However, since these tines are only 2 inches long and fairly straight, they aren't as efficient as the U-shaped blender.

The wires on the traditional pastry blender should be medium-thick and securely bolted to their handle. Most are manufactured in chrome-plated steel with a wooden handle.

Pastry Crimper/Cutter

When lightly floured and run down two sheets of ravioli dough or around the edge of a pasty, pie, empanada, or turnover dough, this tool's two axle-set corresponding crimping disks, which lie flush to the slightly larger central cutting wheel, simultaneously press, pinch, and cut the dough. The wheel's 7½-inch cutting surface needs little time to seal and sever. Its corrugated seal promotes the surest, most leak-proof bond, while the comfortable, contoured wooden handle allows a steady grip.

Pastry crimper/cutters are generally fitted with aluminum wheels and wood handles and measure 7 inches in overall length.

Pastry Cutting Wheel

This pastry wheel is nearly indispensable in a baker's batterie de cuisine. Its 4-inch diameter executes

long, straight trims for Napoleon layers; a keen edge cleanly cuts puff pastry so it can rise properly; a perpendicularly set blade permits meticulous work; and the inflexible round blade won't buckle under pressure.

Fine-fluted pastry wheels—also called jaggers and used most often to create lattice-work pies and tarts and to cut ravioli—have the same features, and the zig-zag edge is very well defined.

Both wheels are available with diameters from 1½ to 4 inches and in such materials as chrome-plated steel, brass, plastic, and stainless steel. The latter is the metal of choice; a 4-inch diameter is the most useful size.

Either tool's wheel should turn smoothly but not loosely, the axle attachment should be secure, and, for safety's sake, the handle should be fitted with a finger guard.

Pizza Wheel

Most agree that there's no better tool for cutting pizza than a wide, sturdy, single-beveled wheel with an offset handle. Its strong blade won't bend or wobble under pressure, a 4-inch diameter easily rips across a 14-inch-wide or 1½-inch-deep pie, a single bevel executes ramrod-straight cuts, and an obliquely set wheel allows for a comfortable, lateral slicing angle.

Dielike cutters for sweet or savory doughs are, clockwise from top: a set of vol-au-vent cutters (see page 55), a doughnut cutter (page 53), a set of fluted pastry cutters, a cookie cutter, and a ravioli cutter (page 52).

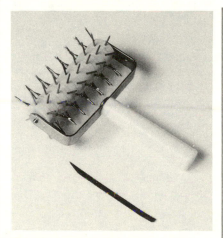

The roller docker at top is used to prick pastry dough to check its rise; the baker's blade at the bottom is used to slash bread dough so that it expands evenly.

Select a pizza wheel with a large diameter—the 4-inch wheels slice faster than the 2½-inch ones. Also check to see if the wheel rotates smoothly and easily. You'll notice that pizza wheels are attached to their handles with only a single steel arm; ideally the wheel should be secured to it by a screw so it can be dismantled for cleaning, sharpening, or replacement.

All pizza-wheel blades are manufactured in stainless steel and have handles with flayed finger shields that prevent the hand from slipping onto the blade. These handles can be crafted in wood, cast aluminum, or plastic.

Roller Docker

Looking more like a vintage tool of torture than a device to prepare delicate pastries, this medium-width, nail-studded roller pricks to prevent puff-pastry and short-crust doughs from rising or blistering as they bake. Its 6-inch barrel breadth covers the typical fruit tart or dartois width; evenly spaced rows of nails ensure uniform, overall piercing; and the handle distances hands from sharp, spinning spikes.

A roller docker, or pastry pricker, is available in all plastic, with a wood barrel and carbon-steel nails, or, ideally, with a plastic barrel and stainless-steel nails.

Inspect and rotate the barrel; the most effective nails are sharp and narrow, and a proper roll should be smooth but not loose.

Baker's Blade

This thin 5-inch strip of steel with its slightly turned-up tip is traditionally used by bread bakers to slash the tops of risen bread doughs so they expand evenly as they bake. A bare ¼-inch depth won't readily pull at sticky dough, an upwardly arced tip expands the forward cutting surface for nearly horizontal strokes, and a short, 1-inch cutting edge slashes ½-inch-deep rings around country couronnes or shallow, ¼-inch diagonals down baguettes.

A baker's blade, or *lame de coup* (blow of the blade), is also available with a straight, hooked, or beaklike profile to contend better with the higher or lower bread contours caused by risings in narrow pans or wide bannetons. The blades are available only in carbon steel and tend to be difficult to find, but a razor blade will do the same job.

Cookie Cutters

It's believed that such animal cookies as the pig and cow were originally made as offerings to the deities by peasants who couldn't afford the expense of ritually killing a live animal during their fertility festivals. Some of these shapes are still baked and served during the same seasons. Finland's gingery, pig-shaped *nissu nassu*, for instance, remains a late-November treat; a horseback-riding knight continues to proclaim the end of the herding and harvesting seasons throughout Italy's Veneto and into Czechoslovakia. And other shapes, like the German crescents and stars that prevail from mid- to late December, may have been featured at solstice celebrations.

The size, scope, and quality of the cookie-cutter repertory has since grown considerably, with the most functional and durable forms being moderately sharp, inflexible, and reinforced.

A lightly floured, relatively keen edge best cuts neat dough forms; an unyielding metal withstands continued stamping; and a folded metal cuff or external brace adds further pressing strength and support.

Stick with either stainless-steel or tin-plated cutters. The better of these are proportionately heavy for their size, with finely soldered or welded joints.

Cookie cutters can range in length from 2 to 8 inches.

Pastry Cutters

At first glance, the only difference distinguishing cookie cutters from pastry cutters is shape: The more whimsical stars, snowmen, and ships are reserved almost exclusively for cookies, while the classical ovals, squares, and circles rarely cut anything but pastry. However, those designed to cut the more delicate puff-pastry bouchées, vol-au-vents, talmouses, and fish fleurons have a heavier steel gauge and a slightly beveled, sharper cutting edge.

That external bevel cleanly separates fragile dough from scraps, a keen edge cuts the neater dough forms that rise eight times their height during baking, a heavier, less yielding shape withstands forceful stamping, and a brace strengthens the form.

Pastry cutters range from 1½ to 6½ inches long, are manufactured in tin-plated or stainless steel, and are available either singly or in sets of graduated sizes. The sturdiest are heavy for their size and are securely spot-welded. Some forms—notably those that cut large fish, squares, scallop shells, and windmills—also have raised handles to facilitate removal after cutting.

Ravioli Cutter

A corrugated pastry wheel can be used to shape the smaller, appetizer portions of ravioli almost as well as a ravioli tray, but to achieve truly flawless entrée-sized, pillowy squares and circles, it's best to use a rigid, heavy, definitively zig-zagged stamp. An unyielding form withstands pressure, and a ⅛-inch-deep, clear-cut flute severs and shapes two thinner layers of pasta.

A top-notch ravioli cutter measures 2 to 2½ inches wide. The longer-wearing chromed steel is recommended over aluminum; the metal should be fairly thick and heavy, have a well-defined cutting edge, and be securely attached to its knoblike wooden handle.

Goat-Cheese Ravioli with Tomatoes, Thyme, and Garlic

Alfred Portale, Executive Chef: Gotham Bar and Grill

6 servings

RAVIOLI DOUGH

5¼ *cups all-purpose flour*

1 *teaspoon salt (or to taste)*

4 *large eggs*

4 *large egg yolks*

⅓ to ⅔ *cup water*

Combine the flour, salt, eggs, and egg yolks in the bowl of a food processor and pulse to mix lightly. Gradually add the water—a few drops at a time—and process; add only as much water as it takes to have the dough form a ball on the blade.

Turn out onto a lightly floured surface and knead 10 to 15 minutes or until the dough is smooth and firm. Cover with plastic and refrigerate 1 hour before rolling and cutting.

GOAT-CHEESE FILLING

1 *pound fresh goat cheese*

2 *large eggs*

Salt to taste

Freshly cracked black pepper to taste

Combine the cheese and eggs in a medium bowl and beat to cream: Season to taste with salt and pepper.

Divide the ravioli dough into four equal pieces, then roll out each until paper thin. Trim to identical shapes.

Use a teaspoon to mound the goat cheese filling onto two pasta sheets at regular intervals to correspond with the size and shape of the selected ravioli cutter. Brush the dough with water between the fillings, cover with the remaining sheets, and press down around the mounds to seal. Stamp with the cutter. Transfer to a lightly semolina- or flour-dusted baking sheet and allow to dry 2 to 3 hours before cooking.

GARLIC BUTTER

8 *ounces butter*

1 to 2 *garlic cloves, minced*

½ *teaspoon fresh savory*

½ *teaspoon fresh thyme*

Salt to taste

Freshly ground black pepper to taste

Combine the butter, garlic, savory, and thyme in a medium bowl and beat to cream; season to taste with salt and pepper. Cover and refrigerate until ready to use.

ASSEMBLY

3 *ounces rich chicken stock*

1 *medium tomato, peeled, seeded, and cut into ¼-inch dice (approximately ½ cup)*

1 *tablespoon finely chopped parsley*

1 *tablespoon finely chopped chives*

Cook the ravioli 5 minutes or until tender in a large pot of boiling water, then remove with a slotted spoon.

Prepare the sauce as the ravioli cooks: Bring the chicken stock to a boil in a small saucepan and reduce to half. Add the garlic butter and whisk to mix. Add the tomato and, if necessary, further season with salt and pepper.

Divide the ravioli among 6 warm soup plates. Spoon a little sauce over each, then sprinkle parsley and chives over all.

Axle-held pastry cutters include the croissant cutter on the left and the lattice cutter on the right.

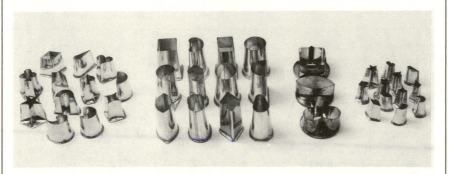

Size is the main distinction between these various cutters that are frequently sold in sets. Shown from left are gelée cutters, fondant cutters, canapé cutters, and truffle cutters (see page 54).

Croissant Cutter

Allegedly created in homage to the Austro-Hungarian bakers who helped defeat the Turks, the croissant mirrors the crescent of the Ottoman flag.

This rolled triangle of yeast puff dough is best shaped with an open, slatted, rolling pin–like croissant cutter. The cutter's curved metal strips, dusted with flour, perpendicularly press, cut, and cleanly sever uniform triangles, which a dough scraper or chef's knife always seems to pull. These are then rolled, curled, set on a baking sheet, then proofed and baked.

The traditional long, narrow, 4″×8″ triangles made by some cutters are not too practical because, once rolled and baked, they tower rather than curve properly. Select instead a cutter that produces near-equilateral triangles—roughly 5½ inches per side—because they are better balanced and, if desired, can then be sliced in half for a tea or canapé size. Croissant cutters are manufactured in tin- or nickel-plated steel or the more durable stainless steel.

Lattice Cutter

Among the most visually tempting pastries are surely a criss-cross topped blueberry pie and grilled apple flan, but the retiform pastry on each takes an inordinate amount of time to cut and weave without a lattice cutter.

Oblong pastries benefit best from a rolling cutter whose 6-inch-wide axle holds 17 evenly notched wheels. Held perpendicular to the dough, the wheels cut narrow strips to be stretched over a filling, creating a uniform, netlike pattern. Round pastries are better served by a two piece, 11-inch circular grid. To use, separate the grids, center the rolled round of dough atop the flat grid, then cover with the cutting grid and compress to punch out and form the latticework.

Both cutters are readily available in plastic, although the professionally preferred axle cutter can occasionally be found in the sturdier, more clean-cutting stainless steel.

Doughnut Cutter

Some people use two glasses to cut doughnuts—a large one to make the initial cut and a small one for the hole—but any mistakes, such as off-center holes, unclean cuts, and misshapen circles, are amplified when the doughnuts rise during frying. The best doughnut cutter is a heavy, double-ringed tool that looks from the side like a tumbler with two side holes. Its heft and rigidity aid downward pressure, a floured external-edge bevel neatly penetrates sticky dough to create a clean ring during the down-drive, a smooth top promotes a comfortable grip, and finger holes on either side break suction for easy dough release.

An internally braced, double-ringed tool fitted with an arced central handle will also suffice. It's light—inappropriate for quantity cutting—but will suit the occasional doughnut maker.

Be sure the two cutting surfaces align to ensure complete cuts and that its internal ring is well centered. The recommended cutter is stamped from a single piece of nickel-plated steel, while the other is tin-plated, composed of four pieces, and usually fairly well soldered. Cutters range in diameter from 2 to 3½ inches, the most popular being a 2 ¾-inch size.

Canapé Cutter

Canapé, whose Latin base means a fine gauze bed-covering, first signified a simple covering, then later a covering for bread. The canape's function mattered first, but ornamentation and its quick application naturally evolved—like the quickly cut clover-, quatrefoil-, ellipse-, and otherwise-shaped canapés that add sparkle and style to cocktail party and reception hors d'oeuvres. All that's needed is a reasonably sharp, rigid, reinforced cutter.

A truly keen edge couldn't withstand the constant stamping through thinly sliced pumpernickel; inflexibility allows drives through chilled shrimp butter and sliced Edam, and a bracketed cap guarantees uniform pressure and easy lifts after cutting. But don't restrict these cutters to hors d'oeuvres: You can also make decorative turnip and large carrot slices for elegant side dishes and more emphatic aspic accents for cold platters.

Be sure the canapé cutter is well soldered or welded and that it measures at least 1 inch high for enough clearance from the canapé top.

These implements usually cut 2-inch shapes. They are manufactured in both tin-plated and stainless steel and, surprisingly, the former are generally more securely braced and joined.

Truffle, Gelée, and Fondant Cutters

Only size distinguishes these nearly rigid, deep, flared cutters, each of which is the crème de la crème of its class. Their vertical inflexibility cuts easily through quivering jellies or pliant taffies; a 1-inch to 2-inch height provides a good purchase and distances hands from tacky fondants or chocolates; a conical profile strengthens the smaller cutting surface and fosters even stamping; while a thin metal edge cuts through sliced black truffles or rolled marzipan.

These cutters are most often found in multishape sets. Those that measure 1-inch-high cut truffles into ½-inch-wide forms; aspic, or gelée, which doesn't have the truffle's veined texture and therefore won't break with a doubly large expanse, has 1³⁄₁₆-inch-tall cutters, and the firmer fondant, which can retain 1½-inch-wide shapes, has cutters that

---

Croissants

Bernard Clayton, Jr.
Bernard Clayton's New Complete Book of Breads

24 to 30 croissants

3 *tablespoons all-purpose flour*

1½ *cups butter, at room temperature*

3 *cups all-purpose flour (approximately)*

1 *cup cake flour (approximately)*

2 *teaspoons salt*

2 *tablespoons granulated sugar*

2 *¼-ounce packages active dry yeast*

1⅔ *cups hot milk*

⅓ *cup cream, warmed*

1 *large egg plus 1 large egg yolk, beaten*

Sprinkle 3 tablespoons of flour over the butter and blend on a work surface. Form into a 6-inch square on a sheet of aluminum foil; wrap and chill 2 to 3 hours.

Meanwhile, prepare the dough: Combine the two flours and add 2 cups to a large bowl containing the other dry ingredients. Add the hot milk and cream and stir 2 minutes or until blended to a batterlike dough. Stir in the balance of the flour—¼ cup at a time—to make a soft dough. Knead 5 minutes to form a solid mass. Empty into a bowl, cover with plastic wrap, and refrigerate at least 1 hour.

Be sure the butter and dough are about the same temperature—ideally 65°F—then shape: Place the dough on a lightly floured work surface and press it into a 10-inch square. Unwrap the butter block and place it diagonally on the dough. Overlap the dough points onto the center to enfold the butter and make a neat package. Using a heavy rolling pin, roll the dough into an approximately 8″×18″ rectangle. Fold the dough length into threes—as though folding a business letter—then turn it so that the open ends are at 12 and 6 o'clock. Roll again into a rectangle, this time folding both ends into the middle and then closed, as one would a book. The dough will now be in 4 layers. Wrap in a cold damp cloth and refrigerate 1 to 2 hours.

Remove the dough and roll out on a lightly floured surface for the final time; fold again in three, as for a letter. Redampen the cloth, wrap loosely around the dough, place in a plastic bag, and refrigerate 6 to 8 hours or overnight.

Roll out the dough on a lightly floured surface to a generous 10″×38″ rectangle and, most important, about ⅛ inch thick. Trim to make the rectangle uniform in width, then cut it lengthwise to make two 5-inch strips. Cut with a croissant cutter or mark each strip into triangles, 5 inches wide on the bottom, and cut with a knife or pastry cutter. Place the triangles on a baking sheet and refrigerate 15 to 20 minutes.

Place the first triangle on the work surface—point facing away from you—then pull that point gently out ¾ inch. Roll the triangle from the bottom to the point, slightly stretching the dough sideways with your fingers as you roll. Set on a baking sheet with the tip of the point to the pan, but not underneath the body of the croissant; bend into a crescent shape. Repeat to shape the remaining triangles, then cover loosely with waxed paper and allow to set at room temperature 1 to 2 hours, or until double in volume.

When the croissants are two-thirds raised, remove the waxed paper and brush them with the egg wash. Leave uncovered for the remaining rising time.

Preheat the oven 15 minutes before baking to 425°F.

Place the baking sheet on the bottom shelf. After 10 minutes move to the middle or top shelf for an additional 12 to 15 minutes. Croissants at the edge of the pan brown more quickly than those inside, so remove them early from the oven and shuffle those remaining. Return to the oven for a few additional minutes. Transfer to a rack to cool.

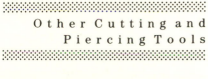

Among the more popular nonindustrial cutters for candy are the caramel cutter at left and a set of nougat cutters at right.

measure nearly 2 inches high. Some are available in stainless steel but the tin-plated cutters are more carefully crafted, with clean joints, superb bead soldering, and the flared caps that allow firm grips, presses, and removals.

Vol au Vent Cutters

Carême, the creator of the filled puff-pastry case, said it should be eaten "with pleasure for its extreme delicacy and lightness." Two of these lightweight, circular templates can properly shape these treats. Their average 4-ounce weight won't compact carefully layered dough during cutting or scoring; the rolled round edge prevents accidental nicks that hinder the dough's rise; the raised centered hole allows clean placement and removal, while 12 circular templates that range in diameter from 4¼ to nearly 10 inches permit the chef to create an appetizer, first course, entrée, or buffet-sized case.

Vol au vent templates are available only in tin-plated steel and should not be confused with the stamplike doubled scallop, fish, and square-shaped puff-pastry cutters that are also used to prepare the more decorative vol au vent cases—or the spring-loaded 1⅝- to 3½-inch-wide plain, fluted, or hexagonally shaped pastry-case cutters that cut and compress the central well in one operation.

Caramel Cutter

This shallow rectangular tray with its 2-handled grid insert will quickly cut inch-square blocks of chewy caramel. A lightly oiled 5″×8″, ⅝-inch-deep straight-sided pan neatly molds a molten sugar-and-cream mixture. Once set, the lightly oiled pressed grid produces 40 bite-sized squares of caramel that are ready to be individually wrapped.

A caramel cutter, available only in tinned steel, can also be used to cool and score small amounts of toffee and dried and fresh fruit pastes. The finest cutter has flush joints and careful soldering in addition to a grid whose rectangular shape is reinforced with a thick wraparound copper wire and further strengthened by spot welding.

Nougat Cutter

This thick steel ring should really be called a white-nougat cutter, as it usually cuts only that Provençal confection. Its distant cousin, black nougat, is also made in the south of France as one of the family's thirteen traditional Christmas treats. The two nougats also differ in consistency and shape: The near-crystalline white resembles a thimble while the more heavily honeyed black is chewy and square-cut. Consequently, different cutters are needed—a confectioner's knife is fine for the black nougat while a heavy,

chamfered, fairly short ring should be used to cut the white.

Extra weight helps to drive uniformly through a firm, nut-studded mass, a distinct angle to the cutting edge cleanly penetrates and separates, and a generous 1-inch height more than adequately tops this rolled candy. An additional thickened neck around the ring creates a ridge that facilitates removal after cutting.

Nougat cutters, which can also be used to weight terrines and gravlax, range in diameter from 1¼ inches to nearly 4 inches; they are available only in nickel-plated steel.

Ice Pick

This sturdy, awllike tool with its weighted handle reduces large blocks of ice to small pieces. It also scores carvers' guide marks onto ice faces and bores small holes. A strong chrome plate allows the shaft to withstand powerful thrusts to a hard surface, a 5-inch length diminishes the chance of bending, and a dull, needlelike tip creates the small impact point that best shatters a crystalline structure.

To break apart a large block of ice, hold the pick handle and stab into the surface at 45-degree angle. To crush the newly made pieces, flip the pick over and smash them with its heavy, tin-capped butt end.

Ice picks are sometimes called 1-point chippers, and their shafts can be manufactured either in carbon steel or the hardier chrome-plated steel. Both are available with various handle configurations, the best being the one that offers you the surest grip.

Ice Chipper

With its moderately wide band of short, strong spikes, this tool looks more like a small, flat hand rake than an important ice-carving implement. Its generous 2-inch span covers enough territory to quickly rough out figures from a melting medium, the six 1-inch-long spikes prompt a close hand-to-ice distance that promotes careful sculpting, and strong steel prevents buckling or breaking during a jarring forward chip or coarse backward draw.

Some manufacturers suggest using their chippers to pierce meat to tenderize or to better accept a marinade, but since puncturing draws out natural juices, reserve your chipper for carving. Ice chippers are available with either the recommended carbon steel or cast-aluminum spikes, which can't be sharpened and break off easily.

Flat Ice Chisel

These two rigid, rectangular blades—one narrow, one broad—scribe, chip, and shape small to medium areas of ice. Each stiff, straight blade front is essential to carve such basic shapes as cubes, cylinders, cones, and spheres from solid blocks of ice; the separate 1¼- and 3-inch-wide tips have enough surface to cut various sizes, and their hollow-ground reverse sides reduce suction and prevent sticking.

Once a pattern is etched onto a large block of ice, that sketch is more emphatically grooved with a chipper or pick before a saw can reduce the block to an approximate shape and the flat ice chisel is then used. A thicker-handled, mallet-driven wood chisel can be employed in place of the more wieldy chisel, but it, too, must be hand-propelled by holding the beveled side against the ice at a 30-degree angle and pushing it across to shave and shape.

Flat ice chisels are usually forged in high-carbon steel with tips that measure from ⅝ inch to 3 inches across and with various features to improve performance. Some blades are faceted down their entire lengths to promote easier gliding, and some have slight, upwardly canted, elongated handles to offer greater, more maneuverable hand clearance from the ice.

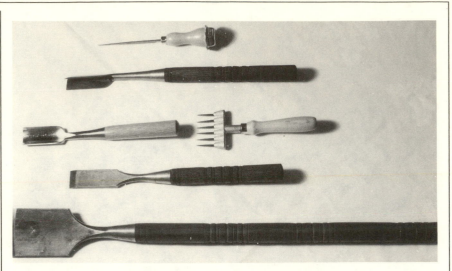

A fine elementary ice-carving set includes, from the top, an ice pick (see page 55), a V-shaped ice chisel, ice gouge, ice chipper (page 55), and small and large flat ice chisels.

A Primer on Ice Carving

John Doherty,
Executive Chef: Waldorf-Astoria

The crowning touch on an important buffet table is surely its glistening ice sculpture. The carved facets are eye-catching and dramatic; the towering height gives visual balance, while the final shape can serve as a vase for flowers, bowl for punch, or salver for seafood.

When many caterers, hoteliers, and restaurateurs plan a buffet, they often recommend a 150-pound ice cornucopia, swan, deer, or dolphin, among others, to their clients.

Whatever form finally graces the table, the chef-cum-carver begins with a 300-pound block purchased from an ice house. Called can ice and measuring roughly 20"×10"×40", ideally it has smooth sides, a level set, and complete clarity save for a small, cloudy core that's the result of injected air to hasten uniform freezing, separate water impurities, and reduce the incidence of large air bubbles.

A well-processed block of ice is one thing, its age quite another, as a young block is more like marble compared to an older block's granitelike state. New ice affords a smoother, tighter grain whose less brittle crystals shave more cleanly and split more evenly.

Using tools on such a medium is a cold, wet task that, to preserve the ice, is best accomplished in an area whose temperature is about 26°F. Dangerously sharp chisels, gouges, and saws are also on hand, so footing should be slip-free and level. For further personal protection, warm, comfortable clothing to fend off flying ice chips—layered shirts and slacks, insulated gloves, boots, and an apron—is often donned during the roughly hour-long procedure.

The art starts with a true-to-size template whose design outline is scribed onto the ice block face with a chipper. Large, unnecessary sections are then sawed off and relief cuts made to reduce internal pressure that could develop—for example, between the handles on a basket or the center of a zero or an omega. Scratching, scoring, chipping, and channeling are then done according to the way the ice melts.

This means carving should be done from the top of the ice block down: to initially rough out the full form, then to return to smooth and to add detail; essentially to complete every part of the sculpture at about the same time so that all parts of it melt proportionally during its average three- to four-hour-long display.

Careful presentation is professionally handled with a large, hard plastic basin that supplies height, built-in drainage, and lighting. Less convenient, but no less workable, is a plain, deep basin with inset blocks, the whole appropriately wrapped in a clean white tablecloth.

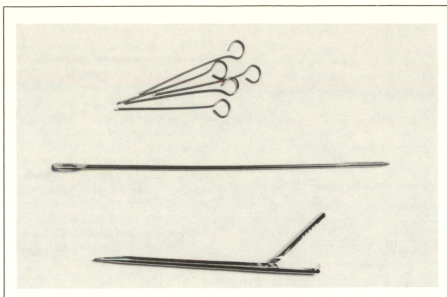

Narrow, sharply tipped needles for preparing food include, from the top, a set of poultry lacers (see page 58), a trussing needle, and a larding needle.

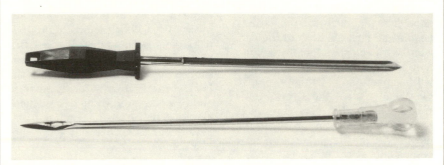

Two tools used to thread either lardoons or twine through beef for braising or roasting are the larding needle at top and, below it, the roast-beef tie tool discussed on the following page.

V-shaped Ice Chisel

The most popular carved-ice centerpieces include swans, boats, and baskets, and while some artists choose to soften and stylize the lines of these objects, others prefer more realistic, detailed effects. The best way to cut feathers, planks, and plaits is with a V-shaped chisel that has a medium spread and an exterior-edge bevel. The third in a beginner's four-chisel set, its nearly 1-inch expanse channels distinct bands and recesses and its exterior-edge bevel allows for a sleek glide and smooth shaving of surface ice.

V-shaped ice chisels are available in high-carbon steel with ½- to 1¼-inch-wide blade fronts.

Ice Gouge

To chisel curved grooves, shave off ice bits for clean detail work, or shape forms, an ice sculptor would do well to use an ice gouge, a troughed steel cylinder whose edge bevel is ground on its exterior, or convex, surface. A ¼-inch breadth creates well-defined coves, a true crescent shape produces gentle, life-like contours, and the external-edge bevel enhances a smooth advance over an ice face.

The blade fronts of traditional ice gouges range in width from ⅞ inch to 2¼ inches, and are usually forged in high-carbon steel. They can be fitted with short or long handles.

Larding Needle

This needle is well designed to thread chilled slivers of bacon or ham or even draw blanched asparagus or carrot sticks through small cuts of meat and poultry. It has ample length to stitch cleanly through any sweetbread or beef fillet, a sharp tip and cone shape to separate flesh for a neat draw, and a toothed clamp to grasp a thin lardoon or vegetable securely.

Curved needles are also available and, although few people condone the addition of fat to meat, poultry, or game, the 15-degree bow at the front of these needles provides the right angle of approach to barely scoop below the surfaces of veal, hare, and pheasant to perform *piquage*—the shallow, surface stitching of fat.

Be sure straight larding needles are long enough to go completely through the item. Also, some clamps flare out, petal-fashion, and these don't seem to hold the lardoon through a complete draw. Both straight and curved needles are manufactured in stainless steel; straight ones range in length from 6 to 12 inches, and the curved come in 7- and 9-inch lengths.

Trussing Needle

This narrow steel length with its fairly sharp tip and large eye is designed to puncture and draw twine through soft, raw flesh. Sewing stuffed meat and fish or trussing poultry and winged game compacts shapes for even cooking and makes for attractive presentations, as well as simplifying turning during searing or roasting.

Trussing, or butcher's, needles are available in 6- to 12-inch lengths of stainless steel. When choosing a length, be sure it will go completely through the item to be trussed. An 8-inch needle stitches stuffed flank steak, veal breast, and small birds like squab; a 10-inch properly suits chicken; and a 12-inch needle is routinely used when trussing capon and turkey.

Curved needles whose tips bow 20 degrees upward are also available; their true value is for slight surface stitching.

Whether using straight or curved needles, thread them with plain, cotton kitchen twine; waxed and synthetic cord may seem easier during the draw, but both melt at high temperatures.

Poultry Lacers

Instead of tying a fowl's legs together to cover its open cavity or to secure the stuffing, many insert these small, stainless-steel skewers, ladderlike, through the skin on both sides of the cavity, then anchor them with twine. Their sharp tips neatly pin skin flaps; their lengths cross the cavity of a 9-pound capon or 1-pound squab with equal ease; while a ringed end that prevents the skewer from being pushed completely through and out the other side also facilitates removal.

Poultry lacers—alternatively made with L-shaped ends—are manufactured only in stainless steel, in lengths that measure from 3 to 4½ inches. The skewers are also used to secure stuffed fish, pork chops, and rolled meats like braciole.

Boeuf à la Mode Needle

Although most people seek fat-free ways with classical dishes, some still insert lardoons into large, lean cuts of meat to lubricate them during long cooking. And to thread strips of fat through beef bottom-round roasts or to push plumped prunes through pork or fresh pineapple through ham, nothing works better than this long, sharply tipped, troughed, handled shaft of steel.

Boeuf à la mode needles are available with either carbon- or stainless-steel shafts in 10- to 21-inch lengths. The troughs of some are equipped with a small, sliding peg that holds the lardoon in the meat as the "blade"

Haunch of Venison with Pears

Anne Willan
French Regional Cooking

6 to 8 servings

½-*pound piece of pork fatback*

1 *5½-pound haunch of venison*

2 *quarts milk (or more if needed)*

7 *tablespoons butter*

Salt

Freshly ground black pepper

2 *pounds fresh pears (or apples)*

1 *to 2 teaspoons ground cinnamon*

1 *cup broth or water*

Cut the fatback into strips small enough to fit easily in the larding needle and lard the flesh of the venison: Sew each strip lengthwise into the venison, holding the strip in place with a finger and twisting to remove the needle. Space the strips evenly so that when the meat is carved, each slice has a pattern. Put the meat in a large, deep dish and cover completely with milk; cover and marinate in the refrigerator 24 to 36 hours.

Preheat the oven to 450°F.

Remove the venison from the milk, dry with paper towels, and lay it in a large, shallow, buttered baking dish. Rub the surface of the meat with half the butter and sprinkle it with salt and pepper. Roast 30 minutes, basting frequently and turning it over several times.

Meanwhile prepare the pears or apples: Peel but leave them whole. Add the fruit to the dish containing the meat, sprinkle it with cinnamon, and dot with the remaining butter. Cook another 30 minutes and baste frequently. To test the venison, insert a skewer in the thickest part for 30 seconds. If the skewer is warm to the touch when withdrawn, the meat is rare; if hot, the meat is well done.

Transfer the meat to a platter; halve the fruit and arrange it around the venison. Pour the broth into the baking dish, stir to dissolve the pan juices, and strain it into a small saucepan; skim off the excess fat. Bring it to a boil, taste for seasoning, and, if necessary, reduce it to concentrate the flavor. Strain a little gravy over the meat and serve the rest separately.

is withdrawn, but this feature is superfluous, as an index finger accomplishes the same trick. Most important is length—be sure the one you select is larger than the cut of meat you plan to lard.

Roast-Beef Tie Tool

The sleek, arrowlike tip, relatively wide shaft, forward eye, and handle on this implement suit it for spearing and binding large masses of meat. Its breadth diminishes the chance of bending and a handle allows for a more efficient pushing, rather than pulling, action. The forward eye makes for rapid trussing: Twine is threaded, pushed through, then looped as soon as it emerges.

Roast-beef tie tools are available in 12-inch stainless-steel lengths and used most often by butchers.

Potato Nails

The reasonably sharp tip and large head of this potato nail ease penetration and extraction, and the 4½-inch length drives nearly through a standard-sized baking potato to conduct oven heat through its interior so that it bakes uniformly.

Some potato bakers have hooks rather than nail-head ends and are meant to hang from an oven's rack, while others appear on stands that vertically hold 6 to 11 potatoes. However, gravity foils the hook-ended nails—once a potato's firm, raw flesh becomes soft and floury, it drops—while the stands take up too much room in the oven when other foods are cooking at the same time.

Potato nails are manufactured in aluminum, a metal that is surpassed only by silver and copper in its quick,

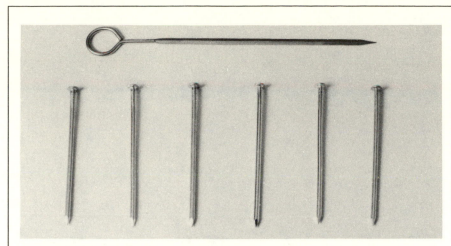

A flat skewer like the one at the top is preferred over a round one for grilling because it more securely holds food during turns. Potato nails, the set of aluminum spikes below it, are used to conduct heat to potatoes' cores so they bake uniformly.

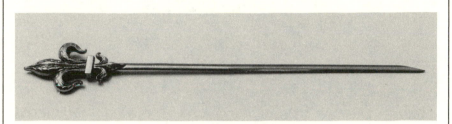

A hâtelet is the batterie de cuisine's most ornamental skewer; thread a few fluted mushrooms and cherry tomatoes onto its shaft, then sink it into a roast capon or chilled galantine for presentation.

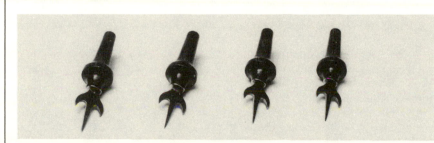

With their sharp tips, three purchase points, and generous grips, these corn-cob holders promise the most secure—as well as the neatest—eating hold.

also prick fatty ducks and geese before cooking; while the 10- and 12-inch sizes are suggested for home kebabs.

Hâtelet

This narrow, silver-plated shaft, topped with a fleur-de-lis or other decoration, is one of the many hâtelets used to present food in stately style. Small, colorful kumquats, cherry tomatoes, turned carrots, and/or carved radishes can be threaded onto the top half of the hâtelet's shaft while the bottom is sunk into a roast duck, aspic-coated beef tongue, or chicken galantine for serving.

Most agree that hâtelets, or attelets, were introduced during the reign of the Sun King, when the buffet became less the functional serving piece and more the ornamental sideboard it still is. With visual attention now fully on the table, the elaborate platters, service plates, eating utensils, even hâtelets that dressed them were commissioned. The silver- and goldsmiths usually emblazoned these items with the owner's (usually royal or noble) heraldic symbol—the dolphin, boar, coquille, and fleur-de-lis among them.

Hâtelets range in overall length from 8 to 10 inches, are now either silver- or gold-plated, and are still used strictly for serving, not preparing, foods. Their pewter-based metal has such a low melting point—roughly 470° F—that disastrous results could occur otherwise.

Corn-Cob Holders

When used in pairs the sharp, stainless-steel trident blade at each end of these wooden handles gives the surest eating hold on cooked corn. The 1½-inch-long razor-sharp tips penetrate rapidly; the three side-by-side purchase points of each blade form the most intractable grip, while the 2-inch-long rosewood handles allow a clean, comfortable distance from hot, buttered kernels.

conductive capability. They are sold in sets of 4 or 6.

Skewer

When you want to thread cubes of lamb, butterflied shrimp, or sausage coils for broiling, grilling, or sautéing, an 8-inch-long, sharply-tipped, narrow, flat steel skewer does the job.

Once the proteins in meat, seafood, and poultry are heated, coagulate, and contract, their flesh pulls away slightly from the inserted skewer. If the rod is round, so, too, is the punctured—but now larger—

hole, so the meat slips rather than flipping easily. The flat, 3/16-inch width creates an uneven axis so foods can be turned to cook fully.

The most functional skewers—with two prongs or with twisted shafts—are rarities in this country, but a wide variety of serviceable ones can still be had in 4- to 14-inch lengths and in carbon steel, stainless steel, or bamboo. (Bamboo should be soaked in water 30 minutes before using.) Four-inch rods work well for appetizer brochettes, cake testers, and poultry or suckling pig lacers; 8-inch rods, which restaurants favor for skewered entrées,

Usually sold in sets for two or four ears, corn-cob holders more often display such modestly effective ends as two offset spikes or a threaded screw. These are usually manufactured in chrome- or nickel-plated steel with plastic or wooden handles.

Corn-cob holders measure from 1½ to 3½ inches in overall length.

Gouge à Jambon

This tool's backwardly bowed blade removes the bone from a ham so effectively that the surrounding flesh remains as intact as possible. The principle behind it is leverage: The 7½-inch blade is longer than the standard-sized pork femur, a narrow trough that gradually arcs 17 degrees mirrors the bone's contours, and a strong, squared-off tip affords ample power to push, scrape, pry, and separate masses of meat from bone.

To bone a ham, free the aitchbone with a boning knife, then invert the gouge à jambon and inch it down the femur, scraping along its length until you come to the ball-and-socket joint above the hock. Free the meat from the femur end, then twist to wrench, pull it out, and either discard it or reserve for a future stock. A boneless ham can be stuffed and is a snap to slice.

A gouge à jambon is available only with a chrome-plated blade.

Manche à Gigot

In heraldry, a manche is a conventional representation of a flared sleeve, a manche à gigot is a flared metal sleeve capped with a handle that fits onto the shank of a roast leg of lamb or mutton to facilitate slicing. Keeping a good grip on a well-rounded leg of lamb is a constant struggle. Each slip on the platter translates into a jagged slice, which some avoid by holding a folded napkin around the frenched shank bone. But the frequent adjustment, in addition to the eventually greasy grip, prompts others to

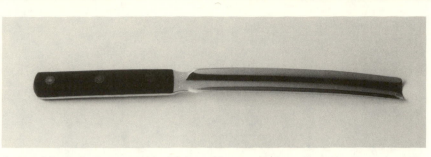

A gouge à jambon's strong, arced trough is used to scrape and pry, thus separating surrounding flesh from a ham's femur so that the bone can then be extracted.

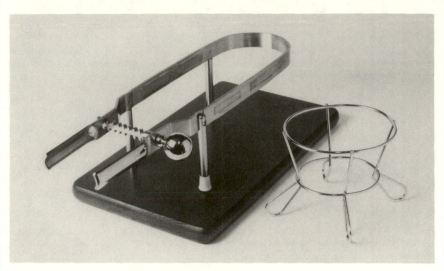

Two effective holders to secure smoked or cured ham during slicing are a prosciutto holder, at left, and a ringed ham holder, at right.

use the more accommodating manche à gigot. When fully open, its 1-inch diameter fits neatly over a trimmed shank and, by tightening the encircling band, six internal teeth bore into the bone to anchor the 5-inch-long carving handle.

The piece is ornamental as well as functional and is available in a variety of materials from silver to stainless steel to bone, while the handle also comes in a number of styles from Louis XV to Georgian to contemporary. Many are found in kitchenware and silver shops, but an inordinate number are also sold in antique stores, testament to the old American tradition of giving the new bride a fine carving set that included a knife, fork, and manche à gigot. In most instances she knew how to use the knife and fork, but not the manche, so it was often given away.

When buying a manche à gigot, make sure its encircling ring is firmly attached, the teeth well-defined, and the handle tightly bonded.

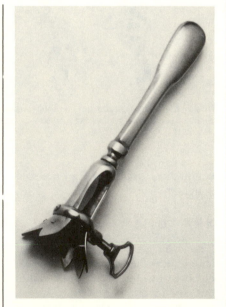

Once fitted onto the shank of a roast leg of lamb, a viselike manche à gigot provides a fine, clean grip for the carver.

Ham Holder

This open, upright ringed frame holds a cooked ham vertically so that it can be easily trimmed and cut. Its two-tiered oblong rings, successively smaller, brace an inserted shank end, as the 6-inch overall height that can contain 40 percent of a standard-sized ham provides a stable hold.

Almost commonplace in delicatessens, ham holders are generally manufactured in chromed steel, the best of which have rings that are well soldered to their frames.

Prosciutto Holder

A large, U-shaped stainless-steel clamp raised above a marble base securely holds a cured ham so that it can be thinly sliced. Its 14-inch hinged jaws that spread from 2 inches to over 6 inches accommodate small or substantial hams; the six inset spikes and end ratchet lock guarantee a firm, fast grip as the 17-

pound weight holds the ham immovable so the carver can easily cut paper-thin slices.

Prosciutto holders are always fitted with a stainless-steel clamp, but wood or granite bases are also available.

Boeuf à la Mode en Gelée
Cold Braised Beef in Aspic

Julia Child et al.
Mastering the Art of French Cooking, Volume I

10 to 12 servings

RED WINE MARINADE

1 *cup thinly sliced carrots*

1 *cup thinly sliced onions*

1 *cup thinly sliced celery*

2 *garlic cloves, unpeeled and cut in half*

1 *tablespoon dried thyme*

2 *bay leaves*

¼ *cup minced parsley*

2 *whole cloves or 4 whole allspice berries*

1 *5-pound beef-rump pot roast, trimmed, tied, and, if desired, larded with fresh pork fat*

1 *tablespoon salt*

¼ *teaspoon black pepper*

5 *cups young red wine with body (Burgundy, Côtes-du-Rhône, Macon, or Chianti)*

⅓ *cup brandy*

½ *cup olive oil*

Place half the vegetables, herbs, and spices in the bottom of an enameled or porcelain bowl just large enough to hold all the ingredients. Rub the meat with the salt and pepper, place it on top of the vegetables, then spread the remaining vegetables and herbs over the meat.

Pour over the wine, brandy, and oil. Cover and marinate at least 6 hours, 12 to 24 hours if refrigerated; turn and baste the meat every hour or so.

Half an hour before cooking, drain the meat on a rack, reserving the marinade. Just before browning, dry the meat thoroughly with paper towels.

BRAISED BEEF

4 to 6 *tablespoons rendered pork fat or cooking oil*

1 to 2 *cracked veal knuckles*

1 to 2 *split calves' feet*

4 to 8 *ounces fresh pork rind, simmered 10 minutes in 1 quart water, rinsed, and drained*

4 to 6 *cups beef stock*

Preheat the oven to 350°F.

In a fireproof casserole or heavy roaster just large enough to hold the ingredients, melt the fat over medium-high heat. When the fat is on the point of smoking, brown the beef on all sides; this should take about 15 minutes. Pour off the browning fat.

Add the marinade to the casserole, bring to a boil, and reduce by half. Then add the veal knuckles, calves' feet, pork rind, and enough stock to come ⅔ of the way up the beef. Bring to a simmer, skim, then cover tightly and set in the bottom third of the oven. Regulate the heat so that the liquid remains at a gentle simmer for 2½ to 3 hours; turn the meat several times. The beef is done when easily pierced with a sharp-pronged fork.

Remove the meat to a platter, discard the trussing, and trim off any loose fat.

ASPIC

2 *tablespoons gelatin (2 envelopes)*

3 *cups cold brown stock*

Salt to taste

Freshly ground black pepper to taste

¼ *cup port or brandy*

Degrease the braising liquid thoroughly, then boil it to reduce to 3½ to 4 cups. Soften the gelatin in cold stock, pour into the braising liquid, and stir over low heat until the gelatin is completely dissolved; season to taste with salt and pepper. Pour in the port or brandy and strain.

ASSEMBLY

2 *pounds quartered carrots, braised in butter*

24 to 36 *small white onions, braised in stock*

Slice the beef into serving pieces and arrange in a rectangular mold, terrine, or baking dish large enough to hold the meat and vegetables; intersperse the slices with the carrots and onions. Pour in the jelly—which need not be cold—and refrigerate 4 to 6 hours or until well set.

When ready to serve, dip the mold in hot water for several seconds. Run a knife around the edge of the aspic, invert onto a platter, and jerk to release the mold. Decorate with watercress, parsley, or Boston lettuce leaves.

3.
Fundamental
(Lever-Based)
Kitchen
Tools

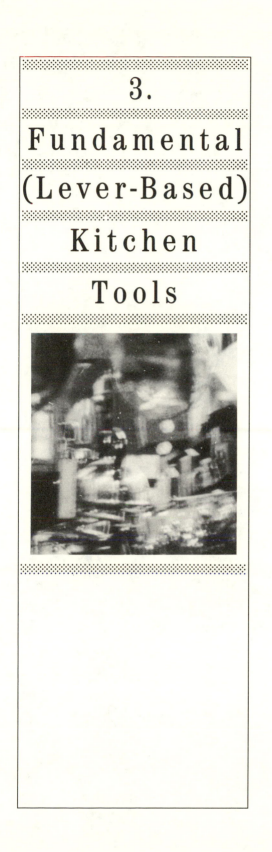

The two most important yet over-looked tools in the kitchen must surely be the chef's right and left hands. With open palms she or he can successfully fold beaten egg whites into a soufflé base, flatten a squab for its turn at the grill, and knead the necessary dough for a bread or pasta. Slightly cupped or spread, two hands quickly shape croquettes and evenly mix a force-meat for a pâté. And with slight finger manipulation, the hands can crimp tart borders, crumble bay leaves, and squeeze sauerkraut.

When a simple length extends the hands' surface, further meshes or separates their shape, or strengthens their grip, the two hands become even more effective implements because they've added the mechanical advantage that allows them to produce more work, to handle large or small masses, fluid or viscous products, and hot or cold foods with equal ease.

Once the chef extends his arm by holding a 12-inch spatula to lengthen his reach, he's creating a simple machine with which to more rapidly ice a cake or turn a crepe. By brandishing a scoop meant to mimic the cupped hand, he more methodically apportions rice or scrapes and shapes sorbet. And with tongs, which enlarge the finger vise, he can better grasp searing steaks or cubes of ice.

And from the moment when the primitive cook held that first, presumably wooden, length to create the lever, the instinctive chef and the tools he then devised to more deftly lift, turn, stir, spread, open, press, and grind were inseparable.

Most of today's kitchen utensils are based on the lever. And while such spinoffs as the bone spoons, spatulas, and earthenware ladles employed in ancient Babylonia and Egypt were clearly elementary extensions, the more durable and specialized leverage-based tools evolved during the Iron Age, shortly after the development of the knife.

Once metalsmiths discovered that they could alter the end forms of their steel lengths, they began to broaden the batterie de cuisine. Through further thinning and shaping, for example, they crafted increasingly effective ladles, then enlarged, perforated, and turned that basic disk into the Roman-handled colanders that led the way to drainers, strainers, and skimmers.

It's not surprising that the tools we use today resemble their rudimentary forebears. Most are longer, with cleaner lines and smoother grips to better extend the range of motion, reduce resistance, and be more comfortable to hold. But others—such as the mortar and pestle, bread peel, and meat tenderizer—remain in much the same shape as they did centuries ago.

This is not to imply that a lever-based tool is simply a length with a tailored-to-task working end—such as a reamer, paddle, or whisk—nor that it has peaked in its design progress. Quite the contrary: When coupled with a screw it forms, among other things, more powerful wine openers, nutcrackers, and garlic presses; together with a wheel and axle it produces rotary beaters and some rolling pins; and when combined with both it serves as the basis for meat grinders and food and pepper mills.

Designwise, we're happily at the start of a new era. More and more of these hand-held complex machines are becoming power driven, to the point where the electric juicers, food processors, and grain mills are further freeing that chef's hands so she or he can enjoy performing more of the creative work.

Flat Spatula

This round-tipped blade that spreads, smooths, and transfers baked goods might as well be called the patissier's right hand. Its 12-inch length has enough surface to ice 9-inch and 10-inch cake rounds efficiently; its 1⅝-inch breadth permits an adequate upward ride for the batter when leveling a soufflé or the buttercream when icing a cake; while a blunt, quasi-rigid span won't pierce a rum-soaked savarin when moving it from wire rack to platter.

Also called palette or icing knives, flat spatulas are most often available in stamped stainless steel with blades that measure 4 inches to the popular 12-inch length.

A fine spatula should be well balanced, with a tight handle-to-blade join and flush rivets.

Offset Spatula

The crook in this spatula's blade, which raises its handle, creates an excellent tool to spread batters in lipped pans and level mixtures on flat surfaces. An average 55-degree bend that lifts the grip above the food permits the chef to work directly over a génoise in a jelly-roll pan or melted chocolate on a marble board. Since no angulation is needed to further distance the hand, there's no surface ridging.

Offset spatulas—which can display angles as high as 70 degrees—are manufactured in 10-inch or the preferred 12-inch length, and although some are equipped with carbon-steel blades, most are stamped in stainless steel.

Wooden Spatula

Because hygienic considerations limit the use of wood in the professional kitchen, this once commonplace flat, wooden length now finds its best use in the home as a stirrer and scraper for foods in tin-lined copper and nonstick-surfaced pots and pans. Like a paddle, its bowl-free face draws through liquids with the least possible drag while the bulbous profile contends with round-shouldered pans and, when turned, reaches equally well into the angled corners of straight-sided ones. More important, its blunt edges don't readily scratch or nick these delicate surfaces.

Wooden spatulas are available in 8-inch to the more popular 14-inch lengths in both beechwood and the slightly denser boxwood.

Rubber Spatula

A near-rectangular, synthetic rubber spatula is one of the true work-horses of the modern kitchen. Its pliancy conforms to any bowl's bow to extract the last bit of batter, a broad flat head allows the cook to press forcemeat into a terrine, while it smoothly channels and folds beaten egg whites and foams into their heavier bases. Those made of high-temperature-resistant synthetic rubber further the tool's practicality, particularly when quickly dislodging browned bits from coated skillets and sauté pans during deglazing.

Manufactured only after World War II, when the then burgeoning synthetic rubber industry began to apply its products to civilian uses, synthetic rubber spatulas are available in lengths from 10 inches to slightly over 20 inches and with head sizes that graduate from 1″×2″ to nearly 3″×5″. Ten-inch-long rubber spatulas with 1″×2″ and 2″×3″ heads are the most popular sizes. One with a plastic handle can be more thoroughly cleaned than one with a wooden handle and is less likely to buckle and pull away from the synthetic rubber head.

Stir-Fry Spatula

The exaggerated bow front and flat, wide blade of this shovellike spatula make it the perfect stir-frying tool. Its arced profile easily glides down a wok's concave sides, the flat, 4-inch blade front slides under, scoops, and flings full portions of shrimp, beef shreds, or bean curd, while a slight wraparound rim breaks the sweep momentum.

Stir-fry spatulas are generally 15 inches long and are manufactured in either black steel or the more practical stainless steel. Both are usually capped with wood to temper conducted heat, and this junction should be tight and smooth.

Both the long, flat spatula on the left and its offset version on the right effectively spread, smooth, and occasionally lift soon-to-be- or fully-baked goods. Both are discussed on page 65.

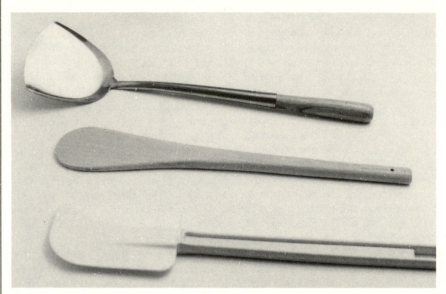

Top to bottom are spatulas to help in cooking or basic food preparation: a stir-fry spatula, wooden spatula, and rubber spatula.

Bench Knife

The chef scrapes, lifts, and cuts malleable dough or syrups with a blunt-edged, rectangular steel blade. Its dull edge withstands constant draws over marble to aerate a fondant's sugar syrup; its inflexibility notches a Danish's yeast-puff dough; a 6-inch length presents ample surface on which to pull, lift, and fold supersoft brioche dough, while a 3-inch depth allows the dough's upward kneading ride.

Select a bench knife, or dough scraper, with a textured plastic handle; it's more hygienic than wood, less likely to split, and, due to the ridging, offers a slip-free grip. A stainless-steel blade is easier to care for than carbon steel and more durable than the nylon and polypropylene scrapers, although some chefs like the flexibility of these plastics.

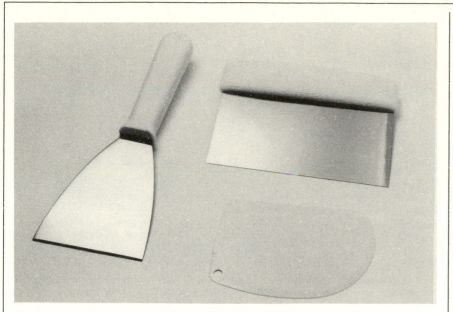

Clockwise from the left are three full-faced blades that extend the cook's hand: a griddle scraper, bench knife, and bowl scraper.

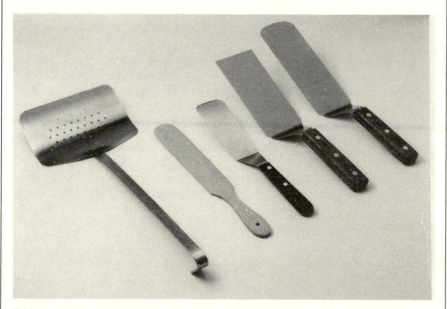

Tools to turn, lift, and/or transfer partially or fully cooked foods include, from the left, a fish lifter (see page 68), crepe turner (page 68), small rounded-tip turner, squared-tip turner, and large rounded-tip turner.

and other flat surfaces. The 3½-inch-wide front cuts a broad path to reduce scraping time; its stiff, straight profile and beveled edge most readily glide, pry, and peel off residue, while its slightly off-center set creates a corner perfect for reaching into the angle joint of a griddle's base and rim. A pumice stone is recommended to scrape off any minute food particles that may remain.

Although griddle scrapers were originally designed as sturdy cleaning implements, their wide, inflexible, beveled fronts make them ideal for driving into and under a tempered strip of still pliant chocolate to make rolls or ruffles.

Griddle scrapers are available with stainless-steel blades that measure from 3 to 4 inches across the front and with either a smoothly molded or, for a better grip, a textured molded plastic handle.

Squared-tip Turner

This blade's straight tip, beveled edge, and limited flexibility make it more efficient than a rounded-tip blade to turn and lift grilled and griddled foods. When hamburgers stick to the pan, that bond is best broken with a direct, unyielding thrust; the bevel buffers this forceful impact while a 60-degree handle offset distances the hand from the hot surface.

Squared-tip turners are available with carbon- or stainless-steel blades that range in size from 2½″×2¼″ to 8″×3″. A medium 5″×3″ blade is the most practical for the home, although you may also come across similarly sized straight-bladed tools that are really griddle scrapers .

Rounded-tip Turner

This relatively long and wide, semi-flexible steel blade with its offset handle carefully lifts, flips, and transfers thinly sliced or partially set foods that have a delicately high proportion of surface to volume. Its

Bowl Scraper

This palm-sized plastic sheet's wedgelike profile and modest pliancy make it a fine tool to remove and transfer the last bit of batter, dough, or icing from mixing bowl to board or pastry. Its long, lightly bowed side arcs up and around, creating a curved front that conforms to most bowl shapes for thorough scraping, as the roughly 5″×3½″ size supplies sufficient lifting leverage and support surface. The back side's tapered working edge promises smooth thrusting and sweeping, while the slight pliancy facilitates scooping.

Bowl scrapers are most often manufactured in polyamide in an index-card size.

Griddle Scraper

This rigid, near-trapezoidal blade effectively removes excess grease and burned-on bits of food from griddles rounded corners prevent pan gouging, flesh punctures, and drained juices, and a 45-degree offset handle raises the hand for more dexterous maneuvering in shallow sauté pans.

Also manufactured with perforated and slotted blades that simultaneously lift and drain, fine rounded-tip turners are most often available with 8″×3″ and 5″×2″ carbon- or stainless-steel blades. Avoid those with exceedingly flexible nylon blades, selecting instead the firmest available nylon or, better yet, a wooden spatula for use with coated pans.

Crepe Turner

Although it looks like a diminutive cricketer's bat, this well-tapered wooden length trims, turns, and removes cooked crepes from their pans. The tapered edges clip any messy trails left by excess batter, a blunt 2-inch width can't readily tear a partially set crepe, and its 10-inch span supplies more than enough surface for a balanced transfer.

Crepe turners are most often available in beechwood with 13-inch or 15¼-inch overall lengths.

Fish Lifter

Although most people use two hands and two spatulas to carefully remove a medium-sized red snapper from its court bouillon or a trout from its steam bath, this fish lifter's slightly bowed, perforated blade accomplishes the task single-handedly. Its 6½-inch width and 4½-inch depth provide the necessary surface, the central bow securely cradles a braised bass, while some perforation allows the fish to drain.

Also available in stainless steel is a similarly efficient half-moon-shaped blade that requires a side approach.

Perforated Spoon

This spoon's low-rimmed, honey-combed bowl lifts and drains small amounts of delicately textured foods. The bowl's 4-inch length neatly slips

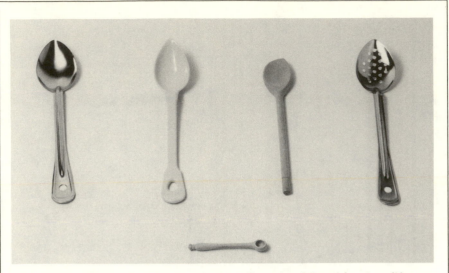

No kitchen is complete without a variety of spoons. Shown from left to right are a solid spoon, tasting spoon, mustard spoon, straight-edged wooden spoon, and perforated spoon.

Fish Waterzooie

Raymond Ameye, Chef-Proprietor: Flamand

6 servings

2 tablespoons butter

2 large carrots, peeled and cut into a 2-inch julienne

3 medium celery ribs, cut into a 2-inch julienne

2 medium leeks, white part only, cut into a 2-inch julienne, rinsed, and drained

1 bay leaf

2 quarts water

8 ounces sole fillets, cut into 1-inch strips

8 ounces sea scallops

8 ounces large shrimp, shelled and deveined

8 ounces monkfish or turbot, cut into 1-inch chunks

Coarse salt to taste

Freshly ground white pepper to taste

2 cups heavy cream

4 large egg yolks

Freshly grated nutmeg to taste

½ cup finely chopped chervil

Melt the butter in a sauté pan set over medium-low heat, add the carrots, celery, leeks, and bay leaf, and sauté 10 minutes to soften; set aside.

Bring the water to a simmer in a casserole, add the vegetables, fish, and shellfish, and season to taste with salt and pepper. Return the water to a simmer and cook 10 to 12 minutes. Transfer the fish, shellfish, and vegetables to a tureen and keep warm; discard the bay leaf.

Meanwhile, reduce the poaching liquid to half its volume. Add the cream, return to a boil, then reduce the heat to medium. Ladle some of this mixture into a bowl containing the egg yolks to temper them; whisk constantly. Pour into the casserole and cook a few minutes to thicken; stir frequently. Season to taste with nutmeg. Pour over the fish, garnish with chervil, and serve with boiled new potatoes.

Deviled Crab Cakes

Leon Lianides, Proprietor: The Coach House

4 to 6 servings

1 *cup clarified butter (or as needed for sautéing)*

⅞ *cup finely diced celery*

⅞ *cup finely diced onions or scallions*

1 *pound fresh lump crabmeat, cleaned of shells and cartilage*

⅓ *cup finely chopped parsley*

¾ *teaspoon finely chopped dill*

Generous pinch cayenne

1 *large egg yolk, lightly beaten with 1 teaspoon dry mustard*

5 *teaspoons heavy cream*

Juice of 1 lemon

1 *tablespoon Worcestershire sauce*

Dash Tabasco

2 to 2½ *cups very fine fresh bread crumbs*

1 to 1½ *cups all-purpose flour*

1 *egg yolk mixed with ½ cup milk*

Melt 2 tablespoons butter in a large fry pan set over medium heat, add the celery and onions, and sauté until transparent; stir occasionally. Cool, then add the crabmeat, parsley, dill, cayenne, egg yolk–mustard mixture, cream, lemon juice, Worcestershire and Tabasco. Sprinkle in 1 cup bread crumbs, toss lightly to mix, and refrigerate 40 minutes.

Place the remaining bread crumbs, the flour, and the egg yolk–milk mixture in three separate bowls and set aside.

Gently shape the crabmeat mixture into 12 plum-sized balls, then dip, one at a time, into the flour, the egg mixture, and then the bread crumbs; be careful to prevent them from falling apart. Flatten slightly, then set in a waxed paper–lined pan and refrigerate 1 hour before cooking.

Heat about half the remaining butter in a large sauté pan set over medium heat, add the crab cakes, and sauté about 4 minutes on each side or until lightly browned; add more butter as needed.

Serve with either diable, rémoulade, tartar, or garlic sauce.

into a simmering broth to bring out perfectly poached cubes of halibut and monkfish for their bourride; its bare ⅜-inch depth provides plenty of roll-resistant surface to safely pluck endives from their braising liquid, and a perforated face drains the water from a scooped spinach dumpling or quenelle.

Not nearly as popular is the slotted spoon, which has 10 percent less surface area and is best used to remove foods that overcook easily unless scooped and quickly separated from their cooking fluid.

Aim for single-piece construction, ideally in stainless steel. It is less pliant and longer lasting than nylon and won't react chemically to some foods as aluminum does. A 14-inch-long spoon suits home use.

Solid Spoon

This oval-bowled spoon is one of the handiest kitchen tools. Its ta-pered tip slips among and separates veal, carrots, and onions to stir a blanquette, a 4-inch-long face removes rising impurities from the surface of soup, rigidity provides leverage to transfer baked beans from their pot, while a generous 3-tablespoon bowl hastens basting.

Solid spoons are available in sizes from 11¾ to 15½ inches long, with the most popular measuring 13¼ inches. Select the simplest spoon, one stamped from a single piece of stainless steel. If there is no bowl-to-handle joint, that means there's no weld to possibly break.

Straight-edged Wooden Spoon

This spoon's nearly flat front edge and shallow bowl make it more a scraper than a tool to taste or transfer food. A blunt 2-inch-wide tip pries, pushes, and peels browned bits of

chicken from the bottom of a sauté pan; one right front angle dispenses with pieces lodged in straight-sided pan corners while an alternate curved angle contends with those in rounded pans. A bowl set back from the edge with a 1-teaspoon capacity further precludes sampling or substantial lifting.

Straight-edged spoons—which measure approximately 10 inches long—are available in beech or boxwood, the finer boxwood ones being somewhat heavy for their size and well finished.

Tasting Spoon

This spoon's two-tablespoon capacity offers a sufficient sampling of soup when checking for seasonings; its nonreactive porcelain promises true tastes, and its 13-inch length distances the hand from a simmering broth.

Tasting spoons are available in porcelain or wood, but the latter tend to absorb flavors that eventually render them ineffective.

Mustard Spoon

Before the eighteeenth century it was common to serve mustard in powder form, which is when this small wooden scoop was practical. Its ¼-teaspoon-capacity wooden scoop apportioned pungent powder or peppery seeds without imparting foreign flavor. Yet with mustard now usually served as paste, this spoon's design is rather obsolete; its slight portioning may still suit some tastes but the bowl is so spherical that, once filled, the near air lock created prevents quick, clean releases.

For a truly utilitarian mustard-serving tool, overlook this popular spoon style and select instead a tiny, 4¼-inch mustard spatula that's available in wood, bone, or porcelain.

When selecting a fine wood-capped stainless-steel Chinese ladle like the one at the top, make sure it has a clean and comfortable handle join; the best Occidental ladles are of single-piece stainless steel construction, as shown in foreground.

Ladle

The broad, calibrated cup and long handle let this ladle effectively scoop and transfer measured amounts of stocks, soups, and very fluid batters. Its 3¼-inch-wide bowl with a 4-ounce capacity doles out the ideal amount of beaten egg to an omelet chef while the 13-inch-long handle facilitates long reaches into a standard-sized stockpot.

Select a ladle constructed from a single piece of stainless steel—no joints means no weak spots—whose relatively thick handle has rounded borders for a comfortable grip. The most popular ladle sizes for home use are the 4- and 6-ounce capacities.

Chinese Ladle

The broad, shallow 4-ounce bowl on this long-handled ladle makes it a versatile tool when cooking with a wok. Its 4-inch disklike face supplies ample surface on which to quickly turn or transfer foods and its 50-degree set to handle effects an easy work reach.

Forgo tradition and select a stainless-steel Chinese ladle over the easy-to-rust carbon-steel variety. Examine the 10-inch steel-and-wood handle to be sure it fits snugly.

Fried-Food Skimmer

Because the hot fat that seals, sets, and cooks just as quickly burns fritters, croquettes, and some dumplings, most chefs use an open-wire, saucer-shaped skimmer to remove these foods from the fat. A 5½-inch face easily retrieves two dozen smelts at one time; well-spaced wires allow efficient draining, while a bowed, shallow disk need only graze the surface to snap up a golden beignet or banana fritter. The long handle distances the chef from splattering fat.

Fried-food skimmers are manufactured in two styles: One has a grid face while the other's concentric circles prompt its colorful "spider" nickname. Both are available in tin-plated or the preferred stainless steel with sizes that range from a 5-inch face to an industrial-sized 12 inches. Opt, when possible, for the streamlined stainless-steel grid over the spider, whose wire-wrapped face and multirod handle are more difficult to clean thoroughly.

Risotto ai Funghi Porcini

Italian Rice with Porcini Mushrooms

Nicola Civetta, Proprietor: Ristorante Primavera

4 servings

2 *quarts unsalted chicken stock (see page 210)*

6 *tablespoons butter*

1 *large onion, coarsely chopped*

2 *garlic cloves, coarsely chopped*

3 *medium porcini mushrooms, brushed or wiped clean, with the heads and stems chopped separately (approximately 12 ounces)*

1½ *cups Italian arborio rice*

1 *cup dry white wine*

1 *tablespoon tomato purée*

½ *cup grated Parmesan cheese*

1 *tablespoon finely chopped parsley*

Salt to taste

Freshly ground black pepper to taste

Bring the chicken stock to a simmer in a medium saucepan set over medium heat, then reduce the heat slightly to a bare simmer as you prepare the rice.

Melt 2 tablespoons butter in a large saucepan set over medium heat, add the onion and garlic, and sauté 8 minutes or until the onions are transparent. Add the porcini stems, cook 2 minutes, then add the rice, stir to coat with the melted butter, and cook 5 minutes. Add the wine and cook until the rice absorbs all the liquid; stir frequently.

Add a 6-ounce ladleful of stock and simmer until the rice absorbs it; stir frequently. Repeat this procedure until all of the stock has been added.

Add the tomato purée and porcini caps, stir to mix, and cook an additional 2 minutes to heat through; stir constantly. Remove from the heat, add the remaining butter, Parmesan cheese, and parsley, and stir to mix; season to taste with salt and pepper and serve immediately.

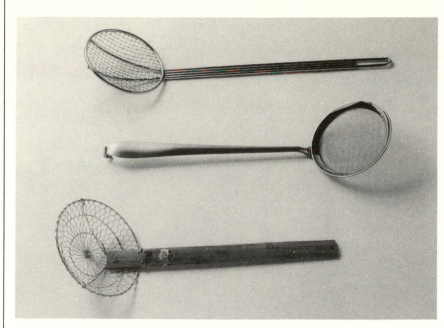

Efficient skimmers have similarly long handles and wide, saucer-shaped heads. Shown from the top are fried-food, mesh, and Chinese skimmers.

A bread peel's full, flat tapered-front face neatly slips under and retracts from proofed or baked loaves.

Chinese Skimmer

This long-handled tool's shallow brass-mesh bowl retrieves deep-fat–fried foods from a wok. Its 5-inch diameter holds two portions per draw; the bowl's curve mirrors the wok's, permitting a smooth sweep and efficient scooping, while open mesh immediately drains off the hot oil.

A traditional Chinese skimmer, or strainer, is fitted with a long, relatively flat bamboo handle that is as easy to grip as it is comfortable to hold, because the woody stem can't conduct heat. However, bamboo does stain and absorb odors, and its bowl is so poorly attached with wire that it can't be thoroughly cleaned. Consequently, the less bowed but more functional Western stainless-steel grid- or spider-style fried-food skimmer is suggested for wok frying and tempura work.

Wooden Bread or Pizza Peel

Period drawings confirm that, except for its smaller size, this flat, shovellike wooden tool has remained virtually unchanged since the Middle Ages. Its tapered edges and thin, tonguelike shape smoothly slip under or retract from a proofed or baked loaf, its 14-inch-square face ably supports standard-sized loaves and today's popular pizzas, and its near 1-pound weight is easy to wield.

Wooden, specifically basswood, bread peels (which should be lightly dusted with semolina before use) generally have 8-inch-long handles with blades that measure 12 to 16 inches square. They should be distinguished from the commercial, stainless-steel peels that have larger blades and up to thrice the handle length for industrial-sized ovens.

Ice-Cream Scoop

Its slightly beveled rim, hemispherical shape, and cog-regulated, spring-release blade allow this scoop to methodically apportion single serv-

Mesh Skimmer

This wide, saucer-shaped mesh skimmer rapidly removes the albuminous particles from meat, fish, or poultry that would otherwise cloud their simmering broths or bouillons. Its nearly 5-inch diameter quickly retrieves scattered surface particles, a saucer shape that glides along the top of a stock most effectively snags impurities, while a full, fine-meshed face scoops and strains them with no liquid lost.

The mesh skimmer is recommended over a perforated disk skimmer. Since the latter's face has more metal, it skims less efficiently. The finest mesh skimmer is manufactured in stainless steel, has an 11¼-inch angled handle spot-welded to the working head, and a mesh face securely clamped between the head's single-piece folded frame. While a 6-inch diameter is also available, the 5-inch size better suits the small-scale stockpots used in the home.

ings of soft to semi-soft foods. The bare bevel slices through like a knife to separate quenelles or cooked rice; a concave face directs and shapes ice cream or sorbet and then releases it rapidly and cleanly with a retracting blade set flush to the bowl.

When looking for a round, tower, or oval scoop, make sure the lever is smoothly set. You'll notice that the oval, whose cog/ratchet/spring mechanism is activated by a handle squeeze, can be difficult to grasp firmly and drive through hard-packed ice cream without triggering the blade's release. The sturdiest scoops are constructed entirely of stainless steel or stainless steel with a plastic handle; their parts are usually welded rather than soldered together, and the cogs and ratchets carefully coincide. The bowls, called dishers, most often range in diameter from 1½ to 3 inches.

Insulated Ice-Cream Scoop

The tapered rim of this thick-handled aluminum scoop smoothly penetrates a mass of hard- or soft-packed ice cream. Its open sides, which encourage the recommended lateral roll, pull, and shaping motion, also prevent suction from developing, while a body heat–warmed, salt-based fluid that's rapidly conducted through its aluminum housing facilitates speedy scooping and easy release.

Available with dish, or bowl, sizes numbered from 10 (4 ounces) to 30 (1 ounce), insulated scoops are also manufactured with polymer-coated bowls that won't be pitted by the higher salt content in some water supplies. Due to the expanding nature of the internal defrosting fluid, the manufacturer advises that this dipper not be exposed to temperatures above 140°F.

Ice-Cream Spade

A relatively wide-bladed spade is better equipped than a scoop to remove large quantities of ice cream

The most functional spades and scoops have smooth, bowed or bowled faces with tapered rims. An olive scoop is at top, with, from the left, an ice-cream scoop, insulated ice-cream scoop, and ice-cream spade.

quickly from a carton and then pack it into a bombe or mold. Its $3'' \times 3½''$ face easily balances transfers, a curved front with a slight bottom bevel facilitates shovellike downward thrusts, and an offset handle keeps the hand above a frosty surface and increases leverage.

The most durable ice-cream spade on the market is outfitted with a heavy stainless-steel blade that's well bonded to its plastic handle.

Olive Scoop

This long-handled wooden scoop's perforated bowl fetches Ligurian or Niçoise olives from their brine cures. Its generous tablespoon portions those ripe olives to add sharpness to an herbed lamb salad or sparkle to an anchovy tart; a deep bowl holds the olives during near-vertical retreats from their crocks while perforations drain away the brine. Its 6-inch handle makes it easy to reach to the bottom of that standard serving container.

Larger scoops, measuring nearly 17 inches long with perforated 3½-inch-wide bowls, are meant to retrieve such fruits as peaches or cherries from brandy. Both sizes are available in beech, boxwood, or, ide-

ally, the denser olivewood; the best have well-drilled perforations and neatly turned handles.

Butter Paddles

The well-grooved rectangular faces of these wooden paddles shape and compact a half tablespoon of butter into a ridged ball for chilling and serving or for a final dusting of paprika or minced herbs. Their tight crenulation promotes smooth rolls and neat impressions as the two $2'' \times 4½''$ faces provide ample rolling area.

Occasionally called Scotch hands or butter spades, these paddles, which must be soaked in ice water before using, are most often available in boxwood or the hardier cherrywood. Some have concave faces but the straight pairs are less apt to knock together during rotations. Any pair you buy must be free of rough spots and splinters.

Raclette Paddle

The bowed, nearly flat-fronted head on this paddle may resemble a diminutive wooden spatula, but it's best employed to scrape melting cheese from the heated face of a

Carefully inspect any wooden kitchen tool before buying to be sure it is free of rough spots and splinters. Shown at left are grooved butter paddles and at right a raclette paddle.

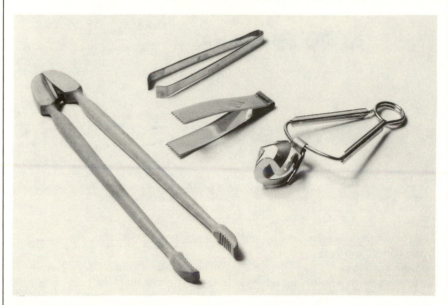

Tongs' distinctly bowed, beveled, or notched jaws are tailor-made for special tasks. Clockwise from left are cornichon tongs and fish tweezers, a pastry crimper, and escargot tongs (see page 74).

Clockwise from top right are jar-lifting tongs, the recommended general-purpose spring-action tongs, and pom tongs.

Spring-action tongs, which are manufactured only in stainless steel, are most often available in 9½-, 12½-, and 16½-inch lengths. For the home, the medium size is the most practical.

Pom Tongs

The 15-degree central crimp and slight, bulging jaws, serrated at their cropped ends, allow these bent metal tongs to grip, turn, or transfer sizzling hot foods. The final curve of the jaw creates a vertical angle of approach for secure grips, and arms up to 12 inches long provide comfortable distance from splatters.

Pom tongs, shortened from the French *pommée* (having arms with knoblike ends), are inexpensive but they have their problems. Since they are so lightweight—only an inch wide—the arms tend to shift laterally through use, and the serrated teeth can pierce meat or poultry, losing some juices.

Pom tongs are available in stainless steel in 6-inch, 9-inch, and 12-inch lengths.

Jar-Lifting Tongs

The scissor-set arms on these tongs form an oval-shaped head to pluck

half-wheel of raclette, a Swiss après-ski specialty. The paddle's 1-inch width and dull, barely tapered edge can remove only properly melted cheese. A slight central bow directs the cheese onto a warmed plate for a single serving with potatoes and pickles, while the wood can't conduct heat, so it remains comfortable to handle even close to a flame or grill.

A raclette paddle generally measures 7 inches long; its wood should be well finished.

Spring-Action Tongs

These utility tongs are a favorite among chefs. Their 3-inch heads are ample for clutching and turning a pork loin roast or plucking a custard cup from its bain marie; the uneven surface of the scalloped edges provides a fast hold and lessens the chance of piercing gripped flesh. A bent steel band behind the end pivot point creates a retraction for release, while the rigid arms keep the heads and pivot properly aligned.

narrow- and wide-mouthed jars from simmering water baths, balanced by a near-central fulcrum. Eight-inch arms distance hands from hot water while a plastic coating guarantees slip-free traction.

Jar-lifting tongs are available only in partially coated stainless steel in 8½-inch lengths.

Cornichon Tongs

These medium-length (nearly 10-inch) wooden tongs with their small, ridged, concave jaws and cropped tips can snatch and serve the last cornichon from its traditional 9-inch-deep brine-filled jar. Internally crimped inch-long heads securely hug a gherkin, and dull tips won't pierce the other small pickles in the jar.

The most functional cornichon tongs are spring-set, which, with the accompanying tiny, inset metal dish, ensures that the jaws balance and that coil/recoil actions are lively.

Pastry Crimper

These tiny tongs' narrow arms, each ending in a jagged edge, are designed to notch, seal, and promote a flaky short-crust pastry. Their 4-inch length prevents the warm hand contact with the dough that promotes toughening gluten formations yet ensures close hand-to-dough proximity for neat flutes. A ⅝-inch width pinches a properly rolled two-crust pie rim while two toothed edges securely grasp, squeeze, and shape the dough.

Pastry crimpers are manufactured in chrome-plated or the more durable stainless steel.

Fish Tweezers

The abruptly angled jaws on these fist-sized forceps are ideal for removing bones from raw, cured, or smoked fish fillets. The sharp, 90-degree meet at the end of 4-inch-long arms prompts the tight finger-to-jaw proximity that promises precise extraction; ½-inch-wide be-

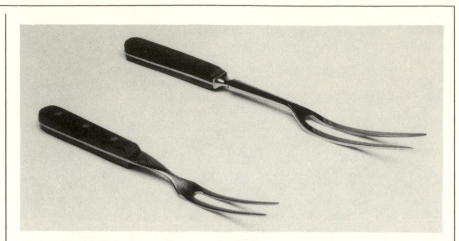

Like a fine knife, a fine fork should have a full tang and a well-attached handle. Two of the most common kitchen forks are the smaller-shafted and pronged pot fork at left and the longer, stronger chef's fork on the right.

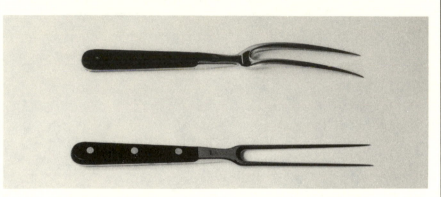

Because a carving fork should anchor, not pierce meat, the two shapes that follow general roast configurations are the curved carving fork at top and bayonet fork beneath it.

veled jaws that close perfectly flat firmly clutch and withdraw small to medium vertebrae.

Fish tweezers are manufactured only in stainless steel.

Escargot Tongs

The slotted, irregularly shaped 1½-inch-long cups on these tongs are tailor-made to grasp securely the shells in which buttered snails are often cooked and served. The hollows nearly correspond to the shape of the shell while interior slotting accommodates its bulges. The metal arms cross twice, which means that when squeezed, the jaws open to grab or release, then close to hold.

Select tongs whose wire arms loop at their base rather than those that simply bend there; that extra loop creates greater tension for firmer grips. Both varieties are available in silver, tin-plated, or tarnish-free stainless steel and measure roughly 6 inches in overall length.

Chef's Fork

The two-tined chef's fork is longer and stronger than the two-tined pot fork. The chef's shaft and tines, which constitute roughly 60 percent of the overall length, are thick, rigid, and substantial to offer the necessary leverage to remove large roasts from pans or to turn and properly drain whole roasting geese. Chef's-fork tines are lightly bowed, which means that rather than lifting foods spoon-fashion from above, they better suit a lateral approach to turn and reposition foods in shallow pans and roasters and on grills.

Chef's forks are almost always 12 inches or the recommended 14 inches long and forged in carbon or stainless steel. Some manufacturers attach a very long, 15-inch hardwood handle to their basic fork form to create a broiler fork.

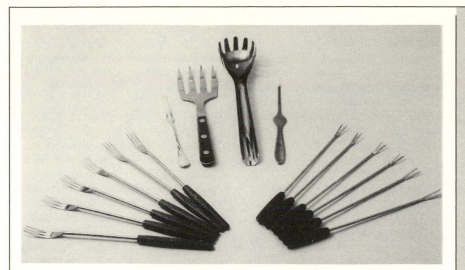

Fork tines can be variously configured to pierce, pluck, or snag certain foods. Shown from left are a cheese fondue fork set, snail fork, choucroute fork, pasta fork, lobster fork, and a meat fondue set (see page 76).

Pot Fork

The long, insulating handle on the two-tined pot fork enables the cook to get in comfortably close to turn pieces of searing meat and chicken; an abbreviated shaft and prongs maneuver small pieces of meat and poultry for braises, stews, and fricassees; and a tight, spoonlike prong curve enhances dexterity to work from a high angle of approach in tall, straight-sided pots like Dutch ovens and doufeus.

Pot forks are usually 12 inches in overall length and are most often stamped in carbon or stainless steel. Smaller versions—nearly 8 inches—are simply called kitchen forks, while those with three prongs are known as granny forks.

Curved Carving Fork

A long, two-pronged fork is as necessary to carving as a sharp knife; it prevents the meat from slipping and, because of the distance it creates from a roast, protects the carver's hand from any slips of the knife. This curved-prong fork, whose bow aligns with the general contour of a large roast, will, when inverted and pressed against the meat, create an anchor that's secure enough to hold even the most wily roast.

Some carving forks still display the traditional hilt or hinged back guard that snaps out for additional hand shielding, but these safety features are becoming rarer. Curved carving forks range in overall length from 10 to 13 inches—most have 6-inch prongs—and are usually forged in carbon or stainless steel.

Bayonet Carving Fork

Although curved-prong forks are preferred for carving, the straight-prong variety, which are commonly called bayonet forks, should not be discounted entirely. Long, flat, grilled butterflied leg of lamb, skirt steak, and London broil, for instance, are better anchored by the longer surface area of a bayonet's unbent tines. Use this fork as you would a curved-prong one; don't puncture the meat, but firmly press the sides of the prongs against it as you carve.

Bayonet forks' prongs measure about 5½ inches long with overall fork lengths between 10 and 12 inches; they are generally available in stainless steel.

Pasta Fork

The 1-inch-long blunt-tipped prongs on this scooplike "fork" adeptly snare and lift cooked pasta without crushing or severing it, while the slots in the wide-fronted spoon drain off water or excess sauce.

Since this fork is limited to snagging small amounts of long noodles, which then cool quickly, its best use is at a buffet table to apportion single servings of already sauced pasta such as fettuccine, linguine, and tagliatelle.

Choucroute Garni

Annemarie Huste, Caterer

6 servings

1 8-ounce bacon slab, rind removed, sliced, and blanched 5 minutes

1 large onion, coarsely chopped

8 juniper berries

1 bay leaf

3 pounds sauerkraut, rinsed, drained, and squeezed of excess liquid

4 cups dry white wine, preferably Riesling

1 large Granny Smith apple, peeled, cored, and coarsely chopped

3 kassler rippchen

3 pairs bratwurst

3 pairs frankfurters

3 pairs knackwurst

1 1-pound kielbasa ring

Freshly ground black pepper to taste

Sauté the bacon in a large sauté pan set over medium heat until lightly crisp. Add the onion and continue to cook until transparent; stir occasionally. Add the juniper berries, bay leaf, sauerkraut, wine, and apples. Increase the heat and bring to a boil; reduce the heat and simmer, covered, 1½ hours.

Add the sausages, first pierced with a fork, then re-cover and continue to cook 20 minutes longer. Season to taste with pepper, and serve with boiled potatoes.

Note: Smoked pork chops can also be added, as well as a teaspoon of caraway seeds. You can also substitute 2 cups of wine with 2 cups of chicken stock.

How to Use a
Carving Fork

To use a carving fork, press the prongs firmly against the meat to anchor it securely as you carve. It may be tempting to pierce the fork into the meat while carving, but by doing so, precious juices will be lost, making the roast progressively drier as more piercing and cutting are done.

Pasta forks, also called spaghetti rakes, generally measure 12 inches in overall length. Select a sturdy, hygienic, single-piece stainless-steel tool over any made in wood, which will stain and absorb sauce colors and odors.

Choucroute Fork

If you prepare the Alsatian smoked-pork-and-sauerkraut specialty called choucroute garni, include coleslaw on your picnic table, or accompany the Christmas goose with braised red cabbage, you'll find this fork quite useful. Its 2½-inch breadth is ample for picking up shredded vegetables; four sharply tipped tines separate strands from their mass, and a slight dip at the prong/handle juncture can't accidentally transfer unwanted juices from pot to platter.

Select a choucroute, or slaw, fork made in stainless steel as opposed to wood, which will discolor and absorb odor through use; it should feel heavy for its size and have a full tang.

Fondue Forks

The most functional fondue fork measures 9½ inches long and has a stainless steel shaft and tines and a color-coded wood or plastic handle. The length protects hands from hot oil, cheese, or warm chocolate; metal withstands heat, and an insulated handle remains cool throughout cooking.

Styles of fondue forks differ: Two-tined forks with inset barbs are designed expressly to hold meat or fish; their tiny end flanges prevent raw cubes from slipping off. Three-tined, barbless forks are best used for bread and cakes; an extra prong better grips delicately textured, leavened foods.

As a rule, fondue forks are sold with the appropriate pot, but they can also be purchased separately in sets of six.

Lobster Fork

The two short, angled prongs at the end of this fork's long, narrow shaft efficiently prize the last morsel of meat from a cracked lobster claw or leg. Their ⅜-inch length easily enters the tops of spindly legs; two angled tines effectively anchor to provide the most secure extraction while the narrow 3-inch shaft allows long reaches into claws.

Lobster forks can be applied with equal authority to crabs and snails. Be sure the prongs are tightly set to maneuver into small recesses and that the handle offers a good grip. The best of these, manufactured in stainless steel, measure a total of 8 inches long.

Snail Fork

When ancient Romans enjoyed cultivated snails they may have used pronged skewers or small spoons called *cocleare*, meant for eating eggs, but whose pointed handles could easily extract the meat from snails and shellfish. The more efficient, two-tined, narrow snail fork appeared centuries later. In the classic style, the prongs' tight, ⅛-inch combined work front assures ready entry into a snail shell; their nearly 2-inch upward curve guarantees a long reach to secure meat, as two purchase points provide a fine foothold.

Occasionally called an hors d'oeuvre fork and available with prongs that either bow more broadly or have sleeker or wider profiles, snail forks are manufactured in silver-plate, stainless steel, ebony, or

Blanquette de Veau

*Claude Franques,
Executive Chef: René Pujol*

6 servings

2 *pounds veal shoulder, cut into
1-inch cubes*

1½ to 2 *quarts chicken stock (see
page 210)*

3 *medium carrots, sliced*

4 *medium onions, each cut into
eighths*

1 *medium leek, white part only,
sliced*

1 *garlic clove*

1 *medium celery rib*

8 *parsley sprigs*

4 *fresh thyme branches*

1 *bay leaf*

2 *cups heavy cream*

2 *tablespoons arrowroot mixed
with 2 tablespoons water*

Salt to taste

*Freshly ground black pepper to
taste*

Place the veal in a medium bowl, cover with cold water, and refrigerate overnight. Drain and rinse in fresh cold water.

Place the veal in a large saucepan, cover with water, and parboil 5 minutes. Drain and rinse off in fresh cold water.

Return the veal to the pan, cover with chicken stock, and add the carrots, onions, leek, and garlic. Tie the celery, parsley, thyme, and bay leaf together and add to the ingredients in the stew. Bring to a simmer, partially cover, and cook 1 to 1½ hours or until tender.

Use a slotted spoon to lift out the meat and vegetables—but not the aromatics—then reduce the cooking liquid to a third of its volume. Remove the herb bouquet, add the cream, and reduce a little more. Whisk in the arrowroot mixture to thicken; the sauce is ready when it can coat a spoon. Season to taste with salt and pepper and serve with white rice.

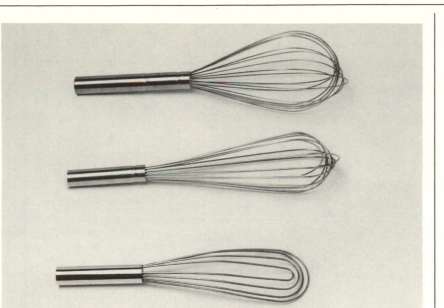

When buying a whisk, make sure it is made of stainless steel, fitted with a comfortably thick handle, and hygienically capped with silicone at its wire-handle join. From the top are balloon, sauce, and flat whisks.

boxwood. All measure about 6 inches long, with any of the more tapered metal forks preferred over the wooden ones, whose more widely splayed and duller-tipped prongs are less effective.

Flat Whisk

This near-flat group of looped wires is best described as a roux whisk. Its nearly 3-inch splay creates a considerable impact area to incorporate flour quickly into melted butter as its light, upward bow offsets the handle for comfortable working reaches across a pan.

Flat whisks usually measure 12 inches long and are manufactured in the preferred stainless steel or tin-plated steel, which is known to snap from its central wire's solder points.

Sauce Whisk

This whisk's nine fairly rigid wires loop into an elongated pear shape to mix, emulsify, or aerate sauces. Slight stiffness separates binding egg proteins in a thickening hollandaise to prevent coagulation; multiple wires increase per stroke capability, and a gently bowed pear shape enlarges the primary contact area.

When buying a sauce whisk—also called a piano-wire whisk—select one with a moderately wide cylindrical handle for a comfortable grip. You will also see whisks that have fewer yet thicker wires, one of which loops around the others at the tip to restrict pliancy. These are called French whisks and are used mainly to whip mashed potatoes or to prepare polenta. Sauce whisks range in overall length from 8 to 18 inches, with the 14-inch size being the most popular.

Balloon Whisk

The pliant wires that loop to form this whisk's distinctive bulbous shape masterfully whip egg whites or heavy cream. Nine wires increase single-stroke efficiency, considerable flex

Chicken Hash

"21"

8 servings

1 large onion, coarsely chopped

3 medium carrots, scrubbed and coarsely chopped

2 medium leeks, trimmed, thinly sliced, and rinsed

2 quarts chicken stock (see page 210)

8 boneless, skinless chicken breasts (approximately 5 pounds)

16 tablespoons butter

1½ cups all-purpose flour

1 cup heavy cream

1 cup dry sherry

Salt to taste

Freshly ground black pepper to taste

Simmer the onions, carrots, and leeks 45 minutes in the chicken stock. Add the chicken, bring to a bare simmer, and poach 30 to 35 minutes. Remove the breasts, cool, and cut into a ½-inch dice. Strain the stock and set aside 1 quart for the sauce.

To make the velouté: Melt 12 tablespoons of butter in a large saucepan set over low heat, add the flour, and whisk to mix; cook about 1 minute. Add the reserved 1 quart stock and whisk constantly to mix. Increase the heat and bring to a boil, then reduce the heat and cook about 20 minutes or until no taste of flour remains; whisk frequently. Whisk in the cream, return to a boil, then whisk in the remaining butter and set aside.

Reduce the sherry by half in a small saucepan, pour over the diced chicken, and toss to coat. Empty into the velouté, toss to coat, and bring to a simmer; season to taste with salt and pepper.

Serve the chicken hash surrounded by a ring of wild rice, then place 3 small mounds of sautéed spinach, equally spaced, around the wild rice.

Although the above recipe was graciously submitted by the "21" management, aficionados would know that it varies from past recipes long since published. The major difference seems to be that the chicken hash used to be served in individual gratin dishes, each topped with an egg yolk–enriched Béchamel sauce first flavored with Parmesan cheese and a little chopped parsley, and then broiled until golden.

whips but doesn't overwhelm, and a well-bowed shape expands the amount of contact surface to speed aeration.

Balloon whisks are available with overall lengths from 8 to 18 inches in both tin-plated and the stronger stainless steel. When buying a first-class balloon whisk, count its wires: The more there are, the better it operates. The handle should be uniformly thick and the wires should be welded together inside the handle, then silicone-capped for hygiene's sake. A 14-inch balloon whisk generally suits home use.

Coiled Whip

This tool, more a whip than a whisk, mixes and aerates small quantities of thin batters. Its low, forwardly set coil promotes a thumb-first, croplike grip, the narrow handle supports quick, staccato flicks, and a light, tightly set spiral encompassing the crescent head works well enough with something like egg whites but clogs up when attempting to beat anything less fluid.

A balloon or sauce whisk is more practical than this limited tool, but if you buy one, be sure the semicircular head is soldered completely shut to its frame. Some open on one side, paper-clip fashion, but the coiling tends to slip off. Coiled whips are available only in tinned steel and measure 11½ inches long.

Churn Beater

This conically coiled, medium-length, tightly set spring, with a maximum 3½-inch diameter, is more pump than whisk for agitating thin batters in small containers. A compressed 5½-inch coil slaps and churns scant cup measures, while a tense spring that quickly recoils reduces the cook's beating effort by half.

Occasionally called a diable whisk, French for jack-in-the-box, this tool's limited use makes it superfluous to own. You're better off using a bigger bowl and the standard sauce whisk to achieve the same end. Churn

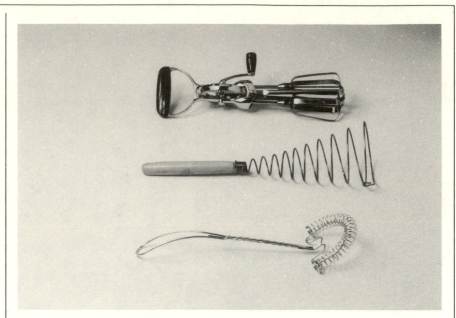

Three whisks that aerate or mix fairly fluid batters are, from the top, the favored rotary egg-beater, a churn beater, and a coiled whip.

Because of its size and light weight, a hand-held mixer is superb for mixing small quantities or combining ingredients over heat or ice.

The Japanese suribachi with surikogi on the left is as adept at pounding, crushing, and grinding as the more common Western mortar with pestle on the right.

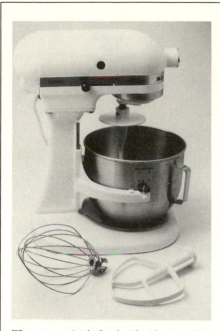

When appropriately fitted with either its whisk, paddle, or dough hook, this high-quality standing mixer can quickly mix, aerate, or knead light to heavy batters or doughs with equal ease.

beaters are manufactured only in chromed steel with 11-inch overall lengths.

Rotary Eggbeater

With its ratchet wheel that turns interlocking cog caps to rotate two four-bladed beaters, this well-braced tool whips or mixes small to moderate amounts of fairly fluid batters. One complete turn of the wheel powers five revolutions of the blades on the two 3-inch-long heads, which easily accommodate three- and four-cup quantities.

Most cooks would acknowledge the rotary beater's efficient yet limited use and stick with their whisks for light batters and electrically operated hand-held or free-standing mixers for heavier ones. However, if you buy such a beater, the sturdiest now on the market has a chrome-plated ratchet wheel and housing, nylon bearings, and stainless-steel blades and frame. A rotary beater can be outfitted with a side-set or the more popular straddling handle.

Hand-Held Mixer

This lightweight, compact hand mixer aerates egg whites, whips

heavy cream, and emulsifies sauces. Its well-balanced form drives the blades through creamed doughs and whipped potatoes; variable speeds are within easy reach of the thumb of the working hand. A 6-foot cord allows sufficient mobility and cleaning.

Some hand-held mixers have detachable cords while others are completely cordless; some are packaged with such optional attachments as dough hooks and whisklike wire beaters. Make sure the portable mixer of your choice is lightweight to maneuver easily, has a comfortable grip, is well-balanced, and is angled to rest on its heel.

Standing Mixer

This heavy-duty countertop mixer, with the most complete beater action available, is designed for the serious home baker. Its 5-quart bowl capacity processes large quantities of light cake batters or heavier pastry doughs; when fitted with its accompanying whisk, paddle, or dough hook, it aerates, beats, or kneads, while the planetary motion of the fitted rotating head continuously forms successive circles greater than the radius of the bowl to thoroughly mix the batter so close to the side of the bowl that little or no scraping is necessary.

At 25 pounds, this enameled stainless-steel unit is nearly immovable, a point its manufacturer has turned into an advantage by offering such optional attachments as a food grinder, shredder, slicer, citrus juicer, grain mill, and can opener to make it more versatile.

A fine standing mixer ideally has a 5-quart capacity, is powerful enough so it won't overheat while processing, moderately hefty so it won't vibrate or walk as it mixes, and has the three working heads (paddle, dough hook, and whisk). A spare work bowl would be a prudent investment so successive ingredients that may require preparation can be added without extra cleanup.

Mortar and Pestle

With its modest depth and unpolished interior, this hefty 3-inch-wide,

The fine pepper mill (see page 80) on the left and salt mill on the right have easy-to-turn top-knob handles and stainless-steel bases.

2-inch-deep bowl, the precursor of which predates recorded history, remains unsurpassed at reducing herbs, spices, and nuts to powders or pastes. Its rough surface furnishes the necessary traction to crack, shear, and crush ingredients as 2 pounds of marble readily withstand the impact and friction.

In addition to the preferred marble, mortars and pestles are also manufactured in porcelain, wood, and brass with diameters that measure from 3 to 7 inches. Shapes range from bell to barrel to apothecary in addition to the simple bowl.

Suribachi

Most recognize this as the name of the extinct volcano scaled by the flag-raising marines on Iwo Jima; it's likely Mount Suribachi was so named because its crater resembled this traditional Japanese mortar. The distinct ridging that covers its unglazed earthenware face allows the chef to crush sesame seeds or to further grind chopped shrimp or chicken into the coarse, granular pastes that enliven sauces or dumplings. Small furrows hold the seed while creating a graterlike surface

This grinder can conveniently store and grind whole nutmeg kernels.

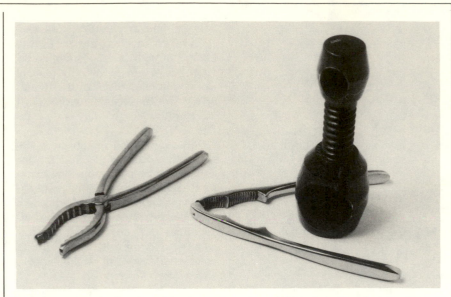

Tools designed to clinch and crack hard carapace and nut shells include, from the left, a lobster cracker, hinged nutcracker, and wooden nutcracker.

to snap it. A 9-inch width that accommodates a pound of chicken or porgy also encourages long, smooth strokes to readily crush them, while a moderately low, concave bowl face provides a comfortable surface on which to rotate a pestle.

In addition to the recommended earthenware, *suribachis* are also manufactured in plastic with diameters from 5½ to 12 inches. The 9-inch *suribachi* best suits the home and is best complemented with a separately sold 10-inch-long pestle called a *surikogi*.

Salt Mill

This mill reduces salt crystals to fine grains to more uniformly flavor a steak, pommes frites, or salad. The angle-set blades compress and crush the gravity-fed flakes; small, parallel slots ensure even dispersal, while the substantial top knob that secures the vertical axle prompts a comfortable twist-turn motion.

A near necessity in humid climes where salt tends to cake, salt mills are most frequently manufactured in wood in heights from 3¾ to 7 inches, with stainless-steel or plastic grinders. A straddling bar or side-set thumb screw offers an alternative to the top-knob handle, but neither works as well as the knob. The mill's base should be stainless steel and have the slotting that harbors its fanlike grinder. This is less likely

to clog than the threaded conical mechanism.

Pepper Mill

With its hollow shaft, bottom-based conical grinder, and vertically set regulating axle, this pepper mill stores, funnels, and grinds such peppercorns as black tellicherry, lampong, and white muntok. The double-threaded cone and similarly ridged surrounding ring easily snag, compress, and crack rough berries. A loosened top screw drops the grinding head to allow contact with widely spaced threads, creating the large "butcher" grind, while a tightened screw exposes the tighter threads to grind finely.

Both top-knob and crank-handle pepper mills are variously manufactured in wood, porcelain, aluminum, acrylic, chrome-plated, or stainless steel with either chrome-plated or stainless-steel mechanisms and in such classic shapes as the elongated, hour-glass hostellerie and the bulging, bottlelike auberge. When buying, overlook shape and examine the grinding mechanism: Those with the smoothest, most easily fed actions are drop-set rather than recessed into their shafts.

Nutmeg Grinder

The spring-set three-pronged shaft that holds a whole nutmeg flush to

the rough-edged slot on this tool's base plate grinds and sparingly dispenses aromatic shavings to flavor sautéed veal, spinach, or cheese soufflé.

Nutmeg grinders—extensions of the personal silver graters of the late-eighteenth- to early-nineteenth-century—are manufactured in wood or acrylic with heights from 3½ to 7 inches. They can be outfitted with a top pin, crank, or knoblike handle, the latter being the smoothest to operate. Unfortunately, it is also the hardest to find in this country, but a fine alternative is the crank-driven acrylic grinder with a practical top-storage feature.

Wooden Nutcracker

This double-headed oak nutcracker carefully cracks shells to free full nutmeats for candying, pastry decoration, or eating plain. Once a walnut is placed in the large head well, or a filbert in the small one, the turned empty head drives the threaded, spindle-loaded connecting shaft into the opposite bowl to crack and shell. Since wood is difficult to twist, it prevents the undue pressure that cracks the kernels. The tool is thick to sustain the press-vice action and carved from hardwood to minimize the expansions and contractions caused by weather changes.

Wooden nutcrackers are also available in beech, cherry, olive-

A topnotch food mill is made of rust-resistant stainless steel and sold with interchangeable plates that produce differently textured foods.

A single-purpose tomato press separates that fruit's seeds, stems, and skin from its pulp and juice when filled and cranked.

wood, and walnut. A single-headed style is also available and both work equally well but the double-headed model is preferred because it holds two nut sizes.

Hinged Nutcracker

These two hinged lengths make it easy to hold, crack, and enjoy the wide range of hard-shelled butternuts to near–paper-covered pecans. Two pivoted 7-inch lengths supply ample breaking leverage and a comfortable grip. The small and large arc insets grip diminutive filberts or bigger walnuts while interior pivot-directed ridging prevents slips.

Nutcrackers—which also crack lobster and crab claws—are manufactured in enameled, nickel-plated, or the sturdiest stainless steel. The once-popular double-hinge style that reverses to crack smaller versus larger nuts is also available. The furrows on the ridged gripping surface should be well defined and moderately tightly set for either style.

Lobster Cracker

The pivot that opens this tool's large, flat-tipped jaws like a pair of pliers makes it easy to grab, hold, and crack a lobster or crab claw. The jaws clinch forward rather than wrap around a claw; their serration gives added traction, while a 2½-inch length compresses claws from the most desirable 1- and 2-pound lobsters. The dull, clipped tips can't be blunted through unavoidable knocks against hard shells.

There are many styles of lobster crackers available, the best of which is the 8-inch-long plierlike device. However, since its jaws' widest opening is limited and must be worked gradually across a standard-sized claw, you're better off with the more finely designed pair of lobster pincers discussed on p. 35.

Food Mill

This mill easily strains or purées vegetables and fruits and mashes cooked fish or fowl for soups, sauces, or forcemeats. A bar that straddles the hopper compacts its underlying spring to keep a constant downward pressure on the blade it directs. The semicircular blade has an upwardly angled front and, when cranked, oversweeps, compresses, scrapes, and crushes apples, tomatoes, or beets against the cutting plate, retaining seeds, skin, and fiber but pushing the flesh through one of three interchangeable cutting plates for supersmooth to slightly textured results.

Food mills, or mechanical sieves, are most often manufactured in either tin-plated or the sturdier stainless steel. Capacities vary from 1 to 5 quarts, the smallest of which best suits the home. Choose a model that has interchangeable cutting plates; not only will you be able to enjoy a variety of textures, but disassembly eases cleaning.

Tomato Press

The hopper that straddles this press's flanged drum and underlying perforated screen makes it easy to feed, strain, and separate fresh tomato pulp and juice from seeds, stems, and skin. A 2-quart hopper ably accommodates home harvests. When cranked, the drum snags, pulls, and presses quartered tomatoes onto a perforated plate that funnels off only pulp and juice. A second flange scrapes, sweeps, and directs all leavings toward another chute.

Tomato presses are manufactured in either aluminum and stainless steel or plastic and stainless steel. While the former is more durable, its aluminum drum reacts to the acidity in tomatoes. If you want the best, most practical machine to process tomatoes, forgo this specialty press and purchase a stainless-steel food mill and use it with the coarse plate.

Spätzle Mill

When its hopper is filled with egg dough and the circular blade crank-turned, this machine speedily shapes

The large perforations on this spätzle mill's base plate shape similarly sized dumplings that cook uniformly.

A sturdy, free-standing electric grain mill can produce over one pound of bread-coarse or pastry-fine flour per minute.

and cuts the small, cylindrical dumplings called spätzle, a southwest German specialty that customarily accompanies stews, fricassees, and roast game. The mill's 1½-quart hopper readily meets most home needs; its spring-set, near upright, S-shaped blade presses dough through a perforated base plate to make uniform scrapings that become the spätzle, as side tabs allow the mill to straddle the pot, dropping the dough directly into the boiling water.

Spätzle, traditionally shaped by cutting flattened dough with a warm, damp knife, can also be made with a flat graterlike device whose hopper is pushed to form and drop the

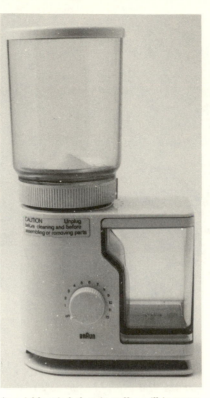

A variable-grind electric coffee mill is unsurpassed at producing evenly sized granules from roasted beans.

dough. But since this tool requires simultaneous lateral and downward pressure to feed and compress, it is neither as convenient as the tinned-steel mill nor as manageable as a simple knife.

Electric Coffee Mill

"Coffee," according to Talleyrand, "should be as black as the Devil, hot as Hell, strong as death and sweet as love"—a goal reached in part by grinding freshly roasted coffee beans just before use to a size that best suits the specific brewing method. The hopper in this mill feeds a controlled amount of beans onto two grind plates, one of which is stationary. When its mate turns, the outwardly angled grooves snag, shear, and grind the beans into evenly sized, coarse to fine granules, depending on the pre-set distance between the burstones. The grounds are flung centrifugally into a removable container.

Almost all freestanding electric coffee mills are fitted with alloy steel burstones and housed in plastic. Some are simply fitted with an ig-

nition and grind regulator while others may also offer a convenient per-cup apportioning feature. Be sure the mill you select can be dismantled for cleaning: Since coffee beans contain oil, the residue must be removed before it becomes rancid.

Electric Grain Mill

This freestanding mill quickly turns such hard, whole grains as wheat, corn, hulled oats, and buckwheat into fresh flours. Gravity makes it work so smoothly: The higher-set hopper funnels kernels into the filtering slot to prevent clogging. Although slight, grain weight directs its own uniform feed onto two nearly flush concave grind plates—one moving and one stationary—whose spiraling furrows distribute, shear, crack, and channel the grain toward the toothed encircling girdle, which further pulverizes it into either a coarse or fine grind as directed by the plates' wider or closer-regulated setting. A chute dispatches the milled flour into an attached bin.

Freshly milled flour imparts a clean, rich flavor to foods, and while it was almost essential to mill one's own grain, particularly wheat, up until fifty years ago, such technological advances as the development of stronger varieties and standard enrichment and bleaching to prolong freshness and create a lighter, more uniformly attractive flour have reduced milling at home to a personally gratifying rather than near necessary task.

When buying a freestanding grain mill, avoid any manual model unless you have stamina and excessive time. Certain free-standing mixers have milling attachments and are equally recommended when processing small amounts. The electric mill described is manufactured in a durable plastic/stainless steel combination that features a 6-cup hopper and a 19-cup flour pan. It measures $11'' \times 9\frac{1}{2}'' \times 6''$.

Meat Grinder

Tuna, duck, venison, and turkey can all be carefully cut or scraped for tartares, terrines, sausages, or forcemeats, but a meat grinder can more quickly produce the most consistent results. The hopper feeds the

A manual meat grinder is most often cast in iron, fitted with carbon-steel blades, and accompanied by one coarse and one fine grind plate.

Three small citrus juicers that completely or sparingly extract the juice from halved or whole lemons or limes are, clockwise from the left, a lemon juicer (see page 84), reamer, and citrus spigot (page 84).

Although called a coffee grinder, this blenderlike machine is also adept at chopping dried herbs and fresh bread crumbs.

flesh onto the wide flutes of the advancing screw; it is then forced through four sharp, rotating blades and onto a perforated disk. The food is nipped into coarse or fine pieces as determined by the preselected grind plate. Gristle can be eliminated, fat regulated, and flavors enhanced by careful spicing.

Although the least laborious noncommercial meat grinders are those that can be attached to a freestanding mixer, there are also a number of crank-driven manual grinders such as this fine one. Save for its carbon-steel blades, it is made of unyielding cast iron and fitted with a firm-footed bolt or clamp rather than a suction base.

Electric Coffee Grinder

The two-armed blade in the bottom of this machine's small container rapidly rotates to chop coffee beans.

Meat Loaf

Bill Blass

6 servings

2 pounds sirloin

½ pound veal

½ pound lean pork

3 tablespoons butter

1 cup coarsely chopped onions

1 cup coarsely chopped celery

½ cup finely chopped parsley

⅓ cup sour cream

1½ cups fresh bread crumbs

¼ teaspoon dried thyme

¼ teaspoon dried marjoram

1 large egg

1 tablespoon Worcestershire sauce

Salt to taste

Freshly ground black pepper to taste

1 12-ounce bottle chili sauce

3 strips bacon

Preheat the oven to 350°F.

Grind the sirloin, veal, and pork together in a meat grinder and set aside in a large bowl.

Heat the butter in a sauté pan set over medium heat, add the onions and celery, and sauté 7 minutes to partially cook; stir occasionally. Add to the meat together with the parsley, sour cream, bread crumbs, thyme, and marjoram.

Combine the egg and Worcestershire in a small bowl, beat to mix, then add to the meat mixture and season to taste with salt and pepper.

Empty into a shallow baking dish and shape into a loaf; top with the chili sauce and bacon strips and bake 1 hour.

An electric juice extractor's internal bucket is very finely perforated so that when spun, it will centrifugally separate the maximum amount of liquid from shredded flesh.

The blades snag, shear, and pulverize up to 4 ounces of beans, starting and stopping when the lid, which regulates ignition, is pressed or lifted.

This blenderlike method of chopping coffee beans is ineffective. There is nowhere to vent granules that are correctly sized for brewing, so they fall to the bottom of the container; some are rechopped, then chopped again, some are not. Better to use this type of coffee grinder to chop small quantities of dried herbs or bread crumbs.

Lemon Reamer

This cone-shaped hand-held reamer extracts juice from fresh lemons and limes. The tapered tip penetrates and separates flesh; the furrows are then turned to crush, squeeze, and juice, while a roughly 3½-inch-long head reaches through the largest Eureka lemon or Persian lime.

Such reamers, available in plastic or the more popular wood, are preferred by many over lemon juicers because the fruit's surface remains unbruised, with no oil released into the juice. Make sure the head has a smooth, conical profile; truncated ones with small front shafts press poorly through flesh and tend to break the far rind, making the juice bitter.

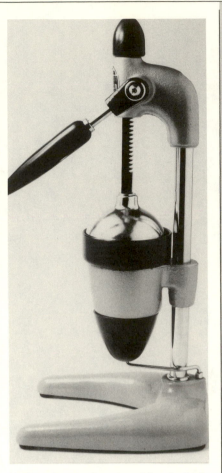

The best free-standing citrus juicer is simple and smooth to operate and strong to compress.

Lemon Juicer

This juicer squeezes, strains, pours, and, if need be, stores juice from lemons, limes, and small oranges. The 2¼-inch-wide cone parts fruit flesh without splitting skin; widely spaced grooves crush, extract, and channel juice into a perforated gulley that separates seeds and pulp from juice. A detachable spouted cup pours the juice or stores it.

Lemon juicers produce a more emphatically flavored juice because oil is released from the skin during squeezing. The juicer should be durable, with stainless steel preferred over porcelain, glass, or plastic.

Citrus Spigot

The tapered, rounded end, top threading, and lengthwise slots along this spigot's 2-inch shaft are ideally suited for inserting and drawing off a few drops of lemon, lime, or orange juice. That tapered tip easily

---

Sea Scallops in Shell with Zucchini Juice

Jean-Georges Vongerichten, Executive Chef: Restaurant Lafayette

4 servings

2 *medium zucchini, washed, trimmed, and quartered*

32 *medium sea scallops (approximately 1½ pounds)*

Salt to taste

Cayenne to taste

6 *tablespoons olive oil*

2 *garlic cloves, peeled and coarsely chopped*

4 *teaspoons fresh thyme, chopped*

Coarse salt

Juice the zucchini in a juice extractor and skim off the foam. You should have about 1 cup of juice.

Season the scallops to taste with salt and cayenne, then sauté in a large (dry) sauté pan set over high heat 20 seconds per side.

Heat one tablespoon olive oil in a saucepan set over medium heat, add the garlic, and sauté until golden brown. Add the zucchini juice and thyme and bring to a boil. Remove from the heat and whisk in the remaining olive oil.

Pour a thick layer of coarse salt in the middle of each of 4 serving plates, top with a scallop shell, then divide the scallops evenly among the shells. Pour the sauce over the scallops and serve.

---

drives through citrus peel into the flesh, light threading locks the tap under the skin, while two slots channel out juice when the fruit is squeezed.

Citrus spigots, which measure 3 inches in overall length, are manufactured in clear acrylic or the more popular cast aluminum.

Citrus Juicer

This juicer is the most efficient manual model on the market. Smooth rack-and-pinion gearing exerts about a thousand pounds of pressure to

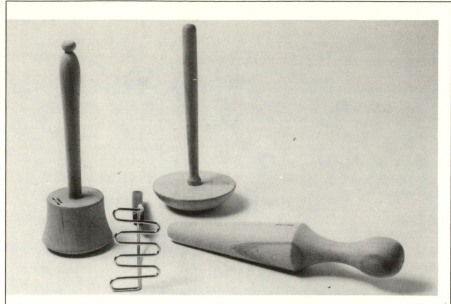

A good vegetable masher has a large, dull working head to quickly reduce food to a pulp. Shown from left are a wooden potato masher, wire potato masher, wooden champignon, and conical pestle.

ensure clean pressing; a form-fitted concave cap promotes uniform squeezing, and a perforated, fluted dome separates seeds and pith while straining off the juice.

Other manual juicers are manufactured, notably a free-standing unit whose hopper/strainer cradles peeled fruit segments to be compressed by a flat face, and a ricerlike, hand-held hinged cap and perforated pail. Both require inordinate time to clean the fruit and energy to operate satisfactorily.

There are two fine manual juicers on the market. A nearly 20-inch chrome and enameled-steel model performs large juicing tasks, and a finger-length semicircular tool has two stainless-steel blades for squeezing single lemon or lime segments for tea or soda.

Electric Juice Extractor

When hard, raw vegetables, fruits, or even herbs such as parsley are fed into the chute of this electric juicer, its rapidly rotating cutting disk shreds their fibers to expose as much flesh as possible. The pulp is then thrown forcibly to the sides of a surrounding spinning strainer basket. Centrifugal force pulls the juice from the pulp through pinpoint perforations and into an encasing jacket, from which it is then funneled out and into a bowl.

Although it is far more convenient and produces juices with generally purer, more intense flavors and colors than those rendered by alternate juicing methods, an electric extractor is fairly expensive, so its potential should be seriously considered before buying. The most durable machine has a 2-quart stainless-steel processing bowl and jacket set above a plastic motor housing.

Conical Pestle

This snub-nosed wooden cone is specially designed to press cooked or partially cooked foods through a chinois. Its 7-inch head readily reaches into a similar-sized conical strainer (see page 89); a clipped tip that rests on the chinois's small, flat base fosters smooth rotation, while a mirror-image shape presses black beans and their broth or soon-to-be-soubise onions through perforations.

A conical pestle, which comes only in wood in lengths to match the chinois, should have at least a 2-inch diameter, the necessary breadth for an efficient scrape/sweep motion. These wider pestles also give the chef a more substantial, comfortable working grip.

Wooden Champignon

This modestly domed hand tool, which looks like an abstract version of the mushroom for which it is named, presses puréed fruits, vegetables, fish, poultry, and flour through a tamis (see page 91) to refine texture. Its 5½-inch diameter and gentle contours—which won't harm taut mesh—break down, spread, mash, and force the food through the sieve.

Most people rely on the greater immediate surface contact furnished by a round-edged rubber scraper or spatula; the wooden champignon also tends to absorb odors. The finest champignon has a wide handle that supplies a comfortable working grip.

Wooden Potato Masher

The drum-shaped working head of this wooden tool is used to purée cooked potatoes and other root vegetables. Its nearly flat face's 3½-inch diameter easily pounds and presses to coarsely cream a mealy vegetable and its 2½-inch backup adds force as the 8-inch turned handle provides a sure, comfortable working grip.

Successfully used in conjunction with a tamis to sieve, wooden potato mashers are, however, definitely surpassed at their intended purpose when compared to the more efficient, multiedged wire tools that allow for the crushed vegetable's upward as well as lateral motion. Both, however, pale before ricers, their benefit being that the vegetable can be worked in the saucepan before reheating with butter.

Potato Masher

This masher is designed to reduce such high-starch cooked vegetables as potatoes and parsnips to soft, fluffy masses. An inflexible wire nicks, separates, splits, and exposes a mealy-textured food to drying air; well-spaced zig-zagging, which allows a vegetable's upward ride, in turn facilitates further penetration, and a nearly 9-square-inch impact surface can mash in the same pot in which the drained vegetable was cooked.

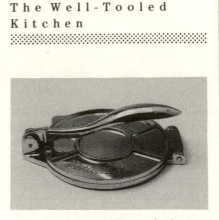

When closed, this tortilla press's aluminum disks uniformly flatten dough so it can then be quickly and evenly cooked.

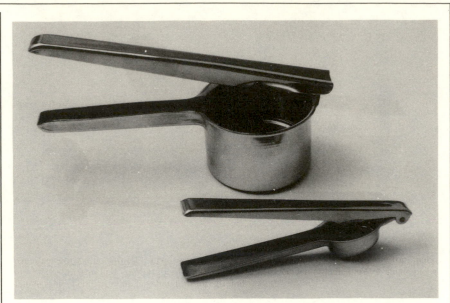

The garlic press in foreground and potato ricer at rear produce lightly textured pressings rather than a mash or a paste.

You'll also find a spring-set masher whose primary face retracts 2 inches up the handle to meet a secondary face and another with a simple perforated disk face. While the first holds promise, the open-ended handle into which the masher retracts can't be properly cleaned, and the latter's large metal face demands greater exertion.

Potato mashers are most often available in nylon and chromed, tinned, or the recommended stainless steel.

Potato Ricer

This hinged tool contains, compresses, and creates soft, semidry, ricelike particles from peeled and cooked root vegetables and puréed chestnuts. The 1-cup capacity holds two generous servings of carrots or potatoes; its perforated base plate cleanly mounds chestnuts into a decorative Mont Blanc, while the plunger's flat face compresses and evenly compacts quartered turnips or sliced parsnips.

Potato ricers are available in cast aluminum, or chrome-plated or stainless steel with one of two container styles, the recommended cup that neatly shoots its pressings directly downward and the V-shaped container whose two perforated sides disperse them more widely. The finest cupped potato ricers, manufactured in stainless steel, come with interchangeable fine and coarse perforated plates.

Garlic Press

The small, perforated oval container and plunger that lie near this tool's two handle ends rend fine pressings from garlic to spike soups, salad dressings, and butters. Its elliptical 2-teaspoon container accommodates up to six cloves per crush; a flat, fitted face crushes the garlic and prevents it from squeezing up and dodging the impact surface, while two 7-inch-long hinged handles that distance hands from the clinging aroma also supply generous leverage.

Garlic presses are manufactured in cast aluminum, some of which have the reverse-pin self-cleaning feature, or stainless steel, which is sturdier but harder to clean.

Butter-Pat Press

When this two-part, palm-sized wooden hand press is chilled in ice water for 30 minutes and the 1½-teaspoon cylindrical cavity is packed with soft butter, the pistonlike plunger can eject well-shaped and -decorated single servings of butter to be chilled before serving. Icing the wood prevents sticking and ensures perfect individual servings.

Butter-pat presses are commonly available in wood with plunging disk faces carved to stamp flowers, fruit, birds, or boats.

A wooden butter-pat press's carved, pistonlike plunger face neatly embosses single servings of butter.

Tortilla Press

These two hinged aluminum disks with their pivoted handle methodically flatten walnut-sized balls of *masa harina* dough that, once grilled, wrap tacos and enchiladas or, cut and fried, serve as tostaditas. Set between plastic and slightly toward that hinge for a more angular spread, the dough ball is easily compressed between the two flat faces. The 6½-inch diameters render the traditional-sized flatbread while a pivoted handle set to further squeeze two plates together ensures the most perfectly flat tortilla.

The sturdiest tortilla presses, of cast iron, are rarities north of the border, but their equally efficient cast-aluminum alternatives are readily found.

Irons to make tantalizingly crisp waffles and wafers are, clockwise from the left: A Belgian waffle iron (see page 88), pizzelle iron, krumkake iron, two pizzelle shaping cones, and a rosette iron.

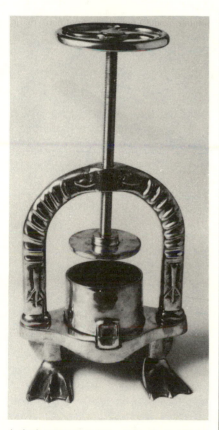

A duck press is indispensable to the grand ceremony of preparing and serving *canneton rouennais à la presse*.

Duck Press

Stately and elaborate, this pistonlike press adds ceremony when preparing the extravagant smothered duck dish called caneton rouennais à la presse. The bird, dispatched by strangulation to retain the blood that enriches and flavors its flesh, is carefully cleaned, then roasted rare. Its breast is then removed for poaching, its legs for grilling, and its carcass for its run through this tall, wheel-powered press. The machine's nearly 17-inch height mainly lends drama but it also provides ample room to crush and compact the remaining carcass; its wheel-regulated shaft that slowly lowers the flat crushing face simultaneously means to whet an appetite while a heavy single-vent bucket that holds a carcass and liver neatly funnels out the pressings that, together with burgundy and cognac, later poach the breast.

Duck presses, which have hardly changed since the presumably medieval dish was rediscovered in France during the late nineteenth century, are most often manufactured in brass, nickel-, or silver-plate.

Rosette Iron

Once preseasoned, preheated, dipped into a sweet, loose batter, then returned to a deep fat fryer, this cast aluminum rose shapes the crisp cookies called *sockerstruvor* in their native Sweden but rosettes almost everywhere else. The rose's multiple edges, which create a sizable metal-to-batter ratio, guarantee rapid frying; cast aluminum's superb heat conduction promises the batter will set immediately and evenly, as a nearly 11-inch, L-shaped handle keeps hands away from splattering fat.

Rosette irons are perhaps more sturdily made, but harder to find, in cast iron with longer, easier-to-grip handles. This iron has two arms, but others have one, and both are often packaged with similar 3-inch-wide interchangeable forms that could include butterflies, bows, trees, or cups called timbales.

Krumkake Iron

This iron's two hinged, heavy aluminum disks evenly and quickly cook krumkakes, the paper-thin Scandinavian wafers that are then rolled into cones to hold whipped cream. The krumkake iron is heavy to retain the high heat necessary to cook a batch of 30 or more and is cast in aluminum to conduct that heat uniformly. It has a burner ring on which to rest and direct heat to its inset press and a small wooden cone on which to wrap and shape the still pliant, warm wafers.

Krumkake irons, once manufactured only in cast iron, are now most readily available in the lighter-weight aluminum.

Pizzelle Iron

The two decorative metal disks at the ends of these hinge-set handles make it easy to transform a fairly liquid batter into the thin, crisp Italian wafers or cones, usually for dessert, known as *cialde* in Florence, *brigidini* in northern Tuscany, and *pizzelle* throughout southern Italy. Frequently ridged or waffled, but always incorporating a daisy design, one of Italy's three national flowers, those symmetrical patterns also strengthen the structure of the biscuit. Heavy metal ensures uniform compression and quickly conducts the high heat, and 10-inch handles distance hands from heat to prevent burns.

Pizzelle irons, usually packaged with medium-sized wood cones to shape the still warm wafer, can be electric but they're most often available with cast-aluminum disks and plastic or, ideally, wood-capped handles.

Belgian Waffle Iron

Over the centuries various religious impressions and familial crests made their way onto the faces of iron waffle plates, but none has had the broad appeal nor—as evidenced by Hieronymus Bosch's fifteenth-century drawing of Mardi Gras waffle bakers—the staying power of the simple, deep pockets on this efficient waffle iron. Each ⅝-inch-deep grid increases metal-to-batter contact for rapid stovetop baking; a wraparound runnel catches and sets excess, runoff batter; the plates' tight pivot eases turns, and 2½ pounds of aluminum sustain an even, high heat while being easy to wield.

Electrified and stovetop waffle irons with the more common smaller and shallower grid surfaces are also available, as are the less common Scandinavian interlocking hearts, usually manufactured in cast iron.

Croque Monsieur Iron

The two heavy aluminum scalloped plates at the hinged ends of this tool's 8¼-inch-long handles compress and heat croque monsieur, the French version of a grilled ham-and-cheese sandwich. Two pounds of aluminum rapidly conduct a stove's high grilling heat as butter-slicked plates that decoratively crimp sandwich-sized slices also increase the available surface for a crisp crust.

Like a cassoulet or vinaigrette-based salad dressing that has as many permutations as there are chefs, a croque monsieur can be dipped in beaten egg, laced with mushrooms, or its Emmentaler substituted with mozzarella or gruyère. The grilling iron should be heavy for its size, with long, plastic-capped handles for easy maneuvering.

Bird's-Nest Fryer

When clamped together, these two openwork hemispheres nest to form lightly floured julienned potatoes,

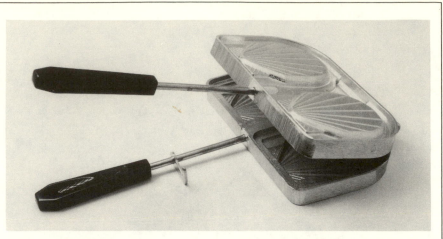

A good croque monsieur iron has heavy cast-aluminum plates to uniformly compact and cook as well as long plastic- or wooden-capped handles for ease in maneuvering.

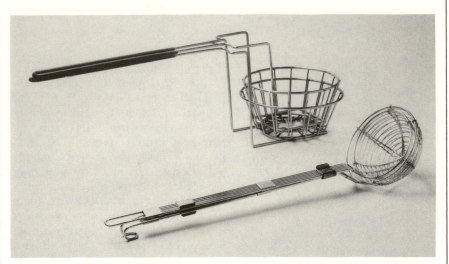

The open-air frame of the bird's-nest fryer in foreground and tortilla-basket foyer at rear expose as much food as possible to hot oil so that it cooks quickly.

leeks, taro, or cooked noodles into tidy baskets for deep frying. The open-wire bowls expose most of the food to hot oil for rapid, even cooking and browning, clips that hold the handles together during frying promise consistent portions, and the 14-inch handles ensure total immersion and distance from splatters.

Bird's-nest fryers are also available with mesh bowls that aren't as sturdy as the preferred wrapped wire ones. Both are manufactured in tinned steel with exterior basket diameters that measure from 3¼ to 5 inches.

Tortilla-Basket Fryer

This long-handled tool's small, open-wire basket and larger, clamp-on companion neatly sandwich to hold and mold a soft flour or corn tortilla during deep frying so it can be used as an edible container for seviche, chili, guacamole, or grilled shrimp. Its nearly 5-inch-diameter basket base accommodates commonly available 6-inch or 9-inch round flatbreads; the medium-thick open wire, which won't buckle in high heat, provides free fat access for even crisping, as foot-long handles that drop 6 inches assure total immersion and safe distance from hot fat.

Tortilla-basket fryers—both the less hazardous larger model and a smaller, shorter-handled, more shallowly dropped version—are manufactured only with chromed-steel wires and insulating plastic-coated handles.

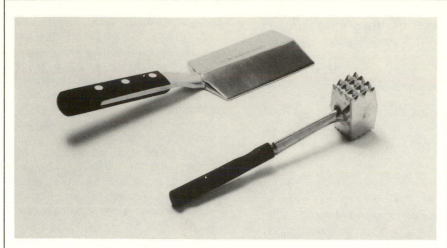

Both the meat pounder on the left and meat tenderizer on the right have heavy heads and thick shafts to withstand pounding.

The two conical sieves found in the professional kitchen are the China cap on the left and the bouillon strainer on the right; the most durable are manufactured in stainless steel.

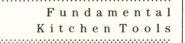
chemically. But since food researchers say that these treatments tenderize only the surfaces of the meat, the most logical tenderizing methods seem to be extended braising, stewing, or, in the case of flank steak, cooking it to its maximum flavor level and then slicing it very thinly across the grain.

Wooden tenderizers tend to crack; opt instead for one of the more durable, single-piece cast-aluminum models.

Bouillon Strainer

The superfine mesh on this reinforced conical strainer allows the chef to strain sauces and clear stocks of sediments or aromatics. The strainer's wide top cuff and external frame support a pestle, small whisk, or ladle as well as protect the mesh from banging against a sink's sides, while its 8-inch mouth easily accepts and directs liquid into a saucepan or bowl.

A bouillon strainer, often (albeit incorrectly) called a chinois, is manufactured in either tin-plated or rust-resistant stainless steel. Top diameters range from 6 to 9½ inches; the 8-inch is most practical for home use. The two most durable are easily recognizable: One strainer has a twill-like woven mesh pattern with a roughly 2-inch-deep top cuff, external reinforcing rods, and a triple-bolted handle. The other's stiffer, proportionately smaller mesh surface is more strongly reinforced, with a 4-inch-deep cuff onto which the frame and handle are spot-welded.

China Cap (Chinois)

This 8-inch-diameter conical sieve with its perforated metal body can purée such soft and semisoft foods as cooked pumpkin, apples, and white beans. Its 2-quart cone shape funnels food downward to assure quick crushing and venting by a pestle while coarse perforations rend near-granular fennel pressings to add character and thickness to a sauce.

Meat Pounder

This broad tongue of heavy steel compresses veal, chicken, or beef to a uniform thickness to cook evenly and look attractive. The 5″ × 4″ strike surface and 2-pound level weight require few downstrokes to completely flatten a full scaloppine or half suprême.

Meat pounders also tenderize tough meat cuts and such shellfish as conch and abalone. They are manufactured in stainless steel, brass, and cast iron, some of which are simply round disks with a perpendicularly set handle. Flatteners can weigh anywhere from 1½ to 7 pounds, the most functional of them fitted with a high-set or perpendicular handle to raise the hand above the strike plane.

Meat Tenderizer

The fine- and coarse-toothed striking faces on opposite sides of this well-balanced hammer head tenderize the tough muscle structures in certain meat cuts. A repeatedly struck 1¼-inch-square face simultaneously makes rump or shoulder steaks thinner and cleanly pierces and clips the fibers. The hammer's thin neck and heavy head distribute weight to the faces to promote accurate blows.

Of course, mechanically tenderized meat is notoriously dry because that riddling drains juices. Most forgo it in favor of an acid marinade or a sprinkling of pepsin, a derivative of the papaya's papain enzyme, both of which act on the protein molecules in meat to break down its muscle

This conical sieve, technically named a chinois, is manufactured in aluminum, tin-plate, or stainless steel with fine, medium, or coarse perforations and measures 6½ to 12 inches in its top diameter. There are two styles, what is commonly called a food press, which fits into an accompanying stand to straddle a pot or bowl, and the more wieldly bracket-handled sieve that clamps onto and in its pot or bowl. An 8-inch china cap with such a handle best suits the home, and the most durable is fabricated from a single sheet of seamless stainless steel finished with a rolled rim and welded-on handle.

Wire Strainers

The coarse stainless-steel mesh (over 200 holes per square inch) on this 9½-inch-wide, flat-bottomed framed bowl strainer quickly and conveniently drains liquids from solids. The flat bottom, which promises an even spread, helps prevent the emptied foods from being crushed, while thick top and base bands plus reinforcing rods help to maintain shape.

Bowl strainers can be placed in the sink during use to free both hands although strainers with handles, generally smaller and with round bottoms, are most often available with different gauges of mesh, the finer of which are superb for straining tea.

Choose a bowl- or handle-fitted strainer of rust-resistant stainless over tinned steel, and one braced with cross-wires or rods. They range in size from 4 inches to 14 inches in diameter with the medium 9½-inch size among the most practical for all-purpose home use.

Tea Strainer

The tight weave of the small, proportionately deep wire-mesh bowl set in the center of this stainless steel lozenge-shaped frame is designed to strain out the last little

St. Jacques Grillées au Fenouil
Grilled Scallops with Fennel

Christian Delouvier, Executive Chef while at The Maurice

4 servings

2 *medium fennel bulbs, cored*

1 *large egg yolk*

Juice from ½ lemon

½ *cup plus 2 tablespoons olive oil*

½ *teaspoon Pernod or Ricard*

Salt to taste

Freshly ground black pepper to taste

1 *pound celery root, peeled*

¼ *cup extra-virgin olive oil*

20 *large sea scallops (approximately 1¾ pounds)*

1 *bunch chives cut into 3-inch lengths*

Leaves from 1 bunch chervil

Chop one fennel bulb in a food processor, empty into a coarse-holed china cap, and press through to extract the juice. Combine it with the egg yolk and lemon juice in the top part of a double boiler set over an inch of simmering water. Whisk 2 minutes or until thickened, then very slowly add ½ cup olive oil, whisking constantly to emulsify. Whisk in the Pernod, season to taste with salt and pepper, and set aside.

Cut the celery root and remaining fennel bulb into bâtonnets, sticks measuring about ¼" × ¼" × 2½–3" each, blanch each 2 minutes in boiling water, then transfer to cold water to halt further cooking. Heat the extra-virgin olive oil in a sauté pan set over medium-high heat, add both drained vegetables, and sauté briefly; season to taste with salt and pepper and set aside.

Preheat the oven to 400°F.

Heat a ridged grill until very hot. Brush the scallops with the remaining olive oil, season to taste with salt and pepper, then grill momentarily to mark them. Transfer to a large baking dish and bake 3 minutes, or until barely done.

For each serving: Spoon a small amount of the sauce on a hot serving plate, mound a few vegetables in the center and surround with an even amount of scallops; garnish with chives and chervil.

particle of tea leaf as freshly steeped tea is poured from pot to cup. The frame's side tabs rest on a cup's rim to straddle the strainer, and the accompanying base provides a tidy support between pours.

The correct way to prepare a pot of tea is to allow the leaves to steep freely a few moments to several minutes in freshly boiled water so that they unfold fully. This unfolding, called "the agony of the leaves" by professional tasters, exposes maximum surface to water for the most complete flavor extraction.

To make a single cup of tea, the more practical device is a two-part perforated stainless-steel spoon whose jaws open to fill and empty by squeezing the handle, which is actually a hinged tension spring that opens and closes the spoon's jaws.

Sifter

When the four arced rods of this sifter are cranked to brush against the hemispherical mesh face, they clear flour through it to produce an aerated baking flour of uniform density. The density of flour in a given container can vary 25 percent or more due to moisture and the way it was milled—factors that a sifter balances out. Repeated agitation against the 400 holes per square inch of screen clear lumps and coarse grinds. The bowed face directs the flour down into the path of the sifting rods.

Sifters are manufactured in plastic, or tinned or stainless steel with single, double, or triple screens and 1- to 8-cup capacities. They can be battery-powered, spring-set, or

The drum sieve on the left is traditionally used to purée foods; the sifter on the right removes lumps and uniformly aerates flour for baking.

Sieve frames are manufactured in plastic, wood, aluminum, or stainless steel with diameters from roughly 7 to 11 inches. Meshes are made of nylon, silk, stainless, or tinned steel with counts from 8 to 70 wires per centimeter to successively sift flours, purées, crushed spices, and confectioners' sugar. Counts of 20, 30, and 40 are the most common.

This colander's perforated-sheet face supplies enough smooth surface to support soft, high-starch pasta or delicately fleshy strawberries.

Bowl-shaped wire strainers run the gamut from the tiny tea strainer on the left to the large, multipurpose one on the right.

Colander

This large, perforated, footed, stainless-steel hemisphere quickly strains liquids from foods. Its 11½-inch diameter, twice its depth, creates easy pouring access and a modest food spread; the bowl's large, overall perforations rapidly drain water from cooked pasta, blanched vegetables, and rinsed fruit.

Some colanders are equipped with a long handle and no base and others have a base ring that more easily separates or fect that are generally more sturdily attached. They are manufactured in tinned steel, tin-lined copper, enameled steel, porcelain, plain and anodized aluminum, and nylon as well as the preferred stainless steel in sizes from 2 to 14 quarts. A 4- or 5-quart colander is fine for home use.

Gravy Separator

Fat rises above the heavier liquid with which it is combined, and this cup's long, low-set spout—a sleek, single-vent version of the famous French gras-maigre gravy boat—neatly pours off that underlying liquid layer as it retains the fatty upper one. The tall, bottom-based spout, as high as the cup, allows maximum filling while its 60-degree angle promotes dripless pouring.

Gravy separators are usually molded in see-through plastic with either 1½- or 4-cup capacities.

Simple tools to help the aspiring cook include the egg separator (see page 92) on the left and gravy separator on the right.

the preferred crank-operated sifter, whose fewer parts mean less breakage. A single screen is all that's necessary to clear flour, and a 3-cup capacity is sufficient for home use.

A sifter's screen should have a medium-fine mesh for proper sepa-

ration, the rods should barely brush against it for efficient processing, and the handle should be large and comfortable to hold.

Drum Sieve (Tamis)

To produce the smoothest sauces or soups from pastes or purées or to remove the lumps from large amounts of flour or sugar before baking, they should be passed through the taut, medium-fine mesh of a drum sieve, or tamis. Its close, 30-count weave, measured by the number of wires per centimeter in one direction, catches and crushes semiwoody stalks or clumped sugar, while the 9-inch-wide sieve base is broad enough for rapid clearance.

Egg Separator

The easiest, most convenient and efficient way to separate an egg white from its yolk is through the fingers of a cupped hand; the palm cradles the yolk while the more fluid white filters out. Barring that, there is this small, shallow, tiered cup, which looks like a tiny bull's eye target. Its 2-teaspoon bowl barely contains a yolk; the slots on the slightly higher tier siphon off the white as a third tier—actually a wraparound rim—allows it to be set atop a cup or jar.

Few distinctions exist among egg separators save for composition, with the less-likely-to-dent stainless steel preferred over aluminum or plastic.

Salad Spinner

According to the nineteenth-century American writer Charles D. Warner, lettuce, like conversation, needs a good deal of oil to avoid friction and to keep the company smooth. Lettuce also needs to be thoroughly dried after washing to hold the oil—a task for this three-part plastic spinner. The slotted basket is set into the outer bowl and loosely filled with greens, covered, and the gears in the lid are cranked. They rotate the basket rapidly to create a centrifugal force that pulls the greens to the basket's sides while the water is flung out through the slots.

Enclosed spinners are far more practical, neat, and convenient than the open wire baskets that are energetically shaken to get rid of water. The spinners are always manufactured in plastic in two styles, the recommended hand crank or a cord pull that tends to break with use. The crank model is sometimes fitted with a vented jacket to simultaneously wash, spin dry, and drain, but its use is restricted to the sink. A nonperforated container that is portable and often held to turn is more usable. Salad spinners are available with 1½- to 7-quart capacities; the 4-quart size is fine for home use.

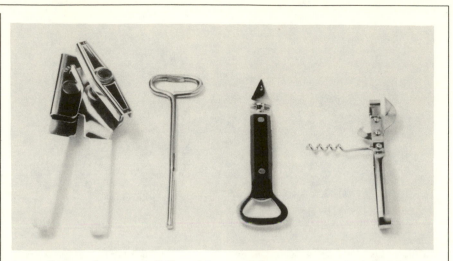

Among the manual openers available to fully or partially open cans are, from the left, a fine gear-driven can opener, sardine can and bottle opener, bottle opener and can tapper, and a manual can opener.

Bottle Opener and Can Tapper

Small, simple, and efficient, this opener pops off crown caps, punctures cans, and pries out the inset lids on paint cans. The tool's open oval end with its slight inset flange reaches under and over the small curve of a pinched crown cap to pry it open; the downwardly angled arrowhead end with its inset metal tab gains enough foothold under and on a can edge to forcibly pierce and open it. The 5-inch handle furnishes the required leverage.

Some hand openers are available with a single open end, others with the addition of a coiled wire worm for pulling corks out of bottles. They are most often manufactured in nickel-plated steel with a plastic-covered handle.

Manual Can Opener

Every GI and Boy Scout has this basic tool to open tin cans, lift off crown caps, and uncork bottles. Its dropped short blade punctures the can, then, with the nearly 6-inch metal body as a lever, it is rocked forward to rip around the perimeter of the lid to open the can. The side hook slips under the pinched rim of a crown cap to pry it off as the coiled wire worm screws into a bottle's cork to extract it.

Manual can openers are most often manufactured in nickel-plated steel.

A fully enclosed salad spinner effectively spin-dries greens for subsequent tossing.

Sardine Can and Bottle Opener

This steel tool, which resembles a barrel key, opens sardine cans and crown-capped bottles with a simple twist or flip. The shaft's almost centrally set parallel flange grips a sardine can's tab, the wide oval end turns the 5½-inch lever to peel and discard the tab, while the wide, flat hollow end simultaneously reaches under and compresses a crown cap to lift it off.

Sardine cans now come with their own keys, so this opener's days are numbered. But if you intend to buy one, overlook any with central eyelets; they thread and peel away a tabbed, flat lid but can't release it.

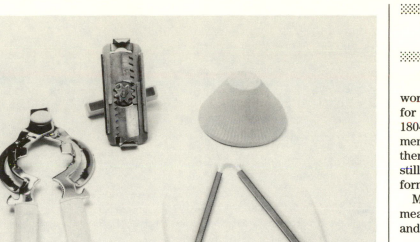

Devices that supply extra leverage or a rough grip to unscrew tight jar lids are, clockwise from the left, a jar wrench (see page 94), retractable jar opener, textured rubber jar opener (page 94), and a mounted V-shaped jar vise (page 94).

Manual Gear-Driven Can Opener

This crank-powered hand tool's small, canted cutting wheel is clamped with plierlike handles over the rim of a can to puncture the lid. As the crank is turned, the synchronized gears advance the cutting disk, whose inward angle, flush to the can rim, creates a broad opening while bending the cut metal of the lid downward to bury its edge.

Can openers have seen a metamorphosis since the Frenchman François Appert first developed a workable method of preserving foods for his country's military forces in 1804. And while many of the elementary openers that developed soon thereafter, like the hooked lever, are still to be found, they are in sleeker form.

Manual gear-driven can openers measure 7 inches in overall length and weigh 8 ounces.

Retractable Jar Opener

This retractable opener easily grips and loosens screwtop lids. The turning cog sets in motion two dropped steel arcs to accommodate any standard-sized lid from ½ to 4¼ inches wide; those arcs clench the sides of the lid for sure traction, and a gripped handle controls the cog and its clamp simultaneously to assure a strong, uniform, steady-powered twist-off.

Retractable jar openers measure 3 inches long and are most often available in nickel-plated steel with plastic-covered handles.

Black Bean Soup

Leon Lianides, Proprietor:
The Coach House

6 servings

3 cups black beans, soaked in water to cover overnight, drained and rinsed

3 quarts water

5 strips bacon, coarsely chopped

2 medium celery ribs, coarsely chopped

2 large onions, coarsely chopped

2 tablespoons all-purpose flour

Rind and bone from a smoked ham or 2 split smoked ham shanks

3 pounds beef marrow bones

3 sprigs Italian parsley

2 bay leaves

2 garlic cloves, halved

2 medium carrots, scrubbed and coarsely chopped

2 medium parsnips, scrubbed and coarsely chopped

½ cup Madeira

Salt to taste

¼ teaspoon freshly ground black pepper

2 large hard-cooked eggs, finely chopped

Combine the beans and 3 quarts water in a large pot set over high heat, bring to a boil, then reduce the heat and simmer, covered, 1½ hours.

Sauté the bacon in a medium stockpot set over medium heat 5 minutes, add the celery and onion, and cook until tender but not brown. Add the flour, stir to blend, and cook 1 minute. Add the ham and beef bones, parsley, bay leaves, garlic, carrots, parsnips, pepper, and the beans and their cooking liquid, bring to a bare simmer, cover, and cook 3 hours. Add more water if necessary.

Discard the bones and rind, then press the soup through a sieve. Return to the stockpot and reheat.

Just before serving add the Madeira and season to taste with salt and pepper. Ladle into warm soup bowls and top with the chopped eggs.

Mounted V-shaped Jar Vise

This flat, V-shaped vise is attached under a cabinet to open screw-top jars. Its two wedge-shaped grips hold a ¼-inch- to 4-inch wide lid; one smooth bar allows easy entrée and braces the lid to twist as the toothed bar clenches when the jar is turned.

These vises measure nearly 6 inches long and are usually manufactured in plastic and stainless steel. Some are packaged with adhesive strips for mounting, but it is better to mount them more securely with screws.

Textured Rubber Jar Opener

This palm-sized, flexible ridged rubber cone provides the extra traction needed to unscrew jar lids smaller than 3½ inches. It has internal horizontal rings and external vertical flutes both to hold fast to the lid and to secure the grip while twisting.

Rubber jar openers, also produced as flat, textured rubber sheets, are quite limited because recalcitrant jar lids more often than not need the stronger grip and traction of a retractable jar opener.

Jar Wrench

The three narrow- and wide-toothed bows created by this tool's serpentine working sections grip, loosen, and open standard-sized screw-top lids. They first appear to be set for the metric system, but the two tiered, concentric, and third oval bows ably grip any 1- to 3-inch cap across its diameter in the English system; the inset serration creates the traction for twisting, while the nearly 10-inch handles, which furnish generous leverage, power the turn. A side hook on each handle and an extended tip tab lift crown caps and pop out inset lids.

The best jar wrenches, some of which are simply two lengths of metal with corresponding crescent-

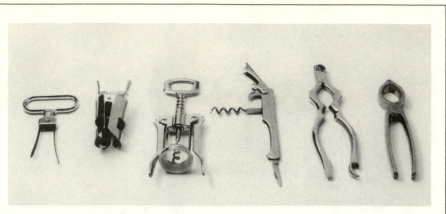

Diverse cork-pulling and bottle-sealing tools include, from the left, a cork puller, champagne stopper, winged corkscrew, waiter's wine opener, bar tender, and champagne pliers.

shaped bows, are manufactured in chromed or nickeled steel with plastic cushion grips in 9½-inch lengths.

Waiter's Wine Opener

This simple, compact tool with its short, coiled wire worm, perpendicular handle, hinged arm, and two small knife blades set at opposite ends dependably removes a cork from a bottle of wine. The small bird's beak or straight knife blade slices off the lead or foil cork covering; the ⁵⁄₁₆-inch wide spiral works its way through the cork in a helical fashion to cover the greatest possible area and the hinged arm then hooks onto the bottle lip to supply leverage for pulling out the cork.

This corkscrew is manufactured in stainless steel with a milled handle for the surest grip. Nickel- or chrome-plated steel waiter's wine openers are also available. All measure approximately 4½ inches long and the finest have a ⁵⁄₁₆-inch wide, nearly 2-inch-long, open coiled wire worm.

Winged Corkscrew

This corkscrew's coiled worm, like the waiter's wine opener, gains a secure hold on a wine bottle's cork, but is simpler to insert, and two-armed leverage gives more power. The centrally set shaft is easy to aim and the frame rests on the rim of the bottle to keep it aligned. A turned capping eye drives the coil downward as it raises the ratchet-set wings. When the wings are then

pressed down, they draw up the cork and extract it.

Manufactured in brass- or chrome-plated steel, winged corkscrews measure 7 inches long, and the best have the coiled worm rather than the augerlike screw style with spirals down a center shaft.

Cork Puller

With some practice and a little exertion, the two small, flat, flexible metal prongs that protrude from this tool's handle neatly remove an unpierced cork from a bottle of wine. The blades slip cleanly between cork and bottle; their outward splay deters penetration or crumbling of an aged cork during entry and their parallel set fully embraces it for successful twisting and extraction.

Few distinctions exist among the cork pullers on the market; they all measure about 4½ inches long with nickel-plated handles and carbon-steel prongs.

Bar Tender

By combining snips, pliers, and a screwdriver, this two-armed tool is a sturdy multimedium opener. Its small snip-front easily nips foil from wine bottles and bails from champagne; the tight, ridged, internal bow created by the double-arced arms unscrews caps, uncorks champagne, and cracks nutshells as the wider bow unscrews larger lids. One arm's hooked end lifts crown caps while the other arm's flat end serves as a screwdriver.

Bar tenders measure nearly 8 inches long and are manufactured

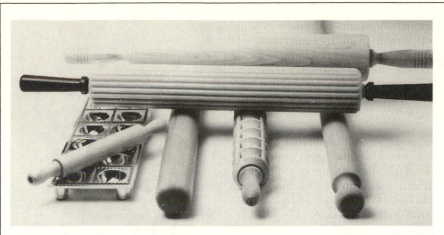

Rolling pins to contend with any variety of doughs are, clockwise from the top, a two-handled rolling pin, puff-pastry pin, pasta pin (see page 96), ravioli pin (page 96), the favored French-style rolling pin for general use, and a ravioli tray and pin (page 96).

in either nickel-, chrome-, or gold-plated steel.

Champagne Pliers

Because the pressure in an unopened bottle of champagne is estimated at 90 pounds per square inch, a chilled bottle must be uncorked with care—a feat stylishly accomplished by these bow-jawed pliers with inset waffling. The long, blunt, internally ridged tips easily twist and free a cork's wire bail covering; oval-shaped jaws that confront a cork's cross axis equally grip the progressively larger corks of splits, magnums, and nebuchadnezzars, while the inner ridging supplies traction to twist them off.

It is believed the first toast ever made was given by the age-blinded old monk and master vintner Dom Perignon, upon the first sip of his bubbly creation. "Come quickly," he reputedly cried to his assistant, "I'm drinking stars."

Champagne pliers measure just over 6 inches long and are most often available in nickel- or gold-plated steel.

Champagne Stopper

When revelers can't quite finish a bottle of uncorked champagne, this spring-loaded, short-armed stopper preserves those remaining bubbles. Its tiered rubber face partially juts into the necks of a broad range of bottle sizes to create an effective seal; once closed, the arm's inner flanges securely clamp below the

bottle's neck rib. The clamp/spring mechanism facilitates capping and removal.

Spring-free champagne stoppers are also available, the best of which are heavy for their size and open smoothly and widely. The finest, however, have springs. They measure about 3½ inches long and are manufactured in either nickeled or gold-plated steel.

French-Style Rolling Pin

This lightweight wooden cylinder is preferred by chefs as their all-purpose pin to roll short crust and creamed cookie doughs, flatten yeast-raised pastry dough, and shape freshly baked tile cookies. Its 20-inch-long barrel covers most expanding dough sheets and the tight, 2-inch diameter keeps hands close to pastry for the careful work that prompts a uniformly thinned sheet. The 1¼-pound weight is not only easy to handle but also helps convey to the chef the pastry's degree of smoothness.

Twenty-inch-long, French-style wooden rolling pins are most often manufactured in beech or boxwood. Check for the nicks and splinters that could hinder level rolling.

Two-handled Rolling Pin

Professionals favor a smooth, simple, lightweight pin without handles for most of their rolling tasks but

most laypeople think a larger, heavier, two-handled pin is best. It is better equipped to flatten yeast-raised doughs: The barrel's 3-inch diameter, which requires fewer revolutions over a pastry sheet, promotes a smoother, more quickly accomplished job; the 4-pound weight better overpowers the drag of a soft, airy dough, while two bearing-set handles make rolling easier.

Heavy two-handled rolling pins—available with stationary, dowel-set, or the recommended bearing-set handles—are manufactured, in order of preference, in wood; marble, which may seem promising but is most often mounted on a dowel that sometimes advances and sometimes doesn't; aluminum, which discolors egg-enriched doughs; or hollow plastic, which is meant to be filled with ice water to keep the dough cold as it is being flattened but frequently sweats and ruins the pastry.

Two-handled hardwood rolling pins are commonly available with 13-inch to 18-inch barrels. A 15-inch well-balanced pin suits most needs.

Puff-Pastry Rolling Pin

This ribbed cylinder is designed to incorporate butter and air into a sheet of dough so that when baked as a vol-au-vent, turnover, fleuron, or tart shell, the evenly spaced fat melts and bubbles as the trapped air expands to make the pastry rise uniformly. The pin's nearly 16-inch barrel easily covers a standard-sized dough sheet called a *détrempe;* its 4½-pound weight requires no further pressure to ensure even compression, while ⅛-inch-wide lengthwise channels evenly distribute butter and air.

Puff-pastry rolling pins are manufactured in plastic and measure 25 inches in overall length. Examine its ribbing to be sure there are no gashes to cause uneven incorporation and layering.

Pasta Rolling Pin

A long, thin, lightweight wooden pin is well designed to roll kneaded, fist-sized dough balls into sheets for such pastas as fettuccine, ravioli, and farfalle. This one is a generous 3 feet long and more for flash than for function; a roughly 2-foot length would better suit the home: That stretch completely covers most non-commercial dough sheets, while its 3-pound weight permits a keen feel for the dough being worked to promote uniform thickness.

Pasta rolling pins, which have one end shaped to resemble a doorknob, can measure up to 35 inches long. They are manufactured only in wood, which should be examined for gouges and splinters before buying.

Ravioli Pin

Once you have rolled this patterned barrel across a previously flattened pasta sheet, spot-filled it, then topped those fillings with a second sheet of pasta, this long, segmented wooden cylinder can do its work: to rapidly compress and form ravioli for final cutting. Its 14-inch length scores a substantial amount of pasta in one run, and the 1⅜-inch squares apportion the most popular, first course–sized pieces of ravioli. But this pin's shallow segments allow only meager fillings which must be very accurately aligned, and the wooden cross-slats that shape specific squares neither lay level nor press evenly, which may later cause the ravioli to separate.

Better to buy a fine ravioli cutter or tray than to rely on this pin; the time, effort, and attention will be about the same but the results produced by the cutter or tray will be dependably better than those of the pin. If you're still in the market, however, you'll find that most are manufactured in beech and measure just over 20 inches in overall length.

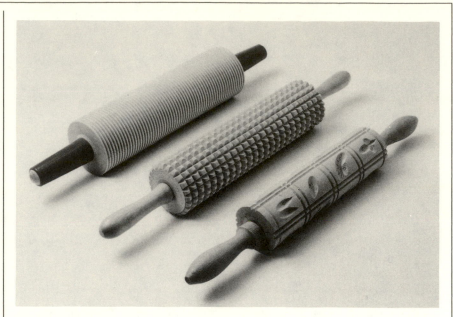

Three pins that flatten and/or emboss their special doughs are, from the left, a lefse pin, hardtack pin, and springerle pin.

Ravioli Tray

This cast-aluminum sheet's twelve evenly spaced, shallow bowls and their surrounding zig-zag ridging let the cook rapidly shape, seal, and cut moderate amounts of uniform packets. Its scant tablespoon indentations turn out parcels that all cook at the same rate; the centered depressions that are bordered by wide, flat edges prompt generous contact between the layered dough sheets to foster thorough sealing, while raised ridges that surround each ravioli allow them to be cleanly severed.

Ravioli trays are most often cast in aluminum and available in two sizes—the nearly 2-inch squares for entrées and the roughly 1-inch squares for appetizers or additions to some soups. They are frequently sold with a smooth, doll-sized rolling pin.

Lefse Rolling Pin

This rolling pin's long ribbed face scores the surface of a flatbread dough so that it rises evenly when cooked. The barrel's shallow pattern suits the paper-thin, unleavened dough of the Norwegian lefse. The 10-inch cylinder notches uniform disks in one run and the 3-inch diameter requires few revolutions.

Lefse rolling pins, which invariably seem to float loosely over their dowels, are most often available with maple cylinders. Don't confuse them with the smaller, narrower, and generally better-made wooden marzipan rolling pins. Including handles, lefse pins measure 16½ inches long.

Hardtack Rolling Pin

To maximize the yield from their brief grain-growing season and because that harvest often remains green, Scandinavians traditionally bake it into flatbreads for the most prudent winter storage and eating. When lightly floured, this long, hobnailed wood cylinder notches the rye or oat *knäckebröds* known simply as Swedish hardtack. This 10-inch pin quickly imprints standard-sized loaves with one pass; ⅜-inch-deep knobs score the dough to restrict its leavened rise.

Hardtack rolling pins, most often manufactured in maple, generally measure 17 inches in overall length.

Springerle Pin

The 16 shallow designs carved into this lightweight barrel emboss the leveled, spiced sugar dough for springerle, the most renowned southwestern German holiday cookie. Bare 1/8-inch-deep carvings clearly imprint an already thin dough; the 8-inch barrel rapidly marks a typically small home batch, while the 12-ounce weight prevents accidental squashing.

Some attribute the traditional birds, bees, flowers, and fruits that appear most often on springerle pins to ancient festivals that celebrated an oncoming growing season. With harvesting done and seeds sown, it's not surprising that the anticipated flora and fauna would be incorporated into the feasts.

Springerle pins are best, albeit rarely, fitted with sectioning disks and raised frames that cut as they emboss. Pins that simply impress are easier to find; be sure the carvings are smoothly finished and gouge free.

Caramel Rolling Pin

This ribbed aluminum cylinder is designed to roll cooled caramel thinly for layering onto or around nougat. Its 1 1/4-pound weight produces even pressure; a nearly 9-inch length quickly covers and spreads the typically small candy batch, while channels increase the pin-to-candy contact surface for authoritative rolls and to score it for later processing.

With expandable confectioners' bars available that frame and shape a hot sugar syrup as it cools, this pin may seem frivolous. But confectioners know that by containing this syrup to a relatively small area, less surface is exposed and less moisture lost—important for a creamy candy.

Caramel pins—which are handle-free to better allow the chef to gauge the pressure he or she exerts—are available only in the 8 3/4-inch length. They should be lightly coated with vegetable oil before use.

Nougat Rolling Pin

This stainless-steel pin is used to roll fresh-from-the-pot nougat between spaced confectioner's bars. Its 14-inch, 6-pound barrel is easy enough to wield and substantial enough to compact. Its inch-wide

---

Classic Puff Pastry

Flo Braker
The Simple Art of Perfect Baking

2 1/2 pounds

3 cups plus 2 tablespoons sifted all-purpose flour

3/4 cup sifted cake flour

2 ounces sweet butter, chilled and cut into 1/2-inch cubes

3/4 teaspoon salt

1 cup ice water

14 ounces sweet butter, chilled

Combine the flours in the top part of a triple sifter and sift into a mound on a large work surface; measure off 2 tablespoons and reserve for the butter package. Scatter the cubed butter over the mounded flour and, with a pastry blender, cut it in until it is the size of peas. Roll a rolling pin 1 to 2 times over the mixture to flatten the butter particles, gather into a mound again, then use the pastry blender to cut until powdery with some oatmeal-shaped flakes throughout; remound.

Form an 11-inch-wide well in the center of the flour mixture. Add the salt and water to the well, stir to dissolve the salt, then slowly push the flour over the water to cover it. Pick up large pieces of dough and pull apart to further disperse the moisture, then gather the loose pieces together in a mass. Gently fold the dough on top of itself 7 to 11 times and shape into a 6-inch square; the dough may be cohesive but not smooth. Score its surface with the tip of a sharp knife in a grid pattern, wrap in plastic, and refrigerate at least 12 hours.

Lightly dust the work surface with the reserved 2 tablespoons flour, place the butter on top, and pound with the end of a rolling pin until it is one malleable unit, yet still cold. Place between 2 sheets of waxed paper and roll into a 9" × 5 1/2" × 1/2" rectangle and refrigerate until cold yet supple.

Lightly dust the work surface with all-purpose flour, place the dough package on top, then, working from the center, use a rolling pin to roll it out evenly to an 11-inch square. Set the butter block on half the dough, allowing a 1/2-inch border of uncovered dough, then fold the other half on top and press to seal the edges to enclose totally. (This package is known as a *pâton*.)

Rotate the *pâton* 90 degrees to the left and lightly dust the work surface under the dough with flour. Start at the center and, with a rolling pin and evenly pressured strokes, roll out, stopping short of the edge; similarly roll the other dough section, stopping short of its edge, then roll out the *pâton* until it measures 7" × 16" × 1/2". Square the corners by rolling carefully over the thicker edges. With the short end of the dough facing toward you, fold one third of it up and over the center, then flap the top third down over the bottom until the dough resembles a folded business letter. (This is called a single fold.) Rotate the dough 90 degrees counterclockwise, lightly dust the top and work surface with flour and roll to measure 7" × 16" × 1/2". Brush off the excess flour and make another single fold. You have just completed two "turns." Wrap in foil and refrigerate 45 minutes.

Lightly dust the work surface with flour and place the chilled dough on top so that its last fold is perpendicular to you and the flap on top opens like a book. Roll again until it measures 7" × 16" × 1/2"; brush off any excess flour and make a single fold again, business-letter fashion. Rewrap in foil and refrigerate 45 minutes.

Repeat the rolling, folding, and chilling three more times, extending the chilling period to 1 hour after each successive turn.

Roll to a more manageable 8" × 11" × 1/2" block, wrap in plastic, and refrigerate at least 4 to 6 hours before using.

diameter allows a feel for the paste to achieve uniform thickness, while the milled finish thwarts adhesion.

Nougat rollers, which should be coated lightly with vegetable oil before use, can also be used to flatten gum paste and fondant. They are available only in stainless steel in that 14-inch length.

Basketweave Rolling Pin

This narrow, 1-pound cylinder with its basketweave design is used to make the final impression on a marzipan sheet. Its 8½-inch length scores marzipan pieces large enough to cover up to 9-inch leveled and apricot-glazed cake rounds or squares. The pin's tight barrel must make many revolutions to mark a sheet, encouraging greater attention and precision.

Basketweave rolling pins measure 12½ inches overall; other similarly long wooden marzipan pins with slightly wider barrels have finely checkered faces or grooves. Basketweave rolling pins are manufactured in plastic and should be predusted with confectioners' sugar to prevent sticking.

Manual Pasta Machine

This machine's two smooth, 6-inch-wide, hand-cranked rollers, like those of a mangle, snag, pull, and press a ball of dough into a uniformly thin sheet for slicing through one of its two accompanying cutting rollers. The six graduated openings—from ¼ inch to 1/32 inch—knead and press the folded and refolded dough to its desired thickness to be cut into such pastas as tagliatelle or fettuccine.

Electric pasta machines make it a cinch to knead and cut dough and, if extrusion types, to premix the flour and eggs for the dough before pushing it through a preselected cutting disk. The manual version, however, is the more practical investment for home use. The best have 6- to 8-inch-long rollers. These should be

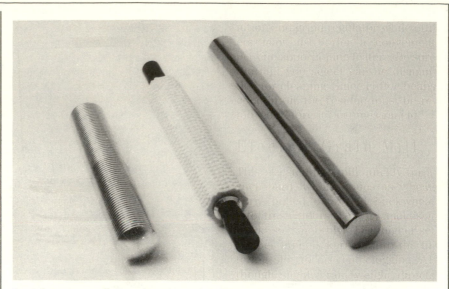

Special-purpose confectioner's and baker's rolling pins are, from the left, a caramel pin (see page 97), basketweave pin, and nougat pin (page 97).

Most experts prefer the texture of hand-worked pasta to that extruded by an electric machine. A manual pasta machine to hasten the rolling and cutting should have easy-to-regulate, perfectly-aligned rollers.

easy to regulate, hold securely, and align exactly so a dough sheet won't pull, wrinkle, and tear. There are additional blades that expand its cutting ability to such shapes as capellini and lasagne. Most manual pasta machines are manufactured in chromed steel and fitted with a base clamp.

Food Processor

The labor-saving food processor has become a near necessity in the professional and serious home kitchen. Its powerful, direct-drive, S-shaped,

The food processor, which rapidly shreds, minces, grates, slices, and kneads, is the true workhorse of the contemporary kitchen.

wave-cut blade snags, penetrates, and severs meat, vegetables, and herbs; it creams soups and emulsifies sauces that are either pressed or poured through the feed tube or added directly to the work bowl. When the central shaft is fitted with an alternate slicing blade, cutting disk, or dough blade, the machine does a fine job of grating, shredding, or kneading.

A powerful commercial bar blender's narrow container keeps foods close to its blade for quick contact and liquefaction.

Food processors normally come equipped with a durable plastic work bowl, an interlocking lid capped with a chimneylike feed tube, the multipurpose double-scimitar blade that does 90 percent of the tasks, and a plastic pestle with which to push solid foods into the work bowl. Bowl capacities range from 1 to 16 cups, with the larger machines being more powerful and sturdier. The best of the larger models sit atop the direct drive rather than next to the belt-driven motors. The machines are regulated by on/off or pulse buttons, feature a brake action that brings the blade or disk to halt, and could be fitted with a larger feed tube to shorten the processing time. Optional attachments generally include french-fry and ripple-cut disks, juice extractor, thick-slicing blade, and a citrus press.

Commercial Bar Blender

To make the smoothest milkshakes, silkiest purées, and most satiny sauces, many forgo the food processor in favor of a blender. The best have large, durable containers and powerful drives to direct four strong, stout rotary blades.

The narrow 44-ounce carafe, when properly filled only half full, keeps foods close to the blades so they liquefy rapidly. Its two speeds—18,000 and 14,000 rpms—turn out a fruit frappé, vichyssoise, or pancake batter, while its thick, straight, angle-set blades just as easily cut through ice as through mayonnaise.

Blenders are available with various lidded containers—glass, which is breakable; stainless steel, which is opaque; and polycarbonate, which is not as durable as stainless steel but is transparent. Some blenders

Fresh Pasta

*Anna Teresa Callen,
Food Writer and Teacher*

approximately
1 pound pasta

2 to 2½ cups all-purpose flour

2 large eggs

Mound 2 cups flour on a pastry board, make a well in the center, and add the eggs to the well; beat them with a fork, then use your fingers to incorporate the flour gradually into the eggs. The dough should be relatively firm yet still pliant.

Gather the dough into a ball and knead 5 minutes or until smooth and elastic; add more flour if necessary. Cover the dough and allow it to rest 30 minutes before rolling and cutting.

Divide the dough into two parts; cover one and work the other: Flatten it with your hands, then divide it in two to portion correctly for the pasta machine. Sprinkle lightly with flour.

With the machine's cylinders fully open, crank the handle to pass the dough through them to further knead and flatten. Fold the flattened dough in thirds, lightly flour, and reroll. Repeat the folding and rolling four times or until the dough is smooth and not sticky. Flour lightly if necessary.

Decrease the cylinder opening on the pasta machine. Lightly flour—but do not fold—the dough and pass it once through this slot. Continue to decrease the size of the machine's cylinder opening, passing the dough through each gap until you reach the desired thickness; lightly flour if necessary. Set the sheet aside about 10 minutes to dry. Repeat with the remaining dough.

Pass the dough sheet through the appropriately spaced cutting blades for the noodles of your choice, then set the noodles aside to dry.

Tagliatelle al Fumo

Smoked Noodles

*Anna Teresa Callen,
Food Writer and Teacher*

4 to 6 servings

1 recipe fresh pasta

8 ounces smoked mozzarella, diced

8 ounces mozzarella, diced

¾ cup heavy cream

Freshly ground black pepper

Freshly grated Parmesan cheese

To prepare tagliatelle from the thinnest possible pressed pasta sheets, separately pass each dough sheet through the pasta machine's tagliatelle cutters or large blades, then set them aside on linen napkins to dry.

Bring 4 quarts of salted water to a boil in a large pot set over high heat, add the fresh pasta, and cook only until the noodles float to the surface of the water.

Reserve 1 cup of the water in which the pasta was cooked, then empty the remaining contents of the pot into a colander to drain.

Transfer the pasta to a shallow serving bowl, add both mozzarellas and the cream, and season to taste with pepper; toss to mix. (If the pasta is too sticky, add a little of the reserved water.)

Serve immediately accompanied by the Parmesan cheese.

are equipped with up to 16 speeds, but in general, the fewer the speeds, the less confusing and less likelihood of breakage.

Ice-and-Salt–Chilled Ice-Cream Machine

When this narrow aluminum freezer barrel is set into its brine-filled wood bucket, fitted with the dasher, and filled with custard, it churns up to 6 quarts of ice cream or, with different mixtures, sherbets or sorbets within 90 minutes. Its nearly foot-long metal barrel supplies over 210 square inches of freezing surface, and the S-shaped stationary dasher scrapes newly formed ice crystals from the rotating canister walls to mix, aerate, and set the mixture. The 16½-quart wood bucket holds the necessary 24 pounds of ice and salt.

Because of the effort required to prepare, maintain, and drain this electric or similarly styled hand-cranked unit, most opt for a tiny refrigerator unit called a sorbetier or compact manual freezer. But if the sorbetier's high price or the dense consistency of the manual freezer's product deter you, a brine-chilled machine is your only other option. Check to see what it needs to operate; some require the less convenient crushed ice and rock salt instead of ice cubes and table salt. Choose a model with a see-through lid so you can monitor the ice cream's progress.

Compact Manual Ice-Cream Freezer

When this aluminum bucket liner, which has a concentrated salt solu-

Two popular ice-cream makers are the compact manual freezer on the left and the ice-and-salt–chilled machine on the right.

Smoked Salmon with Trout Mousse in Savoy Cabbage with Red Pepper and Maui Onion Confit

Seppi Renggli, Executive Chef while at The Four Seasons

8 appetizer servings

SMOKED SALMON/
TROUT MOUSSE

2 1-*pound trout, filleted and skinned (1 pound flesh)*

Salt to taste

Cayenne to taste

2 *large egg whites*

⅔ *cup heavy cream*

1 2-*pound head savoy cabbage, cored, with the outer leaves removed*

¾ *pound smoked salmon, sliced into 8 3½-inch-square slices*

Freshly ground black pepper to taste

Leaves from 1 bunch fresh dill (approximately ¾ cup leaves)

Red Pepper and Maui Onion Confit (recipe below)

Cut the trout into 1-inch chunks and freeze to firm up the edges. Place in a food processor fitted with a metal blade, sprinkle with salt and cayenne, and process until smooth. With the machine running, add the egg whites and slowly pour in the cream. Empty the mousse into a small bowl and refrigerate as you prepare the cabbage.

Drop the cabbage into a large pot of boiling salted water; once the leaves wilt and blanch, transfer them to a bowl of ice water to halt further cooking. Trim off and discard their thick ribs and pat dry; there should be 8 large green and 8 small yellow leaves.

Arrange the 8 green leaves rib-side down on a work surface and place the yellow ones on top. Season with pepper and lay a slice of salmon on each. Cover with the dill, then with a large spoonful of the trout mousse. Roll the cabbage, tuck in the sides, and steam 5 to 7 minutes.

Arrange on 8 serving plates topped with a heaping tablespoon of Red Pepper and Maui Onion Confit.

RED PEPPER AND
MAUI ONION CONFIT

2 *tablespoons olive oil*

1 *cup coarsely chopped Maui or Vidalia onions*

2 *garlic cloves, finely chopped*

1 *dried hot red pepper, crumbled*

2 *cups ¼-inch-diced sweet red pepper*

¼ *cup red wine vinegar*

2 *tablespoons light brown sugar*

Salt to taste

Heat the oil in a medium saucepan set over medium heat, add the onion and garlic, and sauté until transparent; stir occasionally.

Add the remaining ingredients and bring to a boil; reduce the heat and simmer, uncovered, 30 minutes or until almost all the liquid has evaporated; stir occasionally.

Serve either warm or at room temperature.

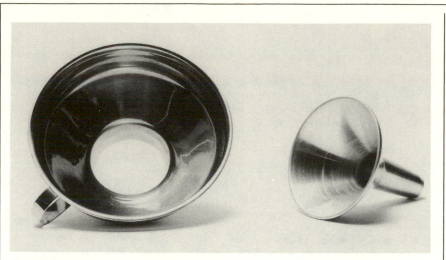

The broad, short-necked canning funnel (see page 102) on the left and the tight, long-necked manual sausage-stuffing funnel on the right are well designed for their particular uses.

and mixes it to further chill, set, and lightly aerate the ice cream.

Compact ice cream freezers, also used to make sorbets, frozen yogurts, and drinks, are manufactured only in plastic with either 1- or 1½-quart capacities, the most efficient of them fitted with narrower canisters. Because there is little churning, there is less "overrun"—air incorporated into the mixture. This creates a dense ice cream that is superb when fresh from the tub but which becomes very hard once frozen.

Manual Sausage-Stuffing Funnel

A meat grinder or multipurpose mixer with a sausage attachment

tion sealed in, is frozen for 8 hours, then set into its thermal jacket, fitted with the dasher assembly, and filled with a prepared custard, it almost effortlessly turns it into a close-textured ice cream. The contained brine frees you from handling ice and salt; the bucket's 5-inch diameter creates substantial contact with the mixture to speed icing, while an occasionally turned dasher scrapes crystallized cream from the sides

---

La Tulipe Marie-Louise

*Sally Darr, Chef–Co-Proprietor:
La Tulipe*

8 servings

VANILLA ICE CREAM

1 *vanilla bean, cut into small pieces*

¾ *cup granulated sugar*

6 *large egg yolks*

2 *cups milk, scalded*

2 *cups heavy cream*

Pulverize the vanilla bean with ½ cup of the sugar in a small electric coffee grinder or a blender; transfer to a small bowl and combine with the remaining sugar.

Beat the egg yolks in the bowl of an electric mixer and gradually add the vanilla sugar; whisk in the scalded milk. Transfer to a medium saucepan set over medium heat and cook to thicken; stir constantly. Pour into a bowl set over ice, let cool, and chill.

Beat the cream until half whipped, fold into the custard, and freeze in an ice-cream maker.

PASTRY CUPS

2¾ *ounces all-purpose flour (about ⅔ cup)*

8 *ounces confectioners' sugar (about 2 cups)*

4 *ounces butter, melted*

1 *cup egg whites (about 8 large)*

1½ *teaspoons vanilla extract*

Preheat the oven to 375°F.

Combine the flour and sugar in a food processor fitted with a steel blade; pour in the butter and blend. With the machine running, pour in the egg whites and vanilla; stop, scrape down the sides, and reblend a few seconds, then strain into a bowl.

Butter several baking sheets. Fill a ⅛-cup measure with batter and pour onto the center of the sheet 5 inches from the end, then repeat at the other end. Tilt and rotate the sheet to form two 6-inch rounds. Bake in the center of the oven 15 minutes, or until golden.

Remove, loosen the edge of one round while hot, peel it off, and immediately press it gently but firmly into a silver coupe or small glass bowl to form a fluted, tulip-shaped

cup. Repeat with the other round. Allow both to stand 1 to 2 minutes, or until they harden; remove and set in a warm, dry spot until ready to use. Use only cool baking sheets, and repeat this procedure to cook as many tulipes as needed.

CHOCOLATE SAUCE

8 *ounces semisweet chocolate*

2 *ounces sweet butter, softened*

3 *tablespoons dark rum*

¼ *cup light cream (or as needed)*

Melt the chocolate in the top part of a double boiler, add the butter, and stir to combine; add the rum and enough cream to thin the sauce to a pouring consistency. Keep warm over hot water.

ASSEMBLY

¼ *cup sliced almonds, toasted (or as needed)*

Set the tulipes in the coupes or bowls used to form them or on individual dessert dishes, fill each with a scoop of vanilla ice cream, and top with almonds. Pour chocolate sauce as desired on top and serve immediately.

can stuff seasoned ground meat into casings, but alternate methods include a cylindrical sausage stuffer that looks and works much like a cookie press, a pastry bag fitted with a plain tube, or this funnel in conjunction with a pestle. Hardly convenient, it is, nevertheless, the only funnel manufactured to hand-stuff sausage. The ½-cup hopper has a 3-inch-wide mouth, and the ¾-inch neck diameter inserts just as neatly into smaller lamb or hog casings as it does into larger beef casings; the neck's 2¼-inch length accommodates up to 10 feet of threaded casing.

A manual sausage-stuffing funnel measures 4 inches in overall length, a bare fraction of the industrial funnels, which, because of their neck sizes, must be hydraulically fed.

Canning Funnel

This low, wide stainless-steel funnel neatly channels salted, spiced, set (properly jelled), or otherwise prepared whole, cut, or puréed fruits or vegetables into containers to be sealed. Its broad 5-inch mouth accommodates liquids and solids; the short, well-bowed body stably rests atop a jar rim while the small neck secures its position.

Canning funnels are usually 4 to 6 inches across the top and are available in plastic or the preferred stainless steel.

Vitello Tonnato with Steamed Vegetables

Lidia Bastianich, Chef–
Co-Proprietor: Felidia

4 to 6 servings

VEAL

2 *pounds lean veal, center cut from the leg*

2 *medium carrots, 1 cut into 2-inch julienned lengths and 1 sliced*

2 *medium celery ribs, 1 cut into 2-inch julienned lengths and 1 sliced*

1 *small onion, cut in half*

1 *tablespoon olive oil*

2 *tablespoons distilled white vinegar*

1 *teaspoon salt*

Use a paring knife to make 2-inch-deep cuts into the meat and insert half the julienned vegetable lengths; tie the meat in cheesecloth.

Bring 2½ quarts of water to boil in a large saucepan. Add the meat, remaining carrots and celery, onion, oil, vinegar, and salt. Bring to a bare simmer and cook, partially covered, 1½ to 2 hours. Remove from the heat and allow the meat to cool in its stock.

SAUCE

1 *6-ounce can tuna packed in olive oil*

3 *anchovies*

1 *tablespoon drained capers*

1 *hard-boiled egg yolk*

2 *tablespoons stock*

½ *teaspoon lemon juice*

1 *tablespoon olive oil*

Salt to taste

Freshly ground black pepper to taste

Boiled carrots, celery, and onion from the cooking water

Combine all the ingredients in a blender and blend until smooth.

To serve: Thinly slice the veal, arrange it in a fanlike manner, spoon sauce over it, and serve with vinaigrette-dressed steamed vegetables (see recipe below).

STEAMED VEGETABLES

2 *cups broccoli spears, florets equally divided and stalks trimmed and peeled*

8 *medium asparagus spears, trimmed, peeled, and cut into 3-inch lengths*

1 *cup green beans, trimmed and julienned*

1 *medium red pepper, stemmed, seeded, deribbed, and julienned*

2 *medium zucchini, seeded and julienned*

1 *medium carrot, julienned*

¼ *cup olive oil*

2 *tablespoons red wine vinegar*

Salt to taste

Freshly ground black pepper to taste

Successively cook the vegetables in a steamer set over a generous amount of boiling water: For al dente broccoli, 7 minutes; asparagus, 6 to 7 minutes; green beans and red pepper, 5 to 7 minutes; and zucchini and carrot, 3 to 6 minutes.

Combine the oil and vinegar in a jar and season to taste with salt and pepper, cover, and shake vigorously to mix, then pour on the cooled vegetables and toss.

4. Stovetop and Ovenware

The variety of efficient outdoor, stovetop, and oven cookware available today is enormous: A sardine grill secures small fish above the fire; a narrow stockpot limits liquid loss; a crepe or gratin pan's low, outwardly angled sides promote quick evaporation and setting; and a pressure cooker's harnessed steam speeds cooking.

Each utensil shape and style is tailor-made to grill, boil, fry, bake, or steam, and while it is not possible to pinpoint when most of these and other cooking methods developed, we can track many improvements in design and variations through classical to contemporary artifacts and illustrations.

Some—save for the materials employed and details applied—have hardly changed since ancient times. The shallow, straight-sided bronze saucepans of Mycenae were just as cleanly profiled as the finest made today. The oval frying pans used in Pompeii may have been deeper and had a slight pouring lip, but they undoubtedly fried fish in much the same manner as do modern ones.

The slight modifications may appear inconsequential, but that is what is so extraordinary, since changes in fuel—from wood to charcoal to gas to electricity—prompted considerable alterations in most pot and pan designs. The iron and bronze caldrons of Homeric, Roman, and medieval times, and the later copper and steel kettles and stockpots of the Edwardian era and the public utility–energized years serve as fine examples. At first round-bottomed, then footed or broad-based to rest atop a trivet, the vessels introduced as much metal as possible to flame to make full use of the available heat. With the advent of a comparably smaller, level stovetop heat source, pot sizes and bottoms in the generally lighter metals followed suit. Body and neck styles also reduced in size to displace weight and further restrict evaporation, and supporting bails gave way to open-ear handles on either side.

Hand in hand with sleeker designs during these periods came a broadening selection based on expanding economies, markets, and trade routes. With regular supplies and more varied foods available, those who could afford them placed less emphasis on the quantities they served in favor of the quality of their preparations, which single-purpose vessels helped to accomplish. Long, oblong vessels to poach large, whole fish began to appear, as did smaller ones for trout and trapezoidal ones for turbot. Tea kettles to heat water or steep and serve the new East Indian teas became more prevalent in Western kitchens, together with coffeepots to decoct, infuse, or percolate Arabian coffees.

On the footsteps of the growing batterie de cuisine came gradual standardization of size as the burgeoning middle class could now refer to recently published works by royal and near royal chefs and, in many instances, hire the same communal smiths and foundries to strike or cast similar vessels to prepare the dishes. These remained individual commissions for decades; greater standardization of capacities and diameters came during the Industrial Revolution.

Metal thickness, or gauge, has always varied, as it still does. Depending on the metal being worked, a different gauge system is used to measure the thickness of the raw stock before it is worked. This measurement may be a fraction of an inch, but it is always given as a whole number to denote, for example, stainless steel's U.S. Standards Gauge or the Brown and Sharp Gauge for aluminum; the lower the number, the thicker the metal and the better the pot. These numbers are rarely used outside the trade, but an informed buyer would recognize that within a specific line of metal pots, the better pot is thicker, heavier, more durable, and more even to heat. (This is not to be confused with, for instance, an $18/10$ or $18/8$ stamped onto many a stainless-steel pot; that number denotes the particular steel's chrome/nickel percent content.)

With product standardization, advancements in the material sciences, and the economics of use, the production of cookware comes of age. Plastic coatings that prevent foods from sticking without the use of oil complement today's desire to eat more healthful foods. Phenolic resins and other plastics molded into cookware for microwave use cater to our desire to speed preparation, and the iron-core cookware that suits the increasingly popular induction cooking process promises great energy savings.

The array makes it clear that no one cookware material suits every method or process, so the following list will help the buyer select the most appropriate material for the task.

Most Common Materials for Cookware

(See also How to Care for Fine Metal, p. 195)

MATERIAL	FREQUENT USES	ADVANTAGES	DISADVANTAGES	CARE
Metals				
Aluminum	Saucepans, sauté pans, fry pans, omelet pans, paella pans, griddles, broilers, stockpots, fish poachers, steamers, couscoussiers, casseroles, pressure cookers, shallow and deep roasting pans, coffeepots, and baking pans	Rapid, uniform heat conduction when the gauge is sufficiently heavy Good corrosion resistance Durable Inexpensive	Reactive with acidic and alkaline foods, which means it can discolor and/or impart a metallic taste, especially with prolonged exposure. Warps easily and heats unevenly when the metal is of a thin gauge.	Wash with soap and hot water; scour with an abrasive when necessary. Remove discoloration by filling the vessel with a solution of 2 teaspoons of cream of tartar to each quart of water and simmering 15 minutes.
Anodized aluminum	Same as for solid aluminum	Anodization, an electrolytic process, produces a hard, dense oxide film that improves aluminum's corrosion resistance.	Same as for solid aluminum	Wash with soap and hot water; avoid scouring.
Brass	Coffeepots (tin-lined) and trivets	Uniform heat conduction Good corrosion resistance Durable Inexpensive	As a copper/zinc alloy, the metal tends to discolor.	Wash with soap and hot water; use a commercial polish as needed.
Copper (unlined)	Sugar boilers, zabaglione bowls, preserving pans, egg-white bowls	Very rapid and uniform heat conduction Good corrosion resistance Durable Unsurpassed at bringing sugar or chocolate to their correct working temperatures	Reacts with the substances in most foods and air to form mildly toxic compounds Low heat retention	Wash with soap and hot water and dry immediately; never scour the interior. Clean unlined pans and the exterior of lined ones with a vinegar and salt solution or use a commercial polish on the latter. Brighten the interior linings with an appropriate polish as needed, then wash before use. Remove the lacquer layer present on some molds with acetone (nail polish remover), then thoroughly wash and dry.
Copper (tin-, nickel-, stainless-steel- or silver-lined)	Saucepans, sauté pans, fry pans, omelet pans, stockpots, fish poachers, crepe pans, gratin pans, chafing dishes, fondue pots, roasting pans, butter melters, and molds	Same as for unlined copper	Implements such as nylon or wood should be used. If tin-lined, do not overheat or the thin layer of tin will blister, wrinkle, and melt. Silver lining blackens on contact with the sulphur compounds in air and some foods. Re-tin, re-nickel, or re-silver when moderate amounts of copper show through. Very expensive	Same as for unlined copper

Material	Properties	Drawbacks	Care
Cast iron	Uniform heat conduction once hot. Retains heat well. Strong. Warp-resistant. Superb for cooking food evenly at high temperatures	Fry pans, chicken fryers, grills, griddles, plett pans, aebelskiver pans, deep fryers, casseroles, cornstick pans, and popover pans	Reactive with acidic foods; discolors and imparts a metallic flavor, especially with prolonged contact. Dense metal is slow to heat and very heavy. As an iron/carbon alloy, the metal is prone to rusting and pitting.	Must season before use to seal the porous surface: Brush all food-contact surfaces with a flavorless oil, add further oil to measure ¼-inch deep in the pan, then heat 1 hour in a 300°F oven. Cool, wipe with a paper towel. Wash with soap and hot water and dry thoroughly; refrain from scouring. Store in a dry place. Brush a thin layer of flavorless oil on the cook surface before each use, then wipe off.
Enameled cast iron	Uniform heat conduction once hot. High heat retention. The borosilicate glass powder (frit) that is fused to the metal prevents corrosion. Very good for long, slow braising or simmering	Saucepans, fry pans, casseroles, gratin pans, and terrines	Cast iron's slow heat absorption precludes quick browning. Nonmetal implements should be used to limit surface scratching. Prone to staining. Brittle coating prone to chipping and cracking	Wash with soap and hot water; avoid scouring. Soak well to remove burned-on food. To remove stains, soak 1 hour in a solution of 1 tablespoon bleach to each quart of water, then wash as directed.
Mild carbon steel (mild steel)	Uniform heat conduction. Durable. Warp-resistant in its usually heavy gauge. Excellent for rapid frying. Suitable for induction cooking	Fry pans, crepe pans, blini pans, paella pans, chestnut pans, deep fryers, and woks	Tends to rust and blacken with age. Reacts with acidic foods	Season before use: Brush the inside of the vessel with a flavorless oil and heat 15 minutes over medium heat. Cool then wipe off the excess oil. Wash with soap and water and dry completely. If scouring is necessary, reseason. Lightly coat with oil and store in plastic. Lacquer finish present on some pans should be removed with acetone, then washed well, dried, and seasoned before use.
Black (or blue) steel	Same as mild carbon steel, but the treatment, a type of annealing, imparts a black (or blue) surface on the untinned steel that makes the metal more corrosion-resistant and more heat absorptive and therefore better able to develop a dark crust on baked goods. Suitable for induction cooking	Brioche pans, tart pans, loaf pans, and baking sheets	Tends to discolor. Reacts with acidic foods	No seasoning required. Wash with soap and water and dry thoroughly; avoid scouring. Some may come with a lacquer coat, so treat as above.

MATERIAL	FREQUENT USES	ADVANTAGES	DISADVANTAGES	CARE
Enameled steel	Saucepans, steamers, roasting pans, and coffeepots	Coating deters metal's reaction with acidic foods. Lightweight. Inexpensive. Suitable for induction cooking	The thin-gauge metal core easily buckles and dents to heat unevenly and eventually chip the finish. Poor for quick, high-heat browning	Wash with soap and hot water; refrain from using abrasives and scouring. Soak well to remove any burned-on food.
Tinned steel	Egg poachers, grills, baking pans, and molds	Uniform heat conduction. Tin coating hinders corrosion. Lightweight. Inexpensive	Tends to discolor. Do not overheat as tin melts at 449°F.	Wash with soap and hot water; avoid scouring and dry thoroughly. Retinning is possible but the expense makes it less practical than buying anew.
Stainless steel	Milk pots, roasting pans, and racks, grills, pot covers, steamer inserts, trivets, bowls, snail plates, and utensils	Nonreactive. Noncorrosive. Durable	Poor heat conduction. Poor heat retention	Wash with soap and hot water; scrub with a nylon pad. Soak off any burned-on food and use a commercial polish when necessary.
Stainless steel with an aluminum disk bottom	Saucepans, sauté pans, stockpots, rondeaus, fry pans, paella pans, pressure cookers, and casseroles	Enjoys the benefits of solid stainless steel with improved heat conductivity. Durable	Can discolor with exposure to high heat. Metal separation of disk from vessel bottom can occur if left empty on a burner	Same as for solid stainless steel
Stainless steel with a copper-cored disk bottom	Same as for stainless steel with aluminum disk bottom	Same as for stainless steel with aluminum disk bottom	Same as for stainless steel with aluminum disk bottom	Same as for solid stainless steel
Cladded stainless steel — Stainless-steel exterior with a layered alloyed-aluminum and aluminum core	Sauté pans, saucepans, fry pans, paella pans, rondeaus, stockpots, chafing dishes, crepe pans, casseroles	Rapid, uniform heat conduction and distribution. Noncorrosive. Strong	Can discolor with exposure to high heat	Same as for solid stainless steel
Stainless steel interior, copper exterior with an alloyed-aluminum and aluminum core	Same as for cladded stainless steel	Same as for cladded stainless steel	Same as for cladded stainless steel	Same as for solid stainless steel

Material	Uses	Benefits	Drawbacks	Care
Stainless steel exterior with a carbon core (or up to 7-ply construction)	Saucepans, sauté pans, fry pans, and casseroles	Same rapid, uniform heat conduction and distribution as the other cladded stainless steels, plus the magnetic core makes it suitable for use on induction cooktops	Same as for cladded stainless steel	Same as for solid stainless steel

Nonstick Surfaces

Material	Uses	Benefits	Drawbacks	Care
Polytetrafluoroethylene (PTFE) (Trade names include Tefal, Teflon, and Silverstone)	Saucepans, fry pans, omelet pans, woks, griddles, casseroles, broiling pans, baking pans, cookie sheets and plaques, and some utensils	Coating does not affect the metal's heat conductivity. High thermal stability. Resists adhesion. Nonreactive. Promises reduced-fat cooking. Easy to clean	Thermoplastic coatings eventually wear off. Implements softer than the coating, i.e., plastic, rubber, or wood, should be used.	As recommended by manufacturers, season before first use: Wash with soap and hot water, rinse and dry. Preheat stovetop pans 30 seconds over low heat then add 1 tablespoon of flavorless oil and rub over its interior surface. Brush the interior of baking pans with oil, then heat 10 minutes in a 350°F oven; wipe clean. Wash with soap and hot water; avoid scouring. Soak well in warm water to remove any burned-on food.
Silicone	Cake pans, springform pans, and tart pans	Same as for PTFE (above)	Same as for PTFE (above)	Same as for PTFE (above)

Ceramics

Material	Uses	Benefits	Drawbacks	Care
Earthenware	Baking stones, baking dishes, soup bowls, mixing bowls, casseroles, and cheese fondue pots	Uniform heat conduction. High heat retention. Nonreactive. Stain-resistant when glazed. Inexpensive. Excellent for slow cooking. Suitable for use in a microwave oven	Unglazed pots must be soaked in water 30 minutes before use. Slow heat absorption. Not flameproof, so must be used in conjunction with a diffuser when placed atop a burner. Unglazed vessels easily stain, absorb and transmit flavors. Fragile: Easily chips and breaks; will crack when subjected to radical temperature changes.	Wash glazed earthenware immediately after use with soap and hot water; soak well to remove burned-on food. Wash unglazed pots by soaking in soap-free water; scrub with either a nylon pad or brush when necessary.
Stoneware as oven-to-tableware	Casseroles, quiche molds, sabots, tureens, and serving platters	Same benefits as earthenware. However, stoneware's high, long firing creates a denser, more durable ceramic. Suitable for use in a microwave oven	Fragile: Will crack at radical temperature changes.	Wash with soap and hot water; soak well to remove burned-on food. Avoid scouring that can scratch the surface.

MATERIAL	FREQUENT USES	ADVANTAGES	DISADVANTAGES	CARE
Porcelain	Double boiler inserts, quiche molds, soufflé dishes, gratin pans, coeur à la crème molds, pots de crème, butter melters, and tea- and coffeepots	Uniform heat conduction Good heat absorption and retention Nonreactive Can briefly sit under a broiler Suitable for use in a microwave oven	Same as for stoneware (page 109)	Same as for stoneware (page 109)
Ceramic/glass: Pyroceram	Double boilers, fry pans, casseroles, baking pans, and gratin dishes	Uniform heat conduction Good heat retention Nonreactive Moderately inexpensive Suitable for use in a microwave oven	Nonporous, crystalline structure can crack at radical temperature changes. Should be used in conjunction with a diffuser when set atop a burner. Not easy to clean	Wash with soap and hot water; scour if necessary.

Glass

MATERIAL	FREQUENT USES	ADVANTAGES	DISADVANTAGES	CARE
Aluminosilicate glass (flameproof glass)	Saucepans, double boilers, and fry pans	Good heat retention Good thermal-shock resistance Nonreactive Suitable for use in a microwave oven	Nonuniform heat conduction Can chip, crack, or break if dropped or if the hot vessel is quickly cooled.	Wash with soap and hot water; soak well to remove any burned-on food; avoid abrasive cleaners that can scratch the surface.
Borosilicate glass (ovenproof glass: trade names include Pyrex and Kimox)	Casseroles, baking pans, pie pans, and measuring cups	Good heat retention Requires 25°F less heat than standard recipe recommendations Nonreactive Inexpensive Suitable for use in a microwave oven	Addition of boric acid makes the glass thrice as heat-shock resistant as regular glass, but it can still crack at radical temperature changes. Should be used in conjunction with a heat diffuser when set atop a burner.	Same as for aluminosilicate glass

Plastics

MATERIAL	FREQUENT USES	ADVANTAGES	DISADVANTAGES	CARE
Phenolic resins	Microwave cookware	Easy to clean Moderately inexpensive Some can withstand low oven heat.	Fair heat resistance Glasslike structure is brittle.	Wash with soap and hot water; scour when necessary.

Size, shape, metal, and weight are all-important in saucepans. Shown from the left are a 2-quart tin-lined-copper slant-sided saucepan; a 1½-quart aluminum-disk-bottomed stainless-steel high-sided saucepan; and a 1½-quart copper-sandwiched-bottom shallow saucepan.

Four special-purpose pans include, from the left, a butter melter, milk pot, bain marie pan (see page 112), and double boiler (page 112).

Slant-sided Saucepan

This flare-sided copper saucepan is the ultimate sauce-reduction pan. Its 6-inch-wide base hastens boiling; splayed sides increase top surface by 25 percent to speed evaporation, while 5 pounds of tin-lined copper supply the fastest, steadiest heat.

Variously called a *sauteuse evasée*, Windsor saucepan, and, mistakenly, *fait tout*, it is manufactured in plain and anodized aluminum, stainless steel with an aluminum-disk base, and the tin-lined copper described above, which is a traditional favorite. Slope-sided saucepans are available in sizes from 1 to 4 quarts; the 2-quart size, which can also be used for sautéing, is the most practical for home use.

The heavier these saucepans are, the more uniform their heat conduction.

Milk Pot

This tall, narrow, spouted vessel is traditionally used in conjunction with a cappuccino maker, whose steam pipe is immersed in it to heat and froth milk for cappuccino, punch, or hot chocolate. When properly half-filled to allow room for the rising liquid, its 1½-cup capacity steams enough for two servings; the narrow, 3-inch diameter ensures even heating and frothing. The 6-ounce pot is durable and easy to clean.

Milk pots are most often available in stainless steel with 1½- or 4-cup capacities.

Butter Melter

This tin-lined copper saucepan quickly heats modest amounts of butter to be clarified for smooth sauces and cleanly flavored sautés. Its 9-ounce capacity holds a cup of butter; the low profile maximizes heat contact to melt, foam, and separate butter rapidly from milk solids, and a lip prevents drips while pouring.

Butter melters, occasionally called

Saucepan

Twice as wide as it is deep, this 1½-quart pan rapidly heats liquids and reduces sauces. Its 6¼-inch diameter creates a generous sauce-to-air ratio for fast evaporation, and the 3¼-inch depth keeps liquids close to the flame.

A low saucepan, or russe, is superb for browning roux and soft-boiling eggs, but sauces are its true métier. They are manufactured in all the standard metals and finishes with the medium-heavy stainless-steel and copper combinations being the most efficient and durable. Capacities range from ¾ to 11 quarts; 1½-, 3-, and 4-quart sizes make a good selection. Whisking will eventually mar the finish of saucepans with coated interiors.

High-sided Saucepan

With its deep, straight sides and narrow profile, this saucepan is perfectly suited to warming or reheating sauces, soups, and stews and blanching small amounts of vegetables and fruits. Its proportionately tall sides, which measure from 25 to 50 percent more than the diameter, restrict air contact and subsequent evaporation while its tight shape and small heating area make the pan ideal for long cooking that doesn't require boiling.

High-sided saucepans are available in aluminum, anodized aluminum, and stainless steel with either an aluminum- or copper-cored bottom; capacities range from ¾ quart to just over 13 quarts.

spouted saucepans, are also used to warm the brandy for hard sauce or café brûlot or the milk for yogurt. They are most often available in nickel-lined copper, anodized aluminum, and the traditional tin-lined copper with 2- to 9-ounce capacities. The copper ones frequently have hammered bottoms; this is purely decorative, as they are often hung when not in use.

Bain Marie Pan

A bain marie is a hot-water bath, generally a low container filled with hot water into which another, food-filled container such as a custard or terrine is set to heat it gently and evenly. This tall, narrow, short-handled pan is usually set in that low container, but it can also be used on top of the stove to warm previously cooked soups and sauces. The tall sides—usually 5 percent taller than the diameter—stand well above their surrounding water to prevent accidental splashes that dilute; the tight diameter, which restricts evaporation and therefore surface skinning, makes it practical to hold heated liquids for extended periods.

Separate pans meant to be set in a bain marie—literally the bath of Mary, to allude to its gentle heating method—are manufactured in heavy-gauge stainless steel, tin-lined copper, or aluminum. Capacities range from 3 cups to nearly 13 quarts.

Double Boiler

This two-part pan—heavy porcelain insert and stainless steel base—is ideal for preparing the silkiest egg-based sauces and pouring custards. The pot simmers 2 inches of water to gently heat the porcelain insert and its contents. That tempered heat so gradually sets egg proteins that they are easily emulsified with butter or oil to produce hollandaise,

Barbecued Squab with Creamy Roast Chili Polenta

Brendan Walsh, Executive Chef while at Arizona 206

6 appetizer servings

SQUAB

3 1-*pound squabs*

Use a boning knife to remove the breastbones, first wing joints, and thigh bones, so that you have boneless squab breasts with the bottom parts of the wing bones attached.

CAROLINA BARBECUE MARINADE

1 *cup cider vinegar*

1 *cup water*

3 *tablespoons Worcestershire sauce*

2 *tablespoons chipotle pepper purée (see below)*

½ *teaspoon cayenne*

1 *teaspoon freshly ground black pepper*

1 *tablespoon kosher salt*

⅓ *cup granulated sugar*

⅓ *cup puréed onion*

10 *garlic cloves, thinly sliced*

Combine all the ingredients in a small, nonreactive saucepan set over high heat and bring to a boil; reduce the heat and simmer 10 minutes. Remove from the heat, cool, and strain. Pour over the squab and set aside 2 hours to marinate; turn once. Remove and pat dry. Reserve the marinade.

To make chipotle pepper purée: Plump ¼ ounce dried chipotle peppers in warm water to cover for 30 minutes. Stem and seed, then purée until smooth in a blender with a little of the steeping liquid.

SQUAB SAUCE

1 *quart chicken stock (see page 210)*

Reserved marinade

Combine the stock and marinade in a medium nonreactive saucepan set over high heat, bring to a boil, and cook until reduced by half, or until syrupy; keep warm for serving.

CREAMY ROAST CHILI POLENTA

3 *cups chicken stock*

½ *cup plus 1 tablespoon cornmeal*

3 *tablespoons masa harina*

5 *tablespoons sweet butter*

⅓ *cup raw corn kernels*

1 *heaping tablespoon each roasted, peeled, seeded, and diced red and poblano peppers*

Kosher salt to taste

Bring the stock to a boil in a medium saucepan set over high heat, then slowly whisk in the cornmeal and masa harina. Reduce the heat and simmer several minutes; stir constantly. Whisk in the butter, corn, and peppers and season to taste with salt; keep warm in a double boiler until ready to serve.

ASSEMBLY

2 *tablespoons olive oil*

Kosher salt to taste

Freshly ground black pepper to taste

6 *fresh tarragon sprigs*

Brush the squabs with olive oil, season to taste with salt and pepper, then grill, breast side down, until crisp and brown. Turn and grill until medium rare; cut in half lengthwise.

For each serving, place ⅓ cup polenta in the center of a 6- to 7-inch plate, top with the grilled squab half, then pour 2 tablespoons of the sauce over the squab. Garnish with a tarragon sprig.

béarnaise, or any of the sauces within their families, including maltaise, mousseline, choron, and paloise.

Double boilers are also manufactured in aluminum and enameled steel without porcelain inserts, both of which should be avoided: The former discolors eggs and the latter chips easily, thereby discoloring and metallically flavoring its contents. A superb stainless-steel version with a very light aluminum bottom is commonly available and not restricted to sauce preparation. A tin-lined copper/porcelain combination is also available but expensive, and an adequate heat-tempered glass one is also made. Sizes range from 3 cups to 2 quarts, which is the most common measurement of both the pot and its insert.

Sugar Boiler

This heavy, unlined copper pot—one of the confectioner's more important tools—quickly concen-trates sugar to any one of its seven stages (see below). Two pounds of heat-responsive metal rapidly conduct and, when removed from flame, swiftly check a syrup at its desired consistency; smooth, straight sides that don't easily hold undissolved grains thwart crystallization, and the spout is well defined for neat pouring.

Sugar boilers, which are always unlined because tin lining would melt at the higher temperatures sometimes required, should be used only

for cooking sugar or chocolate, neither of which react adversely to contact with this bare metal. The pots are manufactured in sizes from just over 3 cups to 4½ quarts; the 5-cup size described above can generally handle the sugar work done at home.

SEVEN STAGES:	°F	USE
Thread	223–234	Fruit pastes, gumdrop-type pectin jellies
Soft ball	234–240	Fudge, certain caramels
Firm ball	244–248	Fondant, marzipan
Hard ball	250–266	Toffee, butterscotch, certain marshmallows
Soft crack	270–290	Soft nougat
Hard crack	300–310	Pulled sugar, spun sugar, nut brittles
Caramel	320–350	Glazes

Poached Lobster with Ginger, Lime, and Sauternes

Gérard Pangaud, Executive Chef while at Aurora

4 servings

POACHED LOBSTER

2 *gallons water*

2 *cups distilled white vinegar*

2 *medium onions, coarsely chopped*

3 *medium celery ribs, coarsely chopped*

1 *medium carrot, coarsely chopped*

3 *garlic cloves, coarsely chopped*

1 *bunch parsley*

10 *whole black peppercorns*

2 *bay leaves*

4 *1½-pound lobsters*

Combine all the ingredients except the lobsters in a stockpot set over high heat and bring to a boil; reduce the heat and simmer 20 minutes. Add the lobsters and cook 4 minutes (based on the suggested 1½-pound weight. If weight differs, adjust cooking time). Remove from the court bouillon and extract the meat from the shells, keeping all the pieces whole. Cut the meat from each tail into six pieces.

GINGER, LIME, AND SAUTERNES SAUCE

3 *ounces fresh ginger, peeled and finely diced*

5 *teaspoons granulated sugar*

1 *cup Sauternes*

2 *ounces fresh ginger, peeled and julienned*

1 *pound cold sweet butter, cut into small pieces*

Zest and juice from 2 limes

Salt to taste

Freshly ground black pepper to taste

Combine the diced ginger with 1 teaspoon of sugar and enough water to cover in a small saucepan set over high heat and bring to a boil; remove from the heat and allow to cool. Repeat this procedure four more times, each time adding another teaspoon of sugar, until the ginger is candied but not caramelized; add more water if necessary.

Combine the Sauternes and the julienned ginger in a small saucepan set over medium-high heat and cook to reduce to a syrup. Lower the heat, then use a whisk to incorporate the butter slowly into the syrup, taking care not to let it boil. When all the butter has been added, whisk in the grated lime zest, then adjust with the lime juice, salt, and pepper.

ASSEMBLY

1½ *pounds fresh spinach, cleaned*

4 *tablespoons sweet butter*

1 *teaspoon granulated sugar*

Salt to taste

Reheat the lobster meat either in the court bouillon or in a steamer set over boiling water.

In the meantime, sauté the spinach in the butter over medium heat; add the sugar and season to taste with salt.

To serve, place an equal amount of spinach in the center of each plate and arrange the hot lobster on top; sprinkle with an equal amount of candied ginger and finish with sauce as desired.

Zabaglione Bowl

This 6-inch-deep solid-copper bowl is perfect for frothing and cooking egg yolks, sugar, and marsala to create zabaglione, as it's known in its native Italy, or sabayon in France. The bowl shape encourages repetitive, rapid-fire dip-scoop-and-sweep whisking as unlined copper reacts chemically to stabilize the aeration and conduct even heat to set it properly.

Zabaglione bowls—which are used either over a double boiler or, more authentically, over a low flame—are available in a 1¾-quart size or the 3½-quart size described above. The better ones are quite hefty and the best—if you're lucky enough to find them in this country—are finished with a rolled, reinforced rim.

Preserving Pan

This unlined copper basin holds and rapidly boils substantial amounts of sugar and fruit for preserves, jams, or jellies so that the important pectin in each has time to develop while flavors remain fresh and colors clear. Its 14-quart capacity, ideally double the amount you should start cooking with, still contains a rising boil. It is twice as wide as it is deep, heightening contact to the heat to most quickly raise the temperature, while 7 pounds of copper evenly maintain it and, when removed from the fire, speedily halt it.

Although excellent for jam-making as well as blanching vegetables, preserving pans should never be used to soak fruits or vegetables in vinegar, as the acid reacts adversely with this unlined metal, much as it does in a sugar boiler. Preserving pans have capacities from 10 to 18 quarts.

Rondeau

This underrated, double-eared pot is one of the most versatile in the professional batterie de cuisine. Its 12½-inch width presents ample surface on which to brown stock bones or a Wellington-bound fillet; that ex-

The batterie de cuisine's few unlined copper pans include, from the left, a preserving pan, sugar boiler (see page 113), and zabaglione bowl.

A pot has two opposite-set, earlike handles while a pan has a single straight one. Clockwise from left are a stockpot, pasta pot (see page 116), and rondeau.

panse, together with 4½-inch sides that encourage steam dispersal for clean searing, can also poach chicken breasts or darnes of salmon. Lidded, it is ideal for browning and braising a pot roast.

Rondeaus are most often manufactured in aluminum, tin-lined copper, or the durable stainless steel with a copper-sandwiched bottom. Diameters range from 8 to 15½ inches, with the medium size described above the most suitable for the home.

Stockpot

"To make a good soup the pot must only simmer, or 'smile,'" says a French proverb. For full flavor and maximum yield, its stock base must "smile" for hours in a deep, somewhat heavy, narrow pot. For home use, an 11-inch height holds considerable bones, meat, vegetables, aromatics, and water; a moderately hefty metal abets even heat dispersal, and an 11-inch width limits evaporation.

Poached Peaches with Zabaglione Cream and Pistachios

Christoper Idone
Glorious Food

8 to 10 servings

ZABAGLIONE CREAM

6 *large egg yolks*

⅔ *cup granulated sugar*

¾ *cup marsala*

Whisk the egg yolks until smooth and lemon-colored in a zabaglione bowl or medium-size bowl. Set the zabaglione bowl over low heat or the medium-size bowl atop a saucepan containing an inch of simmering water. Gradually add the sugar and whisk constantly.

As the mixture becomes thick and puffy, slowly add the marsala and continue to whisk about 20 minutes longer. (If the mixture starts to curdle, remove from the heat and whisk in a little cold heavy cream.) Remove from the heat; cool the mixture over iced water and refrigerate.

POACHED PEACHES

10 *firm, ripe, unblemished peaches*

2 *cups granulated sugar*

Juice from 1 *lemon*

Combine the ingredients in a large nonreactive saucepan, cover with water and a round of fitted waxed paper. Set over medium-high heat, bring to a simmer, and cook until the fruit flesh is easily pierced with a paring knife. Remove from the heat, cool in the liquid, and peel when comfortable enough to handle. Transfer to a bowl, strain the liquid over the fruit, cover, and set aside.

ASSEMBLY

2 *cups heavy cream, whipped to twice its volume*

1 *cup apricot jam warmed with 2 tablespoons water*

¼ *cup shelled pistachios, coarsely chopped*

Add the cream to the zabaglione and fold to incorporate. Pour into a large, deep platter.

Drain the whole peaches on paper towels, arrange on the cream, then spoon some of the apricot mixture on each. Top with a sprinkling of pistachios and serve. This is best prepared no more than a few hours prior to serving because the poached peaches darken with refrigeration.

Stockpots are manufactured in tin- or stainless-steel–lined copper—both beautifully executed, costly, and not necessary for making stock. Choose from more realistically priced, heavy-gauge metals: aluminum, anodized aluminum, aluminum-disk base stainless steel or, ideally, one of the cladded stainless steels. The latter is preferred because of its overall balance and conductivity.

Sizes range from 8 to over 53 quarts; the 18-quart size is the most practical for personal use.

Some of the larger stockpots are fitted with handy spigots to draw off the clear bottom stock. Make sure your pot's handles are comfortably ear-shaped and securely riveted for safety.

Stainless-Steel–Cookware Manufacturers

Professionals prefer heavyweight stainless-steel cookware with either a copper-sandwiched or aluminum-disk bottom because it is easy to clean; quick to distribute high, uniform heat; durable; and, in the long run, economical. The most expertly crafted, well-detailed lines include Sitram's Catering Line, Bourgeat's ¹⁸⁄₁₀ Stainless Steel Cookware, Paderno's Grand Gourmet series, and Lincoln Manufacturing Company's Centurion line. Spring's aluminum-cored Brigade GL series is superb, lighter in weight, and completely clad. The company's equally fine carbon-steel–cored Brigade GLI series suits induction cooking.

Linguine with White Clam Sauce

Elio Guaitolini and Anne Isaak, Proprietors
Giuseppe Lentini, Executive Chef: Elio's

4 servings

1 *pound linguine*

½–¾ *cup olive oil*

6 *garlic cloves, peeled and sliced*

24 *cherrystone clams, shelled, juice strained and reserved, and meat sliced in half*

¼ *teaspoon crushed red pepper flakes (optional)*

2 *tablespoons minced parsley*

Bring 4 quarts of salted water to a boil in a large pot set over high heat. Add the linguine and cook 9 minutes or until tender but al dente.

As the pasta cooks, prepare the sauce: Heat the oil in a medium saucepan set over medium heat, add the garlic, and cook until almost golden; add the clam juice—there should be about 2 cups—and the red pepper, then increase the heat, bring to a boil, and cook until reduced by half. Add the clams, reduce the heat, and cook 1 minute longer.

Drain the pasta, return it to the pot, then add the sauce and parsley and toss to mix. Portion among 4 warm soup bowls.

Pasta Pot

This tall, 8-quart pot with its perforated basket insert cooks, then strains up to 2 pounds of pasta. It holds a generous amount of water to both cook the pasta and accommodate its expansion; its relatively narrow width restricts evaporation.

Pasta pots, also ideal for blanching vegetables, are most often manufactured in stainless steel with an aluminum-sandwiched base; capacities range from 6 to 8 quarts.

Couscoussier

This utensil's two-tiered bulbous pots separately stew and steam the North African semolina-based dish called couscous. The larger, broader-bottomed pot holds copious amounts of lamb, fish, or chicken, and vegetables, maximizes heat contact with the flame, and provides substantial ballast to the smaller top pot. The

Pots designed to suspend food above boiling water or stew to cook it include, from left to right, an asparagus steamer, couscoussier, vegetable steamer, and potato steamer.

footed, perforated bottom of the upper pot vents the underlying stew vapors to flavorfully steam the semolina as its feet keep a tidy work area.

Couscoussiers are traditionally made of earthenware, but in this country they are more apt to be aluminum or stainless steel, the latter with a copper sandwich or aluminum disk bottom. Capacities, measured by the bottom pot, range from 8 to 11½ quarts, and the best—preferably stainless—are moderately heavy with strong, spot-welded handles.

Dilled Chicken and Asparagus Salad

*Paul Neuman and Stacy Bogdonoff,
Chef-Proprietors: Neuman & Bogdonoff*

6 to 8 servings

DILL MAYONNAISE

1 *cup mayonnaise*

2 *tablespoons lemon juice*

1 *tablespoon Dijon-style mustard*

¾ *cup finely chopped dill leaves*

Dash Tabasco

Salt to taste

Freshly ground black pepper to taste

Combine all the ingredients in a medium bowl, stir to mix, and refrigerate until ready to use.

CHICKEN AND VEGETABLES

3½ *pounds chicken breasts*

2 to 2½ *quarts chicken stock (see page 210)*

1¾ *pounds medium asparagus spears*

2 *medium endives, cut in half lengthwise, then cut into ½-inch lengths*

1 *small red onion, diced*

In a large pan set over high heat, cover the chicken with the stock and bring to a bare boil; reduce the heat and poach 30 minutes. Remove from the heat and allow the breasts to cool in their stock, then skin, bone, and cube the meat. (There

should be approximately 2 pounds of meat.) Strain, cool, clear of fat, and store the stock for future use.

Meanwhile, prepare the asparagus: Trim the stalks to uniform length and, if woody, peel the bottom quarter of each. Bring a sauté pan of water to a boil over high heat, add the asparagus, and blanch 45 seconds; remove with tongs to an ice bath. Dry, then cut into 1½-inch lengths.

Combine the chicken and vegetables in a large bowl, add the dill mayonnaise—less than the full recipe if you prefer a dryer salad—and toss to mix.

Chicken Couscous

*Andrée Abramoff, Chef–
Co-Proprietor: Café Crocodile*

6 servings

½ cup olive oil

1 cup coarsely chopped onions

3 garlic cloves, minced

2 3- to 3½-pound chickens, quartered

3 cups water

1 teaspoon cumin

¼ teaspoon ground ginger

¼ teaspoon saffron

1 bunch fresh coriander, coarsely
chopped

Salt to taste

Freshly ground black pepper to
taste

1 pound couscous

½ cup water

1 cup cold water

1 pound carrots, scrubbed and cut
into 2-inch chunks

1 pound zucchini, scrubbed and
cut into 2-inch chunks

1 pound turnips, trimmed,
scrubbed, and cut into 1½-
inch cubes

1 cup cooked chickpeas

4 tablespoons butter

Heat the olive oil in, ideally, the bottom part of a couscoussier or casserole set over medium heat, add the onions and garlic, and sauté about 10 minutes or until tender; stir occasionally. Add the chicken, water, cumin, ginger, saffron, and coriander and season to taste with salt and pepper. Bring to a boil, cover, lower the heat, and simmer 30 minutes.

In the meantime, prepare the couscous: Spread the grains in a large dish or mixing bowl, moisten

them with ½ cup water, and rake with your fingers; if necessary, roll them between your hands to break up any lumps. Place in a couscoussier's steamer section or in a cheesecloth-lined colander and set aside.

Once the chicken has cooked 30 minutes, add the vegetables and chickpeas, return to a boil, then reduce to a simmer and place the steamer or colander over the pot containing the stew. Wrap and tie a wet strip of cheesecloth dipped in flour around the seam between the pot and the steamer or colander, if necessary, so steam can escape only through the couscous. Steam, uncovered, 30 minutes over the simmering stew.

Empty the couscous into a bowl, add the butter, season with salt, and sprinkle 1 cup cold water over the grains; break up any lumps that may form.

Return the couscous to its steamer, reseal the pot's seam with the cheesecloth length, if necessary, and steam another 30 minutes.

To serve, spoon the couscous onto plates, moisten with some of the stew's broth, then top with the chicken and surround with the vegetables and chickpeas. Accompany with a bowl of the remaining broth and a bowl of harissa sauce (see below).

HARISSA SAUCE

1 ounce small, dried red chili
peppers, soaked in hot water
2–3 hours, drained, slit, and
seeded (Use plastic gloves
when handling.)

1 garlic clove

½ teaspoon cumin (or to taste)

Salt to taste

2 to 3 tablespoons olive oil

Grind the chilies to a paste with the other ingredients in a mortar with a pestle.

over an extended area for efficient steaming.

Such vegetable steamers, which are frequently brought to the table, are available only in tin-lined copper with a 2-quart top capacity.

Asparagus Steamer

We are told that when the Romans wanted something done quickly, they would say, "Do it in less time than it takes to cook asparagus." And while cooking asparagus quickly is one thing, doing it correctly can be quite another. This tall, narrow asparagus steamer boils tough stalks as the tender tips steam. The 10-inch height more than accommodates standard-sized peeled lengths, the 5½-inch diameter holds a generous 2 pounds (first tied in bundles), and the wire basket insert simultaneously removes and drains cooked stalks to avoid overhandling.

Manufactured in either aluminum or the preferred stainless steel with a copper-cored or aluminum-disk bottom, the steamers are available in the 3¾-quart size described above or a 5-quart size. They are also used to boil artichokes and corn on the cob, with the most practical fitted with a tight, inset cover to contain steam.

Potato Steamer

Reminiscent of a winner's cup, this bulb-bottomed vessel with a V-shaped top is an efficient potato steamer. Its bulging, 3-cup base increases the water-to-pan heating surface to bring water quickly to a boil; an upright V-shape with a perforated insert plate holds 2 pounds of potatoes and prevents sogginess during steaming by funneling condensation back into the water as the domed lid first collects the drops, then directs them toward the pan's sides.

Also called a *pommes vapeur*, it is most often available in tin-lined copper in a 2¾-quart size.

Vegetable Steamer

This utensil's two stacked vessels, each with its own lid, quickly boils water, then steam-cooks vegetables.

The proportionately tall, narrow, 1½-quart base, really a *fait tout*, limits evaporation to allow prolonged steaming. The bowed top insert with its perforated bottom vents vapors

Steamer Insert

This covered stainless-steel container with its stepped sides transforms a small, medium, or large saucepan into a substantial steamer. Its broad, 4-quart capacity promotes even food distribution for uniform exposure to vapors; the three tiers effortlessly superimpose onto any of three 1½- to 3-quart-sized pans, while the perforated base creates generous steam access.

Single-placement anodized-aluminum steamer inserts are also manufactured to fit pans and pots ranging from 1½ to 8 quarts.

Expandable Steamer Basket

This stainless-steel basket turns any medium to large covered saucepan into a steamer. Its overall perforation permits total vapor access; the three 1-inch-high legs suspend vegetables, fish, or shellfish over water, and 22 overlapping petals that open to 10½ inches wide support 2 ounces or 2 pounds.

Collapsible baskets are manufactured in stainless steel in two sizes, measured by their extended diameters: 8½ inches and the 10½-inch size described above. Look for versatility: Examine the central handle, which should unscrew so such larger flat foods as fish can be steamed.

Bamboo Steamers

When used in conjunction with a wok, these two slat-bottomed, stacked bamboo rounds can steam an entire meal at one time, from dumplings to fish to fowl to meat. The 11-inch width sets neatly above the boiling water in a wok and can easily accommodate a 1½-pound sea bass on a platter, and the 2¼-inch depth can hold custard cups or expanding pearl balls. Slatted bottoms permit steam to circulate up and around each food, while the woven lid allows steam to escape, preventing condensation from dripping onto

An assortment of inserts that turn any number of pots or pans into steamers are, clockwise from the left, stacked bamboo steamers, a bottom-perforated steamer insert, and expandable steamer basket.

food. Two tiers allow quantity cooking.

Bamboo steamers, used as far back as the second century B.C., are most often available with diameters from 4 to 11 inches. Little distinguishes one from another save for an open crossweave or a slatted bottom. Be sure the diameter measures 3 inches less than that of your wok to straddle it properly. Steamers should be soaked 15 minutes, then dried thoroughly before their first use to purge the bamboo scent and its unwelcome flavoring.

Steamed Bass with Black Bean Sauce

Michael Tong, Proprietor: Shun Lee Palace

2 to 3 servings

1 1- to 1½-pound sea bass, scaled, finned, eviscerated, and scored

⅓ cup rice wine

¼ cup black bean sauce (available in Chinese markets)

3 garlic cloves, coarsely chopped

2 tablespoons thinly sliced scallions

2 tablespoons minced fresh ginger

2 teaspoons granulated sugar

¼ cup peanut oil

Sprinkle the fish inside and out with the rice wine, then place on a round or oval platter large enough to hold the fish but one that will fit inside a 10-inch bamboo or metal steamer; set aside.

Bring an inch or two of water to a boil in a wok or alternate vessel, set the steamer containing the fish, covered, on top, and steam 10 to 12 minutes. Pour the accumulated liquid off the platter and empty the water from the wok, if using.

Combine the black bean sauce, garlic, scallions, ginger, and sugar in a small bowl and stir to mix.

Heat the oil until hot in the wok or saucepan set over high heat, add the bean sauce mixture, and heat through; stir constantly to mix. Pour over the fish and serve immediately.

An elongated fish poacher fitted with a rack is essential for poaching a whole fish. A 24-inch-long poacher that can hold a ten-pound fish and straddle two stovetop burners is recommended.

A long, stout, splendid tin-lined-copper trout poacher is traditionally used to cook and serve *truite au bleu*.

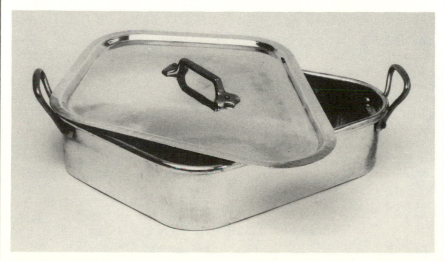

The only vessel in which to poach a whole turbot or halibut is a large, similarly lozenge-shaped turbot poacher.

Fish Poacher

This fish poacher can cook a fish large enough to serve 8 to 10 people. Its 24-inch length straddles two burners for uniform poaching and can accommodate a 10-pound catch. The 7-inch width keeps the fish stationary and intact as the two-handled rack that supports and removes it further protects its flawless shape.

Fish poachers—also called *poissonnières*—are manufactured, in order of preference, in stainless steel, tin-lined copper, anodized aluminum, tinned steel, and aluminum. Popular sizes, measured by length, range from 16 to 40 inches; the 24-inch size is recommended for most home needs.

Trout Poacher

This tin-lined copper kettle is ideal for preparing and presenting truite au bleu, the poached trout dish that aficionados agree is the purest way to savor this fish's flavor. The pan's roughly 14″×5″ dimensions can hold four freshly killed and gutted fish or, with rib cages removed and tails tucked into their mouths, four "enraged" fish; its 4-inch depth accommodates the rack, the vinegar-flecked fish, and court bouillon, while tin-lined copper—one of the finest conductors of heat—provides flair and function.

Frequently called a *truitière*, it is also used to poach small salmon and present steamed baby lobster and crayfish. Fine trout poachers are manufactured as well in aluminum-cored stainless steel and a multiply metal combination that includes copper, aluminum, and stainless steel in sizes from 12″×5″×4″ to 16″×6″×4″.

Turbot Poacher

This lozenge-shaped pan is designed to poach a whole turbot—a firm, white-fleshed, highly prized European flatfish. Its 25-inch length and 6-inch depth easily contain a sizable fish and its milk- or wine-based court

An immersible egg poacher's footed, perforated bowl produces perfectly shaped eggs.

bouillon; the diamond shape matches that of the fish and the inset rack assures intact placement and removal.

Commonly called a *turbotière*, it's more often used on this side of the Atlantic for poaching whole halibut or as a *bain marie* basin. It's manufactured in 20- to 31-inch lengths in aluminum or the preferred tinned steel or tin-lined copper, neither of which will react with the acidic poaching mediums.

Egg Poacher

When brushed with butter, filled with a fresh, raw egg, then immersed in lightly vinegared, simmering water, this small, footed, stainless-steel oval bowl shapes poached eggs for presenting atop toast, hash, or puréed spinach. Its ¼-cup capacity holds medium to jumbo eggs, and the bowl's tight profile and deep back bow center the heavier egg yolk. Four ½-inch-high feet balance the perforated bowl and raise it to permit full hot-water access as the high-set perpendicular wire facilitates removal.

Egg poachers should not be confused with the 1- to 3-shallow-cupped pan inserts that support eggs above simmering water to steam them. True egg poachers are manufactured in tinned or the sturdier stainless steel, either singly or in stands containing up to eight hollows. The latter is totally impractical because its introduction into a pan of properly heated water too radically reduces the correct cooking temperature.

Sauté Pan

Wide, with short, straight sides and a relatively high handle, this pan is designed to lightly and quickly fry food in a limited amount of hot fat.

Crayfish, Zucchini, and Tomato Salad

Jean-Georges Vongerichten, Executive Chef: Restaurant Lafayette

4 servings

CRAYFISH SALAD

48 *crayfish (about 4¾ pounds)*

2 *medium zucchini*

4 *medium tomatoes*

¼ *cup olive oil*

1 *medium onion, finely chopped*

2 *garlic cloves, finely chopped*

½ *bunch fresh thyme, tied together*

Salt to taste

Freshly ground black pepper to taste

½ *cup basil vinaigrette (see below)*

4 *fresh basil sprigs*

Steam the crayfish for 5 minutes, cool, then separate the tails from the bodies and the meat from all but four crayfish, reserving them for garnish; set aside.

Slice the zucchini like coins and blanch 1 minute in boiling water; immediately plunge into a bowl of ice water to halt further cooking, then drain.

Blanch the tomatoes 10 seconds in boiling water, then plunge into a bowl of ice water to halt further cooking. Peel, seed, and chop finely.

Heat the olive oil in a sauté pan set over medium-low heat, add the chopped onion and garlic, and cook 12 minutes or until transparent; stir occasionally. Add the tomatoes and the whole thyme branches and cook 15 minutes. Discard the thyme and set the mixture aside to cool.

In three separate bowls season the zucchini, crayfish tails, and tomatoes with salt, pepper, and basil vinaigrette.

For each serving, overlap an equal amount of zucchini slices to form a large ring on each plate; arrange 11 crayfish tails in the center of each, then spoon the tomato mixture around the outside of the zucchini; garnish with the reserved whole crayfish tail and a sprig of basil.

BASIL VINAIGRETTE

½ *cup olive oil*

Juice of ¼ lemon

1½ *teaspoons sherry vinegar*

6 *large fresh basil leaves*

Salt to taste

Freshly ground black pepper to taste

1 *tablespoon boiling water*

Combine all the ingredients except the water in a food processor or blender. Blend 1 minute, then add the boiling water while the machine is running to emulsify.

Its 11-inch width supplies sufficient surface for a quartered chicken or duck; the 3-inch depth readily confines constantly flipped and shaken foods so every angle is exposed to the heat, while the handle's 35-degree set balances those maneuvers.

Sauté pans are manufactured in all the standard utensil metals, metal combinations, and finishes, with diameters from 6¼ to 14¼ inches and 1- to 10-quart capacities. An 11- or 12-inch size best suits the home, preferably in stainless steel with a copper-cored bottom. The finest is moderately heavy with a well-riveted handle.

To cook food rapidly, a good sauté pan, such as the one shown, is roughly four times as wide as it is deep.

Pans made to quickly fry foods in limited amounts of fat are, clockwise from right, a fry pan (or skillet), oval fry pan, omelet pan (see page 124), and paella pan (page 124).

Fry Pan (Skillet)

Broad, with outwardly sloped, 2-inch-deep sides, this fry pan rapidly cooks generally thin foods in just enough butter, lard, or oil to prevent sticking. Its 11½-inch diameter creates a generous food-to-heat contact surface for clean scrambling, setting, or searing as sloped sides disperse steam to further dry frying.

This pan is manufactured in all the standard utensil metals, combinations, and finishes, but the durable and well-balanced stainless-steel combinations that include copper or aluminum are preferred. They range in diameter from 6 to 14 inches, with a 10- to 12-inch size the most prac-tical for home use. Select a moderately heavy skillet, which resists warping and the attendant hot spots that mar uniform cooking.

Oval Fry Pan

This heavy oval black steel pan, also called a fish fry pan, is the only one a chef reaches for when he wants to fry a fish fillet properly. Its nearly 13-inch length accommodates a full sole, flounder, or perch fillet for uniform cooking; roughly 5 pounds of steel rapidly absorb and conduct high searing heat, while low, outwardly angled sides disperse steam to guarantee a crisp surface.

Farfalle Pasta with Peppar Vodka

Seppi Renggli, Executive Chef while at The Four Seasons

1 serving

¼ cup heavy cream

8 ⅛-inch-thick zucchini slices

1 cup cooked farfalle pasta

1 tablespoon Peppar vodka

Salt to taste

4 wild asparagus spears, trimmed and blanched 30 seconds

2 tablespoons spicy tomato con-casse (see Note below)

4 ½-inch cubes bufala mozza-rella

4 fresh basil leaves

1 tablespoon grated gruyère cheese

Pour the cream into a 6-inch non-stick-surfaced skillet, add the zucchini, pasta, vodka, and salt, and bring to a very slow simmer. Add the remaining ingredients—but do not stir—and cook until the mozzarella melts enough to hold the pasta together. Slide onto a hot plate and serve.

NOTE: To prepare ¾ cup spicy concasse, blanch, peel, seed, and coarsely chop 1 medium tomato, then toss it with a few drops of Tabasco.

This pan's dimensions make it suitable to pan-fry shell steak. Oval fry pans are also manufactured in tin-lined copper and a nonstick-surfaced aluminum in addition to the recommended black steel, which must be seasoned before use. Sizes range from 10¼″ × 7″ to 17¼″ × 10½″, with the 12½″ × 8¾″ the most appropriate for home use.

Simmered Turkey

Jeff Smith
The Frugal Gourmet

1 10-pound turkey, neck and giblets reserved for gravy

Salt, if desired

Freshly ground black pepper, if desired

Place the turkey in a 20-quart stockpot, add enough cold water to cover, then remove the turkey from the pot. Bring the water to a boil over high heat.

Meanwhile, prepare the turkey for simmering by removing its wings and legs and setting them aside.

Once the water comes to a boil, place the body of the bird in the pot and return to a boil. Reduce the heat, cover, and simmer lightly 45 minutes. Add the wings and legs to the pot, re-cover, and simmer an additional 45 minutes. Turn off the heat, but keep the turkey covered and allow it to stand in its cooking liquid 2 hours.

Remove the meat from the bone (season to taste, if desired, with salt and pepper) and serve with a light gravy made by cooking the chopped giblets in some of the stock about an hour before the bird is to be served. Season to taste with salt and pepper, perhaps adding a little sage or thyme. Thicken with roux and serve.

The remaining stock can be saved for later use.

Coniglio in Padella
Stewed Rabbit with White Wine

Marcella Hazan
The Classic Italian Cookbook

6 servings

3 to 3½ pounds frozen cut-up rabbit, thawed overnight in the refrigerator, or fresh rabbit (see Note below)

½ cup olive oil

¼ cup finely diced celery

1 garlic clove, peeled

⅔ cup dry white wine

1½ teaspoons dried rosemary

2 teaspoons salt

Freshly ground black pepper (6 to 8 twists of the mill)

1 bouillon cube

2 tablespoons tomato paste

¼ teaspoon granulated sugar

⅔ cup warm water

Rinse the rabbit pieces in cold running water and pat thoroughly dry with paper towels.

Combine the rabbit with the oil, celery, and garlic in a large sauté pan set over low heat and cook, covered, 2 hours; turn the meat once or twice.

After 2 hours, uncover the pan, increase the heat to medium, and cook until all the liquid has evaporated; turn the meat from time to time. When the liquid has evaporated, add the wine, rosemary, salt, and pepper and simmer, uncovered, until the wine has evaporated.

Dissolve the bouillon cube, tomato paste, and sugar in ⅔ cup warm water, pour it over the rabbit, and cook gently 12 to 15 minutes; turn and baste the rabbit 2 to 3 times. Serve immediately or reheat gently before serving.

If prepared ahead of time, add 2 to 3 tablespoons water and reheat slowly, covered, over low heat, turning the meat from time to time.

NOTE: Do not use wild rabbit in this recipe, only rabbit raised for food. If using fresh rabbit, soak in abundant cold water 12 or more hours, then rinse in several changes of cold water and thoroughly pat dry. It may be refrigerated while soaking.

Tortilla Española

Felipe Rojas-Lombardi, Executive Chef: The Ballroom

6 to 8 servings

½ cup plus 1 tablespoon olive oil

3½ pounds all-purpose potatoes, peeled, quartered, and thinly sliced

1 tablespoon coarse salt

1 large onion, thinly sliced

8 large eggs

Heat ½ cup olive oil in a large fry pan set over medium-high heat, add the potatoes, and sauté, covered, 12 minutes or until semicooked; stir occasionally. Add the salt and onions, stir to mix, cover, and continue to cook until the onions are wilted and the potatoes are tender but not collapsing. Empty into a large bowl and set aside to cool.

Beat the eggs in a separate bowl, then add to the cooled vegetables and stir to mix.

Heat the remaining tablespoon of oil almost to the smoking point in a 10½-inch fry or omelet pan set over high heat. Rotate the pan to coat the sides with the oil, then add the potato-egg mixture and continue to cook over high heat 1 to 2 minutes to partially set the tortilla. Reduce the heat to low and cook 15 minutes, or until the tortilla is set enough to turn.

Cover the pan with a large plate, gently flip the tortilla onto it, then slide it back into the pan and cook the other side an additional 18 minutes, or until the top feels firm when pressed with your finger.

Cover with a serving platter, invert both plate and pan to release the tortilla, and serve either hot or at room temperature.

Beggars' Purses

Barry Wine, Chef-Proprietor: The Quilted Giraffe

24 beggars' purses or
6 servings

CREPES

2½ *ounces pastry flour*

¼ *teaspoon salt*

2 *large eggs*

¾ *cup milk*

1 *tablespoon warm clarified butter*

Combine the flour and salt in a medium bowl, make a well in the center, and break the eggs into it. Gradually add the milk and whisk to mix; pass through a fine sieve, then set aside at least 30 minutes. Stir in the butter just before using.

Heat a lightly buttered small crepe pan over medium to medium-high heat, pour in 3 tablespoons of batter, and spread quickly by rotating the pan; pour off any excess batter, then cook 1 minute or until the crepe slides easily once the pan is shaken. Flip the crepe over and cook 10 seconds longer; rebutter when necessary.

Transfer to a warm dish, stack the crepes one atop the other, and wrap tightly in plastic wrap to prevent them from drying out.

ASSEMBLY

10 *ounces Beluga caviar*

½ *cup crème fraîche (see page 123)*

24 10-*inch-long chives, blanched 10 seconds*

Lay out the crepes on parchment paper and center each with a small mound of caviar, then top it with a teaspoon of crème fraîche. Pull the crepe up around its filling, wrap a chive around the crepe's resultant "neck," and knot it; cut off the excess chive. The bunched crepe purse should have pleats that resemble a ruffle.

Serve while the crepe is at room temperature and the caviar is still chilled.

Crème Fraîche

2¼ cups

2 *cups heavy cream*

¼ *cup buttermilk (active culture)*

Combine the cream and buttermilk in a large glass jar, stir to mix, and place in a warm area 10 hours. Stir to mix, cover, and refrigerate overnight to thicken before using.

Omelet

Rudolph Stanish, Caterer

1 serving

2 *tablespoons water (or beer)*

¼ *teaspoon salt (or to taste)*

Scant ¼ *teaspoon Tabasco*

3 *large eggs at room temperature*

1 to 2 *tablespoons butter*

Combine the water, salt, and Tabasco in a cup and beat to mix.

Break the eggs into a medium bowl and beat lightly until mixed but not frothy. Add the water mixture and beat just to mix.

Heat the omelet pan over medium heat, add the butter, and allow it to foam, then subside. Rotate the pan to grease its sides and bottom. Add the eggs, then with the tines of a fork set flat against the bottom of the pan, stir rapidly in circular motions to fluff the omelet; simultaneously slide the pan back and forth across the burner. Tilt the pan slightly to spread the mixture uniformly over the bottom of the pan and allow to cook briefly until the omelet barely sets and looks glossy.

Change to a palm-up, thumb-toward-the-handle-end grip, then gradually tilt the pan forward as you roll the omelet with a fork toward the far side of the pan and out onto a warm plate.

Sautéed Foie Gras with Apples

Antoine Bouterin, Executive Chef: Le Périgord

1 serving

2 to 3 *tablespoons peanut oil*

2 ½-*inch-thick slices foie gras*

Salt to taste

Freshly ground white pepper to taste

1 ½-*inch-thick slice Rome Beauty apple, cored*

1 2-*inch-wide Rome Beauty apple wedge for garnish*

1 *teaspoon drained capers*

1 *tablespoon port*

¼ *cup duck stock (see page 210)*

3 *sprigs parsley for garnish*

In a small fry pan set over high heat, pour 1 to 2 tablespoons oil and heat until very hot. Season the foie gras with salt and pepper, then add it to the pan and sauté about 30 seconds on each side; set aside to drain on paper towels.

Add the remaining oil, if need be; heat, then add the cored apple slice and cook about 1 minute on each side; reduce the heat and allow to cook 3 additional minutes as you prepare the garnish. Turn once.

Slice the apple wedge into 3 graduated, form-fitting wedges that mirror the initial shape; fit together to form a "stepped" body and set this on the serving plate.

Remove the apple slice to drain on the paper towels.

Add the capers, port, and stock to the fry pan, return to high heat, and reduce to half; season with pepper.

Set the apple slice on the serving plate, top with the foie gras, spoon the sauce over all, add a parsley side garnish, and serve.

Omelet Pan

No other single-service pan has evolved with more design modifications and improvements than this slope-sided, 2-inch-deep omelet pan, which epitomizes the perfect form. Its 10-inch diameter thinly spreads a standard 3-egg mixture for rapid setting, while 4 pounds of aluminum assure even heat distribution and a permanently perfect shape for spirited stovetop maneuvers.

Omelet pans, once seasoned and used solely for omelets, should never be washed, but simply wiped clean, salted, and stored to help the nonstick coating develop. Slightly lighter pans with commercial nonstick coatings are frequently available, as are anodized aluminum ones, but the recommended pan's heft translates into more accurate heat absorption and transfer.

Make sure your omelet pan has an upwardly angled, relatively flat handle; you'll need it to grip the pan securely so it won't twist in your hand.

Paella Pan

This 2½-inch-deep, two-handled pan furnishes a superb surface on which to cook the Spanish national dish, a rustic, saffron-scented paella. Its 14-inch width can sauté the customary pork, chicken, rice, and shrimp, as outwardly flared sides promote evaporation to hasten cooking.

Traditionally made of earthenware, as are the vessels for most provincial dishes, paella pans are also available in elegant and updated versions: tin-lined copper, aluminum, black steel, or the most durable and easiest to care for, cladded, or aluminum disk-bottomed stainless steel. Diameters range from 14 to 20 inches, with the 14-inch size the most popular.

When investing in a pan meant for a specific purpose, don't restrict its use; consider its possibilities, then enjoy it further. This pan can serve as a substantial secondary gratin pan or, given the recommended stain-less-aluminum combination's rapid heat conduction capability, as a secondary fry pan.

Blini Pan

As crepes are to Mardi Gras in Lyon and Liège, blini are to Maslenitsa in Moscow and Minsk: Both these special pancakes star in traditional pre-Lent festivals. The pan suited to a blini's singular batter is 4¾ inches wide to confine a rich, yeast-leavened batter into small rounds; heavy to conduct high heat uniformly; and armed with an offset handle to displace weight evenly and distance hands from heat. Its outwardly curved inch-high sides ensure a clean set and proper rise.

Blini pans are available only in black steel.

Crepe Pan

Except for a shorter handle, this crepe pan's design has remained virtually intact since the early seventeenth century when the Old Master Adriaen Brouwer depicted one in his famous "The Pancake Man." Little wonder, since the design is essential to producing these light-as-a-feather French pancakes. A smooth bottom allows the batter to spread evenly; a near 7-inch diameter shapes

Paella

José Barcena, Chef-Proprietor: Harlequin

8 servings

1 *quart chicken stock (see page 210)*
½ *teaspoon saffron*
½ *cup olive oil*
8 *ounces boneless chicken, cubed*
8 *ounces boneless veal, cubed*
8 *ounces boneless lean pork, cubed*
4 *ounces chorizos, sliced ¼-inch thick*
1 *large onion, coarsely chopped*
4 *garlic cloves, coarsely chopped*
1 *medium green pepper, stemmed, seeded, deribbed, and diced*
1 *cup julienned pimentos*
2 *cups drained canned whole tomatoes, coarsely chopped*
2 *cups short-grain rice*
¼ *teaspoon paprika*
1 *pound large shrimp, peeled and deveined*
4 *small lobster tails, split in half lengthwise*
4 *ounces sea scallops*
1 *cup green peas*
8 *littleneck clams, scrubbed*
8 *mussels, debearded and scrubbed*
Salt to taste
Freshly ground black pepper to taste

Combine the chicken stock and saffron in a small saucepan set over medium heat, bring to a bare simmer, and cover; set aside.

Heat the oil in a paella pan set over medium heat, add the chicken and veal, and sauté 10 minutes or until golden; stir frequently. Transfer to a platter. Add the pork and chorizos to the pan and cook 15 minutes. Add the onion, garlic, green pepper, pimentos, and tomatoes and cook 8 minutes or until the onion wilts and the liquid reduces somewhat; stir occasionally. Add the rice, saffron-infused stock, and paprika and bring to a boil; stir occasionally. Lower the heat and add the chicken and veal together with the shrimp, lobster, scallops, and peas and stir to mix. Sink the hinged side of each clam and mussel into the rice, season to taste with salt and pepper and cook 25 minutes or until the rice is almost tender. (If the rice becomes too dry, add another ¼ to ½ cup stock.)

Either serve immediately or optionally bake 10 minutes at 300°F. Serve directly from the pan.

Pans to swiftly cook special batters are, clockwise from top right, a crepe pan, blini pan, aebleskiver pan, and plättar pan.

a scant ¼ cup of batter; short, flared sides increase the crepe's surface-to-air contact to hasten evaporation and reduce cooking time, and a heavy-gauge steel ensures uniform heat distribution. The shorter handle developed when cookery moved from the hearth to the range, yet its flat shape remains the same for a secure grip to tilt and rotate while spreading batter.

Small crepe pans have 6½-inch diameters and are used expressly for dessert crepes, while the larger ones, with 7¼-, 8¾-, and 9½-inch diameters, are used to prepare entrée crepes. The most durable crepe-cooking pans (as distinguished from the crepe suzette finishing–tableside presentation pans) are manufactured in black steel, which is slightly lighter than cast iron.

Plättar or Plett Pan

This griddle's seven medal-sized indentations shape, set, and bake plättar, those egg-leavened pancakes that, when served with lingonberries, create what some call the Swedish national dish. Each 2½-inch-wide recess neatly accommodates a tablespoon of batter; its outwardly angled sides further evaporation to set the batter cleanly, and 4 pounds of cast iron retain and transfer a medium-high heat while acting as a sure anchor.

Plättar, or plett, pans, also used to make small blini, are most often available in cast iron with 9½-inch diameters.

Aebleskiver Pan

When heated, brushed with butter, and partially filled with batter, this cast-iron pan's seven small, bowl-like depressions create the spherical apple dumplings called aebleskivers that are a Danish specialty. The 3-tablespoon capacity of each pocket assures rapid baking; the hemispherical shape uniformly directs heat to each center for even cooking, while 6 pounds of cast iron easily maintain and conduct a level heat.

The deeply dimpled surface of an aebleskiver pan mirrors that of a cake pan used in ancient Greece. That one was rectangular whereas the aebleskiver pan is round, with a diameter of 7½ or 9¼ inches. The best—those with a wraparound skirt that evenly supports the pan—are manufactured in cast iron. Moderately lightweight aluminum and nonstick-coated aluminum pans are also available.

Chicken Fryer

This heavy cast-iron pan is ideally shaped and weighted to shallow-fry chicken in hot fat. Its 3-inch depth easily holds the generous oil layer that creates even heat contact; the nearly 8-inch base furnishes enough surface on which to brown a split bird, as outwardly sloped sides encourage steam dispersal to promote crisp frying. Six pounds of cast iron convey a steady heat.

Chicken fryers are most often manufactured in cast iron and furnished with either a similarly composed or heat-tempered–glass cover to broaden their use into casserole cooking for all but acidic foods, which react with this metal.

Chicken fryers are measured by their top diameters, generally 10¼ inches, and although not a necessary feature, the most practical have two small spouts on opposite sides from which to pour off fat.

Chestnut Pan

It may look like a frying pan with a perforated bottom, but this broad, shallow pan is a peerless chestnut roaster. Its 10-inch diameter toasts 1½ pounds of cross-cut nuts over a low, 40-minute fire; its large perforations permit sufficient flame-flavoring contact, and its 1¼-pound weight facilitates maneuvering.

Chestnut pans are manufactured only in black steel with diameters that measure 10 inches.

Stovetop Grill

This cast-iron block is flawless at indoor grilling. Even at the necessarily high temperatures, its 15-pound weight can't bend or buckle. The high-set corrugated surface that spot-sears the meat also distances it from rendering fat as the 6-degree tilt chutes grease to a base furrow for clean draining.

Such level stovetop grills as a modestly notched aluminum and an anodized aluminum model that flips to become a griddle are also avail-

The perforated bottom of the chestnut pan at left lets smoke and flames flavor the roasting nuts; the deep chicken fryer at right holds sufficient oil to cook chicken parts uniformly.

Both the stovetop grill on the left and the griddle on the right are cast in iron so they won't buckle at high heat.

able; these measure 11½ inches square up to 20″ × 11″. The preferred canted version measures 17″ × 13″.

Make sure a grill's ridging is well raised and, if tilted, that it drains tidily. A number have removable handles, some strangely anchored at the base gulley where the perforated linkup spots sloppily siphon the rendered fat off onto the stove.

Griddle

Once heated to a high temperature, this flange-rimmed cast-iron disk evenly cooks such short-order foods as bacon, eggs, pancakes, and minute steaks. The 10-inch diameter, which completely covers a single burner, guarantees an unwavering heat; its 5-pound weight resists warping and conducts heat evenly while a shallow flange permits the spatula full, fast access.

Griddles are also manufactured in heavy aluminum with 9- or 10-inch diameters and as oblongs that sit on two burners in 20″ × 9″ to 20″ × 11″.

Wok

The wok was developed as a versatile, brazier-heated cooking vessel, but remains equally effective on today's gas and electric ranges. Its round base and curved sides diffuse heat, extend the cooking surface, and facilitate tossing and stirring; a 4⅛-inch depth accommodates a whole duck or fish for smoking or simmering as well as copious amounts of oil or sauce for deep-frying, poaching, or braising, while a 14-inch diameter provides abundant contact with the hot metal for rapid cooking.

Woks—whose diameters range from 12 to 30 inches—are most often available in stainless steel, aluminum, anodized aluminum, nonstick-coated aluminum, or the heavier carbon steel, which most closely resembles the traditional cast-iron wok's stability and gradient-heat dispersal.

A 14-inch round-bottomed wok with heat-retardant wooden handles

A round-bottomed carbon-steel wok with a 14-inch diameter suits home use. It should be used in conjunction with a burner ring to stabilize it as shown.

A 4-quart black steel deep fryer with a basket insert that can hold a quartered chicken or a few fish fillets suffices most needs.

is most practical for home use. These handles can be either double-eared or single handled–single eared to mirror the southern or northern Chinese provincial styles. It's a good idea also to buy its separately sold domed lid and stabilizing vented reversible ring. This type of wok should be seasoned before use.

Deep Fryer

This black steel pan with its basket insert supplies ready access to enough hot fat to fry, then neatly drain foods. With the pan cautiously half-filled with fat to allow for its bubbling rise, the 4¼-inch-deep basket totally immerses the food; the 9-inch width provides sufficient surface for free floating, while splayed sides give easy access. The wire basket insert simultaneously retrieves and drains crisply done goods.

For accuracy's sake, stovetop deep fryers should be used in conjunction with a deep-fat thermometer. They are often available in stainless steel or aluminum in addition to this black steel workhorse, the larger of which are preferred by chefs. A lower, wider, bow-sided version with two handles is also manufactured in aluminum or black steel, which can have a 2- to 24-quart capacity. For deep frying at home, a 4-quart size is fine.

Smothered Chicken

Craig Claiborne
Craig Claiborne's Southern
Cooking

4 servings

1 3½-pound chicken, split down
   the backbone with the breast
   left intact

Salt to taste

Freshly ground black pepper to
   taste

2 tablespoons butter

2 tablespoons all-purpose flour

1½ cups chicken stock (See page
   210)

Season the chicken with salt and pepper to taste and secure the wings by folding them under the breast; set aside.

In a black iron skillet large enough to hold the chicken comfortably, melt the butter over low to medium-low heat. Add the chicken, skin-side down, then cover with a plate large enough to fit inside the skillet and weight with approximately 5 pounds; cook about 25 minutes, or until nicely browned. Turn the chicken, re-cover, reweight, and continue to cook 15 minutes.

Remove the chicken and discard all but 2 tablespoons of fat from the skillet. Add the flour, whisk to mix, then add the chicken stock and continue to whisk until thick and smooth. Return the chicken to the skillet, skin-side up. Re-cover, reweight, and continue to cook 30 minutes. Cut the chicken into serving pieces, adjust the sauce seasonings, then serve with fluffy rice.

Kung Pao Shrimp

Spicy Stir-Fried Shrimp

Michael Tong, Proprietor:
Shun Lee Palace

4 servings

14 *to* 16 *large shrimp (approximately 1½ pounds)*

1 *tablespoon cornstarch*

4 *garlic cloves, finely chopped*

2 *tablespoons thinly sliced scallions, white part only*

1½ *tablespoons finely chopped ginger*

¼ *cup rice-wine vinegar*

2 *tablespoons light soy sauce*

5 *teaspoons granulated sugar*

1 *teaspoon Szechuan hot bean paste*

Pinch salt

¼ *teaspoon monosodium glutamate (optional)*

3 *cups peanut oil*

2 *teaspoons cornstarch mixed with 1 tablespoon water*

Shell, devein, rinse, and pat dry the shrimp; lightly dust with 1 tablespoon cornstarch, then set aside.

Combine the garlic, scallions, and ginger in a small bowl, toss to mix, and set aside.

Combine the vinegar, soy sauce, sugar, hot bean paste, salt, and, if desired, the monosodium glutamate in another bowl, stir to mix, and set aside.

Heat the oil in a wok set over high heat, then add the shrimp and cook about 1½ minutes; stir constantly. Transfer to a sieve-lined bowl; drain and discard all but 1½ tablespoons of the cooking oil.

Return the reserved oil to the wok and, when hot, add the garlic mixture and cook 10 seconds; stir constantly. Add the vinegar sauce and bring to a boil, then add the cornstarch paste and cook until thickened; stir constantly. Return the shrimp to the wok to both heat through and coat with the sauce. Serve immediately.

A pressure cooker so effectively locks in food and liquid that when heated it harnesses the liquid's higher boiling temperature to cut cooking time by up to one-third.

Pressure Cooker

This tightly sealed pot effectively creates a pressurized environment so that any liquid may be brought to a higher temperature than possible in an open vessel in order to cook food faster. Well-spaced flanges on lid and body rims, together with a gasket to accommodate pressure and temperature distortions, assure sealing; 7 pounds of aluminum-bottomed stainless steel uniformly conduct stovetop heat while the cylindrical shape promises even radial expansion and contraction. Two valves further alleviate danger: One controls the amount of internal pressure by venting excessive steam and the other prevents the vessel from opening should there still be pressure inside.

Pressure cookers (some of which are fitted with pressure valves that are preset to contain 5-, 10-, or 15-pound pressures) are most often available in aluminum or the preferred nonreactive stainless steel with an aluminum- or copper-cored bottom, with capacities from 3 to 17 quarts. The larger ones can also be used for canning, but for a family of four, a 6-quart size is best since the vessel can be only partially filled.

Copperware Manufacturers

The name Villedieu stamped onto the side of many a heavyweight copper pot or pan proudly indicates its origin: a small French village in the southern Norman countryside that, after nearly six centuries, remains one of Europe's preeminent copperware production centers. Flatware, bells for carillons, or boilers for ocean liners are the specialties of such manufacturers as Eugène Havard, Maurice Lefèvre, and Lucien Lecellier. La Maison Armand Mauviel, meanwhile, is the primary producer of heavy-duty tin-, silver-, or stainless-steel–lined copper cookware.

A roasting pan should be medium heavy in weight so it won't warp when exposed to high temperatures. Shown are a shallow roasting pan on top and a covered deep roasting pan (see page 130) below it.

Indoor Hot Smoker

This portable stainless-steel smoke-box gives the urban or otherwise restricted cook a convenient means to impart a smoke flavor to small amounts of fresh meat, poultry, game, seafood, or vegetables. Its 15″ × 11″ × 3″ covered housing sits atop a single burner; the base heats modest amounts of wood shavings, whose fumes waft up and around a drip-pan insert to circulate over the food resting on an inset rack. The sliding cover confines most of the smoke chemicals that flavor food.

One hesitates to compare the product produced in 2 hours by this unit to that smoked for 4 hours to 4 days, but if you like delicately smoked foods, this apparatus does the trick. Smoking should be done in a well-ventilated area.

Shallow Roasting Pan

This pan exposes as much racked meat or poultry as possible to an oven's dry heat for proper roasting.

Its 16″ × 13″ size, which easily accommodates 10- and 12-pound roasts, still allows (in most ovens) a 2-inch wraparound space for even heat circulation, while its 2-inch-deep sides promote heat convection and uniform cooking.

Shallow roasting pans are manufactured in stainless steel, tin-lined copper, aluminum, anodized aluminum, coated aluminum, blue steel, and enameled steel with dimensions from 13″ × 9½″ to 28″ × 22″. The 16″ × 13″ pan is a good general size, but measure your oven and consider your requirements before buying. Ideally, a pan should sit at least 2 inches away from an oven's four walls and the meat should be 1 to 2 inches smaller than each of the pan's sides. Stainless steel is favored for its durability, although not its poor conduction, which—thanks to radiant heat—isn't crucial when roasting. The finest are moderately heavy to prevent buckling and are fitted with strong, well-riveted or spot welded stationary handles.

Ragu alla Bolognese

Bolognese Meat Sauce

Margaret and G. Franco Romagnoli
The New Italian Cooking

Enough for 4 servings of pasta

1 slice lean pancetta or salt pork

½ medium carrot, peeled

1 small onion, peeled

½ medium celery rib with leaves, washed

3 tablespoons olive oil

Giblets from 1 chicken

¾ pound lean beef or mixed veal, pork, and beef

½ cup dry red wine

3 cups peeled plum tomatoes, processed or passed through a food mill

2 teaspoons tomato paste dissolved in ¼ cup water

2 teaspoons salt or to taste

Freshly ground black pepper to taste

Cut the pancetta or salt pork into small pieces, then combine them with the carrot, onion, and celery and either process in a food processor or mince to a fine paste with a knife.

Sauté the mince until golden in the olive oil in an open pressure cooker or heavy pan.

Trim the chicken liver and heart. Skin the gizzard, then either mince in a food processor or grind in a meat grinder.

Add the meat to the pancetta mixture (called a battuto) and cook until thoroughly browned; break up any developing lumps of meat as they form with a wooden spoon. Add the wine and cook until evaporated. Add the tomatoes, tomato paste, salt, and pepper, bring to a boil, cover, and cook according to the pan you are using: 15 minutes at a 15-pound pressure or 3 hours in a saucepan. In long cooking, stir occasionally and cook, uncovered, the last hour to reduce the liquids.

Deep Roasting Pan

Manufacturers in this country call this lidded rectangular pan a roaster but it's actually a brazier. Its snug cover confines food vapors that steam rather than dry-cook the food. Its roughly 19″ × 13″ shape contains large meat cuts or whole birds as its 6-inch height guarantees they will be completely covered during cooking.

Be careful of untreated aluminum pans, which will chemically react if you use acid-based marinades and wine-deglazed pan juices. Since the same hold true for easy-to-nick enameled steel, you're best off investing in tin-lined copper or, ideally, stainless steel. As oven heat is ambient, not conveyed through a pan bottom, stainless steel's poor conductive property isn't a factor in roasting. Your pan should fit comfortably in your oven and be moderately heavy, with sturdy, well-riveted handles. Covered roasters can measure up to 28″ × 18″ × 26″.

Flat Roasting Rack

This rack's level, moderately spaced, raised rods provide meat or poultry with the fewest flesh contact points for the fullest and therefore most uniform exposure to radiant oven heat. The horizontal surface best supports large, even-based crown or standing rib roasts; parallel bars set ¾ inch apart hold such small game birds as squab and quail, while the rack's nearly 1-inch height lifts a saddle for clean roasting rather than simmering in drained juices.

Flat roasting racks, manufactured in chromed steel in sizes from 10″ × 5½″ to 16″ × 12″, can also be used as broiler or cooling racks.

V-shaped Roasting Rack

The raised V-shaped rods comprising this frame securely hold and properly expose unevenly shaped birds and large cuts of meat to oven heat. The ¼-inch-thick rods readily

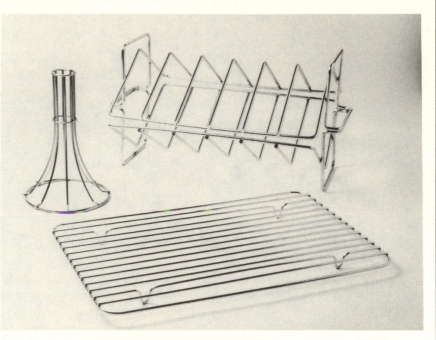

Shaped racks to completely expose variously contoured foods to an oven's ambient heat are, clockwise from top right, a pair of V-shaped roasting racks, a flat roasting rack, and a vertical roaster.

Premeasure your oven before buying a broiler pan; it should match the oven's heating element for economical use.

support a 25-pound turkey; the inch-high set distances a duck from drained fat, while the 120-degree splay that stabilizes a lengthy loin further opens the underlying air space to radiant heat for uniform roasting.

V-shaped roasting racks—occasionally sold in pairs to facilitate, for example, turning a goose—are most often manufactured in chrome-plated steel in a 15″ × 10½″ × 4¼″ size. Don't confuse them with the smaller, adjustable racks, which may

be proficient but, with their bottom-based converting tracks that rest in rendered juices, are more difficult to clean.

Vertical Roaster

Although it looks like a linear model for a trombone, this sturdy, medium-sized stand is a secure means to hold and support an upended chicken or, better still, duck as it roasts. Its 9½-inch height provides sufficient surface on which to mount an untrussed, unstuffed 4- or 5-pound bird; the narrow neck allows easy cavity insertion and extraction, while the 6-inch-wide base prevents toppling.

Smaller stands that accommodate quail and squab are also manufactured, but since their real benefit lies in their ability to drain off fat and these birds are best either frequently basted or preventively wrapped in fat to avert drying, those smaller frames should be used with care. The largest frame, which vertically roasts a turkey or capon, requires a sizable oven that few have.

A vertical roaster saves on trussing time and on the need to turn a bird to expose it evenly to oven heat, but it results in an inelegant splay for the carver.

Vertical roasters are manufactured in chrome-plated steel in sizes from 5½ to 10 inches high, the most durable being the towerlike, cross-braced stand.

Broiler Pan

This 1½-inch deep, rectangular pan and its slotted tray insert expose as much food surface as possible to an oven's heat source, while the tray's downward slots channel rendered fats into the underlying drip pan to reduce splattering and smoking.

Broiler pans are most often available in aluminum—both plain and nonstick-coated—in sizes from roughly 13″ × 9″ to 17″ × 13″ to match the broiling elements of standard ovens.

Magret de Canard aux Épices et Pommes Purées aux Sésames

Sautéed Duck Breasts with Spices and Puréed Potatoes with Sesame Seeds

Jean-Michel Bergougnoux, Executive Chef: Le Cygne

6 servings

DUCK SAUCE

2 *pounds duck bones, coarsely chopped*

1 *medium onion, diced*

1 *medium carrot, diced*

¼ *medium celery rib, diced*

1 *garlic clove, coarsely chopped*

1 *fresh thyme branch*

1 *small bay leaf*

¼ *cup honey*

½ *teaspoon paprika*

¼ *teaspoon powdered cumin*

¼ *teaspoon powdered ginger*

¼ *teaspoon ground mace*

1 *quart dry white wine*

3 *medium tomatoes, quartered*

2 *cups water*

1 *teaspoon butter*

Preheat the oven to 425°F.

Scatter the duck bones in a single layer in a shallow roasting pan and roast 1¼ to 1½ hours; turn once. Add the onion, carrot, celery, garlic, thyme, and bay leaf after the first 40 minutes. Once roasted, skim off the accumulated fat, then add the honey, toss to coat, and return to the oven 9 minutes or until the bones are caramelized.

Stir in the spices, then deglaze with white wine. Add the tomatoes and water, bring to a boil slowly, and reduce the sauce to one-third of its original volume. Strain, reduce to half, then whisk in the butter; set aside.

SAUTÉED DUCK

5 *whole Moulard (or Pekin) duck breasts*

2 *tablespoons corn oil*

Salt to taste

Freshly ground black pepper to taste

Lightly brush the duck breasts with oil, season to taste with salt and pepper, then sauté, skin side down, 15 minutes in a large sauté pan set over medium heat; turn and continue to cook 3 minutes longer. (If using the smaller Pekin breasts, reduce the cooking time by a third.)

Transfer to a platter and let stand 5 minutes before slicing.

PURÉED POTATOES WITH SESAME SEEDS

2 *pounds all-purpose potatoes, peeled*

⅔ *cup heavy cream, hot*

4 *tablespoons butter*

1 *tablespoon sesame oil*

1 *tablespoon sesame seeds*

Salt to taste

Freshly ground black pepper to taste

Cook the potatoes 25 minutes or until tender in boiling salted water. Drain, mash, then work in the cream, butter, and sesame oil and seeds; season with salt and pepper.

ASSEMBLY

15 *green peppercorns*

15 *pink peppercorns*

For each serving: Mold the puréed potatoes in a 3-inch circle in the center of the serving plate. Cover the plate with a layer of sauce, surround the potatoes with duck slices, then sprinkle a few of each type of peppercorn over the potatoes and duck.

Octagonal Grill Rack

"Even an old boot tastes good if cooked over charcoal," says an Italian proverb. That old boot—or oysters, scallops, or skewered lamb—would be securely held over coals in this adjustable octagonal grill. Its generous 14″ × 13½″ face easily sets atop bricks, hearth, or grill, The ¼-inch spacing of the rods together with those that wrap around the side retain slick shrimp or slippery sausage, while a rack insert that neatly adjusts from ½ inch to 1 inch above the bottom rack compresses to hold foods of various thicknesses in place.

The octagonal grill is manufactured only in stainless steel in the aforementioned dimensions and is more practical than racks designed for particular purposes such as kebobs or sardines.

Fish Grill

This wire frame with two sets of feet holds and turns a moderate-sized fish during grilling. The 18″ × 6″ bowed frame easily supports a 5- to 8-pound bass or bluefish; two hinged crosswire faces secure the hold, expose the flesh, and assure intact turns while four pairs of legs—2-inch stationary and doubly long folding ones—allow initial searing, then a judicious distancing from white-hot coals.

Hinged fish grills are most often available in tinned or enameled steel in lengths from 11 to 24 inches. Many come without feet, but results are better with them. Select one with longer legs that fold for storage ease and make sure the frame is hinged rather than loosely joined with metal rings.

Sardine Grill

During a Mediterranean mid-spring when sardines are at their fat, sweet peak, many fry them for beignets, simmer them with fennel to toss with pasta, or simply clean, salt, and

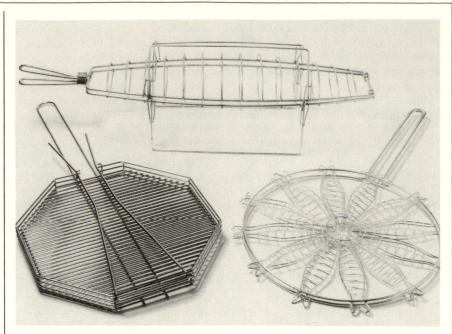

Heavy-gauge wire and rods create such fanciful yet functional grill racks as those shown clockwise from the top: a fish grill, sardine grill, and octagonal grill rack.

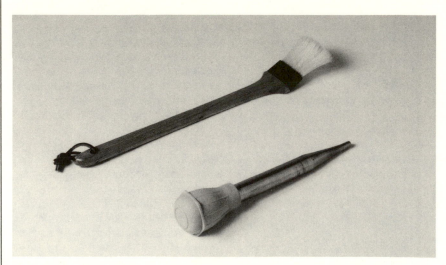

Two tools to further flavor and help moisten grilling or roasting food are the basting brush at top and bulb baster below.

spit them—the final task most efficiently done with this sunburst wire frame. Each 7½-inch fish form emanating from the center secures a 5- or 6-inch sardine; fine, well-spaced cross-wires expose maximum flesh to fire for quick cooking. The frame reduces both grilling time and the chance of torn fish flesh.

On this side of the Atlantic, sardine grills are most often used to barbecue hot dogs. They are manufactured only in tinned steel, measure 14½ inches across, and have 12-inch-long handles.

Basting Brush

This 2-inch-wide brush is a superb tool for applying easily ignited high-fat bastes to grilling meat, fish, poultry, or vegetables. Its natural bristles' flagged ends and barbed shafts expand the available surface to absorb and dispense a marinade or butter baste; their 45-degree angle set conveniently reaches behind drumsticks or across loins, and the 12-inch handle comfortably distances hands from charcoal's intense heat.

Also used to baste broiled and roasted foods, the most durable and hygienic natural-bristle brushes have a tight, seamless nylon ferrule which should be carefully protected from the heat.

Bulb Baster

To keep roast meat or poultry moist and to further flavor it as it cooks, researchers favor a fat-side up or bard wrap that eliminates manual basting, the attendant oven-door openings, consequent temperature reductions, and the extended heating periods that dry and toughen flesh. Basting, however, remains common practice. You can apply melted fat and pan juices to a roast with a syringe such as this one. Its 10-inch tapered cylinder reaches through rack rods and under roasts to siphon off liquid; the end bulb draws ¼ cup through the ¼-inch tip opening.

Glass, nylon, and the durable stainless-steel bulb basters often come with brushes for cleaning and a needle for injecting liquid into meat,

but when such added fluids are heated during cooking, they steam cook it rather than giving you a clean, dry roast. It's best to limit the injector's use to poultry to apply basting liquid just below the skin.

Poularde de Noël

Christmas Chicken Stuffed with Chestnuts and Truffles

Gisèle Masson, Proprietor Gérard Chotard, Executive Chef: La Grenouille

4 servings

1 *large black truffle with approximately 4 thin slices cut off and the rest julienned*

1 *6-pound chicken*

2 *tablespoons butter*

2 *medium shallots, coarsely chopped*

4 *ounces sausage meat*

4 *ounces breakfast sausage links*

4 *ounces bread crumbs soaked in milk to cover for 10 minutes, then squeezed dry*

¼ *cup cognac*

2 *medium mushroom caps, sliced*

¼ *teaspoon dried thyme*

1 *pound chestnuts, peeled, braised in stock, and with all but 8 broken*

Coarse salt to taste

Freshly ground black pepper to taste

1 *medium carrot, coarsely chopped*

1 *small onion, coarsely chopped*

1 *medium celery rib, coarsely chopped*

1 *fresh thyme branch*

1 *bay leaf*

2 *parsley sprigs*

1 *cup chicken stock (see page 210)*

1 *cup port*

The night before, slip the truffle slices under the skin of the chicken, cover, and refrigerate.

Preheat the oven to 350°F.

Melt the butter in a large sauté pan set over medium heat, add the shallots, and sauté 3 to 4 minutes to cook partially. Add the sausage meat and links and continue to cook until the sausage is lightly browned; stir frequently. Add the bread crumbs, cognac, mushrooms, dried thyme, broken and whole chestnuts, and the remaining truffle, and season to taste with salt and pepper.

Fill the cavity of the chicken with the sausage stuffing, truss, set atop a roasting rack in a shallow roasting pan, and roast 1½ hours. After the first 30 minutes, add the carrot, onion, celery, thyme branch, bay leaf, and parsley to the roasting pan.

Transfer the chicken to a serving dish and keep warm as you prepare the sauce. Discard the vegetables and aromatics from the pan and skim off the fat. Set the pan over high heat, add the stock and port, and bring to a boil; reduce to half its volume, scraping off any browned bits that may be on the bottom of the pan. Correct the seasonings, then strain and serve alongside the chicken.

Barbecued Roast Loin of Pork

Karen Lee
Nouvelle Chinese Cuisine

6 servings

MARINADE

1 *tablespoon minced ginger*

½ *cup hoisin sauce*

¼ *cup dark soy sauce*

¼ *cup bottled chili sauce*

2 *tablespoons plum sauce*

2 *tablespoons dark miso (soybean paste)*

⅓ *cup medium-dry sherry*

1 *teaspoon minced garlic*

3 *medium scallions, thinly sliced*

1 *4- to 5-pound pork loin, bones cracked for carving ease.*

Combine the marinade ingredients in a medium bowl, stir to mix, then rub the pork with it. Place the meat and its marinade in a plastic bag, set in a bowl, and refrigerate 12 hours.

Preheat the oven to 350°F.

Bring the pork to room temperature, remove it from its marinating bag, then set it on a rack in a shallow roasting pan. Roast 1½ to 2 hours; after the first 15 minutes, add some water to the roasting pan to prevent the juices from burning.

Transfer the pork to a warm platter and allow it to set 10 minutes before carving. Meanwhile, remove the fat from the pan juices, set them over high heat, and reduce until thick and syrupy. Pour over the sliced pork and serve either hot or at room temperature.

Calamares Rellenos

Stuffed Squid

Felipe Rojas-Lombardi, Executive Chef: The Ballroom

18 calamares rellenos
or 6 servings

SAUCE

3 *tablespoons olive oil*

2 *garlic cloves, finely chopped*

1 *medium onion, finely chopped*

4 *ounces chorizo sausage, finely diced*

1 *medium carrot, peeled and finely chopped*

1 *celery rib, deveined and finely chopped*

1½ *tablespoons fresh thyme leaves*

½ *teaspoon cayenne*

2 *quarts canned Italian plum tomatoes, crushed*

1½ *tablespoons coarse salt*

2 *cups dry white wine*

Heat the oil in a large saucepan set over medium heat, add the garlic and onion, and sauté 3 to 5 minutes or until the onion becomes transparent. Add the chorizo and continue to cook 5 minutes longer; stir occasionally. Add the carrot, celery, and thyme and cook another 5 minutes; stir occasionally. Add the remaining ingredients and bring to a boil; reduce the heat and simmer, uncovered, 30 minutes; stir frequently. Set aside.

SQUID AND STUFFING

18 *4-inch-long squid (approximately 1½ pounds)*

⅓ *cup pignoli nuts*

½ *pound pork, finely ground*

3 *tablespoons raisins soaked in ¼ cup dry sherry*

1 *large garlic clove, finely chopped*

2 *teaspoons coarse salt*

½ *teaspoon ground mace*

⅔ *cup fresh bread crumbs*

1 *large egg*

To clean the squid: Gently pull the head and tentacles from the body. Remove and discard the viscera that come out with the head. Save the heads and set aside. Pop the small, hard, round beak out of the tentacles and discard; reserve the tentacles. Pull out and discard the long, transparent quill from inside the body, then insert your index finger inside the body and pull out and discard any interior waste. Remove the external membrane from the body, then rinse the squid under cold running water.

Reserve the bodies—approximately 1 pound—and finely chop the tentacles for the stuffing; set both aside.

In a small heavy fry pan set over high heat, add the pignoli nuts and toast until slightly golden overall; toss constantly. Immediately remove from the pan.

Combine the chopped squid and toasted pignoli nuts with the remaining stuffing ingredients in a large bowl and stir to mix thoroughly.

Empty into a pastry bag fitted with a ½-inch plain tube and use to fill each reserved squid body ⅔ full; allow a ½-inch clearance at the top and use this area to secure shut with a toothpick.

ASSEMBLY

6 *cups vegetable oil*

½ *cup all-purpose flour*

1 *cup finely chopped Italian parsley*

Heat the oil to 350°F to 375°F in a deep fryer or large, straight-sided pan.

Meanwhile, dredge the squid in the flour and, once the oil reaches the appropriate temperature, add a few at a time and cook 3 to 5 minutes or until lightly golden. Use a slotted spoon to transfer to paper towels to drain. Repeat to cook the remaining squid, then remove the toothpicks.

Combine the squid and the reserved sauce in a large saucepan set over medium-high heat; bring to a boil, then reduce the heat and simmer 5 minutes; stir occasionally. Correct the seasoning if necessary.

Empty onto a serving platter, top with parsley, and serve either hot or at room temperature.

Cassoulet

Jean-Jacques Rachou,
Chef-Proprietor:
La Côte Basque

8 servings

DUCK CONFIT

1 *5-pound duck, boned, bones re-*
served, and meat cut into 6
pieces

1 *teaspoon dried thyme*

3 *bay leaves*

1 *garlic clove*

12 *black peppercorns*

Salt to taste

1½ *pounds rendered duck fat*
(approximately)

Combine all the ingredients in a large saucepan with enough duck fat to cover, bring to a bare simmer, and cook 1½ hours or until very tender. (Optionally, brown the simmered duck in a large sauté pan with some of the fat, then set aside.) Strain the duck fat used for simmering through several layers of cheesecloth and reserve.

LAMB STEW

1 *pound boneless leg of lamb,*
cubed

Salt to taste

2 *tablespoons rendered duck fat*

1 *medium onion, finely chopped*

1 *medium carrot, finely chopped*

2 *medium celery ribs, finely*
chopped

1 *garlic clove, coarsely chopped*

1 *teaspoon dried thyme*

2 *bay leaves*

10 *black peppercorns*

1 *tablespoon tomato paste*

½ *cup dry white wine*

1 *cup brown veal stock (see page*
211)

Preheat the oven to 350°F.
Season the lamb with salt, then sauté in hot duck fat until well browned in a large, oven-going sauté pan. Remove from the pan and set aside. Add the onion, carrot, celery, and garlic to the pan and sauté 10 minutes or until browned; stir frequently. Add the thyme, bay leaves, peppercorns, and tomato paste and stir to mix. Return the meat to the pan, add the wine and veal stock, and bring to a boil. Cover and bake 1 hour. Remove from the oven and set aside.

PORK

1 *pound boneless pork loin, thinly*
sliced and pounded

Salt to taste

Freshly ground black pepper to
taste

2 *tablespoons rendered duck fat*

Season the pork to taste with salt and pepper, then sauté 3 to 5 minutes or until browned in hot duck fat over medium-high heat; turn once. Remove from the pan and set aside.

CASSOULET STOCK (OPTIONAL)

Reserved duck, lamb, and pork
bones, coarsely chopped

2 *tablespoons vegetable oil*

1 *medium onion, coarsely*
chopped

1 *medium carrot, coarsely*
chopped

2 *medium celery ribs, coarsely*
chopped

5 *garlic cloves, coarsely chopped*

2 *teaspoons dried thyme*

5 *bay leaves*

20 *black peppercorns*

Preheat the oven to 400°F.
Toss the bones in the oil and roast 65 minutes in a single layer in a shallow roasting pan. Add the onion, carrot, celery, and garlic after the first 45 minutes. Empty into a stockpot, add the remaining ingredients, and cover with water. Bring to a boil, then reduce the heat and simmer, partially covered, 4 hours. Strain and reserve.

HACHIS

4 *ounces pork fatback, cut into*
½-inch cubes

5 *garlic cloves*

Purée the fatback and garlic until smooth in a food processor fitted with a metal blade, refrigerate until ready to use.

BEANS

2 *pounds Great Northern beans,*
soaked overnight in water to
cover, drained, and rinsed

Salt to taste

Freshly ground black pepper to
taste

Combine the beans in a stockpot with either the stock or water to cover. Bring to a boil over high heat, then reduce the heat and simmer, partially covered, 1½ hours or until tender but not mushy; skim off any impurities as they rise. Add the sauce from the lamb stew and the hachis and bring to a strong boil; stir to thoroughly incorporate the hachis. Remove from the heat and season to taste with salt and pepper.

SAUSAGE

1 *pound saucisson à l'ail (garlic*
sausage) or kielbasa, cut into
1-inch slices

Bake 30 minutes or until well browned in an oiled roasting pan in a 400°F preheated oven; turn occasionally. Drain off the fat and set aside.

ASSEMBLY

2 *bay leaves, crumbled*

1 *teaspoon dried thyme*

½ *teaspoon cracked black pep-*
percorns

Preheat the oven to 425°F.
Use a slotted spoon to place half the beans in an earthenware casserole, top with layers of the duck, lamb, pork, and sausage, then cover with the remaining beans. Add enough of the bean-cooking liquid so that it rises just to the surface of the beans; you may have to add additional brown veal stock to do so. Sprinkle the bay leaves, thyme, and pepper overall, then bake 45 minutes to 1 hour or until a crust is formed on top. Serve immediately.

Baking Stone

Thousands of years have passed since primitive man first baked on a hot stone, yet except for its composition and standardized sizing, this unglazed ceramic slab remains the same and is still unsurpassed at producing bread, particularly flatbread. Its 8-pound weight maintains and transfers steady, high heat for even rising; porous ceramic absorbs water from the dough to encourage crisp crusting, while a 16″ × 14″ rectangle supports four individual loaves or one large round.

Occasionally called a pizza stone, it is also manufactured with a 13- to 16-inch diameter. Select a stone your oven can accommodate in a shape to suit your efforts. Some are packaged with a chrome cooling frame, a nice feature but not necessary.

Marmite

Some suggest that this covered earthenware pot was originally called a marmite—the French base means "murmur"—after the sounds its hearty contents make during long simmering. Its wide surface fosters evaporation for surface crusting when needed; the round shape uniformly diffuses heat over a long period, while a low, domed lid returns

The very thick unglazed ceramic baking stone shown is the best way to duplicate the crisp results of a pizzeria's brick oven.

A low, broad, heavy earthenware marmite is ideal for preparing cassoulets to perfection.

Pizza Dough

Wolfgang Puck
The Wolfgang Puck Cookbook

Dough for 4 individual pizzas

1 ¼-ounce package active dry or fresh yeast
¼ cup warm water
1 teaspoon salt
1 tablespoon honey
2 tablespoons olive oil
¾ cup cool water
3 cups all-purpose flour

Dissolve the yeast in the warm water and set aside 10 minutes.

Combine the salt, honey, oil, and cool water in a small bowl and mix well.

Place the flour in a food processor and, with the motor running, slowly pour in the salt mixture. Then pour in the dissolved yeast and process until the dough forms a ball on the blade. (If it is sticky, add a few sprinklings of flour.)

Turn out onto a lightly floured surface and knead until smooth. Place in a buttered bowl, cover, and set aside 30 minutes to rest.

Divide the dough into 4 equal parts. Roll each into a smooth, tight ball, then set on a dish, cover with a damp towel, and refrigerate for 2 or more hours for the dough to lose its elasticity.

Allow the dough to come to room temperature one hour before baking.

On a lightly floured work surface use the fleshy part of your fingertips to flatten each dough ball into a 6-inch circle; make the outer edge slightly thicker than the center. Lift the dough from the surface and gently stretch the edges, working clockwise to form a 7- to 8-inch circle. Repeat with the other 3 pieces.

The enameled cast-iron Dutch oven on the left and doufeu on the right suit long stovetop or oven braising.

condensation to the bubbling ragout to prevent it from drying out. Earthenware best absorbs and transfers the long, low heat needed for cassoulets.

Although earthenware marmites often sport large ear handles, this one's slight protrusions rank it as an extension of the same family that includes a marmite Vallauris—a squat vessel with one long handle— and a marmite Parisian, a tall, long-handled one.

Marmites are also available in stoneware, and their capacities range from 2 cups to 7 quarts, with the 6-quart size that doubles for marinating, corning, and pickling being the most popular.

Enameled Cast-Iron Casserole (Dutch Oven)

This very heavy casserole, or Dutch oven, is also occasionally called a stew pot because it's primarily used to brown and slowly simmer the various types—from blanquettes and navarins to fricassees and ragouts to salmis. The 12-inch width ensures the contents' close contact with hot metal for uniform cooking and melding of flavor; the 5-inch-high sides hold substantial quantities, as 15 pounds of enameled cast iron evenly absorb and transmit the long, slow heat that tenderizes traditionally tough cuts.

Metal casseroles are manufactured in aluminum, anodized aluminum, tin-lined copper, stainless steel with either an aluminum- or a copper-cored base, cast iron, and the recommended enameled cast iron, which is less prone to rusting than the bare metal. Capacities range from 4 to 10 quarts, with the nearly 9-quart size the most popular.

Doufeu

This enameled cast-iron pot with a deeply indented lid is perhaps the best-made vessel for braising. Its 11″ × 8½″ oval supplies ample surface on which to brown a roaster, then bed its mirepoix; nearly 12 pounds of cast iron retain and distribute a long, low, even heat, while the lid's large, encircling groove— which once held hot coals—now cradles iced water to rapidly condense internal steam. Heat sinks— in the form of interior lid ribs— further augment the cold, condensing contact surface that then directs the formed droplets back onto the braise.

Doufeus—the name means gentle heat—are most often manufactured in enameled cast iron with capacities from 2½- to the more practical 4½- and 6-quart sizes.

Black Forest Ham and Goat Cheese Pizza

Wolfgang Puck
The Wolfgang Puck Cookbook

4 individual pizzas

1 *recipe pizza dough (opposite page), divided into 4 equal pieces*

2 *tablespoons extra-virgin olive oil (approximately)*

1 *teaspoon dried red chili flakes*

1 *cup grated Italian fontina cheese*

2 *cups grated mozzarella or an equal amount of sliced fresh mozzarella*

2 *baby Japanese eggplants, sliced lengthwise into ¼-inch slices and grilled or sautéed in olive oil*

1 *cup cubed goat cheese*

4 *ounces Black Forest ham, julienned*

1 *bunch fresh basil, chopped, with 4 sprigs reserved for garnish*

Preheat the oven with a pizza stone to 500°F 30 minutes before baking.

Working with one pizza at a time, roll or stretch a piece of dough into a 7- to 8-inch circle. Place the circle of dough on a flour- or semolina-dusted wooden bread peel.

Brush the dough with olive oil and sprinkle with dried chili flakes according to how spicy you like your pizza. Arrange a quarter of the fontina and mozzarella cheeses on the dough, then add a quarter of the eggplant, goat cheese, and ham. Sprinkle some chopped basil on top.

Slide the pizza onto the stone and bake 10 to 12 minutes or until the cheese is bubbling. Remove from the oven, transfer to a warm plate, and garnish with a basil sprig. Serve immediately, cut into wedges.

Assemble and bake the remaining 3 pizzas in the same way.

Daubière

This archaic-looking earthenware casserole—first designed for fireside cookery—is still used to slowly braise marinated beef, lamb, goose, pheasant, or turkey with bacon and vegetables. Its 2-quart bulbous body maximizes exposure to heat while still providing sufficient room for ingredient layering, and a cinched neck restricts evaporation and concentrates risen fat for easy removal. Although no longer necessary to set above a bed of embers, the handle's unique, high angulation continues to balance this bottom-heavy vessel.

Daubières—whose lids were first recessed to hold hot ashes for even braising—are manufactured in stoneware or earthenware in 1½- and 2-quart sizes.

Bean Pot

There are height and weight variations, but an earthenware bean pot from Italy, Spain, or Greece closely resembles this typical New England one with its deep, fat body, narrow mouth, and lid. A 5-inch depth economically immerses over 4 cups of soaked navy or kidney beans during 7 hours of simmering; bowed sides expand the actual heating surface and promote uniform baking while a tapered neck topped with a tight cover minimizes moisture loss.

Bean pots range from 2 to 6 quarts, and the described moderate 2½-quart capacity is the most popular. Make sure the glaze is smooth and that the lid fits snugly.

Clay Cook Pot

Salt packs, leaf wraps, or clay seals for baking are among the simplest and most effective means of producing tender, moist chicken, fish, or meat. Each seals in natural juices so that it essentially steam-cooks the food. This unglazed earthenware pot neatly accomplishes the same trick. The pot and cover are first soaked in water, the bottom filled with food, covered, and set in a cold

From left to right, three traditional ceramic cooking vessels are a bean pot, daubière and clay cook pot.

Estouffade d'Agneau au Romarin

Braised Lamb with Rosemary

Daniel Boulud, Executive Chef: Le Cirque

4 to 6 servings

3 *pounds boneless shoulder of lamb, cut into 2-inch pieces*

Salt to taste

Freshly ground black pepper to taste

4 *tablespoons clarified butter*

¼ *cup all-purpose flour*

1 *teaspoon tomato paste*

3 *to 4 cups brown veal stock (see page 211)*

1 *cup dry white wine*

6 *medium tomatoes, peeled, seeded, and diced*

2 *garlic cloves, thinly sliced*

Peel of half an orange, julienned

1 *medium celery rib*

1 *medium leek, trimmed, sliced lengthwise, and rinsed*

2 *fresh thyme branches*

1 *fresh rosemary sprig*

1 *bay leaf*

8 *ounces pearl onions, peeled, with bases nicked*

8 *ounces baby carrots, peeled and cut into olive-sized pieces*

8 *ounces white turnips, peeled and cut into olive-sized pieces*

4 *cups all-purpose flour*

1 *¼-ounce package active dry yeast*

1 *to 1½ cups warm water*

Preheat the oven to 350°F.

Season the meat with salt and pepper, then sauté it until brown on all sides in the butter in a hot, 8-quart, enameled cast-iron casserole. Sprinkle on ¼ cup flour and once it is absorbed, stir in the tomato paste and enough stock and wine to barely cover the meat. Add the tomatoes, garlic, orange peel, celery, leek, thyme, rosemary, and bay leaf, then top with the onions, carrots, and turnips.

Combine 4 cups flour and yeast in a large bowl and stir to mix. Make a well in the center, pour in 1 cup of water, then stir with a wooden spoon to incorporate the liquid with the dry ingredients (add more water if too firm). Turn onto a lightly floured surface and knead until smooth. Roll the dough into a circle whose diameter is larger than that of the casserole, then overlap the bread dough around the entire rim of the pot and pinch so that it will seal to form a cover.

Bake 2½ hours.

To serve, remove from the oven, break the bread crust with the back of a knife, and serve on cooked and buttered fresh fettuccine.

Above is a luxuriously heavy, lidded tin-lined-copper pommes Anna pan.

The most durable ovenproof porcelain is uniformly thick, has a smooth, hard glaze, and is free of chips, cracks, and crazing. Shown with the salamander (see page 140) at bottom are, clockwise from top left, a rectangular baking dish, oval gratin dish, scallop shell, and shirred-egg dish (page 140).

Pommes Anna
Sliced Potato Cake

Jacques Pépin
La Technique

This is a very presentable dish for a party. Begin by trimming the potatoes all around to make long cylinders; use the trimmings in soup, croquettes, or mashed potatoes.

Slice by hand or mandoline into ⅛-inch-thick slices, dry thoroughly, then sauté the slices in butter and oil (or clarified butter) over medium-high heat for a few minutes.

Arrange the slices in overlapping concentric circles in the bottom of a fry pan, cake pan, or pommes Anna pan; if using either of the first two, a nonstick surface is the best. Place the potato slices any old way on top of the bottom layer, seasoning each successive layer with salt and pepper (and basting with a spoonful of clarified butter). Press the potatoes down, then bake in a 425°F preheated oven for 30 to 45 minutes. Let rest a few minutes, drain off the excess butter, and, if using a fry or cake pan, run a knife around the potatoes, and unmold. Remove any slices that stick to the bottom and replace where they belong in the cake.

oven to bake. There, the water absorbed by the porous clay evaporates, condenses, and steam-bastes the food.

Such pots are most efficient when tight to their food, which is why long, shallow vessels are made for fish and tall, bulging ones for chicken. The most versatile, however, is this high-domed rectangular container, so similarly made by individual manufacturers that little distinguishes one from the other. When buying, select for size; the pots can accommodate anywhere from 2 to 14 pounds.

Pommes Anna Pan

This lidded, tin-lined copper pan is as handsome as it is proficient at preparing the elegant sliced-potato cake called Pommes Anna. Seven pounds of metal conduct and retain the high heat needed to turn the potato cake golden on both top and bottom; a round shape distributes heat uniformly; the 3-inch depth contains portions for eight; and a lid that cuffs nearly 1½ inches over the pan's sides soundly compacts a tower of stacked potatoes.

The pans that create this dish—said to be dedicated to the famous courtesan of the Second Empire, Anna Deslions, by its nineteenth-

century creator, chef Adolphe Dugléré of the then renowned Le Café Anglais—vary only in size: a 6½-inch diameter, the described 8-inch diameter, and slightly heavier ones with 9½-inch diameters.

Rectangular Baking Dish

This rectangular porcelain dish is well suited to slowly cook and casually serve such layered and sauced dishes as cannelloni, lasagne, and moussaka. The roughly 15″ × 10″ dimensions provide substantial area to promote evaporation, and the 2-inch depth hastens thorough baking.

The porcelain evenly conducts oven heat and retains it to keep the contents warm at table. Outwardly flared sides make serving easy, while a thick, strengthening rim doubles as a handle.

Equally fine baking dishes are available in earthenware and heat-tempered glass in sizes from 10″ × 7½″ to 16″ × 15″. The medium-large ones—13″ × 9″ and 15″ × 10″—better suit standard recipe requirements.

Oval Gratin Dish

For a bite of the crisp, golden brown topping—usually cheese and/or bread crumbs—that finishes chicken hash, scalloped potatoes, and many another vegetable, egg, or shellfish recipe, a shallow, slope-sided dish is best. Its 1¼-inch depth spreads the ingredients thinly to assure a proportionately high crust ratio while obliquely set sides promote rapid evaporation beneath a broiler.

Oval gratin *dishes* are manufactured in either porcelain or earthenware—oval gratin *pans* are of cladded stainless steel or copper, tin-lined copper, or aluminum. They are most often available in lengths from 10½ to 17½ inches. A nearly 13-inch-long dish serves six to eight.

Salamander

It may look like an archaic metal detector, but when this tool's cast-iron disk is heated until red hot, then slowly swept above a gratin, custard, or meringue, it sets the crust or glaze. The puck's 2-inch-wide face easily covers a crème brûlée in one pass; its ¾-inch depth retains the high heat necessary for searing, while an 18-inch handle safely distances hands from hot metal.

Both manual and longer-faced electric salamanders produce second-rate results when compared to those obtained by a professional's broilerlike salamander, a substantial piece of commercial equipment whose output quality is perhaps matched only by that of the small

Chicons au Gratin

Belgian Endive and Ham Gratin

Raymond Ameye, Chef-Proprietor: Flamand

6 servings

BÉCHAMEL SAUCE

- 6 *tablespoons butter*
- 6 *tablespoons all-purpose flour*
- 3 *cups milk*
- *Salt to taste*
- *Freshly ground black pepper to taste*
- *Freshly grated nutmeg to taste*

Melt the butter in a small saucepan set over low heat, add the flour, whisk to mix, and cook 3 minutes. Add the milk and whisk until smooth. Increase the heat and bring to a boil, then reduce the heat and simmer 45 minutes; stir occasionally. Season to taste with salt, pepper, and nutmeg.

BRAISED ENDIVE

- 6 *large Belgian endive, trimmed and cored*
- 4 *tablespoons sweet butter*
- ½ *cup water*

Combine the endive, butter, and water in a medium saucepan and cover with a fitted piece of waxed paper. Set over medium-high heat to bring to a simmer, then reduce the heat and simmer, covered, 25 minutes; turn once.

Use tongs to remove to a colander to drain and cool. When comfortable enough to handle, squeeze out the excess water.

ASSEMBLY

- 6 *slices boiled ham (approximately 8 ounces)*
- ½ *cup freshly grated Emmenthaler cheese*

Preheat the oven to 400°F.

Roll each endive in a slice of ham and place in a buttered gratin dish. Cover with the Béchamel sauce, then sprinkle the cheese over all. Bake 15 minutes or until nicely browned.

---

propane torch favored by most patissiers.

Shirred-Egg Dish

Although many call this small porcelain vessel a round gratin dish, it's traditionally used to bake—shirr—single servings of eggs. Its roughly 5½-inch diameter maximizes the egg-to-ceramic contact to ensure quick, uniform baking; outwardly flared, 1½-inch-deep sides further expose the egg to heat to set it properly, while porcelain assures even heat absorption and distribution and retains the heat at table.

Also available in earthenware, shirred-egg dishes—which differ technically from round gratin pans made of metal—range in diameter from 4¾ to 9½ inches, with the 5½-inch size being the most popular.

Scallop Shell

Botticelli could easily have had his Venus emerging from this porcelain scallop shell with its wide, clean lines and shallow cup. The real thing provided him with graduated colors but, had he been a chef, this would have provided better balance and superior heat retention. The ringed foot steadies it during broiling or serving; the relatively wide surface ensures sufficient crust development, while the porcelain composition retains heat to keep the contents warm at table.

Less apt to chip and easier to clean than real shells, porcelain scallop shells are manufactured in widths from 3 to 5½ inches. The former, which holds 2 tablespoons, is often used to serve sweet or herbed butter balls or pats and the latter, which holds 1¼ cups, to serve shellfish gratins or salads.

Soufflé Dish

A feather-light, golden-crowned soufflé requires a carefully prepared batter cooked at a high temperature in a round, deep, straight-sided, nearly flat-bottomed dish with an outwardly set lip. A round shape

Porcelain dishes designed especially to bake and serve are, clockwise from the top, a soufflé dish, crème brûlée dish, and ramekin.

most uniformly distributes heat; deep sides offer ample surface-to-batter contact to quickly set expanding egg proteins; straight sides build the soufflé upward, and a very slightly convex bottom allows for thermal expansion and contraction in and out of an ideal 425°F oven. The top lip abets clean rising: Once a channel is made in the batter flush to this edge, the lack of batter-to-dish contact reduces the chance of immediate sticking and an off-kilter rise.

Most soufflé dishes are glazed except for their rims to facilitate even rising. The rough upper edge is the result of a single glazing process: Since this is its only flat area, the dish is inverted onto it during its final firing in the kiln.

Soufflé dishes are available in glass, stoneware, and porcelain—the chef's favorite. All range in size from 1 to 4 quarts, but most professionals prefer the more rapid, even, dependable results given by the 1-quart size—even to the point of buying two instead of one larger.

Ramekin

This heavy porcelain cup is traditionally used to prepare the frothy cheese pudding-cum-soufflé that has the same name as its dish. A typical 6-ounce capacity suits a single serving; its roughly 1½-inch depth and 3-inch diameter provide uniform custard cooking, while 5 ounces of ceramic evenly convey the indispensable bain marie's low heat.

Due to the single-glaze process, a ramekin's flat base remains rough, which secondarily prevents a vacuum and suction from developing with the water-bath tray as it would if the bottom were smooth.

Ramekins, also used to prepare individual pâtés and other egg dishes, come in sizes numbered 1 (6 ounces), 2 (4 ounces), and 3 (3 ounces). Save for slight weight variations and rounded interiors, there are no real distinctions among the ramekins now on the market.

Crème Brûlée Dish

The sole purpose of this small porcelain oval is to prepare and serve crème brûlée—that sumptuous 200-year-old dessert said to have been savored first at King's College in Cambridge. The dish's nearly 6-ounce capacity offers a generous single serving of this cream-based custard; its bare inch depth extends the sur-

---

Soufflé Citron Vert au Sauce aux Framboises

Lime Soufflé with Raspberry Sauce

Jean-Michel Bergougnoux, Executive Chef: Le Cygne

6 to 7 servings

SOUFFLÉ

7 *large eggs, separated*

¾ *cup all-purpose flour*

2¼ *cups milk*

⅓ *cup plus ¾ cup granulated sugar*

Zest and juice from 2 limes

Confectioners' sugar

Preheat the oven to 425°F.

Combine the egg yolks, flour, and ¼ cup milk in a bowl and whisk until smooth.

Heat the remaining milk with ⅓ cup sugar and the lime zest, then slowly add it to the egg yolk mixture to temper it; whisk constantly. Empty into a large saucepan set over medium heat and heat until thick and one or two bubbles surface; whisk constantly. Pour into a chilled bowl, add the lime juice, and stir to both mix and cool.

Butter 2 1-quart soufflé molds, dust lightly with confectioners' sugar, and set aside.

Whip the egg whites until almost stiff, then gradually add the remaining ¾ cup sugar and continue to beat until stiff and glossy. Carefully fold a third of the beaten egg whites into the egg yolk mixture, then fold in the remainder. Empty into the prepared molds, level with a spatula, then run your thumb around the inside rim of each to create a small channel. Bake 20 minutes. Remove from the oven, dust with confectioners' sugar, and serve immediately with Raspberry Sauce (see below).

RASPBERRY SAUCE

3 *pints raspberries*

2 *tablespoons granulated sugar (or more, depending on the ripeness of the fruit)*

¼ *cup Framboise*

Combine the ingredients in a food processor fitted with a metal blade and process until smooth. Force the puree through a fine-meshed sieve to remove the seeds, empty into a small saucepan set over medium heat, and warm.

face area for balanced bites of a caramelized topping. Ten ounces of porcelain promote slow, even, curdle-free cooking and thorough chilling while still withstanding the heat of the final broiling.

Crème brûlée dishes are traditionally oval—purportedly to mirror the shape of the crystal dish in which it was first served. Most porcelain dishes are scallop-edged, but they can also be plain and can hold up to 1 cup.

Snail Cup

This small, stout earthenware cup presents a fine alternative to cooking and serving a snail in its shell. A scant tablespoon capacity provides room for an escargot; a sampling of garlic butter and its 2-ounce weight promotes an even heat that it retains at the table and an open cup shape creates a broad top for easy access.

Also called *godet à l'escargot*—literally, snail mug—it is available in earthenware or porcelain and should not be confused with the more decorative, slightly less utilitarian shell-shaped cup.

Snail Plate

Because health department regulations prevent restaurants in many states from serving escargots in their shells, this double-handled stainless-steel plate is used as both a heating and a serving tray for filled snail cups in commerce and for traditional in-shell presentation at home. Barely ½-inch outwardly sloped sides maximize the snails' exposure to heat and provide easy access for fork and, if used, tongs, while six 1¼-inch-diameter depressions keep a first-course portion neat.

Snail plates are also manufactured in chromed or tinned steels, aluminum, or porcelain with either a half or full dozen depressions. They should not be confused with the preferred deeply indented earthenware dishes or skillets in which shell-

The snail plate on the left and snail cup on the right are two alternate vessels in which to bake and serve escargots.

The custard cup on the left and pot de crème on the right are the very models of perfection for baking and serving single portions of those elegant, egg-rich desserts.

The soup bowl on the left is useful for serving any hearty soup or individual side dish such as baked beans; the oval ovenproof platter (see page 144) on the right is a utilitarian complement to most table services.

free escargots are prepared and, thanks to the ceramic's heat absorption, kept warmer longer at the table.

Custard Cup

With fresh ingredients, a little care, and this porcelain cup, it's almost impossible to cook a curdled custard. An 8-ounce ceramic cup gently conducts the bain marie's moderate heat; the nearly 3-inch-high curved sides expand the custard-to-surface ratio for uniform baking, while the 8-ounce capacity provides a generous single portion.

Custard cups can be used for rice and bread puddings or popovers if, like Ambrose Bierce, you believe that custard is a "conspiracy of the hen, the cow and the cook."

Paupiettes of Dover Sole with Red Pepper Purée

Seppi Renggli, Executive Chef while at The Four Seasons

4 servings

PAUPIETTES

4 *large red peppers*

2 *Dover sole, filleted, skinned, and each fillet cut in half length-wise*

Salt to taste

Freshly ground black pepper to taste

2 *1¼-pound lobsters, steamed, shelled, tail and body meat cubed, tomalley and coral reserved, and claw meat set aside for presentation*

Use a vegetable peeler to remove the skin and a paring knife to peel the tighter recesses of the red peppers. Halve, stem, seed, and derib each, then use a 2½-inch round cutter to make 8 coin-shaped rounds; set these aside, then chop the remaining peppers into 1-inch chunks and reserve.

Place each red pepper round in the center of a lightly oiled 6-ounce ramekin. Season the fillets to taste with salt and pepper, then use them to line the ramekins; this is best accomplished when the fillets are placed inside-out. Pack the lobster meat, tomalley, and coral in the center of each paupiette, then wrap the dish in plastic and steam 6 minutes in simmering water; remove and set aside to cool to room temperature.

RED PEPPER PURÉE

Reserved red pepper chunks

1 *large garlic clove, crushed*

1 *small hot pepper, coarsely chopped*

3 *medium shallots, thinly sliced*

1 *cup sake*

3 *tablespoons rice-wine vinegar*

Salt to taste

Freshly ground black pepper to taste

Lemon juice to taste

Combine the reserved red pepper with the garlic, pepper, shallots, sake, and vinegar in a small saucepan set over medium-high heat and bring to a boil; reduce the heat and simmer, partially covered, 15 minutes. Cool to room temperature, then purée in a food processor and strain through a sieve. Season to taste with salt, pepper, and lemon juice.

ASSEMBLY

Reserved lobster claw meat

4 *bunches radish sprouts, trimmed (approximately 1½ cups)*

½ *cup cooked fava beans*

Divide the purée among 4 serving plates.

Separately unwrap and, holding the open side of the paupiette, flip it over to drain partially, then set it atop the purée; two per plate.

Garnish each serving with a reserved lobster claw, some radish sprouts, and a few fava beans.

Pots de Chocolat

Pierre Baran, Executive Chef: Knickerbocker Club

8 servings

1 *quart milk*

4 *ounces sweet chocolate, broken or coarsely chopped*

2 *large eggs*

6 *large egg yolks*

6 *tablespoons granulated sugar*

Preheat the oven to 350°F.

Boil the milk in a medium saucepan set over medium-high heat, then pour over the chocolate; whisk occasionally until the chocolate is melted.

Combine the eggs, egg yolks, and sugar in a medium bowl and whisk to mix. Gradually add the chocolate mixture and whisk constantly. Skim off the froth.

Pour equal amounts into eight 8-ounce pots de crème or large ramekins. Set in a shallow roasting pan and pour enough boiling water around the pots to come halfway up their sides. Bake 30 minutes. Remove from the hot water bath and serve either warm beneath individual lids or, if cold, cool the pot de crème first, then cap it with its lid.

Pot de Crème

This small porcelain pot with lid is designed to cook, cool, and serve an elegant pot de crème. Its maximum 8-ounce capacity provides a generous offering of this rich chocolate, coffee, vanilla, or almond custard cream; the 2⅝-inch-deep bulging sides expand the porcelain-to-custard surface to properly transfer a bain marie's heat and a refrigerator's chill.

The pots de crème sold in kitchenware stores are almost all equally well made, so selection should be based upon individual preferences. Capacities range from 2½ to 8 ounces, while exterior styles are available in the tête de lion (lion-headed handles), the traditional marmite (two ears), or single-eared cups.

Soup Bowl

This heavy earthenware crock is most commonly used to finish and serve single portions of onion soup gratinée. Its 4½-inch width presents a generous surface for a cheese-encrusted croûte; the slight 2½-inch depth ensures a delightfully high gratinée-to-soup ratio, while nearly one pound of earthenware readily withstands and retains a broiling heat.

Although a porcelain lion's head tureen is de rigueur in an actual bistro, the more provincial earthenware bowl—which also holds pistou, black bean soup, or a simple bean side dish—has become the standard onion-soup service in this country. Bowls are available with handles as well as with covers or without. Individual capacities range from 10 to 19 ounces, with the described 12-ounce capacity being the most popular.

Ovenproof Platter

Porcelain platters come in a variety of shapes and sizes—some suit such special tasks as serving asparagus or brochettes—but most, like this all-purpose oval, provide a fine adjunct to a table service. Its twice-fired vitreous surface resists chips, crazing, and ruptures, the shallow depth and moderate rim provide easy access, while porcelain's superb heat retention continues to warm foods even at table. This platter measures 15″ × 10″ and weighs a hefty 3½ pounds.

A platter's glaze should be smooth, hard, and free of cracks to avert staining. Most of the larger ones have a raised "foot" on the bottom to support the plate face as it's fired.

Ovenproof porcelain is not flame-proof; it can be exposed to radiant or diffused, but not direct heat.

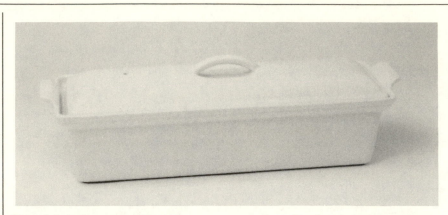

Enameled cast-iron or porcelain terrines are unsurpassed at baking those ground-meat mixtures uniformly.

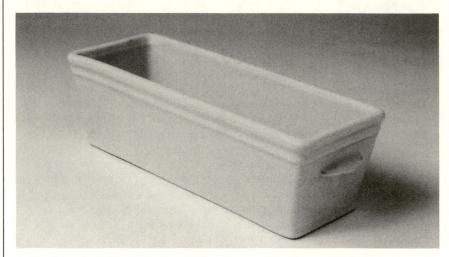

A porcelain galantine mold can serve in the oven as a secondary terrine, but it is designed to hold and shape a poached, stuffed, and rolled boned bird or cut of meat as it chills.

Terrine de Canard

Duck Terrine

Pierre Baran, Executive Chef: Knickerbocker Club

12 to 14 servings

3 *pounds boned and skinned duck meat*

1 *pound pork shoulder*

4 *ounces duck liver*

2 *duck breasts, boned, skinned, and cut into strips*

2 *teaspoons salt*

1 *teaspoon freshly ground black pepper*

¼ *cup cognac*

¼ *cup Madeira*

4 *ounces shallots, peeled and sliced*

2 *large eggs*

4 *ounces shelled and peeled pistachios*

4 *ounces black truffle peelings and juice*

4 *ounces caul, rinsed*

2 *bay leaves*

Combine the boned and skinned duck meat, pork, and liver, toss to mix, and set on one side of a shallow, nonreactive dish. Set the breast meat on the other side. Season with salt and pepper, sprinkle with the cognac and Madeira, and scatter the shallots over all. Cover and marinate overnight in the refrigerator.

Preheat the oven to 375°F.

Attach a medium-sized plate to a food grinder and grind the duck, pork, and liver mixture. Add the duck strips, eggs, pistachios, and truffles to the mixture and mix well.

Line a 2-quart terrine with caul, then use a rubber spatula to carefully pack the forcemeat down. Place the bay leaves on top, then overlap the excess caul.

Set in a water bath and bake 1½ hours. Remove from the bath, weight with at least 5 pounds, and set aside to cool to room temperature. Refrigerate overnight.

A rillettes pot's special inset lid is shallow enough to secure capping yet can't disturb the pâté's top layer of sealing fat.

Terrine

This enameled cast-iron terrine uniformly cooks, shapes, and releases the customarily ground meat, seafood, or vegetable compositions called terrines. A 6½-pound enameled cast-iron body conveys even heat; the 12″ × 4″ × 4″ form enables neat layering and slicing; a vented lid that momentarily contains rising steam to hasten cooking simultaneously prevents a dry top crust from forming, while barely flared sides make for a clean release.

Terrines are also manufactured in earthenware and porcelain and in the round, oval, and octagonal shapes better suited for home use. The exteriors of some oval terrines are decoratively styled to resemble pâtés en croûte with mock pastry-crust sides and lids with a duck, pheasant, rabbit, or woodcock head that ideally indicates the type of terrine within. Terrines generally have 2-

cup to 2-quart capacities, with the larger 1-, 1½-, and 2-quart sizes being the most popular.

Galantine Mold

This porcelain vessel is designed to shape the poached, stuffed, boned poultry and veal packages called galantines. Its 12″ × 4¼″ × 4″ shape creates a tidy, easy-to-apportion, aspic-glazed loaf; nearly 3 pounds of ceramic readily contain a forcemeat-packed capon or duck; the double-ridged rim adds further strength to support a compacting weight inset, while outwardly flared sides facilitate release.

Although the galantine mold has a glazed flat bottom that could develop a vacuum with a water-bath tray if used for a terrine, many avoid this by placing the mold on a small rack. Galantine molds are available only with 1- and 2-quart capacities.

Rillettes Pot

This porcelain pot with its raised-rim lid is traditionally used to pack, store, and serve the well-known shredded-pork pâté that's a speciality of Tours on the Loire River in France. The pot's barely bowed sides facilitate packing and permit easy access with a knife; its 3¼-inch diameter needs only a modicum of fat for a two-week-long seal, and the roughly 3½-inch depth creates a generous surface-to-rillettes ratio to promote safe, cold storage. An inset lid that isn't likely to be knocked off furthers proper storage.

Rillettes pots, which are manufactured only in porcelain, are most often available with roughly 8-ounce to just over 1½-pint capacities; the smaller sizes are the most popular.

Escalopes of Veal with Tomato, Mozzarella, and Basil

Seppi Renggli, Executive Chef while at The Four Seasons

8 servings

8 4-ounce veal loin escalopes, cut ⅓-inch thick

Salt to taste

Freshly ground black pepper to taste

¼ cup all-purpose flour mixed with a pinch of paprika

4 tablespoons clarified butter

1 large beefsteak tomato, peeled, seeded, and cut into ½-inch cubes

4 ounces mozzarella, cut into ½-inch cubes

4 slices prosciutto, cut into ½-inch strips

24 basil leaves

2 cups brown veal stock (see page 211)

1 pound fresh spinach pasta, cooked and sautéed in butter

Preheat the oven to 375°F.

Season the veal with salt and pepper, dredge in the flour, and set aside.

Heat the butter in a large sauté pan set over medium-high heat, add the veal—a few escalopes at a time—and sauté until medium; turn once.

Arrange the escalopes on an ovenproof platter, spoon some tomato, mozzarella, prosciutto, and basil on each, then bake 10 minutes or until the cheese starts to melt.

Meanwhile, reduce the stock to 1 cup and serve this sauce and the spinach pasta with the veal.

Mediterranean Fruit Terrine

Alfred Portale, Executive Chef: Gotham Bar & Grill

1 2-quart terrine

ORANGE WINE

4 *medium oranges, quartered*

Zest of 2 oranges

½ *vanilla bean*

1½ *cups granulated sugar*

6 *tablespoons vodka*

1 *bottle dry or white rosé wine*

Place the oranges, zest, and vanilla in a glass container. Dissolve the sugar in the vodka, then add to the oranges along with the wine. Cover and set aside 1 week in a cool place.

Strain the wine into clean bottles, cork, and let stand 1 month.

ORANGES

20 *medium oranges*

Over a bowl, use a sharp knife to peel all the oranges. Cut between the membranes to release and remove the flesh, and reserve the juice. Reserve the peel of 3 oranges. Lay the orange sections on a kitchen towel to dry.

CANDIED ORANGE PEEL

Reserved peel, scraped free of pith and julienned

1 *cup granulated sugar*

1 *cup water*

First soften the peel: Add it to boiling water, then reduce the heat and simmer 15 minutes; transfer with a skimmer to a bowl of cold water to cool, then drain.

Combine the sugar and water in a medium saucepan set over high heat and bring to a boil. Add the peel, reduce the heat, and cook at a bare simmer 1½ to 2 hours. Spread on a wire rack, separate the strips, and allow to cool, then chop coarsely.

HONEY-POACHED FIGS

Reserved orange juice

½ *cup honey*

1 *tablespoon anise seed*

3 *fresh thyme branches*

3 *fresh mint sprigs*

1 *pound figs, rinsed*

Bring the orange juice to a boil with the honey and a sachet bag filled with the anise, thyme, and mint. Add the figs, return to a boil, and remove from the heat. Let cool in the syrup, then trim off the stems and cut in half.

ASSEMBLY

2½ *cups orange wine, warmed*

6 *gelatin leaves, softened according to the manufacturer's directions and squeezed dry*

Reserved orange sections

Reserved honey-poached figs

Reserved candied peel

1 *small bunch mint leaves, cut into a chiffonade*

Combine the wine and gelatin and stir until smooth; set aside.

Place the orange sections, fig halves, candied peel, and mint into a 2-quart galantine mold or terrine, add the wine, and refrigerate overnight.

To serve: Unmold, slice, and garnish with additional candied orange peel and mint.

Pork Rillettes

Claude Franques, Executive Chef: René Pujol

1½ quarts or approximately 10 servings

1½ *pounds pork butt, cubed*

½ *pound pork fat, cubed*

14 *ounces boned duck meat, cubed*

4 *medium shallots, coarsely chopped*

1 *small onion, coarsely chopped*

3 *garlic cloves, coarsely chopped*

Pinch ground dried thyme

Pinch freshly grated nutmeg

Scant 1 *tablespoon salt*

1½ *teaspoons freshly ground white pepper*

Pinch saltpeter

8 *parsley sprigs*

2 *bay leaves*

½ *teaspoon dried rosemary*

½ *teaspoon dried sage*

1 *quart dry white wine*

Preheat the oven to 325°F.

In a large ovenproof casserole, sauté the pork, fat, and duck over medium-high heat 10 minutes or until lightly browned. Add the shallots, onion, garlic, thyme, nutmeg, salt, pepper, and saltpeter and sauté 4 minutes longer.

Tie the parsley, bay leaves, rosemary, and sage in cheesecloth and add it to the casserole. Add the wine and, if it doesn't cover the meat, add enough water to do so. Bring to a boil, cover, then place in the oven and bake 6 hours or until the meat is tender but not falling apart.

Remove from the oven, discard the cheesecloth, then transfer the meat to a strainer set over a bowl to drain off some of the fat.

Empty the meat into the bowl of an electric mixer and mix very slowly until almost smooth; the rillettes should be slightly rough in texture. You may need to add some of the strained fat to smooth out the spread. Season to taste with salt and pepper.

Pack the rillettes into 3 1-pint or 6 1-cup crocks, pour a little of the reserved fat on top to seal, and refrigerate until ready to use. Serve with toast, crusty bread, or rolls.

The two simplest ways to brew coffee are with the plunger coffeepot on the left, which infuses, and the Turkish coffeepot on the right, which decocts.

From left to right are a filter drip coffeepot (see page 148), a Neapolitan filter coffeepot (page 148), French drip coffeepot, and pumping percolator.

Turkish Coffeepot

Evoking visions of Bedouin fireside breakfasts or afternoon pick-me-ups in sultry souks, this pot simply boils water with coffee grounds and, traditionally, sugar. Its narrow, tapered profile allows substantial metal-to-liquid contact to hasten boiling; the bell-bottom shape that increases the heat-contact surface also brings balance, while the spouted collar facilitates neat pouring. A long, high-set handle distances hands from heat.

Also called an *ibrik* and most often manufactured in tin-lined brass or copper, the pot decocts 16 ounces—or 8 to 10 demitasse cups—of a very bitter brew.

Plunger Coffeepot

Elegant and functional, this filter-fitted framed glass beaker infuses coffee: It allows ground roast beans to steep in near-boiling water and then screen-separates the two. A fitting amount of medium-dark roasted ground beans is recommended, topped with water, then set aside for 5 minutes. Once the brewing is complete, the four-part plunger—two filter screens and two supporting frames—which is attached to the lid by a central shaft, is depressed to compact spent grounds to the bottom of the beaker, and the coffee is poured.

A near-regular on bistro tables, coffee brewed in this manner should be served immediately, as the grounds are not completely separated and there is no way to maintain its temperature. Three- to 12-cup plunger coffeepots are manufactured with plastic or chromed-steel frames; the latter is sturdier, with a more dependably level compressing filter face.

Pumping Percolator

Before the widespread use of automatic drip coffee makers, an aluminum pot with a basket, like this one, traditionally heated and brewed coffee. Its tall, tight profile builds a vigorous boil that shoots water through the central stem and out onto and through the suspended perforated coffee basket; the narrow shape that keeps grounds close to the tube assures proper extraction, while aluminum heats quickly.

Although it produces a hotter and therefore more aromatic brew, the pot has its drawbacks. Since there is no way to prevent boiling water from rising and filtering through the coffee, it refilters to render a bitter brew unless carefully monitored. With the popular 7-cup size, once the water begins to boil, reduce the heat and allow to percolate 8 minutes before serving.

Manual and electric coffee percolators—the latter frequently fitted with a thermostat-controlled on/off switch—are manufactured in aluminum or chromed steel with capacities that range from 2 to over 50 cups.

French Drip Coffeepot

Shortly after coffee was introduced to the Sun King's court, a prototype of this four-piece coffee maker appeared. Then called de Belloy's pot, it was a favorite of Brillat-Savarin, who probably appreciated the comparably mellower flavor than that produced through decoction. The pot works by strict percolation, by allowing hot water to pass through ground coffee and into a waiting receptacle. Its perforated porcelain strainer cap evenly distributes boiled water; the perforated cylindrical shaft, in which the first strainer sits, also acts as a strainer to hold the coffee grounds and is, in turn, inset into the serving pot. Once water is poured, passed, and the brew complete, the two filters are replaced with a lid.

French drip coffeepots, initially made in tinned steel, are manufactured nowadays only in porcelain with capacities from 2 to 8 cups. These fat-bellied pots ably double for tea; they're non-reactive, low weighted, and have a modest flange to keep the lid in position during pouring.

Filter Drip Coffeepot

Most people rely on some version of this two-piece coffee maker with its conical filter and glass carafe. Fitted with a paper cone, filled with ground coffee and then with near-boiling water, the widely splayed filter permits rapid saturation and particle-free passage into a nonreactive glass carafe, ideally kept warm over diffused heat.

Electrified versions of this manual model variously grind, brew, warm, and time. Some have a two-speed brew feature for making one to three cups or four to maximum capacity and some of these provide a stop-drip option that momentarily halts the brewing when the carafe is lifted from its hot plate. Manual filter-drip coffee makers brew 1 to 12 cups and the electric, 4 to 12. You're best off with the simplest one; the less there is, the less there is to break.

A fine tea kettle has a broad base, high-set handle, tight-fitting lid, and an outwardly angled spout.

Neapolitan Filter Coffeepot

This three-part device—two jugs (one spouted and one not) and a basket insert—produce a filter-drip coffee that, thanks in part to medium-fine roasted and ground coffee, is nearly as strong as espresso. Its unspouted container holds water for 9 demitasse cups; the inset basket, which looks like a bottomless sugar dredger, is filled with grounds, capped, then set into the water-filled pot open end downward. The spouted container is then inverted on top and the entire unit set over high heat. When the water boils, the apparatus is upended to filter-drip and serve.

Also called a *machinetta*, it is available in tin-lined brass or copper, aluminum or stainless steel with capacities from 2 to 12 demitasse cups.

Espresso Maker

When this hourglass-shaped apparatus is fully assembled—its base filled with water, inset basket packed with finely ground coffee, and the upper receptacle tightly screwed on—then set to boil, the steam is forcibly funneled up through a central vent and across the grounds to condense as coffee in the top of the pot. Its hefty broad base and top ensure stability and initially increase the water's exposure to heat for rapid boiling, as the constricted waist guarantees the right amount

This well-known espresso maker produces strong, Italian-style coffee.

of steam-to-coffee contact.

A limited number of stainless-steel stovetop espresso makers are manufactured, but by and large, you'll find only the traditional cast-aluminum "moka" model with a 1- to 14-demitasse cup capacity. While dependable and efficient, the pot must be removed from the heat once the steam begins to rise to thwart buckling, and the metal discolors through use.

Tea Kettle

To boil and pour water for teas, tisanes, or filtered coffee, this stout, spouted container comes in handy. A broad base maximizes heat contact to raise temperature rapidly; a

Pot and pan covers that befit warming, braising, general use, or tight kitchen storage are, clockwise from top left, a flat pot cover, dome cover, stepped cover, and universal pot cover.

A splatter screen (see page 150) supplies enough surface to thwart splatters but vent vapors from frying food.

high, well-angled spout allows complete filling, cautiously directed steam, and easy pouring, while a removable lid allows easy filling and cleaning.

Some tea kettles are fitted with a whistle and some are not; some display a curved, swan neck while other spouts are simply angulated. These features are purely options, what shouldn't be optional are a high, thick, stationary handle to furnish a cool, firm grip, a removable lid to allow cleaning of mineral deposits, and a well-flared spout to prevent steam burns.

Tea kettles are manufactured in aluminum, tin-lined copper, an all-too-light enameled steel, and stainless steel with a copper-cored base, with capacities from 2 to 5 quarts.

Stepped Cover

This stainless-steel pot cover—a favorite among chefs—complements all-purpose cooking. Its ½-inch dome returns minimum condensation to the pot, yet effects maximum heat reflection. The small furrow created by the outwardly sloped riser accommodates slight size inconsistencies and also uses rising vapors to create a tight water seal, while the flat edge assures the lid's set.

Stepped covers, also manufactured in tin-lined copper and aluminum, usually have a modest dome. They are frequently sold separately from the particular pots, but it's a good idea to buy one when you invest in that pot. Sizes range from roughly 5½ to 19¾ inches wide and differ slightly from manufacturer to manufacturer, with the better-sealing ones having a tight, more acute riser angle rather than a right angle leading up to the flat edge.

Flat Pot Cover

This rimless, tin-lined copper disk provides a practical pan cover for prepared vegetables or finished soups. Its near-flat, shiny surface that prevents splatters also reflects heat, becoming a secondary heat source, while no rim to contain rising steam means no condensation can develop and drip back onto food. A long, eyelet-ended handle that's easy to hang circumvents the usual lid-storage problems.

Flat covers, available most often in tin-lined copper or aluminum, generally have 9- to 14-inch diameters to match the individual manufacturer's pots. But most buy one—a 12-inch size—that can cover any of eight smaller-sized pots.

Dome Cover

This ringed, high-domed lid directs condensed vapors back to the pot to baste cooking food. Separately sold, the cover transforms many a standard-sized casserole or sauté pan into a modest braiser. The inset edge first develops a water seal by allowing some evaporation to vent up to the cooler pot rim to condense, collect, and block escaping steam. Vapors then rise to the lid's centrally-set heat sinks, concentric rings or ridges that absorb their heat and reduce them to liquid to drip back onto the food.

Equally fine cast-iron and heat-tempered–glass dome lids are manufactured with variations of those heat sinks, as are unridged stainless-steel ones, less appropriate for casserole cooking than for stovetop use. Since the inset edge on the stainless-steel lid invariably rises at a steeper angle than the other two, the larger edge-to-rim gap is not easily sealed. Dome lids are usually available in two sizes to fit pans with an 8- or 10-inch diameter.

Universal Pot Cover

This ringed stainless-steel disk may resemble a bull's-eye, but it serves as a cover for pots with diameters from 6½ to 8½ inches. Its three concentric rings step down toward the center knob, with each level meant to inset into the rim of a smaller pot.

It sounds like a fine, functional acquisition, especially for those short on storage space, but the lid's light, 10-ounce weight dents easily to lie unevenly and therefore seal ineffectually. Aluminum universal lids are also available, and with the same problems. Better to invest in a tailor-made, tight-fitting cover at the same time you buy each of your pots and pans, as manufacturing inconsistencies do occur.

Splatter Screen

Like a shield, this tightly perforated disk covers a fry pan to reduce the amount of grease splattered. Its 11½-inch diameter is wide enough to rest on the rims of seven smaller-sized pans; the 480 holes per inch that rebuff most splatters still allow food vapors to rise, as a medium-long handle eases positioning and removal.

Some manufacturers suggest using these screens as strainers or cooling racks, neither of which you should do. The screen is too weak to serve as a sturdy strainer and the tight mesh still leaves far too much metal contact surface to cool foods properly.

Splatter screens—usually fitted with wire handles with a plastic insert—are available almost solely with that 11½-inch framed aluminum face.

In-Pot Trivet

Water is unsurpassed at uniformly transmitting cold or hot temperature. Sugar, for example, is immediately halted at its caramel stage by immersing the pot in an ice-water bath, and a pudding is evenly steamed in a hot-water bath, best accomplished by using this small, footed ring that transforms any saucepan into a bain marie. In a pan of simmering water, its 5-inch di-

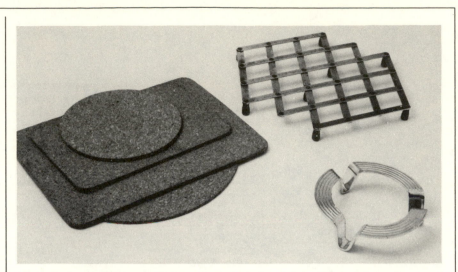

Trivets to protect tabletops or abet cooking include, from left to right, cork hot pads, a metal trivet, and an in-pot trivet.

ameter supports a smaller basin or secondary pan; the 1½-inch-high feet provide full warm-water access, as surface grooves create traction.

In-pot trivets are available only in cast aluminum with a 5-inch width.

Metal Trivet

Its three-footed forebear held a cook pot above an open fire, but this expandable trivet serves instead to safeguard a tabletop from a warm pan, plate, or bowl. Its six metal bands stretch like an accordion to accommodate any standard-sized serving piece, and its bars lie flat to assure balance. But because pan heat is directed both up and down, an exposed table won't be protected. Better to use it as you would a classic brass William and Mary model— with a tablecloth.

This trivet is manufactured in durable stainless steel, most often in an 11″ × 2½″ closed size which can expand up to 14″ × 7″.

Cork Hot Pad

Thin and resilient, a composition cork disk may well be the ideal mat to protect a tabletop from a pan's heat. Its generally ³/₁₆-inch thickness may seem slight, but cork's high k-factor (its insulative value) affords excellent protection as its light pliancy assures slip-free placement.

Remarkably inexpensive, cork hot pads are usually available in packages containing 8- to 12-inch rounds, squares, and/or rectangles.

This heat diffuser's two plates, sandwiched air space, and gridded top all combine to mute temperature to an onset pot.

Heat Diffuser

When set atop a low flame, this inch-high device's two chrome plates with an air pocket between evenly temper and disperse heat to create a safe conduit on which to warm such heat-sensitive materials as heat-resistant glass and porcelain pots. The flame warms the base plate, which heats the air pocket, which then conducts a softer temperature to the gridded top plate. Its rough surface—which reduces the amount of contact with an onset pan—then diffuses what heat remains.

Some manufacturers suggest preparing sauces or melting chocolate in a saucepan set on a diffuser, but heated water, as in a bain marie, remains a far more effective medium. Diffusers in the forms of an enameled cast-iron plate and a simple wire ring are also available.

5. Bakeware, Molds, and Pastry-Preparation Tools

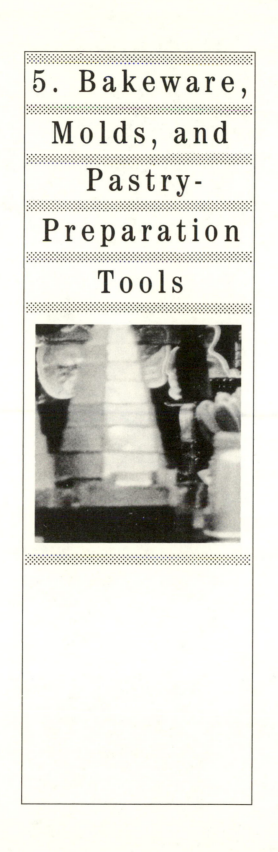

The molds that produce a fluted brioche, crenulated quiche, chocolate rooster caught in full crow, and other elegant, inviting, and whimsical breads, pastries, and confections very likely derive from the neolithic chef. His food supply was the first constant repetition of ingredient combinations that could then be heated as they became predictably more digestible and better tasting. The increasingly confident cook—now less the technician and more the artisan—presumably experimented to improve his diet further: to perhaps sweeten the sustaining grain pastes and doughs with honey and then to notch, plait, or otherwise shape them for baking on hot stone slabs.

The ingenuity that created these finer foods must then have inspired the production of vessels to speed their perfect preparation—as the unearthed Assyrian terra-cotta fireside cake molds and others for Egyptian oven-baked breads attest.

And while those obsolete molds suited the heating methods of that age, others—meant more for assembly than for cooking—are produced today in much the same fashion as their predecessors, such as the negative wooden ones that emboss shortbread, butter, and speculaas and the reed banneton that supports a proofing country loaf.

Most old baking forms served as prototypes for new ones, with the array expanding in the footsteps of an improving oven and advancing metallurgy.

Baking was first accomplished under an inverted, hot earthenware pot whose portable size severely restricted the length, breadth, and diameter of any underlying vessel for batter or dough. The large, domed, cylindrical clay structure that suc-

ceeded it opened the door to hearth cooking, allowing a surface sufficient to support the variously scaled molds then crafted.

Most of these were struck in bronze in uncomplicated, round shapes. Earthenware was simplistically thrown into similarly round, yet lower, forms, the styles of which prevailed until the sixteenth century, when ready supplies of the more malleable and manageable brasslike latten and tin-lined copper allowed chefs to commission the oval, triangular, and trefoil molds illustrated in woodcuts of the period.

Broadening travel and trade increased the decorative batterie de cuisine by making once exotic ingredients available and their preparation tools necessary. The Near Eastern almonds brought back by crusaders and used in marzipan required miniature molding implements or homemade plaster casts for professional presentations. Greater stores of refined Canary and Caribbean islands sugar could be more frequently boiled and blown, pulled, cast, molded, piped, or poured—but the techniques called for special pumps, forms, plaques, and tubes. And New World chocolate—once processed so that it could be eaten out of hand—was rolled, cut, or piped but most quickly and uniformly shaped in sheet molds.

Current technology continues to improve these and the many other pastry and confectionery tools since devised by incorporating more durable metals, coatings, and plastics into their ever-streamlining designs. Plaster marzipan forms that also suit fondant are now lastingly cast in heavy aluminum; the original tinned-steel oeuf en gelée, croquembouche, and bombe molds see sturdier life in stainless steel, while those for

baguettes, brioches, and tarts are often finished in heat-retentive black steel to ensure the development of a golden-brown crust. Fittings, too, are better polished: A springform pan's latch closes more easily and securely; sleeker stainless-steel or polycarbonate pastry tubes promote the smoothest flow while remaining rust-free, and the pastry bags now produced in nylon won't seep.

It's been said that a craftsman's tools reflect his or her culture's demands and this is surely the case with those in the decorative batterie de cuisine, from the elementary forms that meant first to feed and then to flatter to today's high-tech marvels that put the user on the leading edge. Further advances in the state of the art rest with the user.

Baking Sheet

A fine baking sheet with shallowly flared edges and a dark surface bakes and browns such large, dense, frequently filled dough products as croissants, Danish pastries, buns, and round and flat breads that might leak or overflow. This sheet's ½-inch flared edges that securely transport heavier doughs and contain butter or juices still allow an oven's full hot-air access to foods, and 4 pounds of black steel retain and transmit heat to speed the dough's set, rise, steam release, and browning.

Baking sheets are also manufactured in nonstick-surfaced and plain aluminum in sizes from 16″ × 12″ to 28″ × 18″; round sheets in blue steel are available with 8- to 20-inch diameters.

Select as large a baking sheet as will fit in your oven with a 2-inch margin on all sides.

Perforated Baking Sheet

To get the lightest, crispiest pizza, most bakers rely on a ceramic baking stone or perforated baking sheet to help draw off the moisture released by dough through absorbtion or evaporation as it bakes and to heat the bread evenly. In commerce, heavy black steel is preferred; it's more durable, portable, and quicker to heat and conduct. These sheets are also, unfortunately for the home baker, large and are available exclusively in the commercial size—23½″ × 15¾″. To achieve similar results at home, use a lightweight aluminum perforated pizza pan, perhaps atop a household-sized baking stone or black or blue steel baking sheet that would heighten the intensity of the heat conveyed through the pan's perforated face. Perforated pizza pans are available with 13- to 15-inch diameters.

Cookie Sheet

A heavy aluminum sheet is essential and versatile for baking cookies, meringues, and turnovers, among other things. Its level surface encourages a loose batter to spread evenly or a thicker one to maintain its shape; save for two slight end rims for handles, its wide open face allows oven heat to reach the dough or batter from every direction, while 2½ pounds of aluminum, which conducts heat quickly to properly set flat, high-sugar foods, can't warp at high baking temperatures.

Stainless-steel and nonstick-surfaced aluminum cookie sheets are also available. So is a double-layered aluminum sheet with a dead air space that acts as an insulating layer which mutes bottom heat so foods like meringues don't color. Popular cookie-sheet sizes range from 16″ × 12″ to 17″ × 14″; get two of the largest ones your oven can accommodate while still allowing 2 inches of space on each side for

Flat metal sheets with the barest edges allow oven heat to reach every possible angle of a flat cookie, bread, or pizza as it bakes. Shown from the left are a cookie sheet, baking sheet (see page 153), and perforated baking sheet.

Bakers favor a medium heavy, aluminum jelly roll pan with rolled rims that uniformly bakes and retains shape.

Focaccia

*Sandro Fioriti, Executive Chef:
Sandro's*

8 servings

1 ¼-ounce package active dry yeast

1½ cups warm water

2½ teaspoons coarse salt

¼ cup extra-virgin olive oil

4 cups unbleached all-purpose flour

2 tablespoons fresh whole rosemary leaves

Combine the yeast and ½ cup warm water in a large bowl, stir to mix, and set aside 5 minutes to dissolve thoroughly.

Add the remaining water together with 1 teaspoon salt and 2 tablespoons oil and stir to mix; gradually work in the flour.

Turn the dough out onto a well-floured surface and vigorously knead 10 minutes or until the dough is smooth and elastic. Shape into a ball, place in a large bowl, cover with a towel, and set aside in a warm area 1½ hours, or until double in volume.

Punch the dough down, knead briefly, then roll to fit a lightly oiled baking sheet; the dough should measure about ½ inch deep. Use your finger to poke holes in the surface of the dough at 1-inch intervals, then brush with the remaining oil. Sprinkle the rosemary over all and season with the remaining salt; set aside 30 minutes to rest.

Preheat the oven to 450°F.

Bake 15 to 20 minutes or until golden brown.

Cordon Rose Chocolate Christmas Log

Rose Levy Beranbaum
The Cake Bible

1 Bûche de Noël

CHOCOLATE CLOUD ROLL

6 *tablespoons granulated sugar*

6 *large eggs, separated*

4 *ounces bittersweet chocolate, melted*

⅓ *cup finely ground unblanched, sliced, and toasted almonds (optional)*

¾ *teaspoon cream of tartar*

1 *tablespoon unsweetened cocoa*

Preheat the oven to 350°F.

Beat ¼ cup sugar and the egg yolks together in a mixing bowl 5 minutes or until light and fluffy. Add the chocolate, and almonds if desired, and beat to incorporate, scraping down the sides when needed.

Beat the egg whites until foamy in a large mixing bowl, add the cream of tartar, and beat until soft peaks form when the beater is raised. Gradually beat in the remaining 2 tablespoons sugar and continue to beat until stiff peaks form when the beater is raised slowly.

With a large balloon whisk, slotted skimmer, or rubber spatula, fold ¼ of the whites into the chocolate mixture to lighten it. Then gently fold in the remaining egg whites.

Pour into a 17″ × 12″ jelly-roll pan that's been greased, bottom-lined with a nonstick liner or foil slightly extended over the sides, then greased again and floured. Spread evenly with a spatula and bake 16 minutes in the lower third of the oven.

Wet a clean dish towel and wring it out well. Remove the cake from the oven and leave it in its pan. Dust with cocoa, cover immediately with the towel, and allow to cool.

Remove the towel and, lifting by a long edge of the liner overhang, gently slide the cake onto a flat surface. Immediately spread the Perfect Whipped Cream (see below) and roll up, using the liner for support and gently peeling it away as you go. Chill at least 1 hour before final assembly.

PERFECT WHIPPED CREAM

1 *cup heavy cream*

1 *tablespoon granulated sugar*

½ *teaspoon vanilla extract*

Combine all the ingredients in a large mixing bowl, refrigerate alongside beaters at least 15 minutes. Remove and beat until stiff peaks form when the beater is raised.

DARK CHOCOLATE GANACHE

12 *ounces bittersweet chocolate, broken into bits*

1⅔ *cups heavy cream*

¼ *cup sweet butter, softened (optional)*

2 *tablespoons cognac*

Process the chocolate in a food processor until very fine. Heat the cream to the boiling point and, with the processor motor running, pour it through the feed tube in a steady stream; process a few seconds until smooth. Transfer to a bowl and cool completely. Gently stir in the butter, if desired, and cognac. Allow to cool for several hours or until of frosting consistency. If using butter, whisk for a few seconds to aerate.

ASSEMBLY

Cut a diagonal slice from one end of the cake roll and place it on top to form a knot.

Spread the ganache frosting over the log and use the tines of a fork to make lines resembling bark. Make a few round swirls with the fork on top of the knot.

Decorate with meringue mushrooms, marzipan leaves, and any small appropriate figures such as porcelain elves or trumpeters.

Refrigerate until 1 hour before serving.

proper convection. You'll want one sheet to cool and load while the other is in the oven.

Jelly-Roll Pan

This wide, shallow rectangular pan— a standard among bakers—is most often used to bake the aerated cakes and souffléed omelets that are then filled and rolled (if the filling is hot) or simply rolled to shape and cooled before filling. The pan's generous 17″ × 12″ expanse exposes most of the batter to oven heat to speed light, firm setting; inch-high sides are just enough to contain a liquid batter, while aluminum, which reflects some heat, won't overcook the roll's bottom before its center has set.

Jelly-roll pans, which are always prelined with parchment paper to assure the cake is released intact, are also manufactured in tinned and stainless steels and coated aluminum, the best of which are moderately heavy with a rolled rim to reinforce shape.

Brioche Mold

When filled with a buttery, egg-rich yeast dough, then proofed and set to bake, this flared, fluted black-steel mold shapes and evenly colors the luxurious bread called brioche. The mold's top diameter—twice that of its base—creates a desirably high crust-to-crumb ratio. Deep crimps further extend side surface by 90 percent while black steel, which superbly retains and conveys heat, browns and crisps uniformly.

These brioche molds, far more popular in this country than the crinkle-edged loaf style, are also available in stainless steel, heavy tinned steel, porcelain, and heat-tempered glass. Sizes, based on top diameter, range from 2⅓ to 9½ inches and have 2-ounce to 2-quart capacities. An 8-inch-wide mold that holds 5 cups and a single-serving 4-ounce mold serve most recipes; the latter is also used to make fruit tart shells and bran muffins.

Brioche Mousseline Mold

This tin, which resembles a sand bucket, bakes two sumptuous yeast breads—an ultrabuttery brioche mousseline and the cakelike panettone. The mold's specialty lies solely in its sides, which measure roughly 30 percent higher than the base width: Not only does that ratio induce a maximum proofing rise, but it further increases the bread's height during baking by setting the dough's edges long before its center, which then has nowhere to go but up.

Brioche mousseline molds are manufactured only in tinned steel and sold according to their top-diameter measurement—from just over 3 inches to 5½ inches wide. Popular sizes range from 3 cups (for molds with a 3½-inch diameter) to 3¾ cups (4-inch diameter) to 6¼ cups (4¾-inch diameter).

Bread-Loaf Pan

This brick-shaped mold is ideal for forming and baking a neat, crisp-crusted sandwich-type loaf of bread. Its slightly flared sides, which contain, shape, and set dough, later ease its release; black steel quickly absorbs and conveys high heat to assure complete browning, while subtle side and base dimples that don't impress the dough do limit its final metal contact to prevent sticking during release.

Loaf pans are also available in tinned steel, plain and nonstick-surfaced aluminum, and a heat-tempered glass that browns dough almost as adeptly as black steel. Tinned steel and the two aluminums, because each is so heat-reflective, are fine for baking marble and pound cakes, while tinned steel and the coated aluminum, which can't react to acids, better suit baking quick breads with fruit. Sizes range from 3½″×1⅝″×1½ to 10″×3½″×3″, the smallest often combined in plaques for easy, multiple baking.

The brioche mousseline mold on the left and fluted brioche mold (see page 155) on the right are designed to bake variations of that yeast-leavened, egg-rich dough.

Both the pullman bread-loaf pan on the left and bread-loaf pan on the right should be moderately heavy for their size.

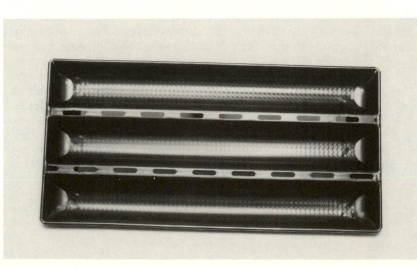

This French bread tray's lengthy black steel troughs uniformly mold, bake, and brown crusty baguettes.

Pullman Bread-Loaf Pan

This long, covered rectangular tinned-steel mold produces a perfect, brick-shaped loaf of bread with a thin, lightly golden crust and close-textured crumb for sandwiches, canapés, and croustades. When closed, the sliding top shapes dough during its final rising, then compacts it during baking to ensure dense texture. Shiny tin that both deflects and transmits oven heat won't overbrown the crust before the bread's center has fully baked.

Alternatively called a *pain de mie*—literally, bread of crumb—or Pullman loaf, perhaps because its compact profile resembles the railroad car's—these pans are also manufactured in black steel, which develops a wonderful, slightly deeper, darker crust, but one that's not always desirable since it's frequently trimmed off. Pullman bread-loaf pans are available in either $13'' \times 4'' \times 4''$ or $16'' \times 4'' \times 4''$ measurements. When cylindrical, they have a $1\frac{3}{4}$- or $2\frac{3}{4}$-inch diameter with a common $11\frac{3}{4}$-inch length. The cylinder with the larger diameter is also available in $9\frac{1}{2}$- and $14\frac{1}{4}$-inch lengths and these are alternately used to steam puddings.

French Bread Tray

This tray's black steel troughs mold and bake high crust–slight crumb breads. Each $17'' \times 2'' \times \frac{3}{4}''$ half-cylinder braces a length of dough during its final rise and subsequent baking; black steel, which rapidly transmits a high heat, assures quick setting, thorough baking, and overall golden brown color, while the perforated strips that separate each trough foster even baking by allowing heat to circulate freely.

This tray shapes baguettes, but wider cylinders are available to create bâtards and thinner ones for ficelles. Solid and perforated tinned steel are notoriously lightweight and prone to buckling and denting. Select black steel instead; it will be moderately light but with a reinforcing, wraparound wire to ensure its shape.

Panettone

Margaret and G. Franco Romagnoli
The New Italian Cooking

4 panettone

3 ¼-ounce packages active dry yeast

¾ cup warm water

1¾ cups granulated sugar

¾ cup milk

7 ounces sweet butter

2½ teaspoons salt

Zest from 3 large lemons

4 teaspoons vanilla extract

8 cups all-purpose unbleached flour (approximately)

6 large eggs at room temperature, 1 of them separated

2 teaspoons vegetable oil

⅔ cup seedless raisins

½ cup slivered citron

1 teaspoon granulated sugar mixed with 1 teaspoon water

Combine the yeast, water, and 2 tablespoons sugar in a 1-quart measure and allow to stand in a warm area 10 minutes or until it has nearly tripled its original bulk.

Scald the milk, then add 4 ounces butter and stir until melted; add the salt and remaining sugar. Empty into a large bowl, add the lemon zest and vanilla, and stir to mix; set aside briefly to cool.

Use an electric mixer or dough hook to beat 2 cups flour into the milk. Beat in the yeast mixture, then 2 more cups of flour and 5 eggs, one by one. Add the white of the sixth egg and beat until smooth.

If not using a dough hook, put aside the mixer and work with a wooden spoon. Add 3 more cups flour and mix until the dough becomes unwieldy.

Turn out onto a floured work surface, add ½ cup flour and knead; gradually work in the remaining ½ cup flour (an additional ½ cup flour may be necessary), kneading until the dough is soft, elastic, and smooth, yet sticky.

Place the oil in a large bowl, add the dough, and twirl it around until both dough and bowl glisten with oil. Cover the bowl with a dry towel, set in a warm area, and allow the dough to rise 3 to 4 hours or until triple in volume.

Cover the raisins with hot water in a 2-cup measure and set aside 20 minutes to plump; drain and squeeze dry.

Punch the dough down when it has risen sufficiently, then knead in the raisins and citron. Divide the dough into four equal pieces.

Butter four 2-cup soufflé dishes, charlotte molds, or small brioche mousseline molds, fit each (except the latter) with a buttered aluminum collar, and set a piece of dough in each. Slash a cross across the top of each, place in a warm area, cover with a towel, and allow to rise 1 hour or until double in volume.

Preheat the oven to 400°F thirty minutes before baking.

Combine the yolk of the last egg with the sugar-water solution, mix well, then brush the top of each panettone with it. Bake 10 minutes, put ½ tablespoon butter in the center of each cross, and return to the oven. Reduce the heat to 375°F for 10 minutes, then lower the heat to 350°F and continue to bake 30 minutes longer or until the panettone are crusty and golden and a cake tester comes out clean after being inserted into the center of each loaf.

Cool completely before removing from their pans. Allow to stand 1 day before cutting.

Deep-Dish Pizza Pan

This moderately heavy black steel pan bakes a crisp-crusted deep-dish Chicago-style pizza. Its 2-inch depth contains a generous filling; outwardly flared sides encourage some evaporation and facilitate slice removal, while black steel, which rapidly conducts high oven heat, sets, browns, and crisps a crust. The medium weight deters buckling at the average 450°F temperatures.

Black steel deep-dish pizza pans are most often available with 5½- to 12¾-inch diameters.

A black steel deep-dish pizza pan is a near necessity to fully set, color, and crisp a layered pizza's bottom crust.

Monsieur Monfort's French Bread

Bernard Clayton, Jr.
The Complete Book of Breads

4 baguettes or 2 medium round loaves

7 to 8 cups all-purpose flour

2 ¼-ounce packages active dry yeast

4 teaspoons salt

3 cups tepid water

In a large bowl combine 7 cups of flour with the yeast and salt; form a well in the center, pour in the water, and, with a wooden spoon, stir to pull the dry ingredients slowly into the liquid. Work into a ball, then turn out onto a lightly floured surface.

Use a pastry scraper to turn and fold the dough; if too tacky, redust the work surface sparingly with some of the remaining flour. Continue to lift, fold, and turn the dough for 10 minutes, occasionally throwing the dough against the work surface to break this rhythmic sequence. The dough will become elastic yet will remain sticky.

Wash the large bowl, grease it, then set the dough in it. Cover tightly with plastic wrap and place in a warm area—70°F—for 2 to 3 hours or until it doubles in volume. Punch the dough down, re-cover, and set aside 1 to 2 hours to again double in volume.

Turn onto the floured work surface, repunch, and briefly knead to press out the air bubbles. Either quarter the dough to make long slender loaves or halve it to make round hearth ones. Form each into a ball and allow to rest 5 minutes before shaping into loaves.

For a long loaf, separately flatten each ball into an oval, then fold it over lengthwise and flatten with the side of your open hand; refold and roll with the palms. If the dough resists, let it rest 3 to 4 minutes as you prepare the other pieces. Return to the partially formed length and continue to roll under your palms until it is shaped; the seam will disappear. The long pieces can be placed directly into lightly greased half-cylindrical French-type pans. Round loaves can be placed on greased baking sheets or, initially, in cloth-lined baskets. Cover with a a sheet of waxed paper supported by water glasses; set in a warm area and let rise 1 hour.

Preheat the oven to 425°F 20 minutes before baking; place a broiler pan or shallow roasting pan on the lowest shelf and, five minutes before baking, pour 1½ cups hot tap water into the pan.

Transfer any basket-raised loaves onto a greased baking sheet, then use a blade to make a series of diagonal slashes on the baguettes or a tic-tac-toe design on the round ones. Brush or spray the loaves with water as you place them in the oven. During the first 15 minutes of baking, spray the loaves every 3 minutes. Do this from the open oven door to prevent too much moist air from escaping. The loaves will be fully ovenproof (expanded) after 18 minutes, at which time the crusts will begin to color. If any water remains in the pan on the bottom shelf at this point, empty it.

Bake the loaves 25 to 30 minutes total or until golden brown. Midway in the baking period shift the loaves to expose them equally to the temperature variations in the oven. Test for doneness by turning over one loaf and rapping its bottom; a hard, hollow sound indicates that the bread is baked. Remove from the oven and set on a wire rack to cool; for a bright, shiny crust, brush lightly with slightly salted water.

Molds that variously shape sweetened yeast-leavened doughs include, clockwise from the top, a kugelhopf mold, savarin mold, baba au rhum mold, and trois frères mold.

Kugelhopf Mold

This deep, fluted tube pan is used to prepare the rich yeast cake—believed to be Ukrainian—that the Austrian-born gastronome Joseph Wechsberg described as a "variation of a pound cake shaped like a derby on which several people have been sitting." Its 4-inch depth contains and directs the dough's proofing rise; the decorative swirls induce a delectably high crust-to-crumb ratio, while the tube that conducts heat to the dough's center assures quick, even setting.

Kugelhopf pans are most often available in nonstick-surfaced aluminum, heavy tinned steel, or the pastry chef's favorite, earthenware, which best retains and transfers heat to better brown the crust. Their top diameters can measure from 6½ to 9½ inches.

Trois Frères Mold

This fluted ring mold is designed to proof, bake, and shape an almond-flavored yeast cake that, when cooled, is glazed with liqueured apricot jam, sprinkled with almonds and angelica, and filled with fruit. Its 2-inch depth exposes considerable dough to radiant oven heat for quick, nondrying setting; the large central tube creates a high metal-to-dough ratio to hasten baking, while flutes extend the cake surface to be soaked.

Named in honor of the Julien brothers—three nineteenth-century pastry cooks—the mold is also used to set aspic and Bavarian cream. It is manufactured only in tinned steel with diameters from 4 inches to the more popular 8¾ inches with its 6-cup capacity. Don't confuse this with a Turk's-head mold, which has similar swirls but has no central tube.

Baba au Rhum Mold

As deep as its top diameter is wide, this tinned-steel cylinder has no peer at producing the classic single serving of the raisin-studded yeast cake that, once baked, dried, soaked in rum syrup, then flecked with candied fruit, becomes baba au rhum. The mold's 4-ounce capacity affords an ideal amount of this rich cake; its flared sides promote clean rising and easy removal. Tinned steel is the best metal for the task as aluminum reacts with the proofing egg-rich dough and stainless steel can't bake it evenly.

Occasionally called dariole molds after the once popular dessert they also shaped, baba au rhum molds are available with heights and diameters from 1⅔ to 2¾ inches. If you're buying a baba mold to bake custard in a water bath for even heat, select the more durable stainless over the tinned steel.

Savarin Mold

This ring mold shapes and cooks a raisinless baba dough to be subsequently soaked in rum, glazed, and filled with fruit or cream. The mold's roughly equal 2-inch trough depth and diameter promise uniform baking; its large central tube, which doubles the dough's contact with hot metal, hastens setting, as outwardly flared sides ease release.

Named after Brillat-Savarin, the renowned French gastronome, savarin molds are also used for aspic, custard, and rice. They are most often manufactured in heavy tinned steel with 2¾- to 10¼-inch diameters; the described 9½-inch mold with its 6-cup capacity is the most popular size. When buying, select a seam- or ridge-free mold for the cleanest shape.

Génoise Pan

This flare-sided tinned-steel cake pan is traditionally used to bake the rich, close-textured génoise sponge cake that serves as the basis for many of the elegant assemblies that are a pastry chef's pride. Its 1½-inch-high sides restrict batter capacity to assure quick heating and setting and a limited rise for a tight, moist crumb; the side's outward angle, which may promote evaporation and an evenly poured icing, were whimsically designed to produce what looked like a fallen cake.

Consequently called a moule à manque—a mistake mold—it is manufactured in equally fine tinned steel or nonstick-surfaced aluminum. Diameters range from 4 to nearly 16 inches, the most popular of which is the 8- or 8¾-inch size.

Manque Rosace Mold

It's said that the handsome praline-coated cake customarily baked in this round, rose-bottomed, flared pan was the result of a mistake—or *manque* in French. When an improperly prepared génoise batter didn't turn out, the story goes, its frugal chef covered it with pralines; the resultant cake was successful, and this mold soon followed to present it more attractively. Its modest depth quickly sets and bakes the batter; the sloped sides, which resemble a collapsed cake, remain easy to coat with the traditional poured glaze, while the rose crown that extends surface for further flavoring assists apportioning because of its raised sunburst pattern.

Also called a rosace droit mold and used to shape aspic and ice cream, it is most often available in heavy tinned steel measuring 7¼ inches wide with a 1-quart capacity.

Round Cake Pan

Round cake pans were once made of different metal and had wide, flat rims and a cover to heat evenly and protect the batter from being flavored during wood-fired baking, but they have otherwise changed little since the Renaissance. Tinned steel is favored by some, especially for batters containing acidic fruit, but professionals usually prefer aluminum because it is easier to maintain and quicker to heat. Uniformly warming a batter is essential in fine cake-baking in order to prevent too thick a crust forming before the batter's center completely sets. Straight sides promote uniform rising while rolled edges and the metal's medium weight preserve clean, smooth lines for level heat.

Round cake pans are also manufactured in stainless steel, as well as anodized and nonstick-coated aluminum, with diameters from 5 to 22 inches. Depths range from ¾ to 4 inches; pick up two of the 9"x2" pans that complement standard recipes.

The sloped sides of both the génoise pan (see page 159) on the left and manque rosace mold (page 159) on the right create spongecakes that welcome a poured glaze.

Professionals prefer easy-to-maintain, quick-to-heat aluminum for both the square baking pan on the left and round cake pan on the right.

Square Baking Pan

This anodized aluminum pan produces professional-looking gingerbread, brownies, and toffee squares—single-layer cakes so richly flavored and densely textured that they are rarely filled or iced, just cut into blocks or bars and served. The pan's 8-inch-square measurement and 2-quart capacity complement most standard spice-cake recipes; the metal's matte surface, which deflects some oven heat, prevents overdried sides and bottoms before the center is set, while the moderate weight prolongs its crisp, clean, even-cooking shape.

Square baking pans are also manufactured in heat-tempered glass and plain and nonstick-surfaced aluminum, most of which are also available in a 9-inch size.

Tube Pan

Many a tall, shiny metal pan can be used to bake an angel cake successfully, but this round-tubed aluminum one is the most traditional and popular. Its 4½-inch depth easily supports the high-sitting, higher-rising aerated batter; the central tube that conducts heat to the batter's core assures even baking, while shiny aluminum promises fast heat and maximum expansion before the batter sets. Once the pan is inverted, the slightly longer central tube allows the cake to cool in the pan with minimal compacting.

Tube pans are also manufactured in medium-heavy-gauge tinned steel with diameters from 6 to 9¼ inches and heights from 2¾ to 3¾ inches, but the lightweight aluminum in the 10" × 4¼", 9-cup-capacity size, fre-

At left, a springform pan for baking densely textured or crumb-crusted cakes; at right, a tube pan for lighter angel-food cakes.

The tiered, hexagonal gorenfloat cake, a mid-nineteenth-century creation, is named in honor of a High Renaissance monk.

Shown above are the forms in which to bake a multilobed Breton cake pyramid.

quently fitted with a loose bottom and occasionally with metal rim tabs to balance the pan for inverted cooling, is appropriate for most standard recipes.

Springform Pan

With its expandable, clip-closed sides and removable base, this nonstick-coated heavy-gauge aluminum pan is superb for baking and releasing dense fruit, honey, and cheesecakes or cakes whose crumb crusts are difficult or impossible to unmold cleanly from standard cake pans. Its 1¼-pound weight, nearly thrice that

of comparable pans, promises fast, even heat conduction for quick setting; sides held fast with a clasp are then opened and spread to release the cake as the smooth-as-glass surface with its silicone coat further hinders sticking.

Springform pans are also manufactured in a medium-lightweight tinned steel with waffled bottoms to deter sticking. They more frequently come with two or three interchangeable bottoms, one of which is always a tube. Pan diameters range from 6 to 12 inches with 2½- to 3-inch-high sides; the described 9″ diameter is the most popular.

Gorenflot Mold

This set's nine graduated hexagonal ring molds and their tiny, fluted dome are used to bake babalike dough layers. These are then soaked in either an anisette or a kirsch syrup and tiered to form the spectacular dessert named for a celebrated High Renaissance monk/gourmand whom Alexander Dumas immortalized in *La Dame de Monsoreau.* Each of this set's pans is designed to carefully cook and present this piece. The central hole helps the yeast to rise evenly and the dough to bake uniformly; angular sides, when stacked and aligned, resemble a monk's flowing robes, while ever-widening layers—2½ to 11 inches—secure the footing for this 19-inch-high pyramid.

Ten-piece gorenflot molds whose specific capacities range from ¼ cup to 11 cups are manufactured only in tinned steel.

Breton Cake Mold

With six-leaf clover shapes, graduated sizes, and—save for the smallest—central tubes, this six-tin set shapes and bakes an almond biscuit batter for assembly into a grand Breton pyramid cake. Each petal profile increases the surface to be sweetened with glaze, fondant, and piped cream; graduated diameters—from 4 to nearly 9 inches—stabilize stacking while the central tube, which speeds baking, also creates a cavity for a traditional hazelnut-cream filling. The full, flat, 1-cup cap is customarily crowned with a molded-sugar—or more accurately, pastillage—horn.

Breton cake molds are manufactured only in tinned steel and sold in sets containing six pans.

Rehrücken Mold

This trough-shaped pan forms a chocolate-almond batter into a cake that—glazed with chocolate and studded with almond slivers—becomes a rehrücken, an Austrian trompe l'oeil of a saddle of venison. Its broad length, which mimics a bowed-back cut of meat, is still uniform enough to set batter; ridges impart a pattern and serve as a slicing guide, and the wide top eases release.

Occasionally used for quick breads, the finest rehrücken molds are manufactured in medium-heavy nonstick aluminum. Lighter weight molds, which are more prone to denting, are also available in aluminum and tinned steel. Lengths generally measure from 8 to 12 inches.

Stollen Mold

This long, ridged, vented tinned-steel mold shapes a well-worked yeast dough for final rising and baking into the Middle European Christmas bread called stollen. Its roughly $15'' \times 5'' \times 3''$ dimensions hold 3 pounds of dough; ridges that impress the stacked sticks or posts connoted by the stollen name still evoke long-gone midwinter fire festivals, and vents that first assist the proofing rise provide egress for steam during baking.

Personal preference remains with traditional methods—careful kneading, folding, and proofing—rather than relying on this incidental mold that duplicates the shape of the final dough mold. The mold is manufactured only in the 15-inch length.

Aluminum-coated Cake Strips

When soaked in water, wrapped around the outside of a cake pan that's then filled with batter, and set to bake, this long, narrow, aluminum-coated strip alleviates the problem of a peaked center by causing the batter to set more uniformly. The strip's three fabrics—aluminum-coated exterior, cotton flannel center, and cotton broadcloth interior—combine to slow the amount of heat conducted to the cake sides so they can rise more evenly with the center.

Two long, troughed, ribbed or ridged forms in which to shape and bake dough or batter are the stollen mold on the left and the rehrücken mold (see page 161) on the right.

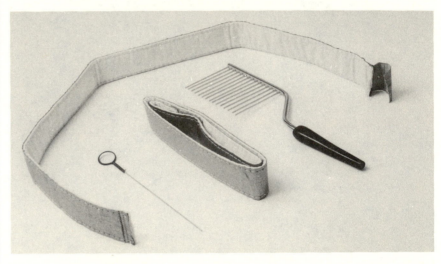

Assorted devices that promise uniform baking, neat apportioning, or clean testing include, clockwise from the top, an unfolded aluminum-coated cake strip, cake breaker, folded cake strip, and cake tester.

Molds are made in different materials to correctly bake specific tarts. Shown clockwise from left are a tin-lined-copper tarte tatin mold, porcelain quiche pan (see page 164), and a more general-purpose black-steel tart form (page 164).

Three processes slow that peripheral setting: The aluminum reflects some oven heat; what isn't deflected evaporates the water in the damp strip to cool the wrapped sides, and when dried, the aluminized textile simultaneously reflects and conducts heat to the sides.

Aluminum-coated cake strips measure $30'' \times 1\frac{1}{2}''$ and are sold in packages containing two or four.

Cake Tester

This loop-ended wire lets the cook gauge the degree of doneness of a baking cake. A straight span promotes clean entry and withdrawal; if the cake is underdone, the $\frac{1}{32}$-inch diameter of the tester supplies sufficient sticking surface for unset batter, while the 7-inch length reaches into an inch-deep sponge or 4-inch-deep angel food cake with equal efficiency. The plastic-coated ringed handle tempers conduction.

Although they are slightly wider, a small skewer, turkey lacer, even a toothpick, can be used in lieu of a cake tester, which is generally manufactured in tinned steel.

Cake Breaker

This cake breaker's comblike teeth penetrate and tear to slice an angel-food or chiffon cake. Its 3-inch-long blunt teeth sink cleanly through a well-risen egg-foam cake; the $3\frac{1}{2}$-inch span cuts cakes produced by standard tube pans, and the wide set of the teeth, which can't compact on the downstroke, then promises a neatly torn slice.

Cake breakers are novelties, since preferences lie with the more prac- tical and versatile baker's knife. They are manufactured in nickeled steel, have plastic handles, and measure 10 inches in overall length.

Tarte Tatin Mold

This tin-lined copper pan reproduces what was originally an accident: an upside-down caramelized apple pie. It's said that at the two Tatin sisters' family inn in the Loire district of France the Tatin who was the cook, forgot to line her pastry tin with dough when baking an apple tart. She capped it midway through with a dough lid and, once

---

Marbleized Spice Cake

Maida Heatter
Maida Heatter's Book of Great American Desserts

12 to 16 servings

DARK BATTER

2 *cups sifted cake flour*

1 *teaspoon baking soda*

1 *teaspoon ground cinnamon*

½ *teaspoon freshly grated nutmeg*

½ *teaspoon ground ginger*

¼ *teaspoon salt*

1 *tablespoon unsweetened cocoa powder (preferably Dutch-process)*

1 *teaspoon powdered instant coffee (or espresso)*

4 *ounces sweet butter*

1 *cup dark brown sugar, firmly packed*

4 *large egg yolks (whites reserved for the light batter)*

½ *cup dark molasses*

1 *cup plain yogurt*

Preheat the oven to 350°F.

Sift the flour, baking soda, cinnamon, nutmeg, ginger, salt, cocoa powder, and coffee together in a medium bowl and set aside.

In the large bowl of an electric mixer beat the butter until soft, then add the sugar and beat to mix. Add the egg yolks all at once with the molasses and beat until smooth and slightly lighter in color. On low speed add the sifted dry ingredients in three additions alternately with the yogurt in two additions; beat until smooth. Set aside as you prepare the light batter.

LIGHT BATTER

2½ *cups sifted cake flour*

2 *teaspoons double-acting baking powder*

¼ *teaspoon salt*

4 *ounces sweet butter*

1 *teaspoon vanilla extract*

¼ *teaspoon almond extract*

1 *cup granulated sugar*

¾ *cup milk*

4 *large egg whites*

Sift the flour, baking powder, and salt together in a small bowl and set aside.

In the large bowl of an electric mixer beat the butter until soft. Add both extracts and ¾ cup sugar and beat until thoroughly mixed. On low speed add the sifted dry ingredients in three additions alternately with the milk in two additions; beat until smooth.

Use clean beaters to beat the egg whites in a separate bowl until they hold a soft shape. Gradually add the remaining ¼ cup sugar and beat briefly only until the whites hold a definite shape. Use a rubber spatula to fold the whites—in three additions—into the batter.

To assemble the cake: Place 4 to 5 large spoonfuls of the dark batter into a lightly buttered and bread crumb–dusted 14-cup tube pan; leave a space between each of the dark mounds. (It's best to use two separate spoons—one for each batter.) Then place a spoonful of the light batter in each space and place a spoonful of the light over each mound of dark; continue alternating the batters. Rotate the pan briefly and briskly, first in one direction, then the other, to smooth the top.

Bake in the bottom third of the oven for 1 hour or until an inserted cake tester comes out clean. Cool the cake 10 minutes in its pan, then invert onto a rack, remove the pan, and cool before serving.

The flan ring on the top and cake ring below it are both used to bake pastries and cakes atop a cookie sheet.

Tarte Tatin

Gisèle Masson, Proprietor
Gérard Chotard, Executive Chef:
La Grenouille

1 tarte tatin
(8 to 10 servings)

8 *ounces puff pastry (see p. 97)*

8 *tablespoons butter*

¾ *cup granulated sugar*

8 *pounds Golden Delicious apples, peeled, cored, and halved*

¾ *cup raisins*

Preheat the oven to 350°F.

Roll out the puff pastry and cut an 11-inch circle to fit an 11-inch tarte tatin mold, then refrigerate it as you prepare the apple filling.

Spread the butter evenly in the mold, add the sugar, set over high heat, and cook until melted but not colored.

Arrange the apples neatly on the bottom and up the sides of the mold.

Set the pan over high heat and cook 10 minutes to caramelize lightly.

Place the puff pastry over the apples and tuck the edge of the dough inside around the edge of the mold.

Bake 25 to 30 minutes or until the pastry is puffed and golden brown and the apples are tender.

Remove from the oven and tilt the excess syrup into a bowl. Invert the tart onto a serving plate.

Combine the raisins and reserved syrup in the mold, set over high heat, and reduce to a thick caramel syrup; pour immediately over the tart and serve.

---

it was baked, flipped it onto a plate to the delight of customers. This 1⅝-inch-deep pan limits the amount of sugar, apples, and puff pastry to ensure thorough, moderately quick cooking at the high heat needed to caramelize sugar; its broad base furthers even baking and a balanced syrup-to-apple ratio, while outwardly flared sides ease release of the tart.

Occasionally used with a water bath to prepare crème caramel, tarte tatin molds are manufactured only in tin-lined copper with diameters from 9½ to 12½ inches.

Tart Form

A crisp, golden-brown tart-pastry shell is best baked in and most easily removed from this black steel pan. Its near-inch depth, which exposes the lion's share of a thin dough to heat, promotes rapid setting and steam release; black steel quickly absorbs and transmits heat to hasten baking and browning, while side flutes virtually double the crust's surface and increase its holding ability and visual appeal. Once baked, a gentle upward push on the base insert removes the shell from the rim for a crumb-free transfer to a cooling rack.

Fluted round black-steel tart pans are manufactured with either the preferred loose or permanently inset bottoms with 4½- to 12½-inch top diameters. Plain rectangular black steel forms measuring roughly 14″ × 4″ are also available, as are similarly sized and styled tinned steel forms that, because of tin's heat-reflective nature, are better used to prepare frangipane and mincemeat tarts that require longer baking but not the very dark crust that black steel would cause.

Select a tart form with medium-heavy, barely flexible metal and nearly straight sides.

Flan Ring

This stainless-steel ring is one of many used to bake quantities of the low, open-faced pies called flans. Durable, easy to maintain, and with no separate base to lose, the hoop is placed on a cookie sheet, lined with pastry, filled, and set to bake. Its ¾-inch depth exposes most of its filling, generally custard, to oven heat to promote rapid setting; rolled edges make the hoop rigid to lie flat on a cookie sheet as stainless steel, although a poor conductor, is used not so much to transmit heat as to shape pastry sides that, once set, then shrink to cook completely.

Equally sturdy, rolled-rimmed and spot-welded heavy-gauge tinned forms in round, multilobe, and rectangular shapes are also manufactured but maintenance restrictions—no scrubbing, and they must be dried immediately after washing—sway most to buy stainless steel. Rings commonly measure 3 to 15 inches across; multilobes have 8- to 15-inch diameters and rectangles most often measure 14″ × 4½″ and 22″ × 4½″.

Quiche Dish

This low, fluted porcelain dish—in truth, a tourtière—is referred to here by its more recognizable, however limiting, name. Terminology aside, it bakes and serves that classic custard pie as it does many another savory tart. Its bare 1½-inch depth exposes most of the filling to oven heat to assure proper setting and evaporation; side flutes that increase the surface area create a stronger crust to better brace a heavy filling, and ovenproof porcelain that evenly absorbs and gently conveys oven heat won't overcook the pastry before the filling is done.

Porcelain quiche dishes, also used for gratins, are available with 5¼- to 12-inch diameters.

Cake Ring

When set on a baking sheet, this nearly 9-inch stainless-steel hoop can bake a torte, flan, or, with some care, set and bake a génoise. It is more often used on a cardboard disk to construct and freeze cakes that include thin layers of baked sponge-cake, ladyfingers, or meringue rounds with various combinations of ice cream, sorbet, mousse, Bavarian cream, fruits, nuts, and chocolate. Its smooth, rigid sides supply substantial support for packing, pouring, and/or pressing; its 1¾-inch height provides for sensibly small portions of generally rich ingredients, while the medium-heavy stainless steel won't buckle from exposure to a propane torch's releasing flame or an oven's heat if used for baking.

Cake rings are also called mousse rings; when their sides measure 1⅜ inches they are called entremet rings, and when 2⅜ inches high they are correctly called vacherin rings because that nutted meringue invariably appears in the layering. The finest dessert rings—even the heart and multilobe forms—are manufac-tured in medium-heavy–gauge stainless steel with diameters from 3 to 19 inches. Some expandable rings are available, but you'd be wise to overlook them since their metal is so thin for spreading or contracting to proper diameter that they frequently flex during assemblies.

For baking, set the appropriately high cake ring on a parchment-lined baking sheet, then pour in a thin layer of batter. Set to bake a few moments, then add the remaining batter, and bake as usual.

Pie Pan

This near-maintenance-free aluminum pie pan is a standard in most commercial kitchens. Its wide edge invites a decorative sealed rim; the short, splayed sides expose more food to heat to encourage quick setting, as rust-resistant aluminum,

which deflects some heat to prevent filled crusts from browning too fast, promotes rapid, thorough baking.

All-purpose pie pans are manufactured in the preferred plain aluminum or an equally good, if less durable, heat-tempered glass, both of which should be medium heavy. When baking a blind crust, however, a black steel pan that conducts heat to better brown it is recommended. Of the frequently available 8- to 11-inch pie-pan diameters, a 9-inch size accommodates most recipes. When you bake filled pies, set the pan atop a baking sheet to catch any overflow.

Tarte à l'Orange

Orange Tart

André Soltner, Chef-Proprietor: Lutèce

1 9-inch tart

PÂTE SUCRÉE

1 *cup all-purpose flour*

3 *tablespoons granulated sugar*

Pinch salt

6 *tablespoons cold sweet butter, cubed*

1 *large egg yolk*

1 *to 2 tablespoons cold water*

Egg wash: 1 large egg yolk combined with 2 tablespoons cold water

Combine the flour, sugar, and salt in a large bowl and stir to mix. Make a well in the center, add the butter, and work it in until it is the consistency of coarse cornmeal.

Combine the egg yolk and water, stir to mix, then add to the pastry and mix well.

Shape into a ball, then roll and fit it into a 9-inch round tart form. Trim, prick the bottom of the pastry shell with a fork, and freeze 30 minutes.

Preheat the oven to 400°F.

Line the form with aluminum foil, weight with pie weights, and bake 12 minutes. Remove the weights and foil, brush the pastry shell with the egg wash, and continue to bake 8 minutes longer. Remove from the oven and cool to room temperature before using.

GRAND MARNIER BAVARIAN CREAM, FRUIT TOPPING, AND GLAZE

4 *large egg yolks*

½ *cup granulated sugar*

1 *¼-ounce package unflavored gelatin*

1 *cup milk*

1½ *tablespoons Grand Marnier*

½ *cup heavy cream*

6 *large navel oranges*

2 *tablespoons warmed and strained apricot preserves*

1 *tablespoon orange juice*

Whisk the egg yolks, sugar, and gelatin together in a bowl and set aside.

Heat the milk in a medium saucepan, then slowly add to the egg-yolk mixture and whisk constantly to mix. Pour back into the saucepan and cook over medium-low heat 5 minutes or until the custard is thick enough to coat the back of a spoon; stir constantly. Pour the mixture into a bowl set over a large bowl of iced water, then stir in the liqueur; stir frequently until the custard is chilled and thicker.

Beat the cream until soft peaks form, then lightly fold into the custard; continue to chill until substantially firmer, then pour into the cooled tart shell and spread evenly.

Julienne the zest from two of the oranges and blanch in boiling water 2 minutes; remove with a slotted spoon and set aside.

Use a sharp knife to peel all the oranges; cut between the membranes to release and remove the flesh, then arrange the freed orange sections over the filling in concentric circles.

In a small bowl combine the strained preserves with the orange juice, stir to mix, then use it to glaze the oranges; sprinkle the tart with the julienned orange zest.

Deep Pie Dish

This oval ceramic vessel holds, cooks, and serves such pastry-capped deep-dish delights as blueberry or steak-and-kidney pie. The 2-inch depth supplies generous room for flavors to mingle and develop; the ¾-inch-wide flat rim that supports a small pastry collar better anchors that moisture-sealing lid, while ceramic, which conveys heat evenly, won't react chemically with any ingredient, a plus when an acidic fruit is included. The flared sides make serving easier and more efficient.

Deep pie dishes are also available in heat-tempered glass and earthenware in lengths from 6½ to 12 inches, with 8- to 24-ounce capacities.

Pie Weights

A bag of aluminum weights helps the cook to blind-bake perfectly formed tart and pie shells so they can be cooled and filled. When evenly dispersed, the pellets restrict a puff or short-crust pastry's upward expansion; their 1-kilogram cumulative weight, meant to cover the bottoms of two or three average-sized shells, prevents pastry blisters from forming, while quick-conducting aluminum—even though present only during the first half of the baking—still fosters thorough setting.

Equally fine pie weights, also called baking beans because their precursors were dried beans, are manufactured in ceramic, usually in 1- to 2.2-pound packages.

Pie Funnel

This porcelain funnel vents the steam that develops below a baking pie's top crust to prevent it from becoming soggy. Its 3-inch height readily clears a standard, two-crust pie; its 2-inch wide and tall shoulders help to support the top pastry as its arced base allows steam to escape easily.

When buying a pie funnel, or pie bird, inspect the opening top vent; it should be at least ½ inch wide to allow steam to escape cleanly.

As is true with the pie pan (see page 165) on the left and deep pie dish on the right, wide-rimmed, slope-sided pie pans ease serving and provide space for crimped pastry edges.

A pie funnel and pie weights lend the baker a hand at producing flawless pies.

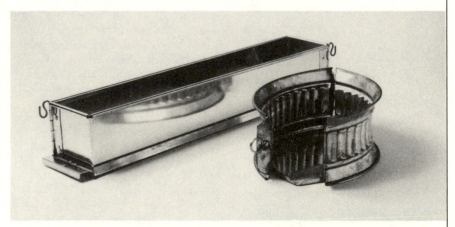

Rough, ground-meat "country" pâtés are prepared in the rectangular pâté mold on the left; more elegant, pastry-covered pâtés require the pâté en croûte mold on the right.

Rectangular Pâté Mold

This smooth-sided tin rectangle could be called a country pâté mold as it is used almost exclusively to bake that rustic ground-meat loaf. Its smooth-as-glass straight sides compact evenly and convey heat uniformly; tinned steel both deflects and transmits heat, promising thorough baking without excessive crust formation, and collapsible sides assure intact release while draining off excess fat.

This three-piece mold is pin-set at two opposite corners, but equally fine pâté molds are also available with slightly flared, hinged sides that fold down. Both are almost always manufactured in tinned steel and range from 8 to nearly 20 inches long, with 1- to 3½-quart capacities. Inspect the base of a three-piece collapsible mold; a number have two upwardly curved ends that block the bottom from sliding out.

Pâté en Croûte Mold

Sturdy and ornate, this eye-shaped tinned-steel mold impresses, bakes, and releases a meat, poultry, game, or fish pie. Its decorative side flutes and bands also create a rough sur-face to discourage the pastry from sticking; the tinned steel, which both reflects and transmits heat, won't overbrown the crust before the fill-ing is done, and the three-part con-struction (two separate sides and a separate base) promises easy re-lease.

Rectangular pâté en croûte molds are also available with slide-away bases and pin-set, herringbone-pat-terned removable sides. The small, tight shape allows for the neatest, most compact slices possible. The forms range in length from 8 to 20 inches and have from 1- to 3-quart capacities. The oval pâté molds measure from 5½ to 12½ inches at their widest axis with 2-cup to 4½-quart capacities.

Petits-Fours Molds

These tiny tinned steel molds—from brioche to lozenge to boat—let the chef create the miniature pastries called petits fours. By allocating 6 petits fours per person, this 50-piece set meets most needs in one oven trip; the less than 2-tablespoon ca-pacity of each mold is standard. Tin-plated steel, which both transmits and deflects radiant heat, assures thorough baking before browning.

Petits fours are generally divided into two categories besides savory

Chicken Pot Pie

*Keith Eldridge, Executive Chef
Dana Brizee, Chef: Between the
Bread*

6 pot pies

PASTRY CRUST

8 *cups all-purpose flour*

2 *tablespoons granulated sugar*

½ *teaspoon salt*

4 *large eggs*

¼ *cup milk*

1 *pound sweet butter, softened to
room temperature*

Sift the flour, sugar, and salt to-gether, empty onto a flat work sur-face, and make a well in the center. Mix the eggs and milk together, then pour into the well and mix in a small amount of the flour. Add the butter and continue to mix until the dough forms a ball. Knead lightly, then wrap in plastic and refrigerate 2 hours or overnight.

CHICKEN AND VEGETABLES

1 3- *to 4-pound chicken, quar-tered*

1½ *quarts double-rich chicken
stock (page 210)*

6 *small red bliss potatoes,
scrubbed and quartered*

24 *2-inch pieces peeled parsnips*

18 *pearl onions, parboiled 30
seconds, peeled, and lightly
cross-cut at base*

24 *baby carrots, scrubbed and
trimmed*

30 *button mushrooms, stemmed
and wiped clean*

5 *bay leaves*

1 *cup roux (½ cup softened but-ter mixed with ½ cup all-purpose flour)*

2½ *cups heavy cream*

Salt to taste

*Freshly ground black pepper to
taste*

1 *cup finely chopped flat-leafed
parsley*

Combine the chicken and stock in a large saucepan set over high heat, bring to a bare boil, then re-duce the heat and poach 35 minutes. Remove the chicken from the stock, cool, then skin, bone, and cube; strain the stock and clear of fat.

Return the stock to a boil and separately blanch the vegetables: potatoes for 8 to 10 minutes, par-snips and onions for 4 minutes, car-rots for 3 minutes, and mushrooms for 2 minutes.

Boil the stock to reduce to 1 quart, then add the bay leaves and roux and stir to mix; reduce the heat and simmer 3 minutes. Add the cream and simmer 5 minutes; stir con-stantly. Remove from the heat and season to taste with salt and pepper.

Evenly divide the ingredients—in-cluding the parsley—among six 14-ounce ovenproof dishes (6-inch di-ameter with a 2- to 3-inch depth), mix well, and top with about 6 ounces of the thickened stock.

ASSEMBLY

3 *large eggs beaten until smooth*

Roll out the dough to ¼-inch thickness on a lightly floured sur-face, then cut circles that are ap-proximately ½ inch larger than the diameter of the ovenproof dish to be used. Reroll the scraps and cut leaves or lengths for braids.

Brush the rims of the ovenproof dishes with the egg wash as well as the rims of the dough circles where their crusts will meet the dish. Gently pat on the crust lid, brush the top with egg wash and decorate with leaves or braids; egg wash the dec-orations as well. Cut steam holes, then refrigerate 1 hour or overnight.

Preheat the oven to 350°F thirty minutes before baking.

Bake 45 minutes or until the crust is golden brown.

pastries: dry, fancy cookies or pastries that can contain chocolate but not cream, and glazed tarts, layered and iced cakes, or sugar-coated fruit. The molds to make the glazed tarts and such diminutive versions of brioche, savarin, and baba au rhum are manufactured in about 20 different styles and are sold singly or in sets containing 8 to 12 styles. The best are stamped in lightweight tinned steel.

Champagne-Biscuit Plaque

The 12 shallow trapezoids, shaped like stylized champagne flutes, stamped onto this reinforced tinned-steel sheet produce the thin, often orange-flavored, crisp champagne biscuits. The plaque's scant depressions maximize the batter's contact to heat to induce quick setting and uniform expansion and color; outwardly flared edges foster even evaporation and hinder surface cracks, called checking, while its thick copper-wire wrap supplies the rigidity for level setting.

The term *biscuit*, whose French base means twice cooked (the original baking method), could still correctly be applied to this cookie since its loose egg batter is warmed as it is beaten.

Champagne-biscuit plaques are available most often with 48-mold tinned-steel plaques.

Boudoir-Biscuit Plaque

The 20 4½-inch-long rectangular forms stamped onto this tinned steel sheet bake the crisp, vanilla-laced, sugar-dusted sponge-cake cookies called boudoir biscuits. Their ¼-inch depth prevents the batter from spreading while exposing most of it to heat so it cooks quickly and rises lightly, while shiny, reflective tin thoroughly bakes the batter before it browns.

Boudoir-biscuit plaques are manufactured only in medium-heavy–

A fifty-piece set of petits-fours molds (see page 167) is used to produce a wide array of miniature French pastries.

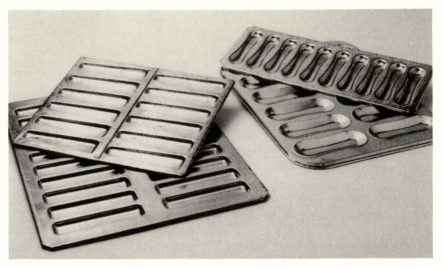

Plaques to make elongated biscuits include, clockwise from top right, a cat's-tongue plaque, éclair plaque, boudoir-biscuit plaque, and champagne-biscuit plaque.

gauge tinned steel with either 20 or 54 depressions.

Cat's-Tongue Plaque

This sheet's 10 scant, finger-length depressions, each of which bears the profile of a supersleek dumbbell, supply the finest surface on which to shape and bake thin, crisp cat's tongue cookies. Each shallow mold, holding a generous teaspoon, checks batter spreading to prompt uniform and rapid baking. Medium-heavy tinned steel won't buckle and, because of its heat-deflecting shine, won't too quickly brown the cookies.

Cat's-tongue plaques are available only in 10-mold tins. They are occasionally called ladyfinger plaques, but that sponge batter, with wider piping and higher setting, can't be properly shaped or baked by this sheet.

Éclair Plaque

The flared aluminum finger-length depressions in this plaque produce model éclair pastry shells: crisp, well-rounded, and as golden as a flash of light. Each mold's bare ¼-inch depth and slight, wraparound lip contain and check the spread of the semi-firm batter while baking; their 1½-

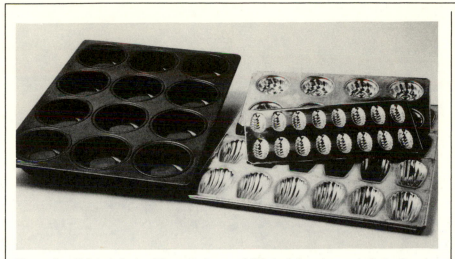

Plaques in which to bake two-bite confections or full-fledged desserts are, clockwise from top right, a visitandine plaque, torsade plaque, madeleine plaque, and shortcake plaque.

inch width creates ample batter-to-heat contact for rapid steam rise, evaporation, and setting, while soft curves promise a thoroughly rounded pastry to be filled. Bright aluminum that deflects as much heat as it transmits thwarts overbrowning.

Éclair plaques, also used to bake an equally aerated ladyfinger batter, are most most often available in lightweight aluminum or tinned-steel sheets with 12 molds.

Torsade Plaque

Almost architectural in their crisp, clean design, this tinned steel sheet's 16 shallow molds, like abbreviated lengths of twisted cording, make the small, egg-rich, sugar-crusted cookies called Rheims biscuits. Each 2-inch length shapes a two-bite confection for its customary accompaniment to crème caramel, fruit salad, and other flour-free desserts in formal French service; the molds' shallow depth abets the batter's quick, nondrying set as the decorative grooves increase the amount of crust and coating.

Torsade plaques are manufactured only in 16-mold medium-heavy–gauge tinned-steel sheets that measure roughly 11″ × 6″.

Visitandine Plaque

Petits fours nomenclature can be quite confusing: When a thick, almond–browned-butter batter is baked in a pastry-lined rectangular mold it creates a financier; when that same batter is prepared—again over pastry—in a boat-shaped mold, it forms a friand; and when piped into one of this sheet's nub-centered, round hollows with swirling sides it becomes a visitandine. Each of this plaque's small, furrowed molds furthers the batter's development. The 2-tablespoon capacities rate as near-standard among petits fours; each 2¼-inch diameter exposes ample batter to heat to quicken setting, as splayed sides aid the inverted release.

The finest visitandine plaques measure 13″ × 7″, contain eight molds, and are manufactured in moderately heavy tinned steel.

Madeleine Plaque

Some say the small, golden, scallop-shaped sponge cakes that provoked Marcel Proust to write *Remembrance of Things Past* are named after Madeleine Paumier, a nineteenth-century French pastry cook. The plaque to bake this special cake-cookie is well designed: Its ½-inch-deep forms, which can hold up to 2 tablespoons, bake the tea cakes in 20 minutes, while the flutes and sloped sides increase the contact of batter to hot metal to hasten setting and evaporation as the batter rises to a central hump. Some achieve that characteristic hump by allowing the batter to rest so that it is

less fluid and less prone to spread; others incorporate a little baking powder into it to effect a similarly high rise, although with air pockets.

Select a madeleine plaque of reinforced tinned steel over the lighter-weight coated or plain aluminum. Black steel plaques are new to the market, but they will overbrown these tea cakes before the center has set. Plaques that shape the 3-inch-long sponge cakes have 8 to 24 molds per sheet, while those that form the 1½-inch-long madeleinettes are impressed with 20 or 40 molds per plaque, the sturdiest of which are braced with a thick, wraparound copper wire.

Shortcake Plaque

This tinned-steel sheet has 12 shallow, level central depressions, each with a deeper ring indented around the edge, to shape and bake the individual sponge-cake bases for strawberry or other fruit shortcakes. The 6-ounce capacity of each makes a single serving, and the raised perimeter around each slight depression multiplies the hot-metal contact with batter for firmer setting and therefore bracing ability to contain fruit and custard or whipped cream.

Called a Mary Ann pan in industry, it draws its style from a fluted German fruit-tart form. Shortcake plaques are most often manufactured in either heavy preseasoned or plain tinned steel. Proponents suggest baking brownies or shaping gelatin in these molds, but it is best to leave them to their main purpose: The raised edge would unappealingly dry that part of the brownie and it would be difficult to release gelatins cleanly and intact.

Dents de Loup Sheet

It may look like a small, tinned-steel accordion bellows, but this pleated sheet was designed to mold and bake the finger-length, triangular, often anise-flavored biscuits called wolf's teeth that bordered the elaborate dessert presentations of yore called pièces montées. Today its 12 angulated troughs are used more frequently to shape and bake orange- and lemon-slice cookies. Each trough's 65-degree crimp, even with a suggested paper lining, distinctly shapes piped batter, while their inch depth and width encourage quick, even setting.

Dents de loup sheets are manufactured only in tinned steel in the 12-inch-square size.

Muffin Tray

Each of the 12 shallow, modestly flared cups pressed into this heavy, tinned-steel sheet speed the baking of a quick bread. Their diameter is twice the depth to expose a generous proportion of batter to heat for fast rising and setting; splayed sides extend top surface by nearly 40 percent to promote evaporation and the quick peripheral setting that then causes a humped center.

Muffin trays generally come in three muffin sizes—mini, regular, and large—the smaller two fitted with 12 or 24 cups each and the larger with 2, 4, or 6 cups. They are most often manufactured in nonstick-coated or plain aluminum; stainless steel; or the popular tinned steel, the strongest of which should be heavy gauge and wrapped with a reinforcing rim.

Corn-Stick Pan

This cast-iron tray's seven decorative depressions shape crisp single servings of cornbread. Each mold's indentations, which resemble ears of corn, produce a proportionately larger surface crust that makes the bread less fragile and less likely to crumble. Four pounds of preseasoned, preheated cast iron won't buckle at the generally very high heat—500°F—but will speed setting, rising, and coloring.

Corn-stick pans are manufactured only in cast iron with 5, 7, or 9 molds.

A crenulated, open-ended tinned-steel dents de loup sheet (see page 169) shapes the ferocious-sounding yet sweet-tasting wolf's-teeth cookies as they bake.

Trays in which to bake an array of quick breads are, clockwise from left, a popover pan, muffin tray, and corn-stick pan.

Four-Grain Muffins

Elizabeth Alston
Muffins

12 muffins

½ cup triticale flour

½ cup buckwheat flour

½ cup all-purpose flour

½ cup oat bran

2 to 4 tablespoons granulated
    sugar

1 tablespoon baking powder

¼ teaspoon salt

1 large egg

1 cup milk

4 tablespoons butter, melted

Preheat the oven to 375°F.

Combine the flours, bran, sugar (as desired), baking powder, and salt in a large bowl and stir to mix.

Lightly beat the egg in a small bowl, whisk in the milk and butter, then add to the dry ingredients and stir just until moistened.

Divide the batter among 12 lightly greased or paper-lined muffin cups. Bake 20 to 25 minutes or until light brown and firm to the touch in the center.

Turn out onto a rack and allow to cool 15 minutes before serving.

Les Madeleines de Commercy

Julia Child
From Julia Child's Kitchen

24 madeleines

2 large eggs, at room temperature and beaten in a 1-cup
measure

⅔ cup granulated sugar

1 cup all-purpose flour

5¼ ounces butter

1 tablespoon all-purpose flour in
a small bowl

Pinch salt

½ teaspoon vanilla extract

Grated zest of ½ lemon

3 drops lemon juice (or 2 of lemon
and 2 of bergamot)

Measure three-quarters of the eggs into a mixing bowl with the sugar and 1 cup flour and beat vigorously with a wooden spoon to blend into a heavy cream—if very stiff, beat in a drop or so of the remaining egg; set aside 10 minutes.

Meanwhile, melt the butter in a saucepan and let it boil until it begins to brown very lightly. Blend 1½ tablespoons into the bowl with the tablespoon flour and reserve. Stir the rest of the browned butter over cold water until cool but still liquid. Finally, beat the remaining bit of egg into the batter and stir in the cool butter. Stir in the salt, vanilla, lemon zest, lemon juice (and bergamot, if you have any). Cover the batter and set aside 1 hour.

Prepare two madeleine plaques, each of which contains 12 3-inch-long depressions: lightly coat the cups with the browned butter–flour mixture, wiping up any pools that form in the bottom of the cups; set aside (refrigerate in hot weather).

Preheat the oven to 375°F.

After its hour-long rest, the batter will be fairly stiff. Using a spoon and rubber spatula, dislodge a rather generous tablespoon lump of batter into each madeleine cup, but do not spread it out; it must stay in a lump in the middle of the cup.

Bake about 15 minutes in the middle level of the preheated oven. Madeleines are done when lightly browned around the edges and when they begin to shrink very slightly from the cups. Unmold onto a rack, hump side up. (When cool, wrap airtight and freeze if not served promptly.)

Serve as is or sprinkle tops with a dusting of confectioners' sugar.

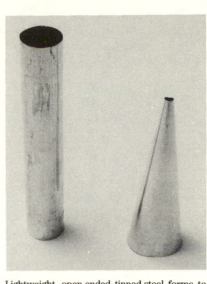

Lightweight, open-ended tinned-steel forms to shape pastry as it deep-fries or bakes are the cannoli form on the left and cream-horn mold on the right.

lengths with approximately ⅝- or 1-inch diameters. They are sold either singly or in sets of four; it's best to buy a total of eight so a cool form is always at the ready during preparation.

Cream-Horn Mold

This tinned-steel cornucopia is used to shape and bake a thin strip of spiral-wrapped puff pastry which, once cooled, can be piped full of pastry cream, whipped cream, or flavored cream cheese. Its roughly 1¼-inch splay allows space for filling and invites an even baking heat; its conical shape, which multiplies metal-to-pastry contact, speeds setting, steam release, and overall browning, while the metal's near feather-weight least interferes with the pastry's rise.

Buy at least six cream-horn molds to bake sensibly. They are available only in tinned steel in 4½- or 6½-inch lengths. Vaguely comparable 5½-inch forms, when more cylindrical, shape the similarly prepared cream rolls called lady locks; when they're widely flared and perfectly conical, they shape ham or salmon slices to be filled and chilled.

Popover Pan

Each tapered cup in this black steel popover frame provides the perfect container to turn a high-liquid batter into a very light, high-rising muffin. When properly preheated, each 2-inch-deep, tight cup promotes the batter's immediate setting around the sides and sealing so the evaporating liquid in the center rises as steam to then expand and set the remaining batter up and out. Black steel assures that the batter sets quickly.

Popover pans are also manufactured in the traditional cast iron, and while it prepares a fine muffin, the forms currently available are slightly shorter than the black steel ones and produce less of a popover and more of a Yorkshire pudding (they use a similar batter). Tinned-steel pans and porcelain cups are alternately used.

Cannoli Forms

A set of lightweight tinned-steel tubes shapes and deep fries the crisp pastry pipes that, when stuffed with sweetened ricotta cheese, become cannoli, perhaps the most renowned of Sicilian desserts. Each roughly 6-inch cylinder doubles the dough's exposure to hot deep fat for fast, thorough frying, while light tinned steel encourages even conduction and provides sufficient pliancy to break pastry contact and ease its release.

Cannoli forms are manufactured only in tinned steel—a bit removed from their allegedly bamboo predecessors—in roughly 4- or 6-inch

Shown above is a cleanly designed teddy bear for producing chocolate molds.

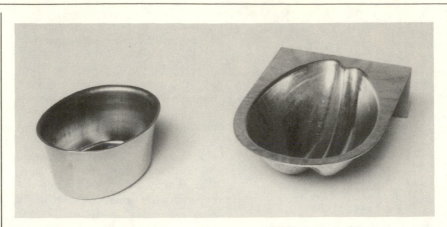

General- and special-purpose molds for food include an oval aspic mold on the left and foie-gras mold on the right.

The smooth, simple, bucket-shaped charlotte mold eases assembly and release.

Oval Aspic Mold

Perfect for shaping elegant individual servings of food is this oval stainless-steel mold. Its 4-ounce capacity suits a single serving of eggs in aspic, trout mousse, or ham persillade; its outwardly flared sides allow careful packing or layering of ingredients and facilitate an inverted release. The 1½-inch height of the unmolded aspic makes it tough to tip over while serving.

Occasionally called an oval dariole, oeuf en gelée, and, when round, a timbale mold, it is also used in conjunction with a water bath to bake custard.

Oval aspic molds are available in porcelain, tinned steel, aluminum, and the preferred stainless steel, which is hard to dent or nick.

Foie-Gras Mold

This double-lobed aluminum mold chills, shapes, and releases single servings of, usually, foie gras mousse. Lightweight aluminum quickly transmits cold to hasten the setting of aspic and mousseline; a rear flange, like a car's spoiler, balances the mold as it chills, while two small bows shaped like a goose liver are easily reproduced, and release cleanly.

Also called a Lucullus mold, after the ancient Roman general known more for his sumptuous feasts than successful campaigns, it is one of many specific molds meant to shape a particular dish. Other shapes include a trussed chicken, lobster, and salmon while more general-use ones designed for gelatins, creams, and aspics bear such shapes as horseshoes, melons, stars, and crowns. Most are available in aluminum and occasionally tin-lined copper with roughly ½-cup (as with this foie-gras mold) to 3-quart capacities.

Chocolate Molds

This vertically halved, well-detailed, stainless-steel mold, which typifies most chocolate molds, sets and shapes a chocolate teddy bear. Its greater width than depth promises a flatter, more uniformly thin layer of chocolate; the smooth scores, nicks, bulges, and bands that form the teddy bear also extend the chocolate-to-metal contact to hasten setting, while two halves encourage an easy release. Each half must be wiped first with melted cocoa butter, then brushed with the molten liquid for a hollow form or brushed with the molten chocolate, allowed to set and, if small, left open-faced or, if large, clipped together to cup the poured chocolate for a solid form.

Free-standing chocolate molds—also manufactured in nickeled-steel or ceramic and in such shapes as paired turtle doves, Christmas logs, Easter bunnies, ducks, and pineapples—range in height from 2 to 18½ inches. Stamped nickeled-steel and plastic plaques that turn out the smaller 1- to 2-inch-high seashells, casks, and turtles are also used to shape individual butter portions.

When buying a free-standing chocolate mold, don't accidentally pick up an open-ended form that won't accept a pour. These shape pastillage, the sugar paste that decoratively covers the plinth supports on some tiered desserts.

Charlotte Mold

This tinned-steel bucket with delicate handles is the simplest, most foolproof vessel in which to create eye-catching aspics, ice creams, custards, and puddings. It is nearly twice as wide as it is deep, with sufficient room for lining or layering, and forms a tough-to-topple turned-out mold; once upended, smooth, outwardly angled sides free the shape as handles distance fingers from the finely formed hot or cold food.

Occasionally sold with a cover, charlotte molds are most often available in tinned steel or tin-lined copper with capacities from 6 ounces to 2 quarts.

Bûche de Noël Mold

Although it looks like a length of roof gutter, this sturdy tinned-steel trough is used to mold a freshly baked and rolled sponge-cake sheet into a neat log to cool before being filled and iced. Its nearly 14-inch length accommodates a cake baked in a standard-sized jelly-roll pan and, when covered with cloth, its tight U-shape binds the rolled cake and prevents the air from drying it out.

Jam-filled cake rolls don't require this mold as their still-warm trimmed cakes are immediately scored, coated with fruit preserves, and rolled, then cooled and iced. It best serves the whipped- or buttercream-filled cake rolls: Since their high-fat fillings easily separate with prolonged exposure to warm cake, that cake should first be cooled to shape before filling.

Bûche de Noël molds are also used to curl tile cookies and chocolate leaves. They are manufactured only in tinned steel with lengths from roughly 14 to 20 inches.

Strawberry-Almond Charlotte Malakoff

Anne Willan
La Varenne's Paris Kitchen

8 servings

CHARLOTTE

14 *to* 16 *ladyfingers*

3 *tablespoons kirsch*

¾ *cup sweet butter, softened*

15 *tablespoons granulated sugar*

1½ *cups ground almonds*

1 *pint strawberries, hulled and cut into pieces*

¾ *cup heavy cream, whipped until it holds soft peaks*

Butter a 2-quart charlotte mold or soufflé dish and line the base with a round of waxed paper. Line the sides of the mold with ladyfingers, trimmed so they fit snugly. Sprinkle the remaining ladyfingers with half the kirsch.

Cream the butter, add the sugar, and beat 3 to 5 minutes or until light and fluffy. Stir in the ground almonds, strawberries, and the remaining kirsch. Fold in the lightly whipped cream. (*Note:* Do not beat or the cream will curdle and separate.) Spoon half the almond mixture into the mold, then add a layer of soaked ladyfingers. Add the remaining mixture and smooth the top. Cover and chill at least 4 hours or until firm. (It can be refrigerated up to 4 days.)

Not more than 4 hours before serving, trim the ladyfingers level with the almond mixture. Unmold the charlotte onto a shallow dish and remove the waxed paper.

STRAWBERRY SAUCE

1 *quart fresh strawberries, hulled*

3 *to* 4 *tablespoons granulated sugar (more if needed)*

1 *tablespoon kirsch or the juice of ½ lemon*

Purée the strawberries in a food processor or blender with the sugar and kirsch or lemon juice. Strain the sauce to remove the seeds and, if needed, add more sugar; chill before serving. (This sauce can be refrigerated up to 3 days or frozen.)

CHANTILLY CREAM

¾ *cup heavy cream, chilled*

1 *tablespoon confectioners' sugar*

½ *teaspoon vanilla extract*

Put the cream in a bowl over ice and water and whisk until stiff. (If the cream is not cold it may curdle before it stiffens.) Add the sugar and vanilla extract and continue to whisk until the cream stiffens again. (Do not beat or the cream will curdle.) Chantilly cream can be stored in the refrigerator up to 12 hours. It will separate slightly on standing, but will recombine if briskly stirred.

ASSEMBLY

8 *to* 10 *whole strawberries*

Scoop the chantilly cream into a pastry bag fitted with a star tube and decorate the top and base of the charlotte with rosettes of whipped cream and top with the strawberries. Serve the strawberry sauce separately or leave the base of the charlotte undecorated and spoon the sauce around the edge. Chill the charlotte until serving.

Tuile-Cookie Mold

This sheet of six moderately tight, deep cylinders holds and shapes a full home batch of the paper-thin, curved cookies called tuiles. The 130-square-inch work surface easily accommodates three dozen freshly baked, still-pliant, single-teaspoon cookies; the U-shape that supports their drape as they cool creates uniform roof-tile profiles while the underlying brackets maintain the shape of the cylinders.

Tuile-cookie molds are available only in tinned steel in the roughly 14″ × 12″ size.

Croquembouche Mold

It looks like a dunce cap, but when the inside of this stainless-steel cone is lightly oiled, then lined with caramel-dipped cream-puff balls, it shapes and releases a croquembouche pyramid that, piped with pastry cream and decorated with candied violets, is traditionally served at French weddings and christenings. Its cone shape welcomes stacking and eases release; spunsteel sides that must be pressed to free sticking caramel retract to remain smooth and snag-free, while the outwardly flared bottom brim clears fingers from the unmolding dessert.

Croquembouche molds are available only in stainless steel with heights from 10 to 23½ inches. The smallest size, because it can fit upright in many freezers, is also used to mold ice cream.

Speculaas Mold

Its Latin-based name and exotic spices may suggest a past conqueror or an eastern trading route, but not the inexplicable origin or ritual of speculaas, an embossed, flat, gingerbread cookie that is a late-fall, Low Country favorite. Animals, birds, fish, and humans are among traditional motifs, all of which are still laid with

Three molds that distinctly shape freshly baked pastries are, clockwise from top left, a croquembouche mold, bûche de Noël mold (see page 173), and tuile-cookie mold.

Molds that shape or emboss cookie doughs are, from the left, an icebox-cookie mold, shortbread mold, and speculaas mold.

a wooden plank similar to this multifigured one. Lightly dusted first with flour, then an appropriate amount of very firm chilled dough pressed into each depression, the board is then rapped to release the shapes which are then baked.

Speculaas molds—available only in wood—measure up to 18 inches long and should be at least ¾-inch deep to withstand the sharp dough-releasing raps.

Shortbread Mold

When dusted with flour and packed with buttery dough that is leveled and turned out, this decorative plaque shapes a shortbread disk that's a traditional Scottish New Year's specialty. Its ½-inch depth assures rapid, thorough baking and, considering the dense crumb, practical serving thickness, while the 1½-cup capacity accommodates most

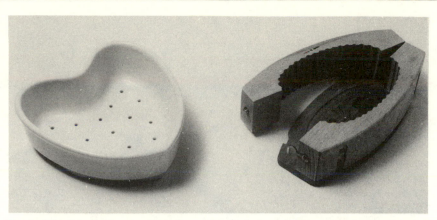

The perforated porcelain coeur à la crème mold at left shapes freshly made, sweetened cheese; the wooden oval butter mold (see page 176) at right shapes blocks of butter for serving.

standard recipes. The thistle and encircling rays—the former is the Scottish emblem and the latter perhaps a holdover from past solstice celebrations—comprise the conventional pattern.

Shortbread molds were once carved almost solely in wood with that time-honored pattern, but now they're available in stoneware displaying inauthentic but ornamental berries, wild flowers, and hearts.

Icebox-Cookie Mold

Like a lunchbox, this double-troughed, hinged, tinned-steel form clasp-closes to shape and chill a soft creamed cookie dough so it can be thinly sliced and baked. With leverage provided by the latches, the mold compacts the dough to shape it. The cool metal case speeds chilling as it protects contents from being knocked, dented, or otherwise marred.

Icebox-cookie molds, which are always prelined with plastic wrap to keep dough moist and free of refrigerator odors, can also be used to store preassembled two-flavored, two-toned spiral, bull's-eye, and checkerboard cookie-dough rolls. The molds generally measure 7½″ × 2½″ × 2½″ and are also available in brick, heart, and hexagonal shapes.

Coeur à la Crème Mold

The early-summer heart-shaped sweetened white cheese that the French call coeur à la crème is best prepared in a porcelain mold with a perforated bottom, raised base, and outwardly sloping sides. The perforations permit the cheese, cream, and egg-white mixture to drain and compact properly; a slightly elevated base lifts the coeur above the fluid accumulation, while outwardly flared sides funnel this liquid and ease unmolding.

Porcelain coeur à la crème molds—available in 3¼- and 6¾-inch lengths—are more durable than the traditional open- or more contemporary closed-weave, heart-shaped wicker baskets that are also on the market.

Coeur à la Crème au Coulis de Framboises

Lydie Marshall, Proprietor: À la Bonne Cocotte Cooking School

10 servings

COEUR À LA CRÈME

2 *cups low-fat plain yogurt, drained overnight in cheesecloth in the refrigerator*

1 *cup granulated sugar*

2 *cups heavy cream*

3 *large egg whites*

Combine the yogurt with ¾ cup sugar in a large bowl and beat to mix.

Beat the heavy cream until stiff peaks form, then fold into the yogurt.

Beat the egg whites until stiff, add the remaining sugar, and whip until glossy. Fold into the yogurt mixture.

Empty into 2 cheesecloth-lined 1-quart coeur à la crème molds or a large colander. Overlap the extra cheesecloth on top of the mixture to cover, then set on a plate and drain overnight in the refrigerator.

COULIS

2 *10-ounce packages frozen raspberries packed in syrup, thawed*

2 *tablespoons raspberry liqueur*

1 *to 2 tablespoons granulated sugar*

1 *pint fresh strawberries, hulled (or any other seasonal fruit)*

Purée the raspberries in a food mill or food processor. (If using a food processor, force the purée through a fine-meshed sieve to separate the seeds.) Empty into a small saucepan set over medium-high heat and boil until syrupy. Remove from the heat, cool, then add 1 tablespoon of the liqueur.

Sprinkle the sugar and remaining liqueur over the strawberries and toss to coat.

ASSEMBLY

Unmold the coeurs à la crème onto a serving dish, drizzle the coulis around them, then sprinkle the strawberries on and around both coeurs.

Oval Butter Mold

As charming and rustic as it is simple and functional, this thick, three-piece carved wooden mold decoratively shapes blocks of butter. First iced for 30 minutes to thwart sticking and then packed, its ¾-inch-thick sides easily withstand filling and compressing; their hinge set and latch lock provide a ready release which is further assured by the removable base plate.

Oval butter molds measure from 6 to 10 inches long and most often emboss a cow or flowers onto the 12-ounce to 1½-pound packed butter-block faces. Since they are manufactured only in wood, examine the mold's carved base and usually fluted sides for rough edges or splinters.

Square Ice-Cream Mold

This stainless-steel form's straightforward lines and two-piece construction—perhaps the most common ice-cream mold—allow swift packing and setting and clean release. Its 4-inch-square base opening accommodates an ice-cream spade or a spatula's head; its depth is nearly half the width, creating substantial metal-to-ice-cream contact to speed setting, while the top's smooth, outwardly tapered rosette relief is readily reproduced and easily unmolded.

Known as a portative mold, it is also manufactured in heavy tinned steel with similar 3-inch- to 5½-inch-square base dimensions that offer just under 1-cup to 1½-quart capacities. The better molds have fine definition, moderately heavy weight, and a well-fitted cap. But if you come across an old mold with a top central vent, pick it up; after filling and freezing, the removal of the cap nut breaks the vacuum to facilitate release.

Bombe Mold

A chef glacier's bombe was once complementary ice creams packed into a flat-bottomed sphere. Today's

Covered tinned or stainless-steel ice-cream molds include, from left to right, a square ice-cream mold, bombe mold, yule-log ice-cream mold, and biscuit glacé mold.

bombe is a prescribed assembly of ice cream and bombe appareil—an otherwise flavored, softer, whipped-cream lightened, often fruit- or nut-laden frozen filling—shaped in a relatively narrow cone. Sides that measure twice the base diameter create a generous cold surface for quick successive setting in the freezer; a ring cap steadies the mold to assure even packing, as a cover prelined with parchment paper fends off freezer odors.

Fluted bombe molds are manufactured in tinned steel; smooth-sided molds are available in stainless and range in height from 3½ to 8¾ inches, with 6-ounce to 1½-quart capacities.

Biscuit Glacé Mold

This three-piece stainless-steel brick provides the simplest, most traditional container to shape and freeze a block of variously flavored and colored ice creams called a biscuit glacé. Similar in base to that of a bombe's filling with sugar syrup and egg yolks mixed with whipped cream, the true biscuit glacé is further lightened with beaten egg whites. The brick's open, 12″ × 3″ face easily accepts gentle, noncrushing pouring, and the tight cap thwarts freezer odors during setting. Once the glacé is firm, the mold is dipped in cold water, the pullaway base and

lid are removed, and a thin knife is run around the inside edge for a smooth release. Evenly spaced base and lid notches allow equal apportioning.

Although a napolitain combining layers of vanilla, strawberry, and pistachio mixtures is the most recognizable biscuit glacé, other popular concoctions include a vanilla and strawberry Alhambra and a chocolate and vanilla harlequin.

Biscuit glacé molds—whose bottoms and lids should be lined with parchment before use—are manufactured only in stainless steel. They measure 11¾″ × 3¼″ × 2½″ and have a 1½-quart capacity.

Yule-Log Ice-Cream Mold

Its name may imply limited use but this footed stainless-steel trough can also freeze and free a half-cylinder of ice cream or poach and release a mousseline. Its 3-inch diameter and 2-inch depth welcome both hand layering and spatula packing; elongated end flaps balance the mold to ensure level setting, while a lid wards off freezer odors or a hot-water bath's condensation.

Yule-log ice-cream molds should not be confused with the wider, unlidded, spot-soldered (and therefore sure-to-leak) yule-log molds that

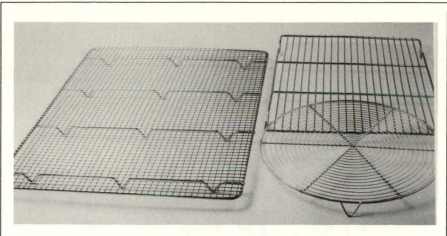

Wire racks for cooling or icing baked goods are, clockwise from the left, an icing or candy grate, baker's cooling rack, and cake-cooling rack.

shape baked rolled sheet cakes as they cool. Those for ice cream are manufactured only in stainless steel in lengths from 7 to 15 inches with roughly 1- to 2-quart capacities.

When shaping ice cream, lightly oil and prefreeze this mold so softened ice cream adheres to it better. You can also pack it with layers of variously flavored and colored ice creams, separating each with a very thin layer of genoise. When it is set and unmolded, you can pipe meringue or whipped cream over the entire length.

Baker's Cooling Rack

The widely spaced wires of this elevated rack cool those breads, buns, pastries, cookies, and pies whose crusts are firm enough to evenly support the settling weight of the whole. The heavy wire's ⅛-inch diameter easily bears three kugelhopf or sandwich-bread loaves; their ½-inch-wide set, which sustains a napoleon's puff pastry or a strip tart, furnishes sufficient air access for quick cooling. The ¾-inch-high feet assure plenty of cool-air contact.

Baker's cooling racks are manufactured in tinned or the more durable chromed steel in sizes from 16″ × 12″ to a professional 26″ × 16½″. For the home, 19″ × 13″ is the most practical.

Cake-Cooling Rack

This rack's close, spiral-set wire face and slight feet create the finest elevated support for cooling freshly baked cakes, tortes, tarts, and cookies. Its 12½-inch diameter holds the most common 9- and 10-inch rounds; the wire's thin spiderwebbing most levelly braces a sponge or pound cake to avert uneven settling, while ¾-inch-high legs ensure ample cool air below to vent steam that would otherwise condense within the cake, creating an irregular textural band.

Circular cake-cooling racks—manufactured in chromed or tinned steel with 8- to 14-inch diameters—are preferred over rectangular ones whose more widely spaced parallel rods provide less uniform support. Two of the larger racks—either 12½ or 14 inches—will handle home needs.

Icing or Candy Grate

Like the wickerwork of its Latin-based name, this raised metal grate's thin rods are fairly tightly woven to create a practical surface on which to rest petits-fours, fondants, or open-faced sandwiches during their final coating, draining, and setting. First placed in a pan to catch runoff for later use, the rods' ¼-inch spacing supports canapés but not their as-

pic; an uneven surface produced by warps and wefts prevents candied peel or rolled sweetmeats from forming the suction bond that hinders cooling and release, while the frame's ½-inch height clears drained glaze and ganache.

Icing grates are manufactured in either tinned or the more rust-resistant chromed and nickel-plated steel in sizes from 14″ × 9″ to 26″ × 18″, with a 24″ × 16″ size best suited to home use. The most durable, permanently level racks are spot-soldered both to frame and to reinforcing crossbars.

Cake-Decorating Turntable

The wide aluminum disk mounted on this cast-iron pedestal rotates to bring the entire surface of a cake within easy reach for icing or decorating. The plate's 12-inch diameter safely balances properly boarded cakes up to 20 inches wide, while the 4¼-pound base provides the counterweight to prevent toppling. The turntable's precise, pivoted setting promises consistently smooth spins and its nearly 5-inch height elevates the cake to a comfortable work level with enough hand room beneath to rotate the turntable.

Similarly durable turntables are also fitted with cast-aluminum bases. Those molded in plastic, notably polystyrene, are adequate for the occasional cake decorator but they tend to drag under heavy weight because of the disk's slight pliancy. The shorter base also reduces the maneuvering area. Turntable platforms can range in diameter from 12 to 16 inches or measure 16″ × 12″.

Pastry-Comb Set

The six scalloped, saw-toothed, and wavy edges of these four decorating combs score diverse impressions onto newly iced cakes, tortes, and florentines. Each 3¼-inch-square sheet of barely flexible plastic supplies enough of a work edge and handle to allow close proximity for fine work, yet sufficient distance from upwardly riding icing as the ¼-inch-deep decorative edge lays a clear pattern.

Often called cake decorating or icing combs and used to finish meringue and whipped-cream toppings as well, they are also manufactured and sold as individual 5″ × 4″ triangles with three slightly shallower serrated patterns.

Pastry Bag

This conical reinforced bag apportions icing onto cakes, sausage into casings, or pastry cream into eclairs. Its 16-inch length can pipe up to 1½ cups of pâte à chou, ladyfingers, or meringue; its lightweight nonporous nylon is quick to respond to pressure and sure to grip, since high-fat contents can't seep through. The reinforced tip further strengthens this bag at its most vulnerable pressure point.

Smaller, more precise jobs such as lettering, piping motifs, and decorating cookies are better accomplished with a parchment-paper cone or icing syringe, but larger chores require a pastry bag. In addition to the favored nylon, pastry bags are also available—in descending order of preference—in a plain woven nylon fabric with a polyurethane coating that sweats, polyurethane-coated cotton that eventually cracks through use, plain canvas that absorbs odors, and disposable polypropylene that saves on cleanup time but needs a textured grip. Lengths range from 7 to 24 inches, with the 16-inch bag a fine all-purpose tool.

Tools to assist a cake decorator's efforts include, left to right atop a cake-decorating turntable (described on page 177), a pastry-comb set, pastry bag, marzipan-modeling leaf (page 180), rose nail, coupler, and pastry decorating tube.

Pastry Decorating Tube

When this small stainless-steel cone is dropped into a pastry bag and the bag filled with icing and squeezed, it creates—depending upon how the tip is cut—lines, garlands, scrolls, flowers, or leaves. Its profile, which aligns with that of the bag, completes a smooth funnel, and its slightly protuding rolled edge fortifies its shape and furthers the leakproof join to the bag.

Tinned steel, nickeled brass, and precision-crafted polycarbonate decorating tubes are also available, either singly or in sets that can contain up to 52 tubes. An elementary set usually consists of 6—a fine writing tube, one open and one closed star tube, a leaf tube, a petal tube, and a ribbon tube.

Basic Choux Pastry

Peter Kump, Proprietor: Peter Kump's New York Cooking School

1 *cup water (or milk)*

4 *tablespoons sweet butter, cut into chunks*

⅛ *teaspoon salt*

1 *cup all-purpose flour*

4 *extra-large eggs*

Combine the water, butter, and salt in a heavy saucepan set over high heat and bring just to a boil. Remove immediately from the heat, add the flour all at once, and stir with a wooden spoon to gather it into a ball.

Set over low heat and begin to dry out the dough: With a wooden spoon smear the dough over the bottom of the pan, then stir to draw it into a ball. Continue to do this 3 to 5 minutes or until the dough starts to feel greasy when pinched with your fingers.

Empty into a mixing bowl, add one egg, then use electric beaters to beat; the mixture will become lumpy and loose. Continue to beat until it tightens up again. Repeat this procedure, adding one egg at a time until you have smoothly incorporated 3 eggs. Test the dough: When you scoop a spoonful and turn it sideways, the dough should retain its shape somewhat as it starts to fall slowly. Add the last egg yolk first, then the white, making sure the dough doesn't become too loose.

Carefully inspect each decorating tube; it should be inflexible and non-corrosive with a deeply cut but burr-free tip.

Coupler

This two-part plastic coupler—threaded conical tube and fitted nut—lets the cake decorator change pastry tubes in the middle of piping. This contrasts with the traditional method of fitting the pastry bag with the tube prior to filling it with pastry, whipped cream, or buttercream. The tube's cone shape—an extension of the bag—assures sealing and smooth flow as the front threads of the cone provide the external twist-on anchor for the coupling nut and selected decorating tube.

Couplers—rarely used in commercial kitchens because professionals own numerous bags with

corresponding decorating tips—are most often manufactured in nylon plastic in two sizes. One has a ½-inch diameter that can hold standard-sized tubes and fit into any pastry bag up to 12-inches long and the other has a ¾-inch diameter that accommodates larger tubes and fits into 14- to 18-inch bags.

Queen Mother's Cake

Maida Heatter
Maida Heatter's Book of Great Chocolate Desserts

12 servings

CAKE

6 *ounces semisweet chocolate, coarsely cut or broken*

12 *tablespoons sweet butter*

¾ *cup granulated sugar*

6 *large eggs, separated*

6 *ounces almonds, blanched or unblanched, finely ground (1¼ cups)*

⅛ *teaspoon salt*

Preheat the oven to 375°F.

Place the chocolate in the top part of a double boiler set over 1 inch of simmering water. Cover until partially melted, then uncover and stir until completely melted and smooth. Remove the top part of the double boiler and set aside, uncovered, to cool slightly.

Cream the butter in the small bowl of an electric mixer. Add the sugar and continue to beat at a medium-high speed about 2 minutes. Add the egg yolks, one at a time, and beat after each addition.

On low speed, add the chocolate and beat only to mix. Then add the almonds and beat to mix; scrape the bowl as necessary with a rubber spatula. Transfer the mixture to a large mixing bowl and set aside.

Combine the egg whites and salt in a large bowl of an electric mixer and beat only until the whites hold a definite shape but not until they are stiff or dry.

Stir a large spoonful of the beaten whites into the chocolate mixture, then fold in the remaining whites in three stages.

Empty the mixture into a buttered 9″ × 2½″ or 9″ × 3″ springform pan fitted with a buttered and bread crumb–dusted round of parchment or waxed paper.

Bake 20 minutes in the bottom third of the oven, then reduce the oven temperature to 350° and continue to bake 50 minutes longer.

Remove from the oven and cool 20 minutes on a damp towel, then remove the pan and lining and allow to cool completely right-side up on a rack. When cooled, level the top with a serrated knife if necessary.

Invert onto a cake plate edged with 4 waxed-paper strips to keep it clean and set on a cake-decorating turntable.

ICING

½ *cup heavy cream*

2 *teaspoons dry instant coffee*

8 *ounces semisweet chocolate, coarsely cut or broken*

Scald the cream in a medium saucepan set over medium heat. Add the coffee and whisk until dissolved. Add the chocolate and cook 1 minute; stir occasionally. Remove from the heat and whisk until the chocolate is melted and the mixture is smooth. Set over cold water to halt further cooking. Cool to room temperature; stir occasionally.

Stir to mix, then pour over the top of the cake. Use a long, narrow spatula to smooth the top and spread the icing down the sides. Smooth the sides with a smaller spatula. Remove the waxed-paper strips and, if you wish, border with chocolate curls.

Gougère

Peter Kump, Proprietor:
Peter Kump's New York Cooking School

12 servings

1 *portion choux paste (opposite page)*

4 to 6 *ounces grated Gruyère or Parmesan cheese*

1 to 2 *tablespoons Dijon-style mustard*

Salt to taste

Freshly ground black pepper to taste

1 *large egg yolk beaten with 1 teaspoon water and a pinch of salt*

Preheat the oven to 450°F.

Add the cheese and mustard to the choux paste and stir to mix; season to taste with salt and pepper—it should be highly flavored.

Drop the pastry by tablespoon (or with a pastry bag fitted with a large round decorating tube) onto a lightly buttered and cold water–rinsed baking sheet in rows 2 to 3 inches apart.

Brush the top of each dollop with the egg glaze and bake 15 minutes, then reduce the oven temperature to 400°F and open the door briefly to let the steam escape. Bake an additional 10 minutes. The gougères must be golden brown and dry before removing from the oven or they will collapse. Serve immediately.

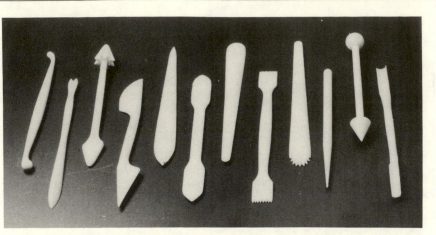

A marzipan-sculpting tool set's twelve pieces help to neatly cup flowers, ridge leaves, score eyes, and notch dimples onto a variety of cake-topping decorations.

Rose Nail

This king-sized nail with its slightly domed head and threaded shaft is used as a tiny turntable by a cake decorator to pipe royal icing into an unfolding bud or full flower. Its 1½-inch-diameter head provides sufficient space for building a high-centered bloom petal by petal; the sloped surface eases access to the widening base for successive petal applications as the threaded shaft assures a slip-free grip to make smooth turns during piping.

Rose nails are the most frequently used of the dozen or so flower nails of different sizes and shapes whose heads better form such cake-topping blooms as dahlias, pansies, and lilies. They are most often manufactured in brass or nickeled steel with 2½- to 3½-inch lengths.

Cookie Press

This tool pushes soft, butter-based cookie dough through a decorative disk into uniformly shaped spritz rings, almond hearts, and vanilla stars. Its 1¼-cup body holds half the batter of the typical home batch; the head's sawtooth shaft, which controls the degree to which the attached lever can move vertically, regulates the amount of ejected dough. A flat pressure plate pushes the dough out evenly as a horizontally set metal stencil shapes it.

A cookie press frequently comes with up to 20 interchangeable disks, a nozzle to inject pastry cream into eclairs, and a small selection of tips to pipe buttercream onto cakes. A few are available in plastic, but the most durable are manufactured in aluminum. Some of the latter have a top knob or crank that allows the chef to self-regulate thinner or thicker dough presses, but the lever style is the most popular.

Icing Syringe

When this tool's double-hook handle is compressed into the cylinder, the piston it directs pushes a regulated amount of icing, whipped cream, or cream cheese through any separately sold, fitted decorating tube to pipe rosettes, latticework, or script. Its 4-inch-long, ½-cup container affords a comfortable, easy-to-guide grip; the handle promotes smooth, single-handed application, and the tube can be changed without having to empty the syringe.

Icing syringes are most often manufactured in aluminum and plastic combinations and generally measure 7 inches long.

Marzipan-Sculpting Tools

These 12 medium-length plastic blades, paddles, and bars with their rounded, pointed, notched, and serrated tips allow the confectioner to press, crease, nick, gouge, and ridge marzipan or gum paste into diminutive vegetables, animals, and flowers to top cakes and tortes and to decorate dessert platters. Twenty-four different tips expand the artist's ability to work with these initially claylike mediums, the marzipan being easier because it remains malleable longer. The 5½-inch length of each tool prompts tight working proximity to foster precision, while the ¼-ounce weight allows the artist to feel each medium's density for more controlled modeling.

Marzipan sculpting tools, once traditionally carved in bone, are now manufactured only in plastic and sold in multiblade sets.

Soft dough is neatly dispensed by the cookie press on the left and icing, by the icing syringe on the right.

Marzipan-Modeling Leaf

With its lifelike size, billow-and-bow face, and rib-and-vein relief, this heavy cast-metal-alloy leaf lets the pastry chef mold marzipan or gumpaste sheets into leaves to set atop cakes and tortes. Its 4-ounce weight withstands all the pushes and presses during forming and accidental knife nicks during trimming while the highly polished dips, crests, and spines of the impression are not deep, steep, nor sharp enough to hinder a clean release.

Leaf molds for marzipan, once commonly made of wood or sulfur, are now available only in the cast-metal alloy, either singly like the rose leaf described above or in sets of three elliptically shaped leaves that more authentically frame such flowers as carnations and lilies of the valley.

Whipped-Cream Siphon

When the canister is filled with cold, flavored, sweetened heavy cream, the appropriate valve fitted with a nitrous-oxide cartridge, and the lever depressed after a quick, vigorous shake and momentary wait, this airtight aluminum cylinder immediately dispenses whipped cream onto sundaes, cakes, and cold soufflés. The design is simple, safe, and efficient: Deep, corresponding threads on cap and gas valve where they meet on the canister plus precision gearing on the outlet valve assure the air lock, as gas increases the internal surface pressure on the cream to roughly 25 pounds per square inch. When the outlet is opened by a strong, spring-set lever, the cream is ejected with such force by the accumulating gas in the bottle that it is aerated in the process; the cartridge contains only enough N$_2$O to empty the canister.

Whipped-cream dispensers are manufactured only in heavy aluminum with plastic fittings. Capacities measure either 2 cups or 1 quart.

Whipped-cream siphon. In less than thirty seconds this nitrous-oxide–loaded canister turns heavy cream into whipped cream.

Mixing Bowls

This decoratively glazed, soft-paste porcelain bowl is perhaps the most efficient vessel in which to hand-beat batters and work doughs. Its width is roughly double the depth to create easy access for mixing or folding; the cinched bottom directs ingredients to a tight, low center to hasten mixing, while its 5 pounds of ceramic withstand vigorous use. The scored exterior pattern creates traction for a nonslip holding grip.

Broader bowls are generally used less for mixing heavy batters and doughs than for combining forcemeats, assembling salads, and whipping cream. Most bowls are manu-

A Cake Decorating Primer

William and Seth Greenberg,
William Greenberg, Jr., Desserts,
Inc.

The final flourish at any well-planned wedding reception, birthday party, christening, or anniversary celebration is its beautifully decorated cake. From a neatly latticed three-tier triumph to a family tree–festooned single layer to another sporting the stylized skyline of a long-past honeymoon view, an elegantly decorated cake personalizes the ceremony, furthers the festivity, and, for the artist, is enormously rewarding.

Few basic tools are needed to produce professional results. First and foremost is imagination; second is practice, and this can be done on an inverted cake pan. A long, rigid, serrated blade best levels the domed top of a cooled, baked cake. A cake board facilitates moving it to a turntable that brings the entire cake surface within comfortable reach. A 2-inch-wide pastry brush removes the crumbs from the newly cut surface. A 12-inch-long spatula promises controlled, even icing when finishing the cake, and a decorating syringe is personally preferred for its single-handed grip, guide, and dispense. This should be complemented with graduated round and star tubes and augmented with leaf, rose, and ribbon tubes. Three primary colors—red, blue, and yellow—from which most others derive—round out the rudimentary kit.

With decorating tools waiting and the trimmed cake set to go, the artist can then enjoy a one- to six-hour-long operation, depending upon the amount of decoration and degree of intricacy. The icing is prepared next; such layered icings as rolled almond paste and fondant may remain in the expert's realm, but others—a stabilized whipped cream, royal icing, meringue, or buttercream—are easy to achieve. Buttercream is the most popular because it colors well, spreads readily, and can be quickly thinned for flat writing or stiffened for higher relief. It also cuts cleanly once dry.

Filling and layering are done next, followed by an especially generous top and side icing to avoid close scrapes and incorporated crumbs. A flawless finish is further assured by rotating the cake on the turntable beneath the sweep of a steady spatula blade, then transferring the cake to a serving platter and setting it aside for the icing to set.

Those with limited experience might want to lightly score a sectioning or geometrical design onto the cake's surface with a length of dampened thin string. This done, a framing top-edge border is first applied so that the center then can be pinpointed for a special sentiment or decoration. Now-evident sections stand ready for stars, swags, or beads, with the desired effect carried over, onto, and down the sides. (Personal preferences lean toward a base border of overlapping thin chocolate mints to finish the design.) New tubes to create different piped shapes can then be fitted as the design dictates. However, it is better to finish one color at a time.

Once completed, the cake is best served as soon as possible so its decorations remain well defined and true in color.

factured in porcelain, earthenware, stoneware, aluminum, heat-tempered glass, polyethylene, polycarbonate, and stainless steel in sizes that can range from 1 to 13 quarts.

It's smart to have a variety of bowls for different tasks; in addition to the described 4-quart ceramic bowl for larger mixing chores, a nest of 1- to 3-quart stainless-steel bowls with rolled rims would accommodate smaller tasks, including chilling gelatin-based desserts and storing. A small, 1½-quart ceramic or stoneware bowl is handy for steaming pudding.

Copper Egg-White Bowl

This wide, unlined copper bowl produces the highest-volume, stablest egg-white foams. Its width is double the depth for a substantial egg white–to–air surface for rapid aeration with a whisk; the sloped sides and round bottom encourage smooth, easy downstrokes and upward whips, while two pounds of copper prolong, shape and, more important, react electrolytically with egg whites to create a stable foam.

Indelicately called a *cul de poule* in French because its profile is allegedly as round as a chicken's rear end, copper egg-white bowls are most often available with 9- to 14-inch diameters. A 12-inch-wide bowl is recommended; make sure it's heavy, with a thick, rolled rim to preserve its shape.

Pudding Mold

When Charles Dickens described a fresh pudding as having "a smell like an eating-house and a pastry-cook's next door to each other, with a laundress's next door to that," he referred to a basin-steamed pudding covered with cheesecloth—to which this fluted, moderately tall pail creates an attractive alternative. Its shallow grooves impress onto the pudding while extending the avail-

Bowls are essential to any kitchen; shown here are a sturdy copper egg-white bowl at left and a more general-purpose porcelain mixing bowl (see page 181) at right.

A low, wide reed banneton shapes heavy country bread dough during its final rise.

able surface to later soak with brandy or rum; the central tube distributes heat to the center of the mixture to set it evenly, while the tight-fitting lid prevents steam from escaping.

Steamed-pudding molds are manufactured almost solely in tinned steel with 3-cup to 2-quart capacities, the better of which are well defined in pattern, medium-light in weight, and secured with hinges rather than latches.

Banneton

When dusted with flour and filled with a hearty rye, whole wheat, or other blended cereal dough for final proofing, this coiled reed basket forms the dough into a neat country-bread loaf. Its low, wide profile induces the shallow rising that best sustains dense, heavy doughs. The coils leave decorative imprints while extending the surface for crusting, as the wrapped reeds ventilate the dough to encourage its yeast rise.

Eight- or 10¼-inch round banne-

A pudding mold's capped central tube conducts heat to its mixture's core, thus assuring uniform cooking.

tons are available, as are 8- or 9-inch ovals, both of which bakers occasionally fit with a canvas or duck sheet before use for easier release, but which also reduces or obliterates the imprint.

Two helping hands for the pastry chef are a naturally cool marble pastry board and a sugar dredger.

Pastry Board

A marble slab is the perfect surface on which to knead or roll dough, work fondant, or quickly set molten candies. Its cooler-than-room temperature hinders pastry or bread dough from sticking, so less flour is needed to create a friction blanket; less is then incorporated into the dough and the ideal fat-to-flour ratio is maintained. For the confectioner, marble's cool, polished surface speeds peanut brittle's or caramel's even crystallization and is excellent for scraping chocolate curls or folding fondant to aerate it.

When prechilled, fine polyethylene boards can serve as adequate alternatives to marble for the dough but not always for the candy work. Marble boards are most frequently available with 14″ × 10″ to 31″ × 23″ dimensions.

Sugar Dredger

When filled with powdered sugar, cinnamon, or cocoa and shaken, this hand-sized, domed canister with its well-perforated screw-on cap sweetens, spices, or flavors cakes, strudels, soufflés, and truffles. Its 2½-inch-wide face promises tidy coating and minimal drifting; the pinpoint perforations allow only a light powder to pass, while a domed head, when inverted, creates the most complete egress for the gravity-dropped granules.

Sugar dredgers—also used frequently for flour to dust pastry work surfaces—are manufactured in stainless steel, aluminum, tinned steel, and tin-lined copper. Most are nearly 5 inches tall with a 1¾- to 2-cup capacity.

Some dredgers have handles so they can be hung near the workplace, but it's best to select one instead on the merit of its cap efficiency. The cap should be domed, not flat, the perforations should be tiny and closely set or, if mesh, tightly woven, and the corresponding threading to canister well defined and secure.

Pastry Brush

Just as an artist's fine oil brushes are absorbent, tightly ferruled, and variously sized for particular purposes, so are a pastry chef's to apply high-fat washes to breads, rolls, and pastries or sealing glazes to cakes and fruit tarts. In both cases, boar's bristle is preferred: Each shaft's split end, called a flag, together with its natural barbing, multiplies the available surface to soak; a tight, cinching ferrule prevents bristles from slipping onto the food or pan and ½- to 4-inch-wide flat or 1-inch round tips are suited to coat-

Floating Islands

André Boissel,
Executive Chef: Les Pleiades

6 s e r v i n g s

2 cups milk

1 vanilla bean, split lengthwise

1 cup granulated sugar

¼ cup Benedictine liqueur

6 large eggs, separated

¼ cup water

¼ cup warm water

Combine the milk, vanilla bean, ¼ cup sugar, and 2 tablespoons Be-nedictine in a saucepan and bring to a simmer; reduce the heat slightly.

Meanwhile, whip the egg whites until they form soft peaks; gradually add ¼ cup sugar and continue to whip until stiff and glossy.

Use two spoons to mold the egg whites into egg shapes and poach about 2 minutes on each side in the simmering milk. Remove to an ice bath to halt further cooking. (Do this in stages so as not to crowd the pan with the meringue eggs.)

Pour the hot milk into a bowl containing the egg yolks to temper; whisk constantly. Empty back into the pan, return to the heat, and cook until the custard is thick enough to coat the back of a spoon; stir fre-quently. Strain into a bowl and scrape the inside lengths of the vanilla bean into the custard; cover and refrigerate.

Prepare the caramel sauce as the custard chills: Dissolve ½ cup sugar in ¼ cup water over low heat, then increase the heat and boil rapidly until amber in color; immediately remove from the heat, stir in ¼ cup warm water, and heat until syrupy. Stir in the remaining Benedictine and serve either warm or at room temperature.

Divide the custard among 6 serving bowls and top each with an equal amount of drained meringue eggs and a drizzling of the caramel sauce.

ing pastry strips with egg wash or cookie sheets with melted butter.

Select an all-purpose pastry brush with a flat, 1½-inch-wide tip. Overlook synthetic in favor of natural bristle and make sure the head is well attached to its generally 4-inch-long handle, ideally with a seamless nylon ferrule.

Goosefeather Pastry Brush

Because of their elongated shape and ability to pick up but not absorb liquids, goosefeather brushes are ideal for applying light glazes on soon-to-be-baked puff pastry. Each brush, generally five feathers, supplies a limited absorptive surface that can dispense only a slight amount; their tight fringe can't spread, so it won't accidentally drip glazes down layered and cut dough sides, and their small overall length, generally 6 inches, creates a close working proximity for sure, steady application.

Although all are quite perishable, goosefeather brushes are either woven together by their lower vanes or twine-bound.

Cheesecloth

This loosely woven, lightweight cotton cloth, which draws its name from its original use as a wrap for pressed cheeses, is one of the most versatile kitchen textiles for its ability to strain, support, and shape. Its diaphanous construction allows liquid but little else to filter through; its weave (versus knit) gives it the greater dimensional stability that prohibits stretching when wrapping a chicken or salmon for poaching.

While knitted substitutes suit most tasks, they shouldn't be used when a truly clean shape—like that of a coeur à la crème—is needed. Cheesecloth can also be called gauze, scrim, or tobacco cloth.

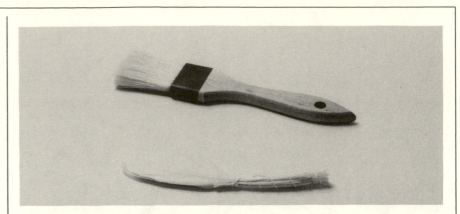

A natural-bristle, flat pastry brush (see page 183) like the one at top is indispensable to the baker for applying heavy coatings; the goosefeather pastry brush below it is better suited for applying lighter coatings.

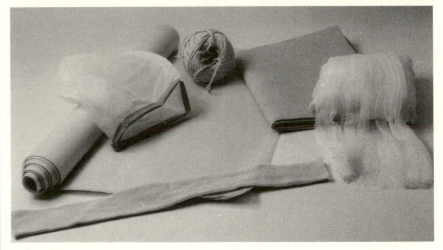

Common kitchen textiles and papers include, clockwise from the left, parchment paper, jelly-straining bag, butcher's twine, a pastry cloth, cheesecloth, and a rolling-pin cover that is often packaged with a pastry cloth.

Jelly-Straining Bag

At one time home canners relied on a thin white-felt or thick white-flannel pocket to strain cooked fruit juice from its pith, pulp, and sediment when making clear jellies. But since both fabrics also retain a considerable amount of liquid in the process, such highly refined, non-absorptive, man-made fibers as the fine-meshed nylon found on this bag are used more often for their economy.

The bag's close knit—a more finely structured marquisette than that used in curtains—supplies sufficient soft surface to block solids but not liquids, and its wide U-shape evenly displaces fruit to minimize compaction and yield the clearest strain.

Jelly-straining bags, almost always used in conjunction with a tripod stand that straddles a bowl during straining, measure 9″ × 8″ and have a maximum 2-quart capacity.

Pastry Cloth

This sheet of plastic-impregnated, lightweight, gray, flat duck provides a satisfactory work surface for occasional bakers and those who have neither the room nor the desire to install or store a marble pastry board. Set on a level surface and lightly floured, its 25″ × 20″ face accommo-

The oven mitt on the left comfortably tempers pan heat during handling; the chef's hat on the right visibly asserts its wearer's mastery.

dates most home-rolled doughs and pastries as its plastic surface precludes the need for the extra flour that would eventually find its way into the rolled dough and offset its proper fat/flour proportions to dry it out as it bakes.

Lighter-colored pastry cloths are also marketed, but the plastic-impregnated, raw-cotton cloth affords smoother, quicker release. You'll find, however, that with use and repeated rinsings, the plastic wears off.

Butcher's Twine

Strong, stout cotton twine is a necessity to truss poultry, secure a steamed pudding's cheesecloth cover, tie a bouquet garni, and compact stuffed roasts. Two types of butcher's twine are now commonly marketed—the preferred cotton and a linen variety. Both are unwaxed; the heavier cotton, three times as wide as the linen, is slightly springy because of its shorter fibers—and more workable, particularly with wet hands. Linen, which has long fibers, produces a beautiful, equally strong twine—but one that can't be stretched.

Butcher's twine is most often available in 50-yard balls.

Parchment Paper

Odorless, tasteless, greaseproof, and with a long-lasting wet strength, parchment paper is a clean, convenient, disposable tool for baking, steaming, and decorating. Parchment-lined pans easily release macaroons, meringues, and cakes; chicken or fish neatly steam in it; and conically rolled, its tip clipped, and filled with icing, the paper encourages fastidious pastry piping.

Parchment paper—a welcome addition to the familiar papers, plastics, and foils in most kitchens—can be waxed, coated, or crinkled, depending on its designated use. It is most often packaged in 20-foot rolls that measure 16 inches wide, 10-inch rounds, 15″×15″×21″ triangles, and 16″×24″ sheets.

Chef's Hat

Depending upon ascending rank in the professional kitchen, one wears a flat-topped calotte, a low toque, or a higher toque called a dodin-bouffant. Each confines hair and visually confirms authority. The dodin-bouffant, lore has it, also declared its wearer's virtuosity: In days when a chef had his toque made, each pleat represented a perfectly prepared omelet.

That may be hearsay, but not the recognition of the finest chef's hat now manufactured: It is always 100 percent cotton. Good quality, permanently pleated polyester-cotton toques are made, but because polyester attracts and harbors dirt, hats that include it can't remain spotless for long.

Chef's hats are marketed in small, medium, or large sizes or in an adjustable, one-size-fits-all model closed by inserting an attached metal arrowhead into any one of the brim's sequential loops.

Oven Mitt

A chef relies on a cloth called a tourchon (a kitchen towel) to protect bare hands when moving hot pots or baking sheets; it's lightweight, compact, easily sized to task, and quickly tucked into an apron. Others feel more comfortable with the fuller protection of an oven mitt, the best of which is silicone- or otherwise nonstick-coated. The covering to forearm particularly suits barbecue and broiler work; the three-ply construction supplies sufficient protection for moderately brief jobs, while the nonstick coating prevents hot masses from adhering, possibly igniting and burning.

Some oven mitts are fitted with a near elbow-length sleeve and all are manufactured in a single large size.

Confectioner's Bars

These four narrow steel lengths contain such freshly poured candies as caramels, butterscotch, and two-layered truffles during their individual slab settings. Placed at right angles, the two pairs of bars—roughly 20 and 30 inches respectively—easily adjust to accommodate large or small batches of syrups, pastes, or chocolates; their generous 6-pound weight contains the flow, while the ⅜- to ½-inch heights provide for various depth settings.

Occasionally called chocolate or caramel rulers, confectioner's bars must first be oiled or dusted with a cornstarch–powdered sugar mixture to prevent cooling candies from sticking, then positioned on either parchment or rice paper. They are available only in nickel-plated steel in the described lengths.

Confectioner's Funnel

This tinned-steel funnel dispenses flavored fondant onto a mat to create wafer-thin mints or prepared cream or syrup into cornstarch molds to produce candy centers that can then be coated. The funnel's tight profile, which is easily balanced when full, limits its contents' contact to drying air to prevent skin from forming on the surface; the ½-inch-wide tip encourages a smooth flow while remaining smaller than the standard negative candy molds, and the long, tapered wooden dowel, which doesn't transmit heat, regulates the flow to deter tailings.

Frequently called a mint dropper, it is most often available in tinned steel with a 1-quart capacity. A more commercial, 2-quart stainless-steel funnel that dispenses drops by means of a spring-operated valve is also manufactured.

Starch-Casting Tray

When filled with cornstarch, leveled with a straight edge, and impressed with a modeling block, this wooden tray creates a superior environment in which to uniformly cast such candies as peppermint patties, candy corn, fruit jellies, and cherry creams. Its roughly 25″ × 14″ dimensions easily support 72 well-spaced candies during their 12- to 14-hour setting, as the generous 1-inch depth, which completely covers individual candies, assures even surface crystallization.

One of the favorite setting mediums of the professional confectioner, cool, dry, reusable cornstarch draws a minimal amount of topical moisture from setting syrups and won't affect flavor but will—because of the dusting left on each candy—facilitate handling during dipping.

Starch-casting trays are manufactured only in wood.

Tools for home and nonindustrial confectioners include, from the left, a starch-casting tray, confectioner's funnel and dowel, and confectioner's bars (see page 185).

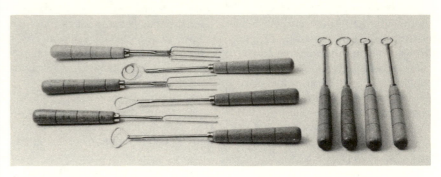

A set of lightweight looped and tined chocolate-dipping forks for balancing any typically shaped or sized candy center as it is coated.

First chilled, then dipped into molten chocolate or sugar, these heavy bronze sugar and chocolate decorating forms quickly set and shape the medium into glorious cake-topping blooms.

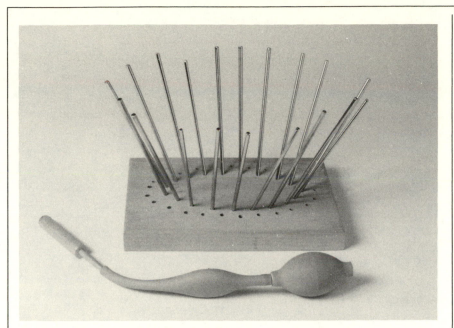

The sugar mandrel at top and sugar pump below it are necessary tools when shaping a specially prepared syrup into a basket or fruit centerpiece.

Sugar Pump

Such simple to complex sugar shapes as peaches, pears, and perhaps a vase to contain them demand patience, a deft touch, and frequently this sugar pump to form them expertly. The carefully prepared sugar compound, still hot but malleable, readily adheres to the pump's milled, hollow aluminum shaft; the bulb feeds air to the smaller reservoir, which in turn provides a constant supply of air through progressive tubes to the parison formed by the sugar mass. Careful stretching and pulling give the appropriate shape, which is then cooled with rubbing alcohol or cold granulated sugar.

The most readily available sugar pump measures just over 17 inches fully assembled, and the best are accompanied by an aluminum rather than a wooden shaft.

Sugar Mandrel

Once this mandrel's steel shafts are inserted into the lightweight wooden slab and both rods and base oiled, they create a superb surface on which to weave the thin, pulled-sugar strands that shape the presentation baskets for blown-sugar fruits and flowers. The mandrel's carefully spaced 7-inch-long bars act as the warp for the sugar's weft, and the wood's light weight eases the constant turning needed as the sugar mass is kept pliant by its heat lamp. With weaving done, the rods are then replaced with additional sugar strands and the basket trimmed and fitted with a pulled-sugar handle.

Two sets of drilled concentric rings in the base allow for the forming of 8½- or 10-inch-wide baskets. A more versatile base produces ovals and squares in addition to the standard circles. Sugar mandrels are manufactured only with wood bases and either nickel-plated or brass rods.

Chocolate-Dipping Forks

These lightweight pronged and looped wire dipping forks let the confectioner neatly coat and decorate any nut, fruit segment, or shaped candy center with a properly prepared syrup, fondant, or chocolate. A four-pronged fork's 1⅛-inch splay easily balances a Brazil nut during dunking and draining, a tear-drop tip scores a lemon jelly's still-wet chocolate sheath, while an average ¾-ounce weight readily hefts a one-bite caramel square or nougat log.

To use a chocolate-dipping fork, drop the center into the couverture, press down lightly with the fork to coat evenly, then slip the fork under the center, lift, and drain before transfer to paper by drawing the fork across the pan's edge.

Chocolate-dipping forks, which are always blunt-tipped to thwart any accidental penetration and a sure-to-follow cracked coating, are manufactured in stainless or the more readily available nickel-plated steels and are boxed in 6- and 10-piece sets.

Sugar and Chocolate Decorating Set

With a set of 17 heavy bronze leaves, multipetaled and lobed forms, the patissier can shape a wide array of sugar or tempered-chocolate lilies, orchids, daffodils, and primroses to top cakes or create centerpieces. Bronze quickly and evenly absorbs and dissipates dipping temperatures and also withstands the knife nicks that release the cooled and contracted shape. Its average 6-ounce weight furthers proper chilling and can't buckle from radically cold to hot immersions, and short, perpendicular handles distance hands while still providing a close working proximity.

Sugar and chocolate decorating sets—which are used almost solely as the time-saving alternative to producing the mattelike turned-and satiny pulled-sugar shapes—are available only in bronze in boxed sets.

Duchess Cake

Flo Braker
The Simple Art of Perfect Baking

8 to 10 servings

CLASSIC ANGEL FOOD CAKE

1¼ *cups sifted cake flour*

½ *cup granulated sugar*

¼ *teaspoon salt*

1 *cup (7 or 8 large) egg whites at 60°F*

1 *teaspoon cream of tartar*

2 *tablespoons granulated sugar*

1 *teaspoon vanilla extract*

⅓ *cup granulated sugar*

Preheat the oven to 350°F.

Pour the flour, ½ cup sugar, and salt into a triple sifter and sift onto a sheet of waxed paper; set aside.

With an electric mixer set on low speed, beat the egg whites 1½ minutes or until frothy, then add the cream of tartar, increase the speed, and pour in 2 tablespoons sugar; whip 2 minutes, or until they reach their soft-peak stage. Add the vanilla extract in the final moments of whipping. Remove beaters from bowl and hand-whip 5 to 10 seconds to ensure uniform foaminess.

Use a rubber spatula to fold in half the ⅓ cup sugar, then fold in the remainder with as few strokes as possible. Sprinkle ⅓ of the flour mixture over the egg whites, fold, then repeat two more times and fold just until incorporated.

Pour into an ungreased 9-inch springform pan, smooth the surface, and bake in the lower third of the oven 25 to 30 minutes or until the top is lightly golden, the cake feels spongy and springs back when touched, and a toothpick inserted in the middle of the cake comes out clean.

Remove and flip, positioning the pan's rim onto four inverted glasses, and allow to cool 1 hour. Remove the pan and set the cake upright onto a fitted, stiff, round cardboard.

MINIATURE BUTTERFLIES

7 *tablespoons sweet butter, room temperature*

1¼ *cups confectioners' sugar*

½ *cup (about 4 large) egg whites at room temperature and lightly whisked*

1 *teaspoon vanilla extract*

¾ *cup all-purpose flour*

Preheat the oven to 350°F.

Use an electric mixer set on medium speed to cream the butter in a warmed mixing bowl until it is the consistency of mayonnaise. Add the sugar—2 tablespoons at a time—and beat until each addition is absorbed by the butter before adding the next; beat until light and fluffy. Gradually incorporate the egg whites, then add the vanilla. Use a rubber spatula to stir in the flour in 2 to 3 installments.

With a homemade 1¼-inch cardboard butterfly stencil set over a nonstick baking sheet, drop, spread, and shape the batter (1 teaspoon) into 8 butterflies at a time. Bake 5 to 7 minutes in the lower third of the oven, then remove and drape over the edge of a cake pan to cool and crimp. Repeat with the remaining batter. When cool, decorate 6 (if so desired) with piped royal icing bodies and antennae. Reserve the remainder for a future use. (Yield: Approximately 6 dozen)

ORANGE SABAYON FROSTING

2 *small sugar cubes*

1 *orange*

1 *cup fresh orange juice*

5 *large egg yolks*

½ *cup granulated sugar*

1 *cup heavy cream, chilled*

1 *tablespoon Grand Marnier*

Rub each side of the sugar cubes against the orange skin to capture its flavor and set aside.

Bring the orange juice to a boil in a saucepan set over medium heat; reduce the heat and simmer 13 minutes or until reduced to half. Add the sugar cubes, stir until dissolved, and set aside to cool partially.

Place the egg yolks in the top part of a double boiler, lightly whisk, then add the sugar and whisk to blend; stir in the orange juice. Set the pan over simmering water and cook 3 to 4 minutes, or until the mixture begins to thicken and registers 175°F on a candy thermometer; stir constantly with a rubber spatula. Empty into a medium bowl, cover the surface with plastic wrap, and refrigerate at least 3 hours.

When cold, whip the cream with the Grand Marnier until near its near-soft peak stage. Fold a few tablespoons into the orange mixture to lighten, then fold in the remainder; use immediately.

ASSEMBLY

Place the cooled angel food cake on a turntable and smoothly ice with the orange sabayon frosting. Refrigerate if not served within 2 hours. Remove from the refrigerator 1 hour before serving. Decorate with the butterflies just before serving.

6. Tableside
Cookware

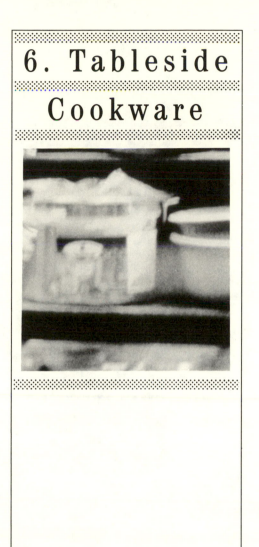

Because the chafing dish is an extension of the bain marie and the flambé pan is akin to the skillet, these and other items for tabletop cooking are mentioned here.

A gleaming chafing dish elicits visions of luxurious dining. In practice, it allows the host or hostess to achieve just that; to present elegantly a dish such as blanquette de veau, shrimp curry, or beef stroganoff to a large group of people with little apparent effort.

The chafing dish doesn't cook, but rather supplies slow, even heat to previously cooked foods by suspending them in a pan over hot water. The foods stay gently warmed and, when covered, they can't burn or dry out.

The design of the chafing dish is elementary and, except for decorative styling and base materials, has remained unchanged over many years. Most have an underliner to protect the table and all have a rechaud—a burner and supporting stand to provide heat and distance from the flame—a hot water pan to ensure a constant temperature, and a blazer pan to hold and cover food.

Despite its aid to the cook, demand for chafing dishes has always been periodic. They were highly esteemed at the court of Louis XIV, when ceremonial meals were divided into three services. First and second services traditionally included soups, fish, roasts, and game, and the third was comprised of desserts. All foods offered during a single service were placed on the table at the start of that course, and the hot items were kept warm on rechauds. Called service à la française, it was popular well into the nineteenth century, when it was replaced by service à la russe. Here, platters of the different foods within a service were arranged in the kitchen, brought to the table, and guests were served from them. Neither rechauds nor chafing dishes were used as frequently and their popularity waned.

Closer to our time, demand for chafing dishes has continued to peak and ebb. They were de rigueur at the Stork Club and El Morocco forty years ago when bar customers were greeted by "chafers" brimming with hot hors d'oeuvres like deviled oysters. Ten years later, chafing-dish suppers were the epitome of fashionable home dining.

Flambé pans, equally elegant but decidedly more showy, followed the same dining trends. When grand-scale home entertaining prevailed, so did the use of silver- or tin-lined copper and silver-plated flambé pans, or poêles.

Pans made of those metals are available today, but they are astronomically expensive. People who want one of these for home use are advised to invest in a stainless-steel one.

It's safe to say that flaming crepes suzettes and cherries jubilee are among the superstars in tabletop cookery; so are bubbling cheese fondue and fondue bourguignonne. The former add final flash to any meal and the latter promote conviviality throughout. Both add immeasurably to a dining experience and, to be carried off smoothly, require proper equipment.

A good flambé pan is designed for fast action. It is light, shallow, and wide to heat quickly and offer ample room for the spirits to spread and the oxygen to feed its flames. Fondue pots are slower and steadier because they cook foods, not just finish them off. The wide, heavy, glazed-earthenware cheese-fondue pot provides gentle heat and a substantial dipping area. The onion-shaped meat-fondue pot is metal for more rapid heat conduction and tall to prevent oil from splattering. And the small, porcelain or enameled cast-iron chocolate-fondue pot is like a butter warmer in conveying only a slight but even heat.

There are three features to consider when buying tabletop cookware: heat source, stand, and handle. For safety's sake, the burner must be reliable and adjustable, the base should be stable and secure, and the handle sturdy and well constructed.

Chafing Dish

This tabletop warming device has long been held dear: Shakespeare mentions one in Richard III, an old English testament cites another's disposition to a family member, and yet another source describes an item much like today's, with frame, fuel compartment, flame adjuster, water pan, and blazer. Simplicity—a heated pan full of hot water to keep foods warm—demands few changes. Some adjustments have occurred through the years: switches from coal firing to wood to denatured alcohol to solid fuel reduced the fuel-housing size. At the turn of the century, the unit was briefly suspended in its frame and called the yachting dish for where it was meant to be used. And most recently, the more durable, tarnish-free cladded metals have replaced the once popular heavy tin-lined copper and silverplate now frequently found in New York's fine auction houses, London's Silver Vaults, and such Parisian shops as Christofle.

Capacities for contemporary chafing dishes range from a diminutive 3 pints to a colossal 38 quarts. For home use, a 3-quart dish is recommended.

Crepes Suzette Pan

Not to be confused with the kitchen crepe pan in which crepe batter is actually cooked, this stainless steel–lined copper pan is meant for showy, tableside finales—specifically the warming, saucing, and flaming of dessert crepes. The utensil is handsome and functional: Its flat copper bottom ensures even heat contact—a necessity for quick flambés; its 12-inch breadth rapidly reduces sauces, and a shallow 1-inch depth makes for easy crepe folding and stacking. Eleven-inch crepes suzette pans, or as they're called, round flambé pans, are available as well, but are not as popular as the 12-inch size. Both are manufactured in the recommended stainless steel–lined copper and the less durable tin-lined copper.

Oval Flambé Pan

Once the preserve of restaurant captains and majordomos for flaming and serving such entrées as steak au poivre, veal kidneys, and crayfish, the oval flambé pan is usually larger than and twice as deep as the round crepes suzette pan. Besides offering visual diversity, an oval flambé's few extra inches are needed to accommodate lengthy steaks, brook trout, and rolled crepes, while a 2½-inch depth prevents their usually generous sauces from spilling and splattering.

Oval flambé pans measure nearly 12 to 15 inches long and 7½ to almost 9 inches wide and are available in various metals and bimetals. Select an aluminum-cored stainless-steel one; it rapidly channels heat, is easy to maintain, looks attractive, and is reasonably priced. Traditional silver-lined copper ones are certainly lustrous, but they command princely prices, and the interiors of tin-lined pans can blister, melt, and/or crack with a flambé's high heat.

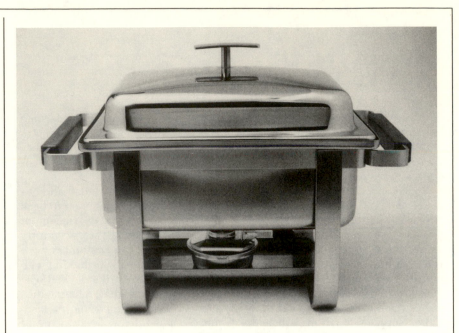

This generous-sized chafing dish (see page 191) is sturdily constructed with a stable base and dependable heat source.

The wide, barely-sided crepes suzette pan is used to flame precooked crepes and their sauce tableside.

This 2½-inch-deep oval flambé pan is substantial enough to cook or flame foods tableside.

This gleaming, silver-lined café diable service is used expressly for preparing and serving post-meal liqueur-laced coffee.

Café Diable Service

As the three devilish telamons that raise this silver-lined copper bowl above its base plate indicate, this piece is used tableside to assemble and serve café diable, a concoction of sugar, orange peel, cinnamon, Kahlúa, and coffee. The broad bowl—whose diameter measures thrice its depth—creates an impressively high surface-to-air-contact for dramatic ignition and quick burnoff of the alcohol, and the nearly 7-inch height sets a visible stage. The 1-quart capacity—of which 24 ounces are usable—serves six. An accompanying double-spouted ladle with an inset strainer on one side facilitates clean straining into separately sold, tall, tight, 6-ounce cups.

Also used to prepare the flaming brandy-laced café brûlot—an ancient brûlot was a fire-bombing warship—café diable services are manufactured only in silver-lined copper in 1- or 2-quart sizes.

Fondue Bourguignonne Pot

Fondue bourguignonne requires very hot oil to cook properly, so the onion-shaped pot should be cast iron, lined copper, or stainless steel for sufficient heat retention. A broad base provides adequate heat contact and a narrower top hinders hot oil from splattering and confines the movement of heat within the pot for temperature maintenance.

A flavorless peanut or corn oil with a high smoking point—450°F—is still favored, but more and more often, those looking to reduce dietary fat are cooking fondues with chicken, beef, or fish broth, which is called fondue orientale after the exotic, broth-based Mongolian hot pot. An occidental meat-fondue pot is a fine, functional alternative to the donut-shaped, funneled, charcoal-burning utensil traditionally stoked on the steppes.

Fondue-bourguignonne pots range from 1½ pints to 2 quarts and are available in a wide variety of materials, including enameled cast iron, stainless steel–lined copper, and aluminum-cored stainless steel. Fondue bourguignonne pots, solid fuel– and denatured alcohol–burning and electric, are usually sold in sets that contain a rechaud, stand, and meat-fondue forks.

Shrimp Curry

Gourmet *magazine*

8 servings

3 *pounds shrimp, shelled, deveined, rinsed, and cut in half lengthwise*

2 *cups heavy cream*

1 *cup light cream*

½ *teaspoon salt*

12 *tablespoons butter*

2 *cups finely chopped onions*

¾ *cup finely chopped green pepper*

1 *garlic clove, finely chopped*

⅓ *cup curry powder*

¼ *cup all-purpose flour*

3 *cups chicken stock (see page 210)*

2 *tablespoons finely chopped green pepper (optional garnish)*

Combine the shrimp, heavy and light creams, and salt in a large bowl, lightly toss, then cover and refrigerate until needed.

Melt the butter in a large sauté pan set over medium heat, add the onions, green pepper, and garlic, and sauté until the onions are soft and golden. Add the curry powder and flour and continue to cook 2 to 3 minutes; stir frequently.

Remove the pan from the heat, add the stock, and stir to mix. Return to medium-high heat and bring to a boil; stir frequently. Reduce the heat and simmer 15 minutes; stir occasionally.

Empty the shrimp mixture into a colander set over a bowl and allow to drain 5 minutes. Reserve the shrimp but add the cream to the pan and let it come to a boil; stir often. Reduce the heat and simmer, partially covered, 30 minutes.

To serve: Transfer the curry to a flambé pan set atop a medium flame and bring it to a bare simmer. Add the shrimp and cook 3 to 4 minutes, or until pink. Optionally garnish with the green pepper and serve with steamed rice, poppadums, various chutneys, scallions, and coconut chips.

Cheese-Fondue Pot

The heavy, traditional cheese-fondue pot, called a caquelon in its native Savoy and Switzerland, is roughly 3 inches deep so the Gruyère, Emmenthaler, wine, and kirsch constantly simmer near hot sides or bottom, 9 inches wide so several forks can be swirled at once, and crafted in earthenware, a material that withstands and conveys only gentle heat. As in any recipe calling for cooked cheese, high temperatures can cause the proteins in cheese to coagulate, toughen, and, in the case of a fondue, become unmanageably stringy.

A standard 2-quart cheese-fondue pot holds enough for four. The recommended material is the customary glazed earthenware, even though fine, enameled-steel caquelons are also made. Both are available alone or in sets containing a stand, rechaud (or electric base), and the appropriate forks.

Chocolate-Fondue Pot

This tiny enameled cast-iron vessel may look traditional, but its design is less than thirty years old. Chocolate fondue and the accompanying pot were developed as part of a Swiss product promotion for the 1964 World's Fair in New York. The pot is thick, heavy, and set over a candle so that only slight heat can be transmitted. Since the cocoa butter and solids in melted chocolate separate easily, with fats rising and solids, which scorch quickly, sinking, chocolate should never be excessively heated.

Chocolate-fondue pots are small, generally 1 pint, because the dessert is so rich that a sampling is usually plenty. The pots are sold in sets with a stand and candle warmer.

The special pots in which to serve fondue are, from the left, a chocolate-fondue pot and fondue bourguignonne pot (page 193) atop their rechauds and a cheese-fondue pot.

A fine tableside butter warmer comes complete with a low, sturdy candle stand that is hard to topple.

Cheese Fondue

Konrad Egli, Proprietor
Dietmar Schluter, Executive Chef:
Chalet Suisse

3 cups or 4 to 6 servings

1 *large garlic clove, halved*

2 *cups dry white wine*

8 *ounces Gruyère, shredded*

8 *ounces Emmenthaler, shredded*

Pinch cayenne

Pinch freshly grated nutmeg

1 *teaspoon cornstarch*

2 *tablespoons kirsch*

1 *to 2 loaves French bread, cubed*

Rub the inside surface of the caquelon (fondue pot) with the garlic, then discard the garlic.

Set the pot over medium heat, add the wine, and bring to a simmer. Add the cheeses and cook until melted and the mixture resembles a light cream sauce; stir constantly with a wooden spoon. Season with cayenne and nutmeg and bring to a boil.

In a small bowl combine the cornstarch and kirsch, stir to mix, then add to the cheese mixture and stir vigorously to incorporate.

Remove the caquelon to its lighted tabletop burner and serve with the cubed bread.

Rechauds to warm food or cook small amounts of it are the denatured-alcohol–fed rechaud (page 196) on the left and the solid-fuel rechaud on the right.

Tableside Butter Warmer

This small, stout pan atop its candle stand warms and serves melted butter, gravy, or heated syrup. Partially filled, its 8-ounce capacity supplies ample sauce for four; its roughly 5-inch breadth and 2-inch depth create a proportionately high liquid-to-hot-metal ratio for continued warmth and easy access, as the candle's three-legged wrought-iron stand/pan support provides steadiness.

Tableside butter warmers, which can have a ¾- to 2-cup capacity, are most frequently manufactured in stainless steel or, ideally, to heat uniformly as well as be decorative, cladded stainless steel. The finest have well-balanced, hard-to-topple stands and secure handles; the separately sold votive candles for warming each have a one-hour life.

Solid-Fuel Rechaud

This solid-gel burner is used tableside with a chafing dish to keep cooked food hot or with a presentation pan to finish off previously prepared foods by flambéing. The unit's 7-inch height elevates food to a more comfortable working and serving level; its 7½-pound weight, mostly bottom-based, makes it hard to topple, and its readily available gel-type fuel is unspillable, clean to burn, and odorless. It does not, however, produce as high a temperature as denatured alcohol nor the hotter-still butane, so if such a unit is pressed into tableside cooking, calculate the preparation time at 20 percent longer than on an alcohol burner.

Solid-fuel burners are manufactured in stainless steel, silver plate, and in combinations that include stainless steel, copper, wrought iron, and nickeled steel. Shorter ones that measure 4 inches in height are tailor-made for fondue: Their lower height is more inviting and the same heat level suits the continued warming of oil, cheese, or chocolate.

When buying a fine solid-fuel burner, select for safety above cosmetics: It should be sturdily built, firm-footed, and bottom heavy.

How to Care for Fine Metal

Copper casseroles, saucepans, flambé pans, and fondue pots, together with silver chafing dishes, are as elegant as they are functional, but to keep them at their sparkling peak, they must be carefully maintained. Their surfaces tarnish because the metals react to the oxygen, nitrogen, sulfur, or chlorine compounds in the atmosphere and in certain foods. Once interaction occurs, a new chemical such as copper or silver oxide, sulfide, or sulfate forms and imparts a characteristic surface color. These colors—black, blue, and green among them—are tarnishes and can be broken down and removed by a polish with a strong reducing agent.

Between polishings, tarnish can be minimized in several ways:

- Rinse the article immediately after use, especially if it has come into contact with egg yolks, citrus fruits, mustard, vinegar, olives, or salt.

- Wash it in hot water and detergent; rinse it in clear water and thoroughly dry immediately. If food particles stick, soak the pan overnight in hot water with detergent, then carefully rub off with a sponge or nylon pad.

- Some recommend removing tarnish electrochemically by lining a sink with aluminum foil, then soaking the item in a detergent-and-ammonia solution. This is not suggested because a dull, luster-less finish results.

Some Italian- and most Portuguese-made copper molds, pans, and kettles designed for cooking—i.e., tin- or silver-lined—are covered with a thin, protective exterior lacquer coating. Leave this on if the item is to be strictly decorative; remove it, however, if you intend to use it to heat or prepare food. To remove the lacquer, moisten a sponge with acetone, then gently rub the article, wash, rinse, dry, and use. (Except for sugar boilers, preserving pans, zabaglione bowls, and bowls in which to beat egg whites, unlined copper is unsuitable for preparing food, so leave the lacquer on these decorative pieces.)

See also the chart on cookware materials, pages 106–110.

Alcohol Rechaud

When its burner is filled with denatured alcohol and ignited, this stainless-steel table stove produces a characteristically tall but low-temperature flame for such modest cooking as light sautés and flambés. The housing is strong and its stand sufficiently broad: Its low, widely spread 3-pound weight stably supports a filled omelet or crepes suzette pan and, when prudently half filled, its 1-cup fuel store supplies roughly 90 minutes of flame that may not be as hot as butane but is more dramatic.

Some lighter-weight alcohol burners—generally silver-plated—are equipped with two heat sources, and some have frames that can be flipped over—oval on one side and round on the other—to support either presentation-pan shape. A gamboled or otherwise convertible burner unit is built in to accommodate both.

Small alcohol rechauds are also available in a copper–stainless steel combination; you'll see that the flame level of each style is similarly adjusted: Two caps, each of whose openings matches that of the gas

A tableside butane-gas rechaud puts out such high heat that it can also be used as a portable cookstove on picnics, porch or patio. It is shown above with a butane canister.

unit, reduce the flame while the complete covering cap snuffs it. Such burners are easily refilled but *never* while they're lit.

Butane-Gas Rechaud

When loaded with a butane canister and set aflame, this rechaud produces such a stable, high-intensity heat that it could be utilized as a portable cookstove, not solely as a food warmer or finisher. Each replaceable butane cartridge supplies enough energy for 1½ hours of cooking; the control regulates output for simmering to searing while its nearly 4-pound enameled stainless-steel casing is sturdy, compact, and, with a drip pan as its single moving part, suited for travel.

Some gas burners are equipped with a grill instead of the standard burner-unit pan supports and others have two burners instead of one. These are options; what shouldn't be are the three all-important safety features: one to shut off the gas-feed should an abnormally high pressure develop within the canister; one to prevent insertion of the cartridge unless the regulating knob is in the off position; and another to temporarily pressure-seal the disposable fuel cartridge to the stove connection to prevent gas leakage.

This elegant caviar presentoir makes its luxurious contents easily accessible.

On Caviar Table Service

Christian Petrossian,
President: Petrossian

With its smooth, lustrous sheen, fleeting sea scent, slight resiliency, and rare, fresh taste, fine caviar—Beluga, Ossetra, or Sevruga—is not so much a food as it is a dream. Mere mention of this carefully treated roe of the three species of Caspian Sea sturgeon evokes visions of festivity, mystique, and grandeur. Aristotle wrote of caviar in the fourth century B.C.; Henry II of England designated the sturgeon a royal fish in the twelfth century; Rabelais spoke of the delicacy in his 1532 *Pantagruel*, around the same time that Pope Julius II praised it.

Such lauding frequently included caviar's traditionally elegant table presentation; the ever-more-sumptuous centerpieces and spoons designed solely to hold and serve it.

The bare essentials appeared first—the sleek, simple spoons made from the Caspian coast's indigenous tortoise shell, animal horn, or bone. Some remain with us, like the carved bone ones that date to the time of the Khanate, and while it is impossible to identify them as specifically meant for caviar, one presumes that if they were, the early Russians who used them knew then of the need for a material that wouldn't react to affect the taste of caviar's processing salt.

Initial rusticity, however, became quite majestic. The country's growing imperial authority, expanding Western contact, and a greater desire to entertain in kind are all evident in the increasingly elaborate Russian tableware, of which the domestically produced nineteenth-century caviar spoons are prime examples. Bowl shapes, at first round, graduated to fig and palette as in Europe. Styles paralleled as well: The now-preferred silver ornament on spoons and their presentoirs progressed from decidedly Russian Byzantine to neoclassical to symbolic.

Yet such exquisite crafting often suffered at function's expense. Too-deep and too-large spoon bowls precluded delicate dipping and dispensing; high, cylindrical presentoirs restricted easy access, and silver altered caviar's flavor. Carl Fabergé's low, broad, glass-lined gilt centerpieces were noteworthy exceptions, as were the more expedient ice-cooled presentoirs designed in France after la Belle Époque.

Personal favorites are contemporary, practical, aesthetic, and of our own design. The wide, slightly raised, very accessible silver presentoir that holds the original caviar tin averts silver's touch and limits handling. Its scant metal-to-tin contact additionally checks ambient heat absorption so the chilled caviar remains cold without ice.

The small ladle's round edge, shell shape, and perforated bow promise gentle scooping, perfect portioning, and complete release, while the individual palette's tapered edges and thumb-sized, thin, flat face slide the caviar smoothly onto toast for spreading. Nonreactive gold graces the working surface of each so caviar keeps its pure taste.

When serving from any presentoir with the appropriate utensils, offer only lightly toasted bread and either iced vodka or brut champagne to drink.

7. Measuring Tools

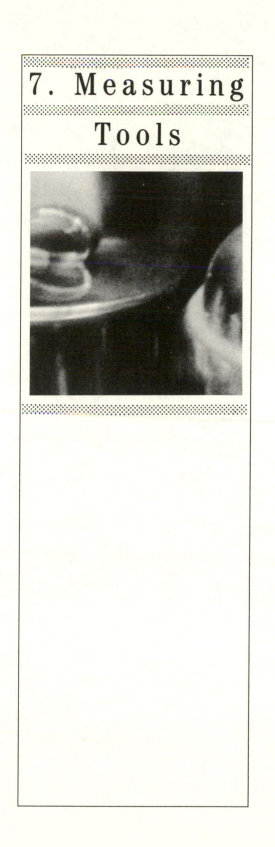

The finest advice a good cookbook can give its readers is in its recipe's details: to poach a whole salmon 10 minutes for every inch of its thickness; to bake a 1-quart soufflé 20 minutes in a 425°F oven; to heat deep fat to 375°F before adding julienned potatoes.

Such direction lets the cook understand that when the suggested ingredients are exactly measured, carefully assembled, sequentially prepared, and cooked at precise temperatures for specific times, they react predictably. And when the aspiring chef realizes the sure response and gains proficiency, his or her increasing confidence opens the door to the creative touches that raise simple food preparation from a task to an art.

With proven techniques that guide the chef to surefire results, it's easy to understand why cooking is as much a science as biology, chemistry, or botany, with repeated successes—whether in a kitchen in Kansas City or a laboratory in London—depending on communicating correct component weights and measures.

And yet specific food weight, mass, time, and temperature are moderately recent inclusions in recipes. Not only did those various units of measure need to be established and standardized, but the tools with which to monitor them had to be invented.

The initial units evolved for trade and commerce and corresponded to the body parts—the foot, finger thickness, and hand span among them. But when man—as Protagoras's "measure of all things"—elected to refine these concrete measures into abstract lengths, container sizes, and grain weights and developed the decimal-based rods, scales, and dials to gauge them, he could then devise the formulary to make uniform tools, medicines, and clay blends and to share further scientific knowledge, including that relating to food.

Food measurements became more precise as culinary advances followed cultural progress and the broadening needs and range of measurement.

Most of the recipes attributed to a cook named Martino which appear in *De Honesta Voluptate*, 1475, by Bartolomeo Sacchi—better known as Platina—merely suggest assembly. A century later Bartolomeo Scappi's *Opera* more specifically recommends weighing many ingredients with an illustrated two-pan balance that was known in ancient Egypt. The author also times certain preparations, most likely with an hourglass, as the relatively new mechanical clock would not yet have been commonplace in the High Renaissance kitchen. In the mid 1600s chefs both on the Continent and in England enjoyed still greater use of weights and measures in La Va-

renne's *Le Pastissier François* and what some say is its partial translation, *The Perfect Cook*, the latter of which compares imperial standards with their continental counterparts. An English pint, according to the English text, was "a Parisian measure which contains two pounds within an ounce." The compiler also likened various avoirdupois and troy weights to the now-obsolete French *choppin*, *septies*, *posson*, and *lition* measures. The first, most thorough and refined recommendations for weighted or measured ingredients appeared in Dr. William Kitchiner's 1817 *The Cook's Oracle* in standardized teaspoon, tablespoon, and pint measures. Also expressed was the wish that "some culinary philosopher shall invent a thermometer to ascertain the heat of the fire."

He did, as others, like Lord Kelvin, devised more precise temperature scalings or such further measurements of sound and shear forces and their tools that food scientists and technologists now utilize and which may more generally appear as kitchenware evolves.

For more elementary use, it took many years of profound consideration by master chefs to develop the tables that follow.

Oven Temperature Conversions

°F	°C CONVENIENT EQUIVALENT	°C ACTUAL TEMPERATURE
250	120	121.11
275	135	135
300	150	148.88
325	160	162.77
350	175	176.66
375	190	190.55
400	205	204.44
425	220	218.33
450	230	232.22
475	245	246.11
500	260	260

Liquid Weights

VOLUME	AVOIRDUPOIS	METRIC: CONVENIENT EQUIVALENT	METRIC: ACTUAL WEIGHT
1 teaspoon	.16 ounce	5 ml	4.8 ml
1 tablespoon	.5 ounce	15 ml	15 ml
2 tablespoons	1 ounce	30 ml	30 ml
¼ cup	2 ounces	60 ml	60 ml
½ cup	4 ounces	120 ml	120 ml
¾ cup	6 ounces	180 ml	180 ml
1 cup	8 ounces	240 ml	240 ml
2 cups	1 pint	480 ml	480 ml
4 cups	1 quart	1 liter	.95 liter

Dry Weights

INGREDIENT	VOLUME	AVOIRDUPOIS	METRIC: CONVENIENT EQUIVALENT	METRIC: ACTUAL WEIGHT
Flour (sifted),	1 teaspoon	.083 ounce	3 grams	2.3 gr
grated cheese,	1 tablespoon	.25 ounce	7 grams	7.08 gr
or chopped	¼ cup	1 ounce	30 grams	28.3 gr
nuts	½ cup	2 ounces	60 grams	56.7 gr
	¾ cup	3 ounces	85 grams	85.05 gr
	1 cup	4 ounces	115 grams	113.4 gr
Granulated	1 teaspoon	.14 ounce	5 grams	3.9 gr
sugar, dried	1 tablespoon	.42 ounce	15 grams	11.9 gr
beans, or	¼ cup	1.68 ounces	50 grams	47.6 gr
uncooked	½ cup	3.36 ounces	100 grams	95.2 gr
rice	¾ cup	5.04 ounces	150 grams	142.8 gr
	1 cup	6.72 ounces	200 grams	190.5 gr
Butter	1 teaspoon	.16 ounce	5 grams	4.5 gr
	1 tablespoon	.5 ounce	15 grams	14.1 gr
	¼ cup	2 ounces	60 grams	56.7 gr
	½ cup	4 ounces	115 grams	113.4 gr
	¾ cup	6 ounces	170 grams	170.1 gr
	1 cup	8 ounces	230 grams	226.8 gr

The three types of scales to help the cook measure accurately by weight are, from the left, a balance, a beam scale, and the favored spring scale.

Measuring tools necessary in every kitchen include, from the left, a measuring-spoon set, liquid-measure cup, and dry-measure cup set, all described on page 204.

Beam Scale

This precise beam scale functions by means of three compound levers whose composite action suspends an empty weight pan, then—thanks to two measuring tares that slide across a horizontal arm—balances any load to provide a faultless weight reading. This scale accommodates a ¼-ounce to a 10-pound load, fine for dieters who monitor their caloric intake and for most baking needs, but to be truly useful, a kitchen scale should register up to 25 pounds to confirm roast and big-bird weights.

The gradations on this and other beam scales are clearly marked, well spaced, and easy to adjust. But adjusting takes so much time to bring the beams into balance that most people prefer to use a spring scale. If you want that unquestionable precision, however, the more finely made beam scales have enameled stainless-steel chassis with chromed trays and fittings.

Spring Scale

Unlike the beam scale that functions by means of leverage, this one operates on Young's modulus, the measured compression caused by a weight set onto a spring coil; the weight is indicated on a divided scale by an attached pointer.

It's convenient, sturdy, and popular in the professional kitchen for measuring baking ingredients and controlling portions. This one's roughly 6″×5″ platform easily accommodates trimmed chops or shaped patties; it can be reset to zero to allow ingredients to be successively incorporated into an onset tray, bowl, or scoop, and its large dial registers up to 50 pounds in 2-ounce increments.

Scales are most often calibrated from 7 ounces to 50 pounds, with a 25-pound scale with 1-ounce divisions generally recommended for home use. The sturdiest are those with enameled-steel or anodized-aluminum chassis, and the best feature an easy-to-read dial and zero-set adjustment.

Balance

With its centrally supported horizontal beam, each end of which bears a separate pan—one for goods and one for weights—this scale indicates an object's precise weight when the beam is brought exactly horizontal by means of correctly weighting the second tray. A variation of the balance known in Egypt in 3000 B.C., it is accurate and modestly weighted for home use. Gravity assures its accuracy, and carefully labeled, hard-wearing brass and iron weights promise consistency over a lifetime, while the 5-pound, separately sold weight set serves most noncommercial chores.

This balance is framed in steel and accompanied by two brass pans but others can be fitted with iron plates and have an optional scoop for such dry ingredients as flour and sugar. They may be precise, but they are also inconvenient due to the enormous amount of time required to bring the beam into balance.

Measuring-Spoon Set

The six elongated measures—from
⅛ teaspoon through 1 tablespoon—
that comprise this three-piece set
scoop and portion those crucial herb,
spice, and zest accents and thickening agents. Each bowl's long,
clipped tip drives, sweeps, and
scrapes against bowl, box, or jar for
a full dry or level liquid measure;
the six measures are half again as
many as most standard oval spoon
sets. The latter's sole advantage rests
in its ring link as opposed to this
set's surprisingly awkward snap-lock
closure.

Both sets are manufactured in
aluminum, plastic, and the recommended stainless steel, which is less
likely to dent and cause inaccurate
measures.

Dry-Measure Cups

This nest of four lightweight cups
with ¼- to 1-cup capacities is essential for measuring by volume. Unlike
liquid-measure cups whose sides—
to avoid spills—are taller than their
top markings, dry-measure scalings
are level to the cups' rims. Once
sugar or sifted flour is spooned to
overflowing into the desired measure, the excess is then scraped off
with a spatula.

Dry-measure cups are almost always opaque and fitted with easy-
to-balance, long, perpendicular handles. They are manufactured in
plastic, aluminum, or the preferred
stainless steel.

Liquid-Measure Cup

This heat-tempered, spouted glass
measuring cup lets the cook quickly
measure and dispense liquid ingredients. Its contents can be read accurately at eye level by aligning the
liquid's convex upper surface—its
meniscus—with the desired mark on
the cup, divided into ounce, cup,
pint, milliliter, deciliter, and liter
units to accommodate American
standard and metric recipe recom-

Thermometers to measure hot or cold temperatures are, from the left, an oven thermometer,
rapid-response thermometer, freezer/refrigerator thermometer (see page 206), and meat thermometer.

mendations, and spouted to pour
driplessly.

Professional chefs understand that
liquid-measure cups can deviate by
as much as ±5 percent due to manufacturing inconsistencies and that
atmospheric pressures can alter volume. They always measure by weight,
which can be time-consuming and,
considering the slight variables and
fractional noncommercial volume,
not usually necessary for the home
cook.

Liquid-measure cups are also manufactured in plastic in 1-, 2-, and 4-
cup sizes.

Oven Thermometer

This folding mercury thermometer
with its 100° to 600°F range is so
dependably accurate that it is used
by servicemen to monitor ovens for
overall and spot-heat fluctuations.
The mercury renders the most precise readings, especially at the higher
range, and its hinged, perforated,
stainless-steel casing protects the
glass tube in storage, then opens to
serve as a sturdy, well-vented stand
while in use.

This is the best of the liquid-in-
glass type of thermometer, first used
successfully in 1714. Its tube's small
end bulb is mercury-filled to gauge

the high temperatures, although
lower ones are better measured by
one of the dyed organic liquids—
alcohol, toluene, and pentane among
them. Liquid-in-glass thermometers
should respond to heat change rapidly and correctly, be well marked,
clearly visible, and safely encased in
a metal sheath.

Meat Thermometer

"Cooks are made, roasters are born,"
according to Brillat-Savarin. If you
aren't among the latter, this bimetallic thermometer, which monitors
the internal temperature of roasting
meat or poultry, can compensate for
that missing gift. The tool's 4½-inch-
long stem drives well into standard-
sized home roasts while the dial's
prominent 120°F to 200°F scale
clearly indicates when a roast has
reached a sufficient internal temperature to kill all food-poisoning bac-
teria.

The thermometer's action is based
on the changes that heat causes to
a bar composed of two bonded metals having different rates of thermal
expansion. One end of the bar is
fixed to the closed end of its metal
case while the other end is attached
to the shaft of a pointer. When heat
rises, the bar's motion prompts the

pointer to register the appropriate temperature on a dial scale.

Meat thermometers are also manufactured as liquid-in-glass types, but their stems are generally broader in diameter and more prone to drain a meat's juices. Their accuracy rate is more precise by roughly 3° but preferences remain with the bimetallic type, the best of which has a narrow probe and large dial.

Rapid-Response Thermometer

With its near instantaneous, 68° to 220°F temperature-measurement scale, this thermometer is a hands-down favorite in the semiprofessional kitchen to spot-monitor anything from the water in which to dissolve yeast to the internal temperature of roasting meat or poultry

or poaching fish. The temperature sensor—located at the tip of its 5-inch-long stainless-steel stem—readily penetrates to the center of any large home roast for the most accurate reading; the sensor then

Grilled Venison Sausage with Leek and Wild-Mushroom Torte

Alfred Portale, Executive Chef: The Gotham Bar & Grill

4 to 6 servings

VENISON SAUSAGE

16 *ounces venison, trimmed of sinew and cubed*

12 *ounces fresh pork butt, trimmed and cubed*

6 *ounces fresh pork fat, cubed*

6 *tablespoons (or 3 ounces) red wine*

2½ *teaspoons (or 14 grams) salt*

½ *teaspoon (or 3 grams) freshly ground black pepper*

½ *teaspoon (or 3 grams) granulated sugar*

⅓ *teaspoon (or 3 grams) ground coriander seed*

¼ *teaspoon (or 1 gram) ground juniper berries*

¼ *teaspoon (or 1 gram) ground dried ginger*

½ *teaspoon (or 3 grams) minced garlic*

2 *tablespoons (or 1 ounce) ice water*

Combine the venison, pork, fat, and red wine in a glass or stainless-steel bowl, cover, and refrigerate overnight. Use a meat grinder to grind half the meat through a coarse plate and the other half through a medium plate. Combine with the re-

maining ingredients, mix well, and either shape by hand into patties or prepare links.

To prepare links: Rinse the amount of small hog casings needed—approximately 10 feet—then soak them 30 minutes in cold water; drain. Slip one end of the casing onto a faucet nozzle and gently run cold water through it; remove any excess water. Slip one end of the casing onto the lightly oiled nozzle of a sausage funnel, slide on all but 3 inches, and knot. Fill the casings with the meat evenly and firmly, but not tightly, letting them gradually slip off the funnel; twist or tie in even lengths.

Grill the links or patties about 8 minutes over medium-high heat; turn once, then serve with the leek and wild-mushroom torte.

TORTE FILLING

3 *tablespoons butter (or as needed for the sauté)*

8 *ounces wild mushrooms (morels, shiitake, and/or chanterelles), wiped and thinly sliced*

3 *medium leeks, trimmed, julienned, and rinsed*

1 *small white onion, julienned*

Salt to taste

Freshly ground white pepper to taste

1 *tablespoon finely chopped parsley*

1¼ *cups heavy cream*

3 *large eggs*

Freshly grated nutmeg to taste

Melt half the butter in a medium sauté pan set over low heat, add the mushrooms, and partially cook 5 minutes.

Melt the remaining butter in a medium sauté pan set over low heat, add the leeks and onion, and sauté 15 minutes to cook without coloring; stir occasionally. Season to taste with salt and pepper. Add the mushrooms 5 minutes before done.

Empty the leek-mushroom mixture into a strainer to drain. Add the parsley and, if necessary, correct the seasoning; set aside.

To make the custard, combine the cream and eggs in a medium bowl and whisk to mix. Strain through a fine sieve, season to taste with salt, pepper, and nutmeg, and set aside.

TORTE ASSEMBLY

6 *ounces puff pastry (see page 97)*

Preheat the oven to 375°F.

Roll out the pastry to ⅛-inch thick in a roughly 10-inch-square shape, then divide this into 4 pieces and use to line four 4-ounce (3 inches wide × 1½ inches deep) tartlet molds. Refrigerate to chill, then neatly trim off the excess with a sharp knife.

Line with parchment paper, weight with beans, and bake 12 minutes or until lightly brown.

Remove from the oven and reduce its temperature to 300°F. Unweight and remove the parchment from each mold, then fill the tart shells with the leek mixture, top with an even amount of custard, and bake 12 minutes. Remove and cool slightly before unmolding.

signals the temperature to its microelectronic circuit to within 1/10°F and it appears in liquid-crystal display numbers on the dial's window. The slim stem finds little resistance when penetrating roasts and won't unduly drain off their juices.

Rapid-response thermometers generally provide 15-second temperature readouts unless their override select button is depressed for 1-second readings. They are battery-powered and measure 5½ inches long with a roughly 1-inch dial diameter.

Freezer/Refrigerator Thermometer

Compact but with a full, bold face, this liquid-in-glass thermometer's −40°F to +80°F scale clearly displays a freezer or refrigerator's internal temperature. Its 5" × 1¼" × ½" size requires little room; the full face gives a crystal-clear readout, while its dyed-alcohol medium (rather than mercury, which freezes at −38°F) provides the safest and surest reaction and readout. Unlike thermometers whose warmed liquid expands to a specific point on a calibrated scale, the dyed liquid in this one contracts to register its low or below-freeze-point temperatures.

Bimetallic freezer/refrigerator thermometers are also manufactured, but the liquid-in-glass type is preferred for its slightly greater accuracy.

Deep-Fat Thermometer

To deep-fat fry successfully, oil must be preheated to the required temperature before adding food for crisp, dry sealing and quick internal cooking. While some chefs can correctly estimate the temperature of hot oil by adding a bread cube and timing how long it takes to brown, a thermometer—like this liquid-in-glass type—is a more reliable guide. Its 95° to 400°F zoned scale easily registers high temperatures; its stainless-steel brace and plastic cap provide support and handling ease,

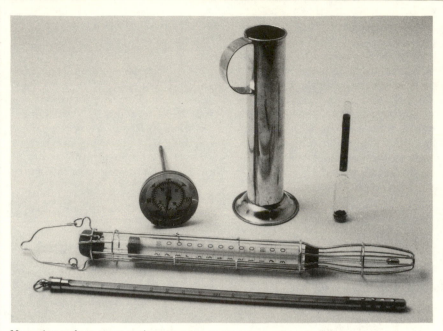

Measuring tools to gauge various stovetop or oven preparations include, clockwise from top left, a meat thermometer, syrup density–meter test tube, hydrometer, candy thermometer, and chocolate thermometer.

while the back clip that attaches to a pan's side keeps it safely out of working range. This thermometer also measures sugar syrup for candy, but if you work frequently with sugar, the more widely spaced confectioner's thermometer is clearer to read.

Bimetallic deep-fat thermometers are not as highly recommended because, while fine for monitoring gradual heat rise, the dial's indicator arrow too quickly flutters and lurches, causing an improper reading when gauging hot fat, which can drop rapidly in temperature when food is added. The better liquid-in-glass type should be sturdily braced and fitted with a pan clip and a well-marked scale.

Candy Thermometer

This mercury thermometer with its 80° to 200°C scale is the finest nonindustrial instrument made to monitor sugar-syrup temperatures. Temperatures in candymaking are critical because they indicate the amount of moisture in a batch of candy. (See page 113 for the seven stages of sugar.) Hard candies require a more concentrated syrup with less water, which therefore boils at a higher point than the syrup bases that make fudge and taffy. This thermometer's

thin capillary of mercury accurately registers a sugar syrup's temperature to let the chef use it immediately once it's reached the correct stage; the 1° scale divisions allow close monitoring, and the bright yellow stem contrasts with the gray mercury for clear reading. The open stainless-steel cage safeguards while promoting precision by permitting free heat passage and distancing the encased bulb from the bottom of the generally hotter pot.

This thermometer is available only with a Celsius readout, which may deter some home cooks, but it is produced for the professional confectioner who relies on that scale. It measures 12 inches in overall length.

Chocolate Thermometer

To achieve high flavor, glossy sheen, and snap, the chocolates for molding, dipping, or piping must first be tempered: melted to a set temperature, additional chocolate added at that point, and then cooled to a slightly lower temperature. Since dark and milk chocolates and compound chocolate coatings all require close but different processing tem-

A kitchen timer should be accurate and easy to read, should time up to two hours and sound a long, sharp alarm. The one above can simultaneously monitor three separate functions.

peratures from 80° to 120°F, most cooks use a moderately low-scaled mercury-in-glass thermometer like this 12-inch one with a 30° to 180°F range. The magnified red-mercury column provides a quick, accurate readout; the scale's 1° increments allow for careful monitoring as its open-faced sauté sheath protects against breakage.

Some chocolate thermometers have tight, hard-to-read scales, others have no casings, and still others are encased in wood, which stains indelibly with first use.

Hydrometer

To measure accurately a syrup's density (or specific gravity), the confectioner pours some of that solution into a tube, cools it to 68°F, then lowers the lead-shot–weighted bulb end of this fist-sized glass gauge to its float/rise position. An imaginary line is then drawn from the liquid's surface to the printed scale in the hydrometer's cylindrical neck to indicate the density or sugar concentration in the solution.

Depending on the specific hydrometric scale, a liquid's alcohol content and the oil in various solutions can also be gauged.

Hydrometers measure 6 inches long.

Syrup Density–Meter Test Tube

This stainless-steel beaker creates an ideal environment for the confectioner to measure correctly with a hydrometer the percentage of sugar in a given syrup. Its roughly ¾-cup capacity is quick to cool to the proper 68°F readout temperature; depending on the liquid's concentration, the 7½-inch tube floats or immerses the hydrometer insert, while its bare 1½-inch width stabilizes the gauge to ensure accurate reading.

Also called eprouvettes, these beakers are manufactured only in stainless steel.

Kitchen Timer

Accurate, easy to read, and equipped with a loud, long alarm, this battery-powered, portable electronic timer that can monitor three functions at once is the quintessential kitchen timer. Each channel can clock a 60-second blanch or a 6-hour braise; the second, minute, and hour liquid-crystal displays read clearly, and the minute-long alarm is sharp and audible. Because it can time extended periods—this one has a 10-hour capability—a digital alarm, even one with a single channel, is more practical than a spring-action timer or a gravity-driven hourglass, the latter's use severely restricted because it is soundless and can monitor only a single block of time.

A digital's sole inconvenience is that its battery must be replaced as needed.

Deviled Roast-Beef Bones

Laurent Losa, Proprietor:
Laurent

6 to 8 servings

Rib bones from 3 standing beef-rib roasts (18 raw bones with the chine removed)

2 to 3 tablespoons corn oil

1 to 2 large bay leaves, crumbled

¾ teaspoon dried thyme

½ teaspoon salt

¼ teaspoon freshly ground black pepper

2 tablespoons spicy brown mustard

⅞ cup Dijon-style mustard

¼ cup minced fresh chives

1 tablespoon minced fresh thyme leaves

¼ cup minced Italian parsley

4 cups fresh white bread crumbs

½ cup melted butter

¼ cup beef broth

Preheat the oven to 325°F.

Trim and scrape to remove the excess fat from the backs of the bones and set aside.

Combine the oil, bay leaves, dried thyme, salt, and pepper in a small bowl, stir to mix, then rub over the bones. Place the bones in a shallow roasting pan and roast 1¼ hours; remove, cool, then cut to separate the ribs. Increase the oven heat to 375°F.

Combine the mustards, chives, fresh thyme, and parsley in a medium bowl and whisk to mix. Generously brush each rib with the mixture, coat with bread crumbs, place in a jelly-roll pan, and chill at least 15 minutes.

Sprinkle the butter and broth over the ribs and bake 30 to 35 minutes in the middle of the oven or until the crumbs are golden. Serve immediately.

Basic Batterie de Cuisine

The following list and the addenda to it suggest the most essential kitchen tools as well as those required by cooks who specialize in grilling, cold-buffet styling, pastry making, or candymaking. These lists are by no means complete, but they do provide a good starting point when assembling a basic or more focused batterie de cuisine.

Knives

Chef's
Paring
Boning
Cleaver
Slicer
Bread
Straightening steel
Whetstone
Polyethylene cutting board

Other Cutting and Piercing Tools

Multipurpose kitchen shears
Vegetable peeler
Four-sided grater

Fundamental (Lever-Based) Tools

Spatulas:
    Flat
    Wooden
    Rubber
Round-tipped turner
Spoons:
    Solid
    Straight-edged wooden
    Perforated or slotted
Ladle
Skimmer
Tongs
Pot fork
Whisks:
    Sauce
    Balloon
Hand-held or standing mixer

Salt mill (or shaker)
Pepper mill
Wire strainer
Sifter
Colander
Bottle, jar, and can openers:
    Bottle and can opener
    Can opener
    Jar opener
    Corkscrew
French-style rolling pin

Stovetop and Ovenware

Saucepans with covers (3 graduated sizes)
Double boiler
Stockpot
Steamer insert (or basket)
Sauté pan
Fry pan
Shallow roasting pan and rack
Broiler pan
Casserole
Rectangular baking dish
Coffee maker
Tea kettle

Bakeware, Molds, and Pastry Preparation Tools

Baking sheet
Cookie sheet
Bread-loaf pan
Round cake pans (2)
Pie pan
Cooling rack
Mixing bowls (graduated sizes)
Sugar dredger
Pastry brush
Butcher's twine
Oven mitt

Measuring Tools

Kitchen scale
Measuring spoon set
Measuring cups:
    Dry
    Liquid
Thermometers:
    Oven
    Meat
Kitchen timer

Batterie de Cuisine: Additions for Baking and Pastry Work

Knives

Baker's
Cake

Other Cutting and Piercing Tools

Apple corer
Cherry and olive pitter
Lemon stripper
Citrus zester
Pastry blender
Pastry cutting wheel
Roller-docker
Cutters:
    Pastry
    Cookie
    Truffle, gelée, and fondant
    Vol-au-vent

Fundamental (Lever-Based) Tools

Offset spatula
Bench knife
Pastry scraper
Bowl scraper
Griddle scraper
Ice cream scoop
Ice cream spade
Pastry crimper
Standing mixer
Lemon juicer
Puff pastry rolling pin

Stovetop and Ovenware

Sugar boiler
Baking dishes:
    Soufflé
    Crème brulée
    Ramekins
    Custard cups
    Pots de crème

Bakeware, Molds, and Pastry-Preparation Tools

Jelly-roll pan
Brioche mold

Cake pans (as needed, but including):
  Kugelhopf
  Savarin
  Square
  Springform
Tart form
Flan ring
Cake rings (various sizes)
Petits-fours molds
Plaques and molds (as needed, but including):
  Madeleine
  Muffin
  Charlotte
  Ice cream
Racks:
  Baker's cooling
  Icing/candy grate
Cake-decorating turntable
Pastry-decoration tools:
  Pastry comb
  Pastry bag
  Pastry tube (assortment)
  Rose nail
Marzipan sculpting tools
Copper egg-white bowl
Marble pastry board
Cheesecloth
Parchment paper

Measuring Tools

Candy thermometer

Batterie de Cuisine: Additions for Grilling

Other Cutting and Piercing Tools

Skewers

Fundamental (Lever-Based) Tools

Square-tipped turner
Chef's fork

Stovetop and Ovenware

Grills:
  Octagonal
  Fish

Stovetop smoker
Basting brush

Measuring Tools

Rapid-response thermometer

Batterie de Cuisine: Additions for Decorating and Cold Buffet Preparation

Knives

Bird's beak paring
Fluting
Slicers:
  Ham
  Salmon
Tomato
Grapefruit
Decorating
Oyster
Clam
Sandwich spreader/cutter

Other Cutting and Piercing Tools

Corers and pitters:
  Apple corer
  Cherry and olive pitter
Lemon stripper
Citrus zester
Melon ball cutters
V-shaped melon cutter
Butter curler
Vegetable garniture set
Curl cutter
Mandoline
Egg slicer
Truffle slicer
Cutters:
  Pastry
  Canapé
  Truffle, gelée, and fondant
Skewers
Hâtelets

Fundamental (Lever-Based) Tools

Offset spatula
Butter paddles
Fish tweezers

Chef's fork
Butter-pat press
Salad spinner

Bakeware, Molds, and Pastry-Preparation Tools

Icing/candy grate
Pastry bag
Pastry tubes (assorted)
Parchment paper

Batterie de Cuisine: Additions for Confectionery Work

Knives

Confectioner's

Other Cutting and Piercing Tools

Cherry and olive pitter
Lemon stripper
Cutters:
  Truffle, gelée, and fondant
  Caramel
  Nougat

Fundamental (Lever-Based) Tools

Offset spatula
Bench knife
Griddle scraper
Standing mixer
Rolling pins:
  Caramel
  Nougat

Stovetop and Ovenware

Sugar boiler

Bakeware, Molds, and Pastry-Preparation Tools

Chocolate molds (assorted)
Icing/candy grate

Pastry decoration:
  Pastry bag
  Pastry tubes (assorted)
Copper egg-white bowl
Marble pastry board
Parchment paper

Various confectionery tools:
  Chocolate dipping forks
  Marzipan sculpting tools
  Confectioner's bars
  Confectioner's funnel
  Starch-casting tray
  Sugar and chocolate decorating
    set
  Sugar pump
  Sugar mandrel

Measuring Tools

Thermometers:
  Chocolate
  Candy
Hydrometer
Syrup density–meter test tube

Basic Stocks

Chicken Stock

Approximately 1½ quarts

4 *pounds chicken parts*

2½ *quarts water*

2 *medium carrots, coarsely chopped*

1 *medium turnip, coarsely chopped*

1 *medium onion, coarsely chopped*

1 *celery rib with leaves, coarsely chopped*

6 *parsley stalks*

6 *whole black peppercorns*

4 *whole cloves*

1 *bay leaf*

¼ *teaspoon dried thyme*

Combine the chicken and water in a medium stockpot and bring to a boil; skim off the impurities that rise to the surface, then add the remaining ingredients. Reduce the heat and simmer, partially covered, 1½ hours.

Strain, cool, clear of fat, and store until ready to use.

Duck Stock

Antoine Bouterin and Elizabeth Crossman
Cooking with Antoine at Le Périgord

Approximately 1½ quarts

2 *to 3 tablespoons corn oil*

2 *large onions, 1 unpeeled and both coarsely chopped*

1 *medium leek, washed and coarsely chopped*

1 *medium carrot, scrubbed and coarsely chopped*

1 *to 2 duck carcasses (uncooked), minus breast, legs, and thighs, trimmed of fat and coarsely chopped*

2 *tablespoons all-purpose flour*

1 *tablespoon tomato paste*

2 *quarts water*

2 *cups dry white wine*

5 *parsley stalks*

5 *basil sprigs*

2 *bay leaves*

1 *teaspoon dried thyme*

12 *black peppercorns*

Heat the oil in a medium stockpot set over medium-high heat, add the onions, leek, and carrot and brown; add the duck, and brown on all sides. Vigorously stir in the flour, then add the tomato paste. A crust will form on the bottom of the pot, then add the water, wine, and a cheesecloth bag containing the remaining ingredients. Scrape the bottom of the pot to free the crust and bring to a boil. Skim off any rising impurities, then reduce the heat and simmer, partially covered, 1 to 1½ hours.

Strain, cool, clear of fat, and store until ready to use.

Brown Veal Stock

Approximately 1 quart

2 *tablespoons vegetable oil*

6 *pounds veal bones, sawed into 2-inch pieces*

2 *medium onions, unpeeled and quartered*

2 *medium carrots, peeled and coarsely chopped*

1 *cup dry white wine*

9 *cups water*

1 *celery rib, coarsely chopped*

1 *large leek, trimmed, halved lengthwise, and rinsed*

6 *garlic cloves*

8 *parsley stalks*

2 *bay leaves*

½ *teaspoon dried thyme*

4 *whole cloves*

2 *medium tomatoes, coarsely chopped*

8 *whole black peppercorns*

Preheat the oven to 450°F.

Combine the oil, bones, onions, and carrots in a large casserole set over high heat and brown 10 minutes; turn several times. Transfer to the oven to roast 1 hour; turn once.

Use a slotted spoon to remove the bones and vegetables to a clean stockpot, pour off the accumulated fat, then add the wine to the casserole. Set it over high heat and bring to a boil; scrape the bottom of the pot to remove the browned bits, then reduce the liquid to half its original volume. Pour into the stockpot, add the water, and bring to a boil; skim off all rising impurities, then add the remaining ingredients. Reduce the heat and simmer, partially covered, 3 hours.

Strain, cool, clear of fat, and store until ready to use.

Quail Stock

André Gaillard, Executive Chef: La Réserve

½ cup

1 *tablespoon butter*

4 *quail carcasses, coarsely chopped*

½ *medium onion, unpeeled and coarsely chopped*

2 *medium shallots, unpeeled and coarsely chopped*

1 *medium carrot, scrubbed and coarsely chopped*

1 *medium celery rib, coarsely chopped*

Salt to taste

8 *black peppercorns*

¼ *teaspoon dried thyme*

1 *bay leaf*

½ *cup dry sherry*

2 *cups water*

2 *medium tomatoes, quartered*

Melt the butter in a medium saucepan set over medium-high heat, add the quail, and sauté until browned. Add the onion, shallots, carrot, celery, salt to taste, peppercorns, thyme, and bay leaf and cook 4 minutes longer; stir occasionally. Add the sherry, increase the heat, and stir to scrape any browned bits that lie on the bottom of the pan; continue to cook until reduced by half.

Add the water and tomatoes, bring to a boil, skim, then reduce the heat and simmer, partially covered, 1 hour. Strain, clear of fat, and store.

Bibliography

Adam, Hans Karl. *The International Wine and Food Society's Guide to German Cookery.* New York: Bonanza Books, 1967.

Alikonis, Justin J. *Candy Technology.* Westport, CT: AVI Publishing Company, 1979.

Amendola, Joseph. *Ice Carving Made Easy.* Washington, DC: National Restaurant Association, 1969.

American Paper and Pulp Association. *The Dictionary of Paper.* New York: American Paper and Pulp Association, 1965.

Andoh, Elizabeth. *At Home with Japanese Cooking.* New York: Alfred A. Knopf, 1980.

Androuet, Pierre. *The Complete Encyclopedia of French Cheeses.* New York: Harper's Magazine Press, 1973.

Apicius. *The Roman Cookery Book* (translated by Barbara Flower and Elizabeth Rosenbaum). London: Peter Nevill Ltd., 1958.

Arbuckle, W. S. *Ice Cream.* Westport, CT: AVI Publishing Company, 1977.

Aresty, Esther B. *The Delectable Past.* New York: Simon & Schuster, 1964.

Bailey, Charles Thomas Peach. *Knives and Forks.* London: The Medici Society, 1927.

Barber, Richard W. *Cooking and Recipes from Rome to the Renaissance.* London: Allen Lane, 1973.

Barnett, Claude. *The Art and Science of Candy Manufacturing.* New York: Books for Industry, 1978.

Beard, James Andrew, et al., editors. *The Cooks' Catalogue.* New York: Harper & Row, 1975.

Besançon, Robert M., editor. *The Encyclopedia of Physics.* New York: Reinhold, 1966.

Bilheux, Roland, and Alain Escoffier. *Professional French Pastry Series.* Volumes 1–4. New York: Van Nostrand Reinhold, 1988.

Bowring, Jean. *Cake Icing and Decorating.* Melbourne: Colorgravure, 1963.

Boyle, Peter T. *Sugar Work.* New York: Van Nostrand Reinhold, 1988.

Brothwell, Don and Patricia. *Food in Antiquity.* New York: Frederick A. Praeger, 1969.

Brown, Dale. *The Cooking of Scandinavia.* New York: Time-Life Books, 1968.

Bruns, Gerda. "Küchenwesen und Mahlzeiten." *Archaeologia Homerica.* Volume 2, Q. Gottingen: Vandenhoeck & Ruprechs, 1970.

Bugialli, Giuliano. *The Fine Art of Italian Cooking.* New York: Quadrangle Books, 1977.

Campbell, Susan. *Cooks' Tools.* New York: William Morrow, 1980.

Carême, Marie Antonin. *Le Pâtissier Royal Parisien.* Volumes 1 & 2. Paris: J. Renouard, 1841.

Carmichael, W. L., George E. Linton, and Isaac Price. *Callaway Textile Dictionary.* La Grange, GA: Callaway Mills, 1947.

Carnevali, Oreste, with Jean B. Read. *Carving and Boning Like an Expert.* New York: Random House, 1978.

Chandler, Maurice. *Ceramics in the Modern World.* New York: Doubleday, 1967.

Child, Julia. *From Julia Child's Kitchen.* New York: Alfred A.. Knopf, 1975.

Clayton, Bernard, Jr. *The Breads of France and How to Bake Them in Your Own Kitchen.* Indianapolis, IN: Bobbs-Merrill, 1978.

Cosman, Madeleine Pelner. *Fabulous Feasts.* New York: George Braziller, 1976.

Davidson, A., editor. *Handbook of Precision Engineering.* Volumes 1–11. New York: McGraw-Hill, 1971.

Del Conte, Anna. *Gastronomy of Italy.* New York: Prentice-Hall, 1987.

Durocher, Joseph F., Jr. *Practical Ice Carving.* New York: Van Nostrand Reinhold, 1981.

Edwards, Iorwerth Eiddon Stephen. *Treasures of Tutankhamun.* New York: Metropolitan Museum of Art, 1976.

Fance, Wilfred J., editor. *The New International Confectioner.* London: Virtue, 1981.

Grabhorn, Robert. *A Commonplace Book of Cookery.* San Francisco: North Point Press, 1985.

Green, Jonathon, editor. *Consuming Passions.* New York: Ballantine Books, 1985.

Harris, H. G., and S. P. Borella. *All About Biscuits.* London: Maclaren & Sons, 1926.

———. *All About Ices, Creams and Conserves.* London: Maclaren & Sons, 1926.

Harvey, John F. *Theory and Design of Modern Pressure Vessels.* New York: Van Nostrand Reinhold, 1974.

Hillman, Howard. *Kitchen Science.* Boston: Houghton Mifflin, 1983.

Himsworth, Joseph Beeston. *The Story of Cutlery.* London: E. Benn, 1953.

Jackson, Albert. *Tools and How to Use Them.* New York: Alfred A. Knopf, 1979.

Bibliography

Jackson, C. J. "The Spoon and Its History." *Archaeologia*. Volume 53. London, 1892.

James, E. O. *Seasonal Feasts and Festivals*. New York: Barnes & Noble, 1961.

Jones, Evan. *The Book of Cheese*. New York: Alfred A. Knopf, 1980.

Kennedy, Diana. *The Cuisines of Mexico*. New York: Harper & Row, 1972.

Kisch, Bruno. *Scales & Weights*. New Haven, CT: Yale University Press, 1966.

Kitchiner, William. *The Cook's Oracle*. London: S. Bagster, 1817.

Lanz, Henry. *Japanese Woodworking Tools*. New York: Sterling Publishing, 1985.

Lawrie, R. A. *Meat Science*. New York: Pergamon Press, 1985.

Larsen, Hjalmar. "On Baking in Egypt During the Middle Kingdom." *Acta Archaeologica*. Volume 7. Copenhagen: Levin & Munksgaard, 1936.

La Varenne, François Pierre de. *Le Cuisinier François*. Paris: Chez Pierre David, 1652.

——— (attributed). *Le Pastissier François*. Paris: Chez Jean Promé, 1662.

Lecoq, Raymond. *Les Objets de la Vie Domestique*. Paris: Berger-Levrault, 1979.

Lees, R., and E. B. Jackson. *Sugar Confectionery and Chocolate Manufacture*. New York: Chemical Publishing Company, 1975.

Lichine, Alexis. *Alexis Lichine's New Encyclopedia of Wines and Spirits*. New York: Alfred A. Knopf, 1985.

Lin, Hsiang Ju, and Tsuifeng Lin. *Chinese Gastronomy*. New York: Hastings House, 1969.

Lloyd, G.I.H. *The Cutlery Trades*. London: Frank Cass & Company, 1968.

Lobel, Leon and Stanley. *All About Meat*. New York: Harcourt Brace Jovanovich, 1975.

Lucas, Dione, and Marion Gorman. *The Dione Lucas Book of French Cooking*. Boston: Little, Brown, 1973.

M. W. *The Queen's Closet Opened*. London: J. Phillips, H. Rhodes and J. Taylor, 1710.

Marnette. *The Perfect Cook*. London, 1656.

Matz, Samuel A. and Theresa D. *Cookie and Cracker Technology*. Westport, CT: AVI Publishing Company, 1978.

McClane, A. J. *The Encyclopedia of Fish Cookery*. New York: Holt, Rinehart & Winston, 1977.

McGee, Harold. *On Food and Cooking*. New York: Charles Scribner's Sons, 1984.

McMillan, P. W. *Glass-Ceramics*. New York: Academic Press, 1964.

Mennell, Stephen. *All Manners of Food*. New York: Basil Blackwell, 1985.

Merriman, A. D. *A Concise Encyclopedia of Metallurgy*. New York: American Elsevier Publishing Company, 1965.

Minifie, Bernard W. *Chocolate, Cocoa and Confectionery*. Westport, CT: AVI Publishing Company, 1980.

Montagné, Prosper. *Larousse Gastronomique*. New York: Crown, 1961.

National Collection of Fine Arts. *Objects for Preparing Food*. Washington, DC: Smithsonian Institution, 1972.

Olney, Richard. *The French Menu Cookbook*. New York: Simon & Schuster, 1970.

Pagé, Camille. *La Coutellerie depuis l'Origine jusqu'a Nos Jours*. Volumes 1–6. Châtellerault: H. Rivière, 1896–1904.

Page, Edward Beynon, and P. W. Kingsford. *The Master Chefs*. London: Edward Arnold, 1971.

Pellaprat, Henri Paul. *The Great Book of French Cuisine*. New York: Vendome Press, 1966.

Platina (Sacchi, Bartolomeo de'). *De Honesta Voluptate*. Venice: Bernardinus Venetus de Vitalibus, 1498.

Pomeranz, Yeshajahu. *Modern Cereal Science and Technology*. New York: VCH, 1987.

Pomeranz, Yeshajahu, and J. A. Shellenberger. *Bread Science and Technology*. Westport, CT: AVI Publishing Company, 1971.

Pullar, Philippa. *Consuming Passions*. Boston: Little, Brown, 1970.

Pyler, Ernst John. *Baking Science and Technology*. Chicago: Siebel Publishing Company, 1973.

Reuther, Walter, Herbert John Weber, and Leon Dexter Batchelor, editors. *The Citrus Industry*. Volume 1. Oakland: ANR Publications (University of California), 1967.

Revel, Jean-François. *Culture and Cuisine*. New York: Doubleday, 1982.

Root, Waverly. *The Food of Italy*. New York: Atheneum, 1971.

Rudolf-August Oetker KG. *Biscuits, Confiserie et Petits Fours*. Netherlands: Editions Chantecler, 1984.

Scappi, Bartolomeo. *Opera di . . .* Venice: Vincenzo Pelagalo, 1596.

Scullard, H. H. *Festivals and Ceremonies of the Roman Republic*. Ithaca, NY: Cornell University Press, 1981.

Sounders, Mott. *The Engineer's Companion*. New York: John Wiley and Sons, 1966.

Stewart, Katie. *Cooking and Eating*. St. Albans: Hart-Davis MacGibbon, 1975.

Strung, Norman. *An Encyclopedia of Knives*. Philadelphia: Lippincott, 1976.

Thiele, Ernst. *Waffeleisen und Waffelgebäcke in Mitteleuropa*. Cologne: Oda-Verlag, 1959.

Toulouse, Julian Harrison. *Fruit Jars*. Camden, NJ: Nelson, 1969.

Ukers, William H. *All About Coffee*. New York: The Tea & Coffee Trade Journal Company, 1935.

————. *All About Tea.* New York: The Tea & Coffee Trade Journal Company, 1935.

Urbain-Dubois, Félix. *Grand Livre des Pâtissiers et des Confiseurs.* Volumes 1 and 2. Paris: E. Dentu, 1883.

Wallace, Evelyn. *Cake Decorating and Sugarcraft.* London: Newnes, 1967.

Weiner, Piroska. *Carved Honeycake Molds,* translated by Pál Morvay. Budapest: Corvina, 1964.

Wolfert, Paula. *Couscous and Other Good Food from Morocco.* New York: Harper & Row, 1973.

Yumoto, John M. *The Samurai Sword.* Rutland, VT: Charles E. Tuttle Company, 1958.

Contributors

The authors wish to thank the following establishments for generously contributing recipes and/or preparation techniques to this book.

RESTAURANTS & CLUBS

Aquavit
15 West 54th Street
New York, NY 10019
(212) 307-7311

Arizona 206
206 East 60th Street
New York, NY 10022
(212) 838-0440

Aurora
60 East 49th Street
New York, NY 10017
(212) 692-9292

The Ballroom
253 West 28th Street
New York, NY 10001
(212) 244-3005

Bellini by Cipriani
777 Seventh Avenue
New York, NY 10019
(212) 265-7770

Between the Bread
141 East 56th Street
New York, NY 10022
(212) 888-0449

Café Crocodile
354 East 74th Street
New York, NY 10021
(212) 249-6619

Chalet Suisse
6 East 48th Street
New York, NY 10017
(212) 355-0855

Le Cirque
58 East 65th Street
New York, NY 10021
(212) 794-9292

The Coach House
110 Waverly Place
New York, NY 10011
(212) 777-0303

La Côte Basque
5 East 55th Street
New York, NY 10022
(212) 688-6525

Le Cygne
55 East 54th Street
New York, NY 10022
(212) 759-5941

Dooky Chase's Restaurant
2301 Orleans Avenue
New Orleans, LA 70119
(504) 821-0600

Elio's
1621 Second Avenue
New York, NY 10028
(212) 772-2242

Felidia
243 East 58th Street
New York, NY 10022
(212) 758-1479

Flamand
349 East 86th Street
New York, NY 10028
(212) 722-4610

The Four Seasons
99 East 52nd Street
New York, NY 10022
(212) 754-9494

La Gauloise
502 Sixth Avenue
New York, NY 10011
(212) 691-1363

Gloucester House
37 East 50th Street
New York, NY 10022
(212) 755-7394

Gotham Bar & Grill
12 East 12th Street
New York, NY 10003
(212) 620-4020

La Grenouille
3 East 52nd Street
New York, NY 10022
(212) 752-1495

Harlequin
569 Hudson Street
New York, NY 10014
(212) 255-4950

Kitcho
22 West 46th Street
New York, NY 10036
(212) 575-8880

The Knickerbocker Club
2 East 62nd Street
New York, NY 10021
(212) 838-6700

Laurent
111 East 56th Street
New York, NY 10022
(212) 753-2729

Lutèce
249 East 50th Street
New York, NY 10022
(212) 752-2225

La Mangeoire
1008 Second Avenue
New York, NY 10022
(212) 759-7086

The Maurice
118 West 57th Street
New York, NY 10019
(212) 245-7788

Oyster Bar & Restaurant
Grand Central Terminal/Lower Level
New York, NY 10017
(212) 490-6650

Le Périgord
405 East 52nd Street
New York, NY 10022
(212) 755-6244

The Plaza
Fifth Avenue at 59th Street
New York, NY 10019
(212) 759-3000

Les Pléiades
20 East 76th Street
New York, NY 10021
(212) 535-7230

The Quilted Giraffe
550 Madison Avenue
New York, NY 10022
(212) 593-1221

René Pujol
321 West 51st Street
New York, NY 10019
(212) 246-3023

La Réserve
4 West 49th Street
New York, NY 10020
(212) 247-2993

Restaurant Lafayette
65 East 56th Street
New York, NY 10022
(212) 832-1565

Ristorante Primavera
1578 First Avenue
New York, NY 10028
(212) 861-8608

The Russian Tea Room
150 West 57th Street
New York, NY 10019
(212) 265-0947

Sandro's
420 East 59th Street
New York, NY 10022
(212) 355-5150

Shun Lee Palace
155 East 55th Street
New York, NY 10022
(212) 371-8844

La Tulipe
104 West 13th Street
New York, NY 10014
(212) 691-8860

"21" Club
21 West 52nd Street
New York, NY 10019
(212) 582-7200

Waldorf-Astoria
301 Park Avenue
New York, NY 10022
(212) 355-3000

SPECIALTY FOOD SHOPS

William Greenberg, Jr., Desserts, Inc.
1377 Third Avenue
New York, NY 10021
(212) 535-7118

Ideal Cheese Shop
1205 Second Avenue
New York, NY 10021
(212) 688-7579

Lobel's Prime Meats
1096 Madison Avenue
New York, NY 10028
(212) 737-1372

Ottomanelli Meat Market
1549 York Avenue
New York, NY 10028
(212) 772-7900

Petrossian
182 West 58th Street
New York, NY 10019
(212) 245-2217

Pisacane Mid-Town Corp.
940 First Avenue
New York, NY 10022
(212) 758-1525

William Poll
1051 Lexington Avenue
New York, NY 10021
(212) 288-0501

Rosedale Fish & Oyster Market
1129 Lexington Avenue
New York, NY 10021
(212) 861-4323

CATERERS

Annemarie Huste
104 East 30th Street
New York, NY 10016
(212) 685-5685

Neuman & Bogdonoff
1385 Third Avenue
New York, NY 10021
(212) 861-0303

Rudolph Stanish
P.O. Box 396
Yukon, PA 15698
(412) 722-3567

COOKING SCHOOLS

Anna Teresa Callen
59 West 12th Street
New York, NY 10011
(212) 929-5640

Peter Kump's New York Cooking
  School
307 East 92nd Street
New York, NY 10128
(212) 410-4601

Karen Lee
142 West End Avenue
New York, NY 10023
(212) 787-2227

Lydie Marshall
23 Eighth Avenue
New York, NY 10014
(212) 675-7736

General
Index

I n d e x

Recipe
Index